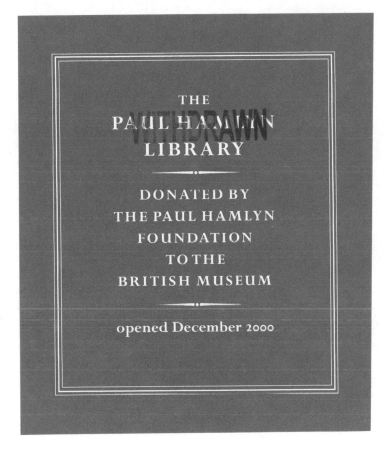

To Walter L. Wakefield, historian of Catharism

The Cathars

MALCOLM LAMBERT

BLACKWELL
Publishers

First published 1998

Reprinted 1998, 1999

Blackwell Publishers Ltd
108 Cowley Road
Oxford OX4 1JF, UK

Blackwell Publishers Inc
350 Main Street
Malden, Massachusetts 02148, USA

British Library Cataloguing in Publication Data
A CIP catalogue record for this book is available from the British Library

Library of Congress Cataloging in Publication Data
Lambert, Malcolm (Malcolm D.)
The Cathars/Malcolm Lambert
p. cm.
Includes bibliographical references and index.
ISBN 0–631–14343–2. — ISBN 0–631–20959–X (pbk.)
1. Albigenses. 2. Heresies. Christian—France—Languedoc—History—Middle Ages, 600–1500. 3. Heresies, Christian—Italy—History—Middle Ages, 600–1500. 4. France—Church history—987–1515. 5. Italy—Church history—476–1400.
I. Title. BX4891.2.L35 1998
272'.3—dc21
97–39153
CIP

Typeset in New Baskerville 9.5pt on 11pt
by Jean Cussons Typesetting, Diss, Norfolk
Printed and bound in Great Britain
by MPG Books Ltd, Bodmin, Cornwall

This book is printed on acid-free paper

Contents

Illustrations

Maps

Acknowledgements

The Alexander von Humbolt Stiftung enabled me to spend six months in the finest of all libraries for medievalists, the Monumenta Germaniae Historica in Munich. I am grateful to the President and staff for their hospitality and especially to the Diplom-bibliothekärin, Frau M. Becker, to her predecessor, Dr H. Lietzmann, to Dr Marlene Polock and to the kindness of Dr H. Schneider and Dr C. Lohmer in sending a series of references and photocopies. Professor G. Rottenwöhrer has been swift and generous with advice and photocopies, and I owe hospitality to the late Professor P. Calmeyer and Frau Dr Calmeyer.

I am grateful to the Centre National d'Etudes Cathares, Carcassonne, whose library was donated by Dr J. Duvernoy, himself an unfailing and kindly resource for references and information on Occitania and the inquisition, and to the kindness of Dr Anne Brenon and Monsieur J. L. Gasc, the photographer of Languedocian Catharism. Monsieur M. Roquebert, whose *L'Epopée Cathare* demonstrates that full-scale narrative history can still entertain and instruct, has sent me advance copies of articles.

I am indebted to the Leverhulme Foundation for the generous grant of an Emeritus Fellowship.

Dr Claire Dutton and the Rev. Dr J. Mary Henderson gave me full access to their theses: I hope both may be published in some form. Dr J. Džambo kindly translated his maps and made them available.

Emeritus Professor W. L. Wakefield has been a support and inspiration for many years and entrusted me with unpublished work. My dedication is a tribute to his humour and wise advice.

I am indebted to Mr John Davey, formerly of Blackwell, for commissioning this work and for his patience and support; I am grateful, too, for the swift response of his successor, Tessa Harvey and her team.

My wife has borne cheerfully with this book's inordinately long gestation, has discussed it, typed it and aided me, as always, at every stage. Her work has been irreplaceable.

M.D.L.
The Yews
Eastcombe
Stroud
GL6 7DN

Introduction

The rise and fall of the Cathar heresy from the twelfth to the early fourteenth century was a major event in Western European history. The reaction which Catharism provoked led directly to the Albigensian Crusade, to the ending of the possibility of a trans-Pyrenean Occitanian state and the effective incorporation of the South under a dynamic French monarchy. Catharism rose just as other heresies did in the twelfth century, but it was feared more than any other by contemporary churchmen, and its recruiting successes, especially in certain parts of Languedoc and Northern and Central Italy, unleashed a crisis in the medieval Church. Accelerated procedures for the investigation and judgement of sinning clergy developed by Innocent III were used in other hands to provide a novel and grimly effective machinery to investigate, judge and repress heresy. Bishops did not forgo their traditional duty to put down heresy, but their work was stimulated, supplemented and sometimes replaced by inquisitors appointed *ad hoc* by the papacy. They were determined men, dedicated to their task and equipped with overriding powers, effectively of life and death. They built up a body of knowledge of heretics, their customs and beliefs, which are enshrined in manuals of procedure, disquisitions on the enemies of the Church, refutations of their tenets and defences of orthodoxy.

Quite possibly, popes thought of these proceedings as a strictly temporary expedient – to be put aside when victory over heretics was won. But this was not to be: the machinery long outlasted the Cathars, becoming known as the Inquisition. Its continuing importance for the history of the Catholic Church needs no underlining.

Catharism stimulated St Dominic, whose first vocation had been as a missionary among the Slav heathen, to found an order of friars dedicated to preaching and refuting heretical beliefs by reason. It reinforced the lay confraternities in Italian cities who incorporated in their statutes duties connected with the refuting or repressing of heresy, providing a strong arm to inquisitors and a focus for a positive, orthodox personal piety designed to override the appeal of the heretics. St Francis of Assisi played a major role in the development of a piety focused on the Holy Family and the humanity and sufferings of Jesus. This worked powerfully against the menace of Catharism, of which he was more aware than is commonly supposed.

The horror of the Cathar heresy was one factor that brought about weighty changes in the Church, leading to dogmatic definitions, extended defences of orthodoxy and a serious attempt to raise standards of preaching, increase its incidence and provide a better instructed laity armed against unorthodoxy.

Despite the importance of its story, Catharism has never received a comprehensive study in English. The nearest approach is the admirably concise survey by Walter Wakefield on heresy and crusade in Languedoc, which came out in 1974, and uses the author's special knowledge of inquisition records. But he ends effectively before the turn of the thirteenth century and Italy is not in his sights. This book is an attempt to provide a synthesis of the whole story of Catharism across Western Europe, its rise and fall, beliefs and customs, its long and bruising struggle with the medieval Church, which affected both the heresy and its opponents.

The survival of source material affects the balance of exposition. There are rich records of heresy in Southern France and Northern and Central Italy: consequently, the story of Catharism in these lands is given much more space. It had an international impact and there were few countries in Western Europe that were not touched by Cathar missionary activity. It is easy to forget that Northern France had sufficient supporters to justify a Cathar bishopric. It would be highly desirable to describe in detail the history of that Church, but persecution was more effective there, early support was cut down and the failure of records to survive in the North means that little can be said about it. I allude briefly to the history of Catharism in other lands, but because of superior source material give pride of place to Languedoc and Italy.

Similarly, in Languedoc's story I give extensive coverage to Autier's revival even though his career as missionary lasted for no more than a decade, but the extensive records give us a rare opportunity to see precisely how Cathar preachers and supporters won recruits. W. I. Wakefield adjudges that the revival had little significance. I cannot agree. Politically, yes, but the degree of support won in a short time shows that the heresy *per se* in the right hands still had potency.

The story of the Bosnian Church makes up the last chapter. It is a historiographical curiosity. The intriguing questions – was it a state Church? was it heretical? – have absorbed historians, partly for nationalistic reasons, for over a century, and given birth to remarkably subtle investigations. These, J. V. A. Fine Jr's book introduces to English readers, but I cannot simply hand my readers over to him. Much as I value his work, I cannot agree with his conclusion.

For much of its history, Catharism was an underground movement and the bulk of extant records for it emanate from its bitter opponents. This has led some historians to argue that we cannot safely reconstruct Cathar history and belief from such tainted materials. I do not take this view. Enough has survived which comes directly from the Cathars themselves to act as a check on what their enemies said. Handled correctly, both the records of bishops and inquisitors and hostile treatises can give us a fair picture of what happened and what Cathars believed. Doctrine mattered within the movement and disputes over creation, salvation and the nature of God which split Italian adherents were disputes with a real content, not just quarrels among primadonnas or expressions of urban rivalries, as some historians have alleged. On the other hand, I believe that doctrinal disunity, though it seriously damaged Italian Catharism, was only one factor in its decline; divisions on dualism, by contrast, hardly mattered in Languedoc.

On this theme I disagree with Arno Borst in his classic, and still gripping, book on the Cathars of 1953. Materials are adequate for the study of Cathar belief, but until recently no trained theologian has given them sustained analysis. Dondaine, a pioneer MS researcher, though equipped for this, never undertook it. Happily, Gerhard Rottenwöhrer, in an encyclopedic reference work, has given heretical doctrine close and conscientious scrutiny. His is a safe pair of hands. By a publishing eccentricity, his work has hardly been reviewed at all, and one object of this book is to make his excellent work better known.

Post-war study has gone a long way in illuminating the context in which Catharism, the exotic intruder born of contacts with a heresy derived from Bulgaria and Byzantium, prospered in Western Europe: the *aperçus* of Violante and d'Alatri for Italy, Duvernoy, Roquebert, Barber and Anne Brenon for Languedoc help us to understand where and why the Cathars gained prestige and support, but few do full justice to the central motivation of the Cathar elite and their most ardent supporters. This lay, above all, in the search for individual salvation. Catharism was pre-eminently a religious movement.

I have adopted the most commonly used form for Christian names without attempting consistency and, though the Holy Office *per se* was not founded until 1542, have found it convenient to use 'inquisition' as a hold-all term for various tribunals or individuals given inquisitorial powers to investigate heresy.

1

The Little Foxes

At the beginning of the eleventh century, leading churchmen in Western Europe had no living experience of heresy. What they knew they had learned from books, above all from St Augustine, who had written on the various forms of heresy, had once been a Manichee auditor and, as bishop of Hippo in North Africa, had had to confront the Donatists. His own attitude towards the use of force, shaped by this experience, was of critical importance for the development of repression in the West.

Churchmen were aware of the words of St Paul in his second epistle to Timothy associating heresies with the perils of the approaching end of the world.

> This know also, that in the last days perilous times shall come. For men shall be lovers of their own selves, covetous, boasters, proud, blasphemers ... traitors, heady, high-minded, lovers of pleasures more than lovers of God; having a form of godliness, but denying the power thereof. From such turn away. For of this sort are they which creep into houses and lead captive silly women laden with sins, led away with divers lusts. Ever learning and never able to come to the knowledge of the truth.[1]

They would also know that in his epistle to Titus, Paul had told his followers to shun a heretic after he had been warned twice.[2] Heresy and heretics were words full of foreboding: but they remained merely words, the Dark Ages providing a kind of *tabula rasa* for orthodoxy. Catholicism triumphed and Arianism, which had been widespread among the Germans, faded out. Enemies of belief remained but they took the form of superstition and paganism: the only heresies to be found were either the work of individual theologians or the casual idiosyncrasies of rustic preachers with no theological training. No heresy at all is recorded after the death of Louis the Pious and the breakdown of the Carolingian Empire.[3]

---

[1]   2 Tim. 3: 1–7.
[2]   Titus 3: 10.
[3]   M. D. Lambert, *Medieval Heresy: Popular Movements from the Gregorian Reform to the Reformation* (2nd edn, Oxford, 1992), pp. 25–6 (ch. 3 of first edition superseded).

When, in the first half of the eleventh century, heresy did reappear in a series of episodes, often ill recorded in chronicles or the proceedings of Councils, Church authorities were alarmed and uncertain. From their book knowledge, the heresy they knew best and feared most was Manichaeism, a universalist religion which originated in Persia in the third century in the teaching of Mani, or Manes, whose adherents, intensely disliked by Roman imperial authorities, in part because of their fear of Persia, were subjected to fierce penalties, including burning alive. The heretics who were uncovered in these episodes were quiet, puritanical groups, often strongly ascetic and dualistic in their teaching, inclining contemporaries brusquely to label them Manichaean.

In his first epistle to the Corinthians, Paul also wrote '*Oportet esse haereses*' – in the Vulgate's translation, 'there must be heresies, that they which are proved may be manifest among you'[4] – and the instruction of churchmen would lead them to believe that heresy was a normal, albeit diabolically inspired, accompaniment to Church life: the cessation of heresy during the Dark Ages was an aberration. St Paul's association of heresy with the approach of the end of the world bore rich fruit in the reporting, principally by monastic chroniclers, of the heretical episodes of the earlier eleventh century. Around 950 Adso of Montier-en-Der wrote a book, *De vita et tempore Antichristi*, which had considerable vogue at the time and was both read and developed further in the eleventh century. He took up Gregory the Great's doctrine of Antichrist as the Devil incarnate, a Satanic antithesis to Christ whose emergence would herald the Last Times, and reinterpreted his vision, creating an Antichrist who was legion, manifest in various guises, within the Church, working wonders and deceiving mankind.[5]

For Raoul Glaber, too, the appearance of heresy was one of the signs of the approach of the end of the world:[6] this credulous Cluniac chronicler wrote about heretics in apocalyptic vein, making free use of such terms as insanity, demoniac possession and the like when referring to their preachers and leaders. The descriptions of four heretical episodes in his *Histoires* spring from a coherent, albeit markedly unhistorical, vision of his

---

[4] 1 Cor. 9: 19; H. Grundmann, 'Opportet et haereses esse: das Problem der Ketzerei im Spiegel der mittelalterlichen Bibelexegese', *AKG* XLV (1963), pp. 129–64, reproduced in H. Grundmann, *Ausgewählte Aufsätze* I (Stuttgart, 1976), pp. 328–63 at pp. 339–40; Lambert, *Medieval Heresy*, 2nd edn, pp. 3–8; F. Morley, 'Heresy in New Testament times', *Theology* LI (1948), pp. 288–93.

[5] A. Vauchez, 'Diables et hérétiques: les réactions de l'église et de la société en occident face aux mouvements religieux dissidents de la fin du Xe au debut du XIIe siècle', *Settimane di Studio del Centro Italiano di Studi sull' Alto medioevo* XXXVI, 2 (Spoleto, 1989), pp. 573–607 at pp. 584–5; N. Cohn, *Europe's Inner Demons* (London, 1975) (account of origins of witch-cult; classic debunking ch. 7), pp. 16–17; Michael Psellos did not write the *De daemonibus* (as Cohn and historians generally); it dates from the twelfth century, P. Gautier, 'Le *De daemonibus* du Pseudo-Psellos', *Revue des Etudes Byzantines* XXXVIII (1980), pp. 105–94.

[6] R. Landes, *Relics, Apocalypse and the Deceits of History, Adémar of Chabannes, 989–1034* (Cambridge, Mass., London, 1995) (subtle, illuminating analysis of Adémar and writings), on apocalypticism and its vogue, pp. 285–308, on Glaber, p. 297. I am grateful to the author for the gift of his book.

own times. All were the work of the Devil operating through his agents: in one case the peasant Leutard whose private parts were penetrated by a swarm of bees, demonic agents; in another, demons in the likeness of Virgil, Horace and Juvenal who worked on the mind of a certain Vilgard of Ravenna; in the other two cases, through women, the fallen daughters of Eve. Heresy was a form of contagious madness, propagated 'by seduction and magic'. The Devil deceived mankind, promising splendid rewards. At Orléans his clerical adherents believed that they attained an inner illumination which gave them angelic visions and a full understanding of Scripture; Vilgard was promised literary glory; heretics at Monteforte were promised eternal life. In the event, the Devil's promises were all deceptions and ended in death: the peasant committed suicide and Vilgard and the recalcitrant heretics of both Orléans and Monteforte were burnt.[7]

Another monastic chronicler from the abbey of Saint Martial of Limoges, Adémar of Chabannes, wrote in a similar vein in an entry for the year 1018 when he described Manichaeans in Aquitaine practising asceticism and called them 'messengers of Antichrist'. His description of their hypocrisy accorded with the stereotype of heresy which descended to medieval churchmen from St Paul's words as elaborated and understood by the Fathers. 'They abstained from food and seemed like monks; they pretended chastity, but among themselves they practised every debauchery.'[8] Heretics were deceivers as well as deceived; they would present themselves as better than others, when in fact they practised secret vice.

Here Augustine especially had a part to play, for although he had once himself felt the attractive power of Manichaeism and had been an adherent for nine years, none the less he accused its Elect of secret vices, having heard from a woman that at a meeting one of the Elect had put out the lamp and tried to embrace her, and in his work on heresies said that the Elect ate a kind of eucharist including human sperm. Jerome did not believe in the guilt of the Manichees on this point, but Augustine's view prevailed and so, when observers in the eleventh and twelfth centuries believed that they had detected modern Manichees, they inevitably attributed to them secret vices: this came to be a natural attribute of heretics in general.[9]

The sober and factual reporter, Paul of St Père de Chartres, describing in detail the heresy and trial of a group of clergy and their supporters at Orléans in 1022, felt impelled to include a passage within his account wholly out of accord with the rest in which he describes how the heretics there chanted the names of demons till one descended 'in the likeness of a little beast', then extinguished the lights, engaged in an orgy and ate a diabolic *viaticum* compounded of the ashes of the body of a baby, burnt as the result

---

[7]   Vauchez in *Settimane* XXXVI, pp. 574–7; tr. W. L. Wakefield and A. P. Evans, *Heresies of the High Middle Ages* (New York, London, 1969) (*WEH*), pp. 72–3, 75–81, 86–9; R. I. Moore, *The Birth of Popular Heresy* (London, 1975), pp. 9–15, 19–21. *WEH* is most frequently used here but there are often parallel translations in Moore.
[8]   *WEH*, p. 74.
[9]   Vauchez, in *Settimane* XXXVI, p. 587; Cohn, *Demons*, p. 17.

of one such orgy.[10] Demons spread their influence: a party of them, having done their work in Orléans, was seen in a monk's vision advancing from the latrines into the monastery at Fleury. It took St Benedict and the relic of his staff to deter them.[11]

After his account of Vilgard, Glaber, sensitive to the currents of his age, wrote 'This accords with the prophecy of the apostle John, in which he said that Satan would be released when a thousand years had passed.'[12] In his *Histoires* he was fascinated first by the year 1000, then with 1033, the point at which a thousand years would have elapsed from the crucifixion, and by the signs and wonders, including heresy, marking the approach of the Last Times. Adémar, more subtle and more aware of Augustine's solemn warning against identification of dates and times of the Second Coming, none the less had the apocalyptic implications of his age clearly in mind. After 1033, apocalypticism and its association with heresy was less dominant, but the strand of Augustine-inspired interpretation linking heresy with magic and orgies continued across the centuries.[13]

In the early twelfth century, Guibert de Nogent, a weak historian like Glaber but a faithful reflector of the currents of thought of his time, attributed to two peasants of Bucy-le-Long, near Soissons, captured about 1114, the consumption of a diabolical *viaticum* compounded of the ashes of a dead child. They also rejected marriage, infant baptism and food produced by coition, called 'the mouths of all priests the mouth of hell' and held secret orgies. Recalling Augustine, he identified their heresy with Manichaeism and commented 'Though this heresy had its origin in former times among learned persons, its dregs sank down to the country folk who boasting that they held to the way of life of the apostles, choose to read only their Acts.'[14] In other words, Guibert, confronted with a heresy more likely to have been sparked off in classic fashion by an independent reading or hearing of Scripture, preferred to interpret it as a recrudescence of the heresy known to Augustine and to treat it as a cloak for vice and magic. The diabolical *viaticum* had the property of securing its eaters, fast bound, to heresy; the same result was reported both by Paul of St Père de Chartres for Orléans and by Guibert for Bucy-le-Long. Here ancient folklore exerted its hold. Ashes had potency, for good or ill: Bede recalled how the ashes of the kings of Northumbria were used as a remedy against disease, and peasants used ashes burned on St John the Baptist's day in their fields to secure fertility. Adémar warned in a sermon against charlatans selling a powder made from the bones of the dead. He believed the outbreak of heresy among the clergy at Orléans to have been caused by a rustic carrying the

[10] *WEH*, pp. 78–9; analysis: Lambert, *Medieval Heresy*, 2nd edn, pp. 9–16.
[11] T. Head, 'Andrew of Fleury and the Peace League of Bourges', in *Essays on the Peace of God: the Church and the People in Eleventh Century France*, ed. T. Head and R. Landes, *Historical Reflections/Reflexions Historiques* XIV, 3 (1987), pp. 513–29 at p. 522.
[12] *WEH*, p. 73.
[13] Vauchez, in *Settimane* XXXVI, pp. 583–4; see Landes, *Relics*, pp. 17–19, 43–6, 93–7, 144–6, 287–9, 320–7.
[14] *WEH*, p. 103: R. I. Moore, 'Guibert de Nogent and his world', in *Studies in Medieval History Presented to R. H. C. Davis*, ed. H. Mayr-Harting and R. I. Moore (London, 1975), pp. 107–17.

ashes of dead children which, once administered, made a Manichaean of anyone who accepted them. When the obstinate heretics were burned, he noted, their bones were completely consumed and only ash remained. The clergy adored the Devil who appeared to them first as an Ethiopian, then as an angel of light.[15] The *viaticum* had an odd scatological fascination. Aubri des Trois Fontaines, a Cistercian chronicler, reports how in 1160 an army of demons in Germany secured their victims against ever returning to orthodoxy by a magnificent feast: 'when the sign of the cross was made, the food turned to excrement and the wine to urine.'[16]

Magic, demonic possession, poison, illness and contagion, excrement, seduction, orgies and the ashes of a dead child were all symptoms and signs of heresy. Some reporters were very much more sober and factual than others, and these rather than the inferior chronicles have been used by modern historians attempting to reconstruct the reality of heresy in the eleventh and twelfth centuries; yet even they shared, and to some extent were swayed by, the common assumption that heresy was of direct diabolical origin. So the bishop of Cambrai/Arras, whose detailed refutation of the views of a group seized at Arras in 1025 is a prime source for their beliefs, set out in a scholarly fashion, called them 'abominable men, bewitched by the spirit of error', and Wazo, bishop of Liège, a rare voice calling for restraint in the treatment of heretics, still called them 'souls deceived by a diabolical trick'.[17]

The assumption of diabolical inspiration is not merely a feature of literary interest to modern investigators: it has a direct influence on the contemporary choice of methods used to deal with heresies and their defenders. If the Devil and his army of demons are the effective force in the field, then resistance to them is the same kind of resistance that churchmen and the faithful believed to be appropriate against witchcraft. The two offences ran closely together. So when Aréfast, the double agent who uncovered the heresy at Orléans, prepared himself for his task, he accepted advice to fortify himself against 'devilish deceit' by prayer, the sign of the cross and daily communion. In the episode described by Aubri des Trois Fontaines the sign of the cross revealed the demons' fraud.

It was not that refutation and exhortation were excluded from the armoury of bishops wrestling with heretics: at Orléans, we are told, the assembled clergy spent a day attempting to reason the leaders into renunciation of their beliefs. At Arras, the bishop ordered the monks and clergy of his diocese to fast before the trial. He put the captured heretics into prison, where they may have been tortured, but he also treated both them and his clergy to a long exhortation on orthodoxy, designed not only to refute the heretics but also to confirm the faith of his clergy.[18] The assumption of diabolical influence did not eliminate rational confrontation, but it tended

[15]   Vauchez, in Settimane xxxvi, pp. 588–90; R. Gorre, *Die ersten Katharer im 11. Jahrhundert: religiöse Eiferer-soziale Rebellen?* (Constance, 1985), pp. 62–73; WEH, p. 75.
[16]   Vauchez, in *Settimane* xxxvi, p. 581.
[17]   Ibid., p. 582.
[18]   R. I. Moore, *The Origins of European Dissent* (London, 1977; Oxford, 1985) (forceful analysis, classic introduction; author's approach, pp. ix–x, 311, n. 4); on Arras, pp. 9–18, 37–8, 43.

to tilt the balance towards supra-rational methods for the defence of orthodoxy and it clearly influenced decisions made about the punishment of the recalcitrant.

Bishops long remained uncertain about the methods that ought to be followed. At Arras, there was no problem: the heretics were simple people who, deprived of their leader, submitted, formally renounced their errors and were given a vernacular copy of the renunciation to which they had assented. A rational approach remained dominant. At Orléans, the recalcitrant were incontinently burned by the decision of the king, Robert the Pious: it was the first burning for heresy in the West and it was characteristic that it was carried out by a lay ruler. The laity tended to see matters in black and white. No doubt the king and queen were anxious to clear themselves as dramatically as they could from any possible complicity with heresy and the king wished to retain his reputation as a pious ruler, determined to ensure the maintenance of orthodoxy. The clergy would have remembered that burning had been the punishment for Manichaeism. But it was also a punishment for sorcery, and the strongest single factor leading to the pyre is likely to have been the fear of pollution of Orléans and of the kingdom. Burning removed all trace of the offenders and their evil and cleansed the site.

Demons were responsible not only for heresy but for other evils. It was well to be utterly rid of their influence: a tolerance of evil could bring down the wrath of God on a locality. The concept of heresy as an illness or contagion pointed in the same direction of thorough cleansing:[19] that alone would remove all the spores that carried infection. However, in the eleventh and twelfth centuries burning was not the only form of capital punishment applied to heretics. At Goslar in 1051, after a hearing in the presence of the emperor Henry III, heretics were hanged after refusing to kill a chicken; in the case of Bucy-le-Long, while the bishop, puzzled as to what to do, went off to seek advice, the crowd broke into the prison and lynched the heretics.[20] But the eventual emergence, over many decades, of burning as the recognized punishment for the obstinate heretic or for the heretic who, after renunciation, relapsed owed much to the notion of cleansing from pollution.

Churchmen were thus the heirs to an amalgam of ideas and preconceptions from the past broadly dictating their views on heresy.[21] Catholic

[19] R. I. Moore, 'Heresy as disease', in *The Concept of Heresy in the Middle Ages*, ed. W. Lourdaux and D. Verhelst (Leuven, The Hague, 1976), pp. 1–11; Moore, *Origins*, pp. 246–50.

[20] *WEH*, pp. 93, 104; H. Fichtenau, *Ketzer und Professoren: Häresie and Vernunftglaube im Hochmittelalter* (Munich, 1992) (valuable details, fruit of wide experience), pp. 30–1, 76–7; on Goslar, G. Rottenwöhrer, *Der Katharismus* III (*GRK* III): *Die Herkunft der Katharer nach Theologie und Geschichte* (Bad Honnef, 1990) (penetrating theological analysis, full bibliography), pp. 219–22.

[21] H. Grundmann, 'Der Typus des Ketzers in mittelalterlicher Anschauung', *Kultur -und Universalgeschichte: Walter Goetz zu seinem 60, Geburtstage* (Leipzig, 1927), pp. 91–107; *Ausgewählte Aufsätze* I, pp. 313–27 (wide-ranging); A. Patschovsky, 'Der Ketzer als Teufelsdiener', in *Papsttum, Kirche und Recht*, ed. H. Mordek (Tübingen, 1991), pp. 317–34.

writers, apologists, chroniclers wrote by and large in order to warn their readers and hearers against an imminent danger to their souls and to society. Heretics formed part of the city of the Devil, the *civitas diaboli*, which stood in perpetual opposition to the city of God. Certain favourite texts explained the nature of heresy: it was cunning and secret, and the characteristic heretic was a wolf in sheep's clothing. Jesus sent his disciples to preach openly; heretics worked in secret. In a scriptural interpretation which went back to Origen, heretics were compared to the little foxes described in the Song of Songs: 'Take us the foxes, the little foxes that spoil the vines, for our vines have tender grapes.'[22] The foxes were the heretics who damaged the vineyard of the Lord; their proliferation had to be checked. They were many, just as heresies were many, their differences a sign that they were of the Devil; Catholicism was one, its unity a sign that it was true and proceeded from God. Heretics could not agree amongst themselves; they were a confusion. Yet, in another sense, all the various heresies were one, forming one enemy of God, united in their purpose of capturing souls. Here another text came in aid, from Judges, where Samson 'caught three hundred foxes and took firebrands and turned tail to tail and put a firebrand in the midst between the tails' and flung the burning fox corpses into the standing corn, crops, vineyards and olives of the Philistines to set them alight.[23] The foxes had different faces but were all bound together into one: so it was with heresy.

Heresy was also associated with moral fault. Pride was held to be its root, causing perverted individuals and groups to stand against the authority of the Church and its teaching. Leaders of heresy might indeed include hypocrites and charlatans, though as far as can be ascertained an overwhelming majority were personalities with a high moral commitment, but to the conventional reporter, high morality was but a cloak, a *species pietatis*, designed to attract victims to the heretics' cause, serving to conceal grave flaws of character. In a similar fashion, Satan could transform himself into an angel of light.

These received notions from the past were all the more influential in the early years of the revival of heresies in Western Europe because of the limited intellectual equipment of Church authority at the time. Stereotypes were potent where practical knowledge and experience were lacking. This has affected the quality of the sources but at the same time, their very frailty has excited interest and provided a challenge to historians, ever interested in problems of origins. The eleventh and twelfth centuries were one of the great creative periods in European history, marked by the beginnings of population growth, the rise of towns and trade, a continued expansion of cultivated land and concomitant dynamic social and cultural change. Church life was transformed. At the same time, there were problems of order and much social dislocation.

Historians have been intrigued by the eleventh century *par excellence*, since it is plainly a starting-point for so many European developments and

[22]   Song of Solomon 2: 15.
[23]   Judges 15: 4–5.

yet suffers from a great paucity of records. Heresy – its rise, its true incidence and the factors lying behind it – is one historiographical problem that runs parallel to the others and for similar reasons has excited interest among church historians since 1953. Understanding the roots of heresy in its first manifestations, it has been held, should give clues to the nature of Western heresy in the Middle Ages as a whole; similarly, the reactions of authority to what was for them a quite novel phenomenon may explain attitudes towards persuasion or repression which came to prevail later on. The questions are intriguing; the sources peculiarly refractory. The challenge has stimulated a high level of investigation, not yet at an end, which has succeeded in scotching old hypotheses and thrown at least a frail, wavering light on the heretics.[24]

It is clear that the heresies which began to appear from c.1000, so often labelled Manichee, had nothing to do with Mani and his movement, which had long died out in Western Europe. They were not the endpoint of a line of ancient heresy: their roots lie in the religious and social history of their own age. They were individualistic, *sui generis*, sporadic, the fruit of particular circumstances, coteries, isolated leaders. Each of the episodes recorded has its own history and has required individual investigation. None, apparently, formed a lasting tradition: most were snuffed out and failed to survive the death or recantation of their leadership.

In one case at Monteforte, the key factor seems to have been an individualistic reading of the Bible by one inspiring leader, Gerard, who created a close-knit illuminist circle, largely or exclusively lay, with strongly ascetic views and startling idiosyncracies, including a rejection of the existence of Christ, who was transmuted into an allegory of the spiritual side of man.[25] At Orléans, a small, closed circle of canons and their followers believed themselves to be directly inspired by the Holy Spirit to an understanding of Scripture which excluded the reality of the incarnation or resurrection and made all the sacraments of the Church superfluous.[26] At Arras, we have one of the best examples of a new kind of textual community in which one charismatic leader creates a community based on a selection of scriptural texts, chosen and interpreted by him: the magister Gundolfo, who was not captured, brought into being a community supported from 'precepts of the Gospels and the apostles', leading a way of holy life, referred to as *justitia*, which did away with the necessity of the sacraments.[27] In Aquitaine, the movement stigmatized as Manichaean by Adémar laid stress on an apostolic

[24]   Bibliography: Lambert, *Medieval Heresy*, 2nd edn, p. 15, n. 21; *Il secolo XI: una svolta?*, ed. C. Violante and J. Fried, *Annali dell' Istituto storico italo-germanico*, Quaderno 35 (Bologna, 1993).

[25]   *GRK* III, pp. 187–207: virtuoso reanalysis, discussion of *animus* crucial, pp. 192–7; see also *canones*, pp. 191, 203–4, *pontifex*, pp. 197–8, *martirium*, pp. 199–202, not comparable to *endura*; elucidates extreme nature of this heresy seeing biblical interpretation as key. Neoplatonism not excluded, p. 205; compare Fichtenau, *Ketzer*, p. 47.

[26]   Lambert, *Medieval Heresy*, 2nd edn, pp. 9–16; sources, *GRK* III, pp. 151–71.

[27]   B. Stock, *The Implications of Literacy: Written Language and Models of Interpretation in the Eleventh and Twelfth Centuries* (Princeton, 1983) (analysis of chroniclers' thought world, originating concept of textual communities).

life, turning their backs on the formal ways of religion, on baptism and the use of the cross, and engaging in a fierce asceticism which rejected marriage and the eating of meat – actions which, not wholly inappropriately, earned them the label of Manichee. Their exasperated asceticism and rejection of ritual had no ancient roots: it seems rather to have been sparked off by a disaster at the basilica of St Martial at Limoges and, more profoundly, by disappointment with the failure of the Peace of God movement to achieve its ideals of reform, peace and order. In this heresy, social as well as religious factors played a considerable part. One root of this anti-Church movement was, indeed, a reaction against the cult of saints, relics and ritual which underpinned the Peace of God; another, the disappointment that the quest for order and reform in a changed society, which had once united all classes, had been distracted into a support for the consolidation of lordship, which worked emphatically against the interests of the powerless in society.[28]

Isolated and idiosyncratic as they were, the eleventh-century heresies are an overture to the much more substantial heretical movements of the twelfth and thirteenth centuries and share some characteristics with them: ethical considerations predominate over intellectual ones, in contrast to the classic heresies of early centuries. The laity are demanding a greater share in religious life and are prepared to break with ecclesiastical authority to secure it; growing literacy and awareness of texts and precedents create the conditions for an appeal to the New Testament, above all to the pattern of the life of the apostles, in opposition to the Church; monastic reform, spilling over into the lay world, helps to create a demand for ascetic communities not under existing Rules, which carry renunciations to the limits of orthodoxy. Rejection of marriage is a recurrent theme: at Monteforte, sexual intercourse was treated as wrong in itself and the leader, Gerard, looked forward to an age in which mankind would be begotten without coition 'like bees'; Adémar's Manichees rejected marriage, as did a group described by Roger II, bishop of Châlons-sur-Marne, in his diocese; at Arras, one tenet of the group was that they should restrain their flesh from 'carnal longings'.[29] A dominant strand in a rising religious zeal of this epoch was the

---

[28]   Landes, *Relics*, pp. 37–9, 67–8; R. I. Moore, 'Heresy, repression and social change in the age of Gregorian reform'; in *Christendom and its Discontents*, ed. S. L. Waugh and P. D. Diehl (Cambridge, 1996), pp. 19–46 at pp. 27–33. I owe information to Professor Moore.

[29]   *WEH*, pp. 84, 88, 90; Moore, *Birth*, pp. 20, 22; R. Landes, 'The dynamics of heresy and reform in Limoges: a study of popular participation in the "Peace of God" (994–1033)', in *Essays on the Peace of God*, ed. Head and Landes, pp. 467–511 at p. 499, trans. conflated version of Adémar's chronicle: *GRK* III, pp. 148, 198–9, 215. Conflict over sacralization of marriage could distort – heretics may have been opposed to this rather than marriage *per se* (Moore, *Origins*, p. 312, n. 9), or reports were blurred by literary reminiscences of Manichaeism. But flight from the corporeal is a salient feature in eleventh-century heresy. B. Töpfer (review, Fichtenau, *Ketzer*, *Mediaevistik* VIII (1995), pp. 366–8) believes Bogomil influence understated, infers possibility of Bogomil missionizing from existence of dualism in Kievan Rus c.1070 (*Jahrbuch für Geschichte des Feudalismus* XII (1988), p. 318ff). For Hamilton on Bogomil influence, see below p. 35.

growth of pilgrimage and the development of shrines, the extension of the influence of Cluny, its impressive liturgy, its lands and its dependent houses. A minor strand, which could issue in heresy, was impatient of the highly corporeal apparatus of the Church's worship, so strongly represented at Cluny, and sought a radical, austere alternative, stressing the simplicity and austerity of the gospels and Acts.

An accusation of heresy was too potent a weapon for it not to be used ruthlessly in Church polemics and political disputes. At Orléans, the heresy of the little illumunist group was real enough, but the occasion of its unmasking was a factional conflict within the kingdom of France, in which an accusation against a group of clergy which included the queen's confessor represented a blow struck at Queen Constance, her husband Robert the Pious and the power and patronage of the court.[30] The accusations launched against the 'Manichaeans' by Adémar and others may arouse suspicion. Adémar records the imposition of torture on heretical suspects and capital punishment on the obdurate.[31] The stakes were high. What dogmatic envelope in fact existed for the defiance of authority by the 'Manichacans' will not emerge from a source content with attributions to Mani and references to Antichrist. There was a serious conflict of views in the phase of decline of the Peace of God movement and, all unconsciously, the true extent and depth of heresy may easily have been exaggerated and distorted in the heat of the dispute.

Monks viewed with unease the emergence of lay groupings with their own Rules (like the *canones* which Gerard recommended to his followers at Monteforte)[32] and were suspicious of men and women leading a supposedly celibate common life. Leading churchmen could become nervous in the face of a resurgence of popular piety and see any resistance to their authority in these circumstances as amounting to heresy.[33] Hence the violent response, of which traces can be detected in several sources.

In the second half of the eleventh century, the Gregorian reform movement occupied the centre of the stage. Great controversies convulsed the Church and reform ideals put forward by a series of popes, beginning with Leo IX and including the inspiring and wayward figure of Gregory VII, awakened in the laity a new sense of responsibility for reform and a higher expectation of moral standards from their clergy. A genie was unleashed which could never again be put back into its bottle. Without the force of lay agitation, boycott and force deployed against a simoniacal and married clergy, the reforms which took place could never have been carried through.[34] But the agitation had profound long-term consequences. It has

---

[30] R. H. Bautier, 'L'hérésie d'Orléans et le mouvement intellectuelle au début du XIe siècle', in *Actes du 95e Congrès National des Sociétés savantes (Rheims, 1970): section philologique et historique* (Paris, 1975) I, pp. 63–88.

[31] Landes, *Relics*, p. 39, n. 91.

[32] *GRK* III, pp. 203–4.

[33] Landes, *Relics*, p. 37; for presuppositions of repression generally, Moore, *Origins*, pp. 243–62; ordeal, pp. 258–61.

[34] K. Leyser, *Am Vorabend der ersten europäischen Revolution. Das 11 Jahrhundert als Umbruchzeit, Theodor-Schieder-Gedächtnisvorlesung. Schriften des Historischen Kollegs, Dokumentationen* 9 (Munich, 1994), p. 6.

been rightly pointed out that Humbert of Moyenmoutier's *Three Books against the Simoniacs*, one of the most influential treatises of the movement, has a revolutionary quality comparable to that of Engels' *Communist Manifesto*.[35] The ideals it put forward, disseminated in sermons and treatises, could not easily be stifled and they lived on in the expectations of dissatisfied laity after the great days of the movement were over. Boycott of the masses of unworthy priests, encouraged by popes, deployed in its heyday with great effect in the social and religious protest of the Pataria in Milan, was a two-edged weapon. It led all too easily to the heresy we may loosely call Donatist: that the masses of unworthy priests were invalid because of their moral failures and were not true masses at all. St Peter Damiani, one of the heroes of the reform, was careful to reject such an interpretation, but the people to whom the reform appealed for support were often untrained, illiterate enthusiasts and were liable to accept Donatist interpretations. It is no accident that when heresies at a popular level are again recorded in Western Europe in the twelfth century the most common single tenet amongst them is that the sacraments of evil-living priests are invalid.

Magnificent in its idealism, the movement demanded of society and mankind objectives that were not realizable given the extensive landed endowment of the Church, the role and expectations of kings and princes and the inadequacy of all arrangements for the selection and training of the priesthood. But it had created a new mood of intolerance towards the practices of simony and clerical marriage; it had stirred consciences across Europe. When, inevitably, the initial impetus for reform ran down and its aims became more narrowly clerical and judicial – when the whole passionate concern that, in the words of Gregory, the Church, 'the bride of Christ ... should return to her true glory and stand free, chaste and catholic',[36] diverted into the lesser issue of investitures, narrowly understood as the right of rulers to deliver the symbols of sacred office to bishops – the reaction of those who now felt cheated of reform ran readily into channels of anticlericalism and heresy.

In contrast to the quiet, underground missionizing of most eleventh-century heresy, in the twelfth century evangelism took a more aggressive tone: there is more open preaching, more demonstrations and more use of force. Where earlier those accused of heresy were generally content to practise their austerities, preach or read their Scriptures within small, closed groupings, a new breed of leaders insists that the Church at large should listen to them and accept their ideas, and are prepared to use force to get their way. Although the best-known leaders – Henry of Lausanne, Peter of Bruys, Tanchelm, Arnold of Brescia – spring from the clergy, they make use of their lay following as a kind of battering-ram against abuse, as they see it, and resistance to their ideas. Henry turned Le Mans upside down, mobilized it against their bishop and used adherents stirred by his revivalism to carry out his reforms. Tanchelm moved about in the Netherlands amongst the crowds he had gathered accompanied by an armed guard. Peter of

---

[35]   Ibid., p. 7.
[36]   Quoted H. E. J. Cowdrey, 'Pope Gregory VII', *Headstart History* I (1991), p. 27.

Bruys used his following in vivid demonstrations, making bonfires of crucifixes or dragging monks from monasteries and compelling them to marry.
At the beginning of his career as an agitator, Arnold of Brescia used the
commune in his native city to set about reforming the clergy, and in the last
phase of his life succeeded in moving the citizens of Rome both to expel the
pope and back his radical assault on the power and wealth of the clergy.[37]

Differ as they might in their teaching, the leaders had in common a
preoccupation with the status and moral life of the clergy. Peter of Bruys
resolved the problem of evil-living priests by cutting away their functions,
rejecting the mass out of hand on the grounds that Christ had not intended
the actions of the Last Supper to be in any sense repeated, and repudiating
the whole apparatus of church buildings and traditional worship. Henry was
similarly drastic, and saw as his ideal a clergy who lived without money and
honours and exercised a preaching function. Tanchelm said the Church
had become a brothel and rejected its sacraments; Arnold, like Henry,
sought to impose poverty on the clergy and denied the hope of salvation to
monks and clergy who had possessions. It is easy to see how the new phase
of heretical outbreaks is linked with the sea-change in public attitudes to the
clergy brought about by the reform movement in the eleventh century and
the inevitable failure in the twelfth to live up to those ideals.

The careers of the best-known agitators of the first half of the twelfth
century also bear witness to changing attitudes to the apostolic life. All are
wandering preachers, generally advocating and practising poverty, sometimes covering considerable distances in their preaching tours: in their
attitudes they form an unorthodox parallel to the hermit preachers of
western France like Robert of Arbrissel or Bernard of Tiron, preaching
penance and attracting great crowds by their eloquence, disinterested zeal
and poverty. Both groups were following a pattern of apostolic life based
rather on Christ's Sending of the Seventy, carrying neither scrip nor staff
and having neither gold nor silver, living off their hearers, in Matthew's
gospel, than on the old, traditional pattern described in Acts of the community of possessions of the early Church at Jerusalem, adopted by monks
living on common property.[38] The ferment which had grown up in the
eleventh century was not over; it had its origins not only in the pronounce-
ments of popes, cardinals and bishops but in a desire for reform among
lesser clergy and lay people, above all in the search for an apostolic lifestyle
to be observed personally, or to be admired and responded to. Pressures for
reform, in H. E. J. Cowdrey's words, 'were welling from the bottom
upwards'[39] and continued to do so. Whether those pressures remained
in orthodoxy or sought expression outside was often dependent on the
presence or absence of a satisfactory orthodox leadership and on the
conditions prevailing in individual churches.

Social tensions aided heretical preachers and helped to give them audiences: towns were growing rapidly in the more advanced areas of Europe,

[37] Lambert, *Medieval Heresy*, 2nd edn, pp. 44–54; full treatment, Moore, *Origins* (see
esp. pp. 82–114); Henry of Lausanne and Peter of Bruys, *GRK* III, pp. 244–80.
[38] Matt. 10: 1–15; Acts 4: 32–5.
[39] Cowdrey, 'Pope Gregory VII', p. 27.

presenting a pastoral challenge to churchmen, often very imperfectly addressed; Arnold was able to use the citizens of Brescia and Rome's wish for independence for his own purposes; dramatic pastoral failure in Antwerp gave a platform to Tanchelm and internal problems had much to do with the success of Henry in Le Mans.

Heresies which first made an appearance tentatively in isolated outbreaks in the first half of the eleventh century, so far from vanishing altogether, had reappeared in a different and more challenging form under resourceful and eloquent leaders, founders of movements, as they may now be called – Arnoldists, Petrobrusians, Henricians.

Western churchmen were no more equipped to deal with heresy in the 1130s than they had been a hundred years earlier. Bishops were the traditional guardians of doctrine, but they were often enough distracted and not trained either to penetrate the statements of heretics or clearly enough to distinguish heresy from orthodoxy. The bishop of Soissons, faced with the task of dealing with the accused peasants of Bucy-le-Long in 1114, found it a hard business. Though he elicited some oddities, he found on questioning them about their beliefs that 'they replied in a most Christian fashion.' He determined to seek the judgement of heaven by resorting to the ordeal by water; while preparations for it were in hand, he entrusted further questioning to Guibert de Nogent, who similarly felt unable to penetrate to their true views, believing he was being put off by fair answers. One of the accused failed the ordeal and was pronounced guilty; the other confessed; two other supposed heretics who had come to watch the ceremony or the ordeal were then pulled in. The bishop still did not feel able to proceed to punishment and went off with Guibert to a synod being held at Beauvais to consult his fellow bishops on what he should do. In their absence, 'fearing clerical leniency', the crowd broke in and burnt the prisoners.[40] There is more to this than meets the eye: the peasants' neighbours may well have been objecting, not only to leniency but to disregard of the communal judgement enshrined in the ordeal procedure.[41] The story is none the less one of confusion on the bishop's part, both on how to recognize and how to punish heresy.

At Liège in 1135 the people wanted to stone certain heretics: some escaped this fate by flight, but three were imprisoned in fetters, two returned to orthodoxy and one was burnt. At Liège again, the clergy narrowly succeeded in rescuing an underground group of heretics whom the crowd wanted to burn. The clergy desired their repentance, but were plainly uncertain what to do. They sent a letter to the pope asking for guidance, at the same time despatching a penitent who wanted to go to the pope.[42] The heresy, which the clergy described as 'varied and

[40]   *WEH*, pp. 102–4. Source conveys the intense popular interest.
[41]   R. I. Moore, 'Popular violence and popular heresy in Western Europe, c. 1000–1179', *SCH* XXI (1984), pp. 43–50 at p. 49.
[42]   G. Despy, 'Les Cathares dans le diocèse de Liége au XIIe siècle: à propos de l'Epistola Leodiensis au Pape L (?)', in *Christianisme d'hier et d'aujourd'hui: hommages à Jean Preaux*, ed. G. Cambier (Brussels, 1979), pp. 65–75; 1135 chronicle entries, p. 70; letter to pope, pp. 74–5; dating to 1140s accepted. Text reproduced (*PL* CLXXIX),

manifold' had spread, they said, from one village, Mont Aimé in Champagne: it was here in 1239, well into the Cathar era, that a great mass burning took place presided over by a distinguished gathering of notables. Its evil reputation to the orthodox as a centre for heresy had evidently lasted for well over a generation. What exactly the heresy at Liège was remains unclear, for though are whiffs of later dualism in the letter's reference to 'auditors' and 'believers' and the rejection of marriage, there are other incongruous elements. The outcome of the application to the pope is unknown.

Peter of Bruys and his heresy was the target of a skilled exposition by Peter the Venerable, abbot of Cluny, but he himself was never captured and interrogated: he was lynched by Catholics, being pushed into one of his bonfires of crucifixes. Henry was at first checked by the decision of the Council of Pisa, which condemned three of his tenets and handed him over to the abbot of Clairvaux; whether Henry ever went as a monk to Clairvaux is unclear – if he did he did not stay long and was soon back preaching. He disappears from record after St Bernard deployed his eloquence against his influence and followers in Toulouse in 1145. Tanchelm was casually killed by a priest. After his defiance of both pope and emperor at Rome, Arnold was captured by the troops of Frederick Barbarossa and then hanged by order of the prefect of the city of Rome.

There was no established pattern for capture, investigation or punishment of heretics. Part of the difficulty is obvious: the lack of an authority experienced in the interrogation of suspects and equipped to decide what was heresy and what was not. The procedures of the ordeal were wholly unsuited – in a case at Ivoy near Trier, the chronicler clearly believed that a suspect, the priest Dominic William, escaped just condemnation by asking to be subjected to a form of ordeal. His request was granted and he was told to celebrate mass; when his turn came to receive communion, his bishop challenged him at this most solemn moment to take the host only if he was not guilty. He took it 'and obtained relief from his present troubles', but on his return home reverted to heresy. The chronicler related with satisfaction that eventually he came to a bad end, but plainly this was not before his heresy had been more widely diffused.[43]

The legitimacy of the use of force was another difficulty. There was precedent. St Augustine, confronted with the Donatist heresy in his diocese in North Africa, accepted the necessity of imperial legislation condemning heresy and subjecting it to various penalties: they formed, he came to believe, 'a teaching by inconveniences' (*per molestias eruditio*), comparable to the series of disasters by which God in the Old Testament disciplined his chosen people. Though he accepted forced conversions, he was opposed to

---

with doctrinal analysis, *GRK* III, pp. 287–93 (ranks and comparison to Everwin, pp. 290–1); *WEH*, pp. 139–41, quotation, p. 140. Despy argues for Innocent II as pope and suggests 1140; Wakefield for Lucius II and 1145.

[43] *WEH*, pp. 105–7; J. B. Russell, *Dissent and Reform in the Early Middle Ages* (Berkeley, Los Angeles, 1965), pp. 54–6.

capital punishment because it cut short the opportunity of repentance; in fact, there were numerous executions.[44]

Wazo of Liège, replying to a request for advice from his colleague, Roger II of Châlons-sur-Marne in the 1040s, made a classic statement of principle about the repression of heresy. Wazo understood 'the fervour of spiritual zeal' burning in Roger 'for souls deceived by devilish fraud'. This he felt should issue in preaching to refute heresy and publicity to warn the faithful. There should be excommunication 'officially and publicly announced to others' but not the death penalty. Wheat and tares should grow together till the harvest, and he warned Roger against premature use of the 'hoe of judicial decision to rid the grainfield' of the tares, a proceeding which usurped God's power of decision and could issue in miscarriages of justice. He urged the example of Christ 'who ... did not come to wrangle or contend but rather to suffer'. Anselm, the author of the history of the bishop of Liège in which Wazo's letter appears, believed that his exhortation had some effect, for 'in a measure he curbed the habitual headstrong madness of the French, who yearned to shed blood. For he had heard that they identified heretics by pallor alone, as if it were certain fact that those who have a pale complexion are heretics.' Anselm believed that executions in the past had killed 'many truly Catholic persons' and he deprecated the hanging after Wazo's death of heretics at Goslar.[45] But Wazo's attitude was not widely followed: violence against heretics continued, often inflicted by the laity in a sporadic, uncoordinated way. There was insecurity and inefficiency – stories of escapes by heretics recur – and confusion. It was in this context of uncertainty and growing dissent that Catharism, a more formidable and durable heresy than anything that had yet been seen in the West, made its appearance.

---

[44] P. Brown, 'Religious coercion in the later Roman Empire: the case of North Africa', *History* XLVIII (1963), pp. 283–305; reproduced in his *Religion and Society in the Age of St Augustine* (London, 1972), pp. 301–31; also his *Augustine of Hippo: a Biography* (2nd edn, London, Boston, 1969), pp. 237, 241.

[45] *WEH*, pp. 89–93; Moore, *Birth*, pp. 21–4. Pallor was allegedly produced by abstinence from meat. See Fichtenau, *Ketzer*, pp. 28–9.

2

The First Cathars

Emergence

St Hildegard of Bingen, abbess and visionary, known to contemporaries as the Sybil of the Rhine, recorded in 1163 a vision about the Cathar heretics, heavily touched by her reading of the Apocalypse. Their appearance in the Rhineland, which she dated to 1140 was interpreted by her as a consequence of the release of the Devil from the bottomless pit, which was followed by the four angels of the winds at the corners of the earth bringing evils to mankind – among which Catharism was a notable menace. 'For twenty-three years and four months have passed', she wrote, 'since through the wicked works of men which are blown out from the mouth of the black beast, the four winds have been set in motion by the four angels of the [earth's] corners, causing great destruction.'[1]

The release of the Devil preceded by decades the unleasing of the winds. Hildegard's dating of this is less clear but can be related either to the capture of St Peter's basilica by the emperor Henry IV in 1083 – an event which would have especially struck the imagination of pro-papal supporters of Gregory VII in Germany – or to the failure of the Crusade of 1101, which ended disastrously *en route* to the newly founded Christian settlements in the Holy Land, which it was designed to reinforce.[2]

Hildegard was well informed: she was a friend of St Elizabeth of Schönau, also a visionary, whose brother Ekbert took the lead in refuting Catharism in a set of sermons in 1163. He was a monk. Once, in the 1150s when he was still a young canon at Bonn, he had come into personal contact with Cathars and could witness to the tenacity of their missionaries who revealed their doctrines to him and one of his fellow canons because of their eagerness to win them over. They had not been dislodged by a serious attempt to destroy

---

[1] Quoted in B. Hamilton, 'Wisdom from the East: the reception by the Cathars of eastern dualist texts', in *Heresy and Literacy, 1000–1530*, ed. P. Biller and A. Hudson (Cambridge, 1994) (*BHL*), pp. 38–60 at p. 43 from St Hildegard, *Ep.* x *De Catharis*, ed. J. B. Pitra, *Analecta Sacra* VIII (Paris, 1882), p. 349.

[2] Hamilton's discussion, *BHL*, pp. 43–4.

them in 1143, which no doubt followed on the first intimations of their presence to which Hildegard referred. Everwin, provost of a house of Premonstratensians at Steinfeld near Cologne, was witness to their trial in the presence of the archbishop, in which two of their leaders whom he described as a bishop and his assistant, resisted all arguments for orthodoxy and were eventually seized by the crowd and burnt out of hand, bearing 'the agony of the fire', Everwin reported, 'not only with patience but even with joy'.[3]

A local chronicle, the Annals of Braunweiler, reports under the same year, 1143, a hearing before the archbishop of Cologne, in which some heretics, being subject to the ordeal, were found not guilty, while others fled. Three who were obdurate were burnt to death at Bonn by orders of Count Otto of Rheineck. The hearing under the archbishop may or may not have been the same as that described by Everwin.[4]

At a date subsequent to his sermons of 1163 on the Cathars, Ekbert was able to use his intimate knowledge of Cathar belief to break down the defences of a group at Mainz, which had apparently existed quietly for some time and even had a burial place of its own.[5] One, whom Ekbert's biographer describes as a heresiarch and master of the heretics, yielded and returned to orthodoxy; the others were recalcitrant and expelled from Mainz. Neither burning, nor expulsion, nor argument succeeded in eliminating the new heresy from the Rhine; authority was uncertain how to deal with it. While the clergy investigated at Cologne, the Cathar bishop and his assistant asked if they could call on their own teachers who they believed could more ably defend their views. The crowd, impatient at their obduracy, took over as Count Otto had done. At other times, provided they were discreet, Cathar representatives were evidently free to debate their beliefs with Ekbert and his fellow canon Bertolph at Bonn, and at Mainz the group, some forty strong, had been able to practise their beliefs with impunity.

Ekbert was quite clear why this new heresy was so dangerous. He identified it with the Manichaeism which had numbered Augustine among its adherents, and did not hesitate to use Augustine's evidence to fill in any gaps in the knowledge he had managed to acquire through interrogations and through his earlier infiltration of the movement. Sometimes this clearly led him into error, as when he attributed the celebration of the *Bema*, the feast held annually in the autumn to commemorate the death of the founder Mani, to the Rhineland heretics; it was their replacement, he said, for the Catholic feast of Easter. No doubt they endeavoured to avoid the celebration of Easter, but they knew nothing of Mani and his feast.

---

[3]   *WEH*, pp. 127–32 at p. 129 (*PL* CLXXXII, cols 676–80); R. Manselli, 'Evervino di Steinfeld e S. Bernardo di Clairvaux', in *Studi sulle eresia del secolo* XII (Rome, 1953), pp. 89–109; Moore, *Origins*, pp. 168–72, 179.

[4]   See *WEH*, p. 680, quoting *MGH SS* XVI, p. 727.

[5]   Ekbert's sermons are in *PL* CXCV, cols 11–98; Moore, *Origins*, pp. 175–82, 187, 195; see A. Borst, *Die Katharer* (Stuttgart, 1953) (classic analysis of doctrines and rites, based pre-eminently on chroniclers and controversialists), pp. 6–7, 94–5; Fichtenau, *Ketzer*, pp. 82, 85, 102–3, 125, 129, 158; assessment, *GRK* I (1), pp. 90–1; (2) pp. 292–6.

Ekbert's reflections on the dualist core of the heresy were also vitiated by his borrowings from St Augustine: we cannot securely infer from Ekbert exactly how the Rhineland heretics understood the origin and nature of evil, for on this point he has let Augustine speak for him. None the less, his thirteen sermons, the first learned attempt in the West to grasp the essence of Catharism, has a great advantage of bringing to the attention of his readers the fact that the heresy was an ideology, with a body of belief and practice, potentially supra-national, impersonal, exceeding in durability the individual, idiosyncratic teachings of this or that charismatic personality, which had hitherto formed the stuff of the heretical episodes recorded by Western chroniclers.

Through his personal contacts, Ekbert had knowledge of the fundamental rite of the Cathars whereby the neophyte was accepted into the ranks of the 'perfect'. 'The wretch who is to be baptized, or catharized', he said, 'stands in the middle [of the meeting] and the archcathar stands by him holding a book which is used for this office. He places the book on his head and recites blessings – or rather curses – while those who stand around pray and make [him] a son of Gehenna ... they call this the baptism by fire.'[6] Ekbert did not know what the book was – it was in fact either a gospel or a New Testament, placed on the head so that its contents might by a kind of osmosis flow into the selected individual.[7] Ekbert was describing the rite of the *consolamentum*, or the act of consoling, whereby entry was made into the small, dedicated elite of the perfect, on whom in great measure the success of the heresy rested. It was described as the baptism of the Spirit, or the baptism by fire, in contrast to the conventional baptism by water, despised as the work not of Jesus but of John the Baptist, which made use of evil matter and, so far from incorporating the baptized into the Church of Christ, put him or her into the power of Satan.

The heresy of the Cathars was more than a reform movement: it offered a direct, headlong challenge to the Catholic Church, which it dismissed outright as the Church of Satan. Only prolonged preparation and a willingness to undertake a lifetime of celibacy, fasting and ascetic practices secured the escape of the individual from Satan's power into the ranks of the perfect, among whom alone – if the renunciations were sustained – salvation was to be found. Catharism lacked the elaboration of ranks to be found in Manichaeism but, like all dualist movements, it shared a profound division between ordinary rank and file adherents and a small, committed elite, who alone carried out the full renunciations demanded by the sect – renunciations which were beyond the powers of ordinary members who remained in the world, married, had children and ate meat.

As in Manichaeism, the rank and file had a duty to care for the elite, whom they venerated. On that emotional link between believers and perfect in Catharism, as between hearers and Elect in Manichaeism,[8] much of the potency of the movement rested. The perfect inspired a remarkable devotion

---

[6]   Moore, *Origins*, p. 177; *PL* cxcv, cols 51–2.

[7]   Fichtenau, *Ketzer*, p. 90.

[8]   For Manichaeism, Moore, *Origins*, pp. 140–6; wise observation on problem of an outsider entering with sympathy into another set of beliefs: 'Few Protestants have

from their followers. In turn, entry to their grade was not easily permitted; in the great days of Catharism, the elite had to give proof of their readiness to endure considerable sacrifices and were encouraged by a considerable *esprit de corps* amongst themselves. Some could always be broken down by pressure, arguments and intimidation and so be brought back to Catholicism, but a nucleus, from the very beginning of our records, stood firm and faced fierce punishment with equanimity. Their resolution has sometimes been treated as a mere *topos* – a convention in the Catholic chroniclers – but there is too much independent evidence of their determination for it to be dismissed as an aberration of the sources. A number of the perfect, well trained in self-mastery through their ascetic practices, observed from the beginning to the end of the movement a potent tradition of martyrdom and thereby gave prestige to their Church.

Both Ekbert and Everwin record another novel and disturbing facet of the heresy: it emerges in the Rhineland as a full-fledged Church with its own hierarchy in contradistinction to the Catholics. Everwin's reference to the 'learned', to whom the bishop and his assistant wished to appeal, implies that the Cathar Church had had time to build up a trained, missionary body and that the young Church was already making a distinction between its formal leadership, with liturgical and directional functions, and its learned men.

Everwin was not as well informed as Ekbert, and he felt helpless before the heresy. His letter is an appeal for assistance from St Bernard of Clairvaux, then known to be working on his sermons on the Song of Songs. Everwin asked for some more reflections on the little foxes that spoil the vines and, in apocalyptic vein, like Hildegard, urges Bernard to 'stand forth against the new heretics who everywhere in almost all churches boil up from the pit of hell as though already their prince were about to be loosed and the day of the Lord were at hand'.[9] They unchurched the Catholics, he said, on moral grounds because of their claim to observe the apostolic life in a way in which the Catholics did not. They claimed no property, 'possessing no house, or lands, or anything of their own, even as Christ had no property nor allowed his disciples the right of possession'. They pleaded that they were persecuted 'as were the apostles and martyrs' and, by contrast, accused the Catholics of multiplying possessions and being 'false apostles'. Their descent, they claimed, was from the apostles themselves: 'we and our fathers, of apostolic descent, have continued in the grace of Christ and shall so remain until the end of time.'[10]

---

contributed much to the history of the Catholic liturgy, and there are no Manichees now to recreate the passions which gave substance to the bare skeleton of prohibitions' (p. 144); S. N. C. Lieu, *Manichaeism in the Later Roman Empire and Medieval China* (Tübingen, 1992).

[9]   *WEH*, p. 128.
[10]   Ibid., p. 129. Borst, *Katharer*, pp. 188–9, 228–9 stresses lack of consistency. See L. Paolini, 'Esiti ereticali della conversione alla povertà: La conversione alla povertà nell' Italia dei secoli XI–XIV', *Atti del Convegno dell' Accademia Tudertina e del Centro di Studi sulla Spiritualità medievale* (dir. E. Menestò) (Spoleto, 1991), pp. 127–86 at pp. 155–61.

Everwin then sketched their dietary practices, rejecting 'milk ... and whatsoever is born of coition',[11] their rite of baptism, rejecting the use of water and making use of the imposition of hands and their use of the pater-noster and ended with a crucial reference to their own understanding of their history. They claimed many adherents 'scattered widely throughout the world', Everwin said, and believed that they had won supporters among Catholic clergy and monks. Everwin referred to the obdurate pair who were burned and attributed to them the belief that their *credo* had 'lain concealed from the time of the martyrs even to our own day and has persisted thus in Greece and other lands'.[12]

Here was a drastic challenge, indeed, resting on a dogmatic core with ascetic practices conflicting with those of orthodoxy, a rival hierarchy, a claim to ethical superiority and a continuous history going back to the apostolic age. Little wonder that Catharism, born of the moral ferment of the twelfth century in the aftermath of Gregorian reform, in an age of much anticlericalism and disappointed expectations, given the capabilities of its leadership and the nature of its appeal in a world which gave great weight to asceticism, soon began to forge ahead of other more transient heresies. The alarm of Hildegard, Everwin and Ekbert was amply justified: a new threat to the Church became visible in the 1140s and it took a very long time of tribulation before it could be mastered and overthrown.

The Bogomils and the Byzantine Church

Everwin's casual reference to Greece has long intrigued historians because of the presence within contemporaneous Byzantium of the heresy of Bogomilism, which has important affinities to that of the Cathars. Bogomil, a village priest whose name 'worthy of the pity of God' was most probably a pseudonym,[13] organized a movement of rebellion in Bulgaria in the tenth century, born, in part, of the sufferings of the peasants at the hands of their masters, of reaction against an alien Byzantine-trained higher clergy imposed on a recently converted people, and in part on the doubts and tensions of an imperfectly instructed populace still close to heathenism and possibly influenced by pre-existing dualist beliefs in the country.[14]

---

[11] Paolini, 'Esiti ereticali ...', p. 129.

[12] Ibid., p. 132.

[13] H. C. Puech and A. Vaillant, *Le Traité contre les Bogomiles de Cosmas le Prêtre* (Paris, 1945) (subtle analysis), pp. 27, 282–3. Dr Lydia Denkova of Sofia will argue in future work that Bogomil was a name assumed, 'friend of God', marking the priest's ascent to a higher grade of perfection, on the analogy of Romil who in fourteenth-century Hesychast sources changed his name three times; see also E. Werner, 'Theophilos – Bogumil', *Balkan Studies* VII (1966), pp. 49–60; and 'Bogomil – eine literarische Fiktion?', *FF* XXXIII (1959), pp. 24–8; T. S. Thomov, 'Les appellations de "bogomiles" et "bulgares" et leurs variantes et équivalents en Orient et en Occident', *Etudes Balkaniques* I (1973), pp. 77–99. I thank Dr Denkova for generous help.

[14] Summary, Lambert, *Medieval Heresy*, 1st edn, pp. 12–17; D. Obolensky, *The Bogomils* (Cambridge, 1948); J. V. A. Fine, Jr, 'The Bulgarian Bogomil movement',

The heresy was marked by a profound hostility to the beliefs and practices of Byzantine orthodoxy, its priesthood, liturgy, churches and Fathers, which it replaced by a simple community of believers, whose prayer consisted solely of the paternoster, repeated four times every day and four times every night. It rejected marriage and procreation and, in the words of Cosmas the Priest, who wrote a treatise against it, Bogomils were in the habit of turning away as from a bad smell, spitting and holding their noses whenever they met children of baptismal age. They believed that the Devil, equated with the God of the Old Testament, was the creator of the visible world of matter, and consequently repudiated the Byzantine sacraments which made use of matter, baptism and the eucharist, and rejected ikons and the veneration of the cross; baptism in water was rejected in favour of an initiation rite based on the laying on of hands. The drinking of wine was condemned and even to touch meat was to obey the command of Satan.

By a strange and rare mutation, Bogomilism passed out of the wild, frontier land of Bulgaria, conquered after hard campaigning by the emperor Basil the Bulgar-slayer early in the eleventh century, made converts within the heartlands of Byzantium and finally, in the imperial capital, aided by a mood of deep depression and loss of confidence in the Empire and its Church following the years of troubles suffered by the Byzantines after the death of Basil and the great defeat of Manzikert, it missionized and won recruits in sophisticated circles in Constantinople. Their leader, a doctor Basil, who no doubt won converts through his medical skills, even aspired to influence the emperor himself, Alexius Comnenus, who with his brother Isaac pretended to be a possible recruit to the heresy and lured Basil into revealing his beliefs while a stenographer, concealed behind a curtain, took down the incriminating details.[15]

The unmasking can be dated approximately to the last years of the eleventh century, probably after the First Crusade and certainly before the death of Isaac which took place, at the latest, in 1104. Tradition had it that Basil had been spreading his views for fifty-two years before he was discovered. A fierce attachment to the New Testament as interpreted by Basil and his most intimate followers, the *theotokoi* (the bringers forth of God in whom the Holy Spirit dwelt who illuminated their understanding of Scripture), led to a rejection of the Old Testament with the exception of the Psalms and the Prophets and of the whole apparatus of Byzantine orthodoxy. One episode from Basil's early career as a seeker after truth, which emerged from the interrogation carried out by Euthymius Zigabenus, the Byzantine theologian employed by Alexius to ascertain and refute his heresy, gives a glimpse of the psychology of underground protest that lay near the heart of Basil's system.

East European Quarterly XI (1977), pp. 384–412 (pungent critique); Y. Stoyanov, *The Hidden Tradition in Europe: the Secret History of Medieval Christian Heresy* (London, 1994) (wide exposition, illuminating on Bulgarian history).

[15]   M. Angold, *Church and Society in Byzantium under the Comneni, 1081–1261* (Cambridge, 1995), pp. 468–501, unmasking, pp. 480, 485–6; background, M. Angold, *The Byzantine Empire, 1025–1204* (London, 1984), pp. 114–35.

Basil had acquired a copy of the gospels. After he had bought it, he met an old man in a deserted place. 'Calling me by name', Basil said, 'he told me that I had bought a great treasure, for this book alone escaped the hands of John Phrysostom.'[16] This was a pejorative way of referring to the master of Orthodoxy, St John Chrysostom. Bogomils believed they were heirs to an authentic, underground tradition of correct interpretation of the deposit of faith, which went back to the age of the apostles and allowed them to escape the falsifications and distortions of Chrysostom and the other Fathers. To recover the authentic beliefs of the early Church, Basil and his followers did not read the gospels in isolation but with the aid of the Apocrypha, which they believed had also escaped the baleful influence of Chrysostom. These mediated to them the heretical tradition of dualism, long latent in Byzantium and intertwining easily with Greek Orthodox monasticism.

Cosmas noticed how the early Bogomils profited from a passion for the ascetic life awakened among the Bulgars and from a flight to monasticism sparked off by the bitter conditions of Bulgarians in the tenth century. Bogomilism made headway in western Asia Minor after Cosmas's day via the missionary efforts of John Tzurillas, described as a pseudo-monk, and infiltrated the Peribleptos monastery in Constantinople in the eleventh century, where Euthymius of Peribleptos uncovered four Bogomils among his fellow monks.[17] Monasticism provided both a camouflage and a refuge for the heretics in Bulgaria and Byzantium and helps to give credibility to the claim of the Cathars of the Rhineland that they had made converts among monks.

Basil clearly developed the Bogomilism he had inherited and made it acceptable to the highest circles in the imperial capital, where a vogue had developed for dabbling in arcane learning. His latest interpreter, Angold, describes it as a blend, not wholly coherent, of dualism, demonology and a New Testament ethic (or, rather, a Bogomil version of this).[18] From his interrogations of Basil, Zigabenus elicited a whole cosmology based on the fall of Lucifer, originally the elder son of God expelled from heaven for his rebellion but retaining, despite all, his divine power of creation. The making of Adam was the result of a bargain between God and the Devil, whereby God would provide the Devil's creature with a soul and they would have joint dominion over him. The Devil, however, seduced Eve in the form of a serpent and lost his divine powers, but God still allowed him to rule over his creation – for a time. The coming of Christ resulted from the Father's taking pity on the human soul which was his creation and sending another son, identified with the Archangel Michael, who entered Mary by her right ear. He only appeared to be man and did not suffer as a man; a true crucifixion did not take place, nor did a resurrection in the orthodox sense. But Christ seized Satan and bound him. Defeated, the Devil had still not lost all his power, however, and a struggle continued which would end, not in a resurrection of body and soul, but in a destruction of the body with all Satan's evil creation and the assumption into heaven of the imprisoned souls.

[16] Angold, *Church*, p. 479.
[17] Lambert, *Medieval Heresy*, 1st edn, pp. 18–19; G. Ficker, *Die Phundagiagiten* (Leipzig, 1908); Angold, *Church*, p. 21.
[18] Angold, *Church*, p. 484.

Figure 1 The ladder to heaven: ikon from St Catherine's monastery, Sinai, showing the stark struggle between good and evil in Byzantine monastic imagination. Black devils with pikes, ropes and bows and arrows drag sinners to perdition: Byzantine monasticism was a seed-ground of Bogomilism.

Photograph: Corbis/Roger Wood

Bogomil interpretation was nourished, not only by apocryphal tales derived ultimately from such sources as Gnosticism and Judaic apocalyptic, whose traditions had lingered on in Byzantium, but also by an arbitrary, allegorical exegesis of Scripture, which ingeniously and fluently glossed away inconvenient references to Christ's humanity or to his use of bread and wine in the Last Supper, and which has been enshrined for us in Zigabenus's extracts from a Bogomil commentary on St Matthew's gospel. Through the rites and prayers of the Bogomils, man might make his escape from the power of Satan. Careful initiation was necessary and not all the inner secrets of Bogomilism were at once imparted to potential recruits, who were taken stage by stage into the *arcana* of the movement, a progressive form of instruction with strong affinities to that customary in Gnostic movements, and with the same attractions.

Zigabenus describes for us a double initiation ceremony before a neophyte became one of the *theotokoi*, or, in Cathar terms, one of the perfect. After a period of preparation, the gospel of John was placed on the candidate's head and the Holy Spirit invoked. There followed a period of retreat and an examination to ensure the candidate's fitness and then a final ceremony, with the gospel again laid on the candidate's head. Those accepted in this fashion maintained as feeble a contact with the visible world of Satan as possible: they were, of course, celibate and renounced the products of coition and fasted every Monday, Wednesday and Friday until the ninth hour. The attraction of an ascetic life and the veneration for those who practised it was a central point in the appeal of Bogomilism.

Holy men circulated freely in the Byzantine Church, were under loose control and were accustomed to widespread respect. Basil was able to profit by this tradition and to exploit the division between the hierarchy and the priesthood, which excited scant affection, and Orthodox monasticism which retained much enthusiasm and imparted a sense of community. He sheltered within this monastic tradition, wearing always a monastic habit. At the core of the life of these informal communities of *theotokoi* was a prayer life of the utmost simplicity in which the tradition of reciting the paternoster, dating back to the priest Bogomil,[19] was continued, in contrast to the elaborations of Byzantine worship and church buildings, dismissed by the movement as the abode of demons.

Alexius Comnenus, determined to restore the role of the emperor after many years of weakness and anarchy, saw action against heresy as one of the traditional duties and prerogatives of the imperial office which he was restoring: his activity against the Bogomils was thus a pendant to his other military and political successes, resurrecting and giving further life to the Byzantine state. But the signs are that he also took the Bogomils seriously in their own right with their long-standing tradition of missionary zeal and was well aware of their insidious power. He took the trouble to commission and support Euthymius Zigabenus and to continue the work of the Patriarch

---

[19] To consider the paternoster to be the only prayer is rare, so I reject Angold's suggestion (*Church*, p. 471) that the Bogomilism of Bulgaria and of Basil the Doctor 'had little more than the name in common'.

Nicholas Grammatikos, who had set up a body of preachers soon after 1084 to protect the populace of the capital from heresy. Alexius took a personal interest in the fate of the heretics, who were rounded up and imprisoned after Basil's heresy was detected. His first intention was to burn them but he met hostility from the crowd and let the majority go free, perhaps after a superficial expression of repentance, kept the closest supporters in prison and put Basil under pressure to yield to Orthodoxy. But he would not and was burned before a great crowd, probably after a final decision made by the Patriarch and his synod.[20]

Although Alexius's disciplinary action did not end the life of Bogomilism, ecclesiastical authority had been alerted and remained vigilant. Sometimes authority turned on suspects who were not strictly Bogomil but held views in some respects worryingly similar, as in the scandal of Constantine Chrysomallos.[21] At other times, Bogomils proper were unearthed, as in the case of St Hilarion, bishop of Moglena c.1134–64; they were bold enough to stone him unconscious.

Bogomilism spread in the European provinces of the Empire and was sporadically persecuted; as late as mid-thirteenth century, the Patriarch Arsenius (1254–60) sent one of his officers to Macedonia to repress them. The Dialogue *Timotheos or about Demons*, once attributed to Michael Psellos but now convincingly redated to mid-twelfth century, shows with probability Nicholas, bishop of Methone, using an imaginary dialogue to refute Bogomil beliefs. Though his work included conventional anti-heretical slanders reminiscent of Guibert de Nogent, the views he attacked, on the Devil as the Father's elder son who held dominion over the earth, and Christ as the younger son, show that Bogomilism of Basil's type had survived and had gone on winning recruits in provinces far removed from Constantinople.[22]

However, Bogomilism never created a crisis in the Byzantine Church in the way in which Catharism did in the Latin Church in the late twelfth and thirteenth centuries. The Byzantine Church was more experienced in grappling with heresy and was never subjected to the intense feeling of powerlessness in the face of a growing heretical menace which afflicted the ecclesiastical authorities in the West and led to dramatic responses. Bogomils proper remained few: they continued to make converts, especially in outlying provinces, to profit by anarchic and extravagant elements in monasticism and to make use of the long Byzantine tradition of eccentric, wandering holy men. Moreover, they gave an outlet to a lay piety unsatisfied

[20]   I follow Angold's interpretation (*Church*, pp. 486–7), preferring Zigabenus to Anna Comnena.
[21]   Ibid., pp. 487–90. Angold supersedes older historians; note Chrysomallos's use of the Orthodox spiritual writer Symeon the New Theologian. See H. J. M. Turner, 'St Symeon the New Theologian and dualist heresies – comparisons and contrasts', *St Vladimir's Theological Quarterly* XXXII (1988), pp. 359–66.
[22]   Gautier in *Revue des Etudes Byzantines* XXXVIII (1980), pp. 105–94; Angold, *Church*, pp. 496–9, seeing discussions of Devil worship as Orthodox travesty of Bogomil beliefs. Sermons of Patriarch Germanos II (1223–40), which seem to be directed against a living Bogomilism, are evidence of survival (Angold, *Church*, p. 551).

by the formalities of the hierarchical Church, which in turn stiffened its reaction against dissent and became less tolerant. Alexius's action was reasonably effective and occasional policing, using the powers of patriarchs and bishops, synodal denunciations with imprisonment and occasional burnings, was sufficient to keep the Bogomils a marginal force.

After the superficial glories of the revival led by the Comnenian dynasty, the Byzantines had other preoccupations; they descended rapidly into anarchy and, after the shock of their conquest by the troops of the Fourth Crusade in 1204, revival in these last centuries of Byzantine independence owed much to Orthodoxy. It was the Church which gave Byzantines a sense of identity as the powers of their state weakened. In these circumstances, Bogomilism in the lands of the old Empire seems to have faded out. It had a much less dramatic history than the sister movement of the Cathars and never achieved the remarkable progress against authority that the Cathars did. While, after a major expenditure of effort on refutation and, above all, police work, the Cathars were finally put down by the Western Church, by contrast Byzantine Bogomilism died a quiet, natural death.

Bogomilism and Catharism

There are striking likenesses between Eastern Bogomilism and Western Catharism, especially in their ritual practices and their attitudes towards the beliefs, order and ritual of the great Churches against which they struggled and protested.[23] Both movements restricted prayer to the paternoster alone, repeated in swathes by their respective elites, on lines reminiscent of monastic prayer and with similar frequency. Zigabenus reported that the Bogomils prayed seven times during the day and five times during the night; Anselm of Alessandria, the inquisitor who gave a narrative account of early Cathar history and a description of their beliefs and practices as he knew them in Italy in the thirteenth century, said that they prayed fifteen times every twenty-four hours.[24] Euthymius of Peribleptos described an infiltration of heresy within Orthodoxy perpetuated by a false monk and priest who, as a blind, built a church on the banks of the Bosphorus but desecrated it by installing his latrine behind the altar; a comparable gesture of contempt is recorded of a Cathar in Toulouse who defecated by the altar in a church and wiped himself with the altar cloth.[25] The psychology was the same. Cathars insisted that Catholic churches were no more holy than any other building and regarded them as sites of idolatry; Bogomils described Byzantine churches as the dwelling place of demons.

Both Bogomils and Cathars rejected the veneration of the cross on comparable quasi-rational grounds, that it was inconceivable that the piece

---

[23] *GRK* III, pp. 74–114, 570–1 (fullest analysis of similarities and dissimilarities between Bogomilism and Catharism); also G. Rottenwöhrer, *Unde Malum? Herkunft und Gestalt des Bösen nach heterodoxer Lehre von Markion bis zu den Katharern* (Bad Honnef, 1986), chs 6, 7; comment, Fichtenau, *Ketzer*, p. 76; Hamilton in *BHL*, p. 38.
[24] *GRK* III, p. 107.
[25] Ibid., pp. 307–8; Angold, *Church*, p. 475; J. H. Mundy, *The Repression of Catharism at Toulouse: the Royal Diploma of 1279* (Toronto, 1985), p. 24.

of wood on which his son was killed would be dear to the king. Both gave an allegorical interpretation of the words of Christ instituting the eucharist. They were alike in having the same weekly fast days, Mondays, Wednesdays and Fridays. Both rejected marriage *per se* as a dirty business which perpetuated the reign of Satan, and believed that salvation was only possible when the marriage partners repudiated each other. Both laid great emphasis on the initiation rite, a baptism of the Spirit or of fire, in contrast to the Satanic baptism in water.[26]

Both movements referred to the members of their elite in the strongest terms. Zigabenus's statement that they were believed to be the dwelling place of the Holy Spirit is repeatedly echoed in Cathar sources and in Catholic treatises about them, above all and most tellingly in the two surviving Cathar rituals. Certain Bogomils called their elite 'Good Christians'; the Cathars did too. They were also known in both movements as 'the righteous' and were held to be simply the Church, those who followed the gospels and the way of the apostles. In the evil creation of Satan, they represented the good and their ascetic practices were the outward and visible sign of their goodness and the guarantee of their perfection, in contrast to the clergy of the Byzantine and Catholic Churches, mired in the world of Satan.[27]

It was a simple and powerful appeal, with an identical force in both Bogomilism and Catharism. In a notable phrase, Fichtenau has referred to the Cathars as being 'living ikons'[28] in the eyes of their followers and this applies equally well to the Bogomils. These protest movements were opposed to the veneration of Byzantine ikons or Catholic images, but they were reared in a tradition of the cult and veneration of saints, to whom appeals and prayers were constantly directed. The perfect or *theotokoi* simply and effectively stepped into the place occupied in both systems by the saints. The sense of attachment to authentic Christianity made visible in a class of true practitioners buoyed up both movements from the beginning to the end of their histories.

The belief that the Holy Spirit was to be found in the elite explains the respect that the rank and file had for their interpretations of Christianity – the creation, the fall and the mission of Christ – and the variation as this or that master, wielding his powers of interpretation, developed a school of doctrine round him. The masters, however, worked within a field of dualistic and allegorical assumptions about Scripture, which led to similar interpretations. The detailed selection of books which were acceptable varied, but in all cases there was a profound suspicion of the Old Testament, which was handled differently from the New and treated in general as the work of Satan.[29]

---

[26]   *GRK* III, pp. 108–9 (cross), pp. 110–11 (eucharist), p. 114 (fast days), p. 114 (marriage), p. 102 (initiation); compare *WEH*, pp. 475–9, 488–90.

[27]   *GRK* III, pp. 86–7; Borst, *Katharer*, pp. 205–8; 242–3; Fichtenau, *Ketzer*, pp. 88–93; W. L. Wakefield, *Heresy, Crusade and Inquisition in Southern France, 1100–1250* (London, 1974) (*WHC*), (concise, reliable introduction), pp. 37–41.

[28]   Fichtenau, *Ketzer*, pp. 86–7.

[29]   *GRK* III, pp. 95–6.

The movements shared a common aversion to matter and a set of vivid, even gross metaphors, allegories and narratives explaining creation, interpreting the Old Testament and allegorizing much of the New. Both had supporters who believed that God the Father ruled only the heavenly sphere; that Satan was the creator and ruler of the earthly sphere, repeating the story of his seduction of Eve and his act of intercourse with her in the form of a snake; that God was divided only for a time into three persons. Rejection of matter led both movements to believe that Christ had no body and that he only appeared to be crucified; that his miracles were not physical events, but only spiritual healings.[30] Proof texts were used to buttress dualist interpretations. The words of Jesus to the woman at the well in St John's gospel, 'My meat is to do the will of him who sent me', were interpreted as a sign that Christ's humanity was only apparent, not real, for he did not need food; and the words of St Paul, 'Flesh and blood cannot inherit the kingdom of God', as a proof against the resurrection of the body.[31] Sometimes the conjunction is such as to lead us to infer, not only that Bogomils and Cathars shared a common approach to Scripture and tradition from which similarities of interpretation inevitably arose, but that Bogomils directly or indirectly influenced Cathars. A case in point is the episode in which Satan grappled with the body which he made for Adam and tried in vain to animate. Euthymius of Acmoneia, reporting on Byzantine Bogomils probably in the early eleventh century, attributed to them the belief that the time-lag in which Satan tried to put life into the body lasted either three hundred or thirty years; the anti-Cathar treatise attributed to Peter of Verona (St Peter Martyr), assassinated in 1252, records it as being thirty years, after which he called on God to do it for him.[32] To explain so detailed a likeness we must infer some channel of influence, personal, oral or written, between these Bogomils and the Italian Cathars of St Peter Martyr's day.

Similarly, Zigabenus recorded that Bogomils in the early twelfth century believed Satan to be stronger than Christ; the late twelfth-century controversialist, Alan of Lille, author of the *De fide Catholica*, attributed the same view to the Cathars, apparently based on the temptation of Christ as the pinnacle of the Temple.[33] That there was a substantial transmission of ritual and ideas from Bogomilism to Catharism is beyond reasonable doubt.

As Everwin describes the early Cathars he knew in the Rhineland, it was a movement which had already established roots in the West by 1143. He mentions casually the reference by the bishop and his assistant to their coreligionists in Greece, but he gives no hint that any of those investigated were Greeks or Slavs or originated in Byzantium; it seems reasonable to infer that if they had been foreigners, he would have said so. The same would apply to Ekbert's evidence. So the assumption must be that these Cathars were native Rhinelanders and that their movement, unmistakably

[30] Ibid., pp. 75–91.
[31] John 4: 34, *GRK* III, p. 99; 1 Cor. 15: 50, *GRK* III, p. 100.
[32] Ibid., p. 89.
[33] Ibid., p. 79.

linked as it was to Bogomilism, had already passed beyond the first missionary phase in which preachers from outside the region sought to win recruits: they had established a native leadership.

Diffusion and development

What other footholds the new heresy had established in the West by 1143 it is impossible to say. The comment of Bernard Hamilton carries weight: 'I doubt whether anybody would wish to claim that all Cathars throughout the west derived from the congregation whose leaders were brought to trial at Cologne in 1143.'[34] No doubt Catharism grew at a number of places and succeeded or faded according to the skill of preachers or missionaries and the receptiveness they found, but other episodes were not detected or records of them have not come down to us.

The private heresies of individuals, spontaneously arrived at, might have given a launching-pad for Catharism. Fichtenau notes with interest[35] the views of John, Count of Soissons, as exposed in the criticisms made of him by Guibert de Nogent, who said that he loved the heretics and held in high regard Judaism (which he none the less did not observe). John was plainly something of a free thinker, who was powerful enough to please himself and say what he thought – suggesting that all women should be shared in common and that it was no sin if they were, and casting doubt on the virgin birth, the omnipotence of God and the nature of creation – was it good or bad? Such ideas probably did not spring from any direct Bogomil or Cathar contact, but they are straws in the wind indicating how in places where they were active, their teaching could find support points in doubts and denials of orthodoxy which already existed in the minds of individuals.

Both Bogomils and Cathars believed that their elite followed the way of the apostles, but in the Rhineland that 'way' was being interpreted in a firmly Western fashion. The belief that apostolic life consisted pre-eminently in wandering preaching in poverty, on the lines of Christ's commands at the Sending of the Seventy, gained ground in the twelfth century in the West at the expense of the older, traditionally monastic view, practising community of goods. Everwin's description of the Rhineland Cathars shows how thoroughly they had taken up this contemporaneous, developing Western concept and treated the poverty and insecurity of their lives and the persecution to which they were actually or potentially exposed as a sign of the authenticity of their way of life and teaching.

Despite the common inheritance of myths and doctrines, Bogomilism and Catharism were far from being identical: there are no signs of irrele-vancies and anachronisms lingering on in Catharism which would have orig-inally been derived from the Balkans or Byzantium – there is no mention of Chrysostom, for example. Catharism is a protest movement rejecting the Western Church. Their leaders are aware of a link to the East, and as the late twelfth-century journeys of Cathar leaders to Constantinople and the

---

[34]   *BHL*, p. 44.
[35]   Fichtenau, *Ketzer*, p. 77.

Balkans indicate, Eastern cradles of belief have prestige, and continue to have it right into the fourteenth century.[36] But it is never subservient to the East: as soon as we have records of its existence, it is unmistakably and thoroughly westernized and develops a life of its own. Stray eccentricities in Bogomilism drop away; Zigabenus tells us, for example, that they saw the Father as an old man with a long beard, Christ as a bearded man and the Holy Spirit as a beardless youth, but these anthropomorphisms were not accepted by the Cathars. Even in dietary practices, where a likeness is striking, there is a certain difference. Bogomils rejected wine, Cathars did not, except during their great forty-day fasts – whether these occurred in Bogomilism we do not know.[37]

The demonology of the Bogomils owed much to the assumptions of the Byzantine Church, which went further than the demonology of the West and is plainly not transmitted to the Cathars. Zigabenus reported the Bogomil belief that God had allowed demons dominion over the whole world, until its end. Christ could not achieve a complete destruction of their power and they were able to do damage against which neither Christ nor the Holy Spirit could wholly prevail.[38] His record of the beliefs of the doctor Basil's circle is unlikely to have been the product of prejudiced interpretation since he was a careful reporter who himself interrogated Basil, whose counsel to his followers was to 'honour the demons, not so that you will benefit from them, but so that they do you no harm'.[39] This placatory caution is nowhere to be found among the Cathars, who excised such a Byzantine attitude.

The Cathar ritual of the *consolamentum* derives from the Bogomil form of initiation of adepts. The two versions of the Cathar ritual which have come down to us are contained in thirteenth-century MSS, but the indications emerging from modern research indicate strongly that the archetype of these MSS was a Latin version made in the twelfth century.[40] In other words, early Cathars had a liturgy in the ecclesiastical language of the West, matching in solemnity that of the Catholics. They also dropped the two initiation ceremonies of the East, with a probationary period in between, preferring just one with the gospel laid on the candidate's head.

At its first recorded appearance, Catharism had the episcopate. Its subsequent history demonstrates that the office carried prestige and was both sought after and quarrelled over. In time, the subordinate ranks of *filius major* and *filius minor* were added, with automatic right of succession, acting, in effect, as coadjutor bishops; there was also a diaconate.[41] A Cathar hierarchy confronted a Catholic one, with territorial titles, where demarcations of diocese evidently mattered. The bishops were elected from the perfect

---

[36] See below, pp. 47–8, 50, 53, 56, 206, 211, 294–6.
[37] *GRK* III, pp. 94, 114.
[38] Ibid., pp. 93–4.
[39] Angold, *Church*, pp. 480–1 (quotation, p. 480), supporting Zigabenus's credibility.
[40] Hamilton in BHL, pp. 46–9.
[41] Borst, *Katharer*, pp. 202–13.

and gave opportunities to leading personalities to exert sway and exercise pastoral duties. Despite quarrels between individuals, noteworthy in Italy, the existence of a hierarchy was a source of strength for the Cathars. Did they develop this hierarchy in distinction to the Bogomils?

It is clear that the Bulgarian Bogomilism described by Cosmas the Priest had no such ranks; there seems to have been a great measure of equality among this tenth-century elite. They confessed sins to each other without distinction of gender.[42] When Bogomilism entered the Byzantine heartlands, the impression given is of groups led effectively by charismatic personalities such as John Tzurillas, who did not claim episcopal rank. Euthymius of Peribleptos describes a simple, *ad hoc* organization with a strong hortatory, inspirational element, dividing up the Byzantine Empire by lot to apportion various regions to individuals for the task of preaching. Zigabenus describes Basil's Bogomils in Constantinople in similar terms. The doctor was the leader and inspiration of the movement with many followers but with a core of women disciples and twelve apostles. His organization was simple, based on the New Testament, but he himself was effectively in charge. There is no mention of bishops or other offices apart from the 'apostles'.[43]

Zigabenus had completed his work before Everwin wrote. The implication is that the Cathars developed some hierarchy of their own before the Bogomils did. They also in the end carried it further, for Bogomils are not recorded as developing a diaconate. Later in the century, when Eastern dualists and Western Cathars came into contact, Western sources attribute an episcopate to the East. How it emerged remains obscure,[44] but by that stage Catharism was the more dynamic movement, making inroads at the expense of Latin orthodoxy.

The evidence is that, though Catharism was intimately linked with and owed much to the Bogomils and their teachings, it none the less emerged as an independent movement with characteristics of its own and, by the time it was detected by Church authorities, had been thoroughly westernized.

Curiously, no evidence has ever emerged to throw light on a Bogomil missionary phase within Western Europe. As far as extant records are concerned, no Bogomil was ever caught preaching, leading a group of neophytes or disseminating literature. Powerful as it is, all our evidence of a link between Bogomilism and Catharism before 1143 is inferential, based on likenesses between ritual, diet, religious practices and doctrines.

That Byzantium and the West came into more intimate contact from the eleventh century onwards is undeniable. Energies in the West were turned outwards in a way that had not been possible for centuries past and the

---

[42]   *GRK* III, p. 105, citing Cosmas.
[43]   Angold, *Church*, pp. 474, 480; Lambert, *Medieval Heresy*, 1st edn, p. 19.
[44]   Key points are (a) lack of detailed information about Bogomilism/Eastern dualism after Zigabenus's account; (b) Western Cathars' lack of detailed knowledge of the East; (c) obscurity in sources about the evolution of early Catharism. See *GRK* III, pp. 567–75 for summary, and personal hypothesis. Borst (*Katharer*, pp. 202–3) speaks of the episcopate as becoming a necessity among the Bogomils 'probably not long before 1140' as the Bogomil Church spread in 'several areas of mission'.

weakness of Byzantium gave them new opportunities. Warriors took land in the Byzantine Empire; Venetians were called in by Alexius to provide a naval defence for the Empire and established a trading position with privileges for their merchants. Alexius suffered the trauma of the First Crusade, when a remarkable expedition of Western warriors passed through his territory on a march to the Holy Land, for a time, at least in Alexius's eyes, threatening Byzantium's very existence. Thereafter, the magnet of the crusade drew down Western attention, often hostile, on to the Byzantine world. On the other hand, Byzantine influence played on Western monasticism. Hamilton has put forward the hypothesis that agents for a Bogomil infiltration might be found among Byzantine monks visiting shrines in the West:[45] Southern Italy, which remained a Byzantine colony into the eleventh century and long possessed Greek-speaking inhabitants, has been mentioned as a possible area of infiltration.[46] And yet it remains true that all positive evidence for Bogomils making a landfall and then spreading their views in the West is missing.

Perhaps this is no accident. A clue to what may have happened is given in the curious reconstruction of Cathar history which Anselm of Alessandria, inquisitor in Lombardy, put at the head of the compendium of useful facts on heresies and how to deal with them which he assembled round about 1266–7 for the use of other inquisitors, in part designed to provide some facts supplementary to the classic, succinct account of Cathars and Waldensians written by Sacconi, once his master and a predecessor in office.[47] The little history, derived no doubt from the oral traditions of prisoners he had interrogated, includes facts given by no one else.

Anselm's weaknesses are obvious. He insists on tracing Catharism back to Mani, who 'taught in the regions of Drugunthia, Bulgaria and Philadelphia',[48] i.e. at sites which in his day were seats of Eastern dualist bishops. The time-lag between the twelfth-century birth of Catharism and Anselm is uncomfortably wide and there is no sign that he has any lost document before him to diminish the gap. His account has just the legendary overtones which one might expect from oral witness, handed on from generation to generation in Cathar circles for over a hundred years. And yet one would be unwise to dismiss it out of hand. Cathars cared about their history and there are signs that the narration they preserved kept the essential contours of Cathar development, despite errors of timing. Its credibility is also enhanced in that it tells us something quite unexpected about the origins of Catharism in Italy – that it was first transmitted from Northern France and not, as geography would lead one to suppose, either by maritime routes from Byzantium to the seaboard or by customary trade routes overland from Cathar strongholds in Languedoc.

[45]   *BHL*, pp. 39–40.
[46]   H. Sproemberg reviewing Borst, *Katharer*, *DLZ* LXXVIII (1957), cols 1095–1104.
[47]   *Tractatus de heretics* (TDH), ed. A. Dondaine, 'La hiérarchie Cathare en Italie', *AFP* XX (1950), pp. 234–324 at pp. 308–10.
[48]   *WEH*, p. 168.

Anselm proceeds:

> Presently, Greeks from Constantinople, who are neighbours to
> Bulgaria at a distance of about three days' travel, went as merchants to
> the latter country; and, on return to their homeland, as their
> numbers grew, they set up there a bishop who is called bishop of the
> Greeks. Then Frenchmen went to Constantinople, intending to
> conquer the land, and discovered this sect; increasing in number,
> they established a bishop who is called the bishop of the Latins.
> Thereafter, certain persons from Sclavonia, that is, from the area
> called Bosnia, went as merchants to Constantinople. On return to
> their own land, they preached and, having increased in number,
> established a bishop who is called the bishop of Sclavonia or of
> Bosnia. Later on, the French who had gone to Constantinople
> returned to their homeland and preached and, as their numbers
> grew, set up a bishop of France ...[49]

Bogomilism in Constantinople was indeed derived ultimately from Bulgaria,
probably transmitted by missionaries rather than merchants, and though
Anselm omits the long stages of development which carried the heresy from
Bulgaria to Asia Minor, and thence to Constantinople, yet the outline of
facts is not strictly incorrect. The use of trade routes to transmit heresy
fits the Bosnian situation fairly, for heresy there spread inland from the
trading cities of the Dalmatian seaboard. But the reference to Frenchmen
coming to Constantinople as crusaders and there succumbing to heresy is
less convincing. Crusaders came for a definite purpose, opportunistic or
idealistic – one would not expect them to be particularly susceptible to
deviant religious views. Some who embarked on the First Crusade did
indeed meet heretics: Bohemond and his Normans came across Paulicians
and their response was to burn the fortified town which they held in the
Macedonian district of Pelagonia.[50]

The crusade which Anselm mentions sounds more like the Fourth
Crusade of 1204 than any other: it was this crusade which, under Venetian
influence, intended to conquer the land, i.e. Byzantium. But 1204 is far too
late a date.[51] If the Latin Church of the heretics in Constantinople is to be
held responsible for missionary activity in the West and the formation of an
indigenous Cathar Church, then the date of its first appearance must lie
behind, and preferably well behind, Hildegard's vision, 1140, or 1143 when
Everwin attended the trial at Cologne. Anselm lacked a strong sense of

---

[49] Ibid.
[50] Lambert, *Medieval Heresy*, 1st edn, p. 23.
[51] As historians using Anselm have concluded. Dondaine (*AFP* xx, p. 240), Borst
(*Katharer*, p. 90, n. 4), C. Thouzellier ('Hérésie et croisade au XIIe siècle', *RHE* XLIX
(1954), pp. 855–72; and *Hérésie et hérétiques* (Rome, 1969), pp. 17–34) believe the
Second Crusade is intended; Hamilton (*BHL*, p. 45) believes it could apply to the
First, or the failed Crusade of 1101 (p. 44, using Hildegard of Bingen). I do not
believe emendation is necessary: Anselm intended the Fourth and was muddled. See
Moore, *Origins*, pp. 172–3.

historical perspective and his account was shaped all unconsciously by his own age: he put down Philadelphia among Eastern dualist Churches simply because of the role it played in the thirteenth rather than the twelfth century.[52] He, and probably the Cathars too, overestimated the place of crusading in the developments of contact between Byzantium and the West. There were many and growing channels, any of which allowed for a conversion of expatriate Franks in Constantinople to Bogomil faith. Anselm may well have been in error on the crusade, but is correct about the role of Western converts to heresy in the Byzantine capital, the 'Frenchmen' or 'Franks' (*Francigene*) who 'established a bishop ... of the Latins', then 'returned to their homeland and preached'. The contact in Constantinople was crucial. Here, we may reasonably surmise, Bogomilism was westernized; its ritual was translated, most probably directly into Latin,[53] so that Frankish converts could compete in liturgical solemnity with the Catholic mass, or with Catholic services of ordination or consecration which they felt it was their destiny to supplant.

A natural focus for early translations of any kind would have been Constantinople, with the underground, heretical Latin Church to which Anselm alludes and natural access to bilingual elements in the population. Evidence is growing that twelfth-century Cathars were already using the Scriptures in Latin. It may be that a kind of Authorized Version of Scripture for Cathar use emerged early through the insertion into the Latin Vulgate of variants derived from the Greek which were more susceptible of a dualist interpretation. As Hamilton observes,[54] translation of ritual or books of the Bible or sections thereof is a skilled, scholarly task, not to be undertaken by warriors and their entourages or by merchants accustomed to using linguistic skills for commercial purposes. Constantinople is a city where one would expect to find the necessary scholarly expertise. Here, we may argue, Catharism evolved from Bogomilism and the missionaries were equipped who transmitted the heresy to the West. Westerners converted Westerners and this facilitated both the arrival of a Byzantine dualist heresy in Western Europe and its early successes.

The response to the Western Church

The level of detail in Anselm's account rises as he describes the birth of Catharism in Lombardy. He tells of the arrival of a 'certain notary' from Northern France and his encounter at Concorezzo, north-east of Milan, with a gravedigger called Mark. The message passed from Mark to his friends John (elsewhere called John Judeus), a weaver and Joseph, a smith, one of whom found another friend at a gateway of Milan 'and led him astray'. Together the little group turned again to the notary who counselled

---

[52] Sacconi's list of Churches in the thirteenth century includes 'Philadelphia in Romania'; the record of the Council of S. Félix de Caraman in the twelfth (below, pp. 48, 211) does not.

[53] Hamilton in *BHL*, pp. 46–52.

[54] Ibid., p. 58.

them to go to Roccavione, a village seven miles from Cuneo on the route overland from Languedoc to Italy via the Alpes Maritimes, Nice and the Col de Tende, and there seek out Cathars 'who had come from Northern France to settle'. Plainly Mark's group wanted more instruction about their faith and, as the bishop was not there but had gone to Naples, they went on down and stayed there a year. The bishop administered the *consolamentum* to Mark and made him a deacon and then sent him back to Concorezzo 'where Mark began to preach. As a result of his preaching in Lombardy, then in the March of Treviso, and later in Tuscany, the number of heretics greatly increased.'[55] A new Cathar Church had been born. Other accounts imply that at some stage John Judeus and Joseph the Smith also received the *consolamentum* and joined the Cathar elite. Concorezzo became a Cathar centre in the first instance because it was Mark's home but it had other virtues, for it lay conveniently in the Milanese *contado* yet was far enough from the centre of archiepiscopal powers in Milan.

It was propitious moment for a heresy which proclaimed the Catholic Church to be the Church of Satan, avaricious and mired in earthly preoccupations. In the 1160s, when Mark and his friends were active, Italy was racked by a contest between the emperor Frederick Barbarossa, the cities and pope Alexander III. In 1159 Barbarossa supported a papal schism, which he kept alive by backing one successor after another, so sustaining two rival obediences, weakening the forces of Catholicism and putting financial pressure on the papacy. Milan opposed the emperor, was besieged and in 1162 razed to the ground. Its population was settled in four localities outside the city. The suffering and confusion and the problems which remained after Barbarossa left Italy in 1167 gave Cathar preachers freedom of movement. The Church often appeared in the darkest of colours.

The years of Barbarossa's terrifying expeditions accentuated trends which had long been in evidence in Northern and Central Italy. Since early in the century, the power of bishops, the natural defenders of orthodoxy with local knowledge and local forces to repress heretics, had been on the wane, weakened by Investitures, by the often justified Gregorian attack on unchaste and simoniac clergy, by the anxious search to recover tithes and lost economic rights and by a growing tension between them and the communes backed by new social forces in the burgeoning cities.[56]

The Pataria, the reform movement opposing an aristocratic upper clergy given to abuses, based in Milan but extending to Brescia, Cremona and Piacenza, had received the support of Gregory VII and had had a lasting effect on public opinion; the name outlasted the movement. It was once used of a dedicated abbot to designate his stoical, unyielding detachment from the passions of the world; it ended up as the customary term for the Italian Cathars. There was no direct connection, but the Pataria prepared

---

[55]   *WEH*, p. 169. On Concorezzo, C. Violante, 'Hérésies urbaines et hérésies rurales en Italie du 11e au 13e siècles', in *Hérésies et sociétés dans l'Europe préindustrielle 11e–18e siècles*, ed. J. Le Goff (Paris, La Haye, 1968), pp. 171–98 at pp. 179–80.

[56]   A. Vauchez, 'Movimenti religiosi fuori dell' ortodossia nei secoli XII e XIII', *Storia dell' Italia religiosa*. I: *L'Antichità e il Medioevo*, ed. G. de Rosa, T. Gregory and A. Vauchez (Rome, Bari, 1993), pp. 311–36.

the way for various radical forms of heresy by its uninhibited demand for a pure clergy and its deep suspicion of the power and wealth of many in high clerical office.[57]

The eloquent canon regular, Arnold of Brescia, who allied himself, in an endeavour to impose an evangelical poverty on all churchmen, first with the commune in his native city and then with the citizens of Rome, was there executed in 1155. But his preaching, which in part rested on a current of opinion stemming from the Pataria, roused echoes among the laity long after his death. Arnoldists in a formal sense are unlikely to have survived the collapse of his movement; the dissatisfaction with the Church to which he had appealed lasted longer, became part of the mental furniture of supporters of the commune movement and provided an opening for the early Cathar perfect who appealed to the simplicities of the gospel.[58]

A traditionalist, Barbarossa gave no succour to heretics and rebels, and indeed had cooperated with the pope of the day to suppress Arnold. When, in 1177, after a disastrous expedition, he recognized defeat and abandoned his headlong attempt to restore imperial power, papacy and Empire could resume their traditional alliance and seek for effective means to put down heresy. But authority found it hard to undo the effects of the intervening years – the time of opportunity for Italian Catharism.

Bernard's reply to Everwin's cry for help resulted in two sermons on the Song of Songs, interpreting the little foxes as heretics.[59] It was powerful polemic written in a flowing and sparkling Latin, blending with capable academic arguments an almost certainly unjustified sexual suspicion and much conventional language about heretics' secrecy and cunning. There is no underestimate of the sinister potential of the heresy, which, Bernard observed, had no named leader and mainspring, as Mani or Sabellius, but sprang 'from the suggestions and artifices of seducing spirits'.[60] 'Women have quitted their husbands, men have deserted their wives ... Clerks and priests, as well as young and old, often abandon their flocks and their

---

[57]   G. Cracco, 'Pataria: *opus* e *nomen*', *RSCI* XXVIII (1974), pp. 357–87 at p. 386; bibliography, Lambert, *Medieval Heresy*, 2nd edn, p. 36; comment, Vauchez, 'Movimenti religiosi ...', p. 315. J. Duvernoy, comment, *Christianisme médiéval. Mouvements dissidents et novateurs. Heresis* XIII, XIV (Carcassonne, 1990), p. 112.

[58]   G. G. Merlo, ' "Heresis Lumbardorum e Filii Arnaldi": note su Arnaldismo e Arnaldisti', *Nuova Rivista Storica* LXXVIII (1994) pp. 87–102. I am indebted to the author for a copy.

[59]   *Sermones super Cantica Canticorum*, ed. J. Leclercq, C. H. Talbot and H. M. Rochais, *Sancti Bernardi Opera* II (Rome, 1957), pp. 172–88; trans. *WEH*, pp. 132–8 (sermon 65); St Bernard of Clairvaux, *Eighty-six Sermons on the Song of Solomon*, trans. S. J. Eales (London, 1895) (Everwin pp. 388–93; sermons 65–6, pp. 393–408); comment, Fichtenau, *Ketzer*, p. 81; Dr Rottenwöhrer generously made available to me his unpublished supplement to *GRK* I on Bernard. B. M. Kienzle, 'Tending the Lord's vineyard: Cistercians, rhetorical heresy, 1143–1229. Part I; Bernard of Clairvaux, the 1143 sermons and the 1145 preaching mission', *Heresis* XXV (1995), pp. 29–61; A. Brenon, 'La lettre d'Evervin de Steinfeld à Bernard de Clairvaux de 1143: un document essential et méconnu', *Heresis* XXV (1995), pp. 7–28.

[60]   Eales, *Eighty-six Sermons*, p. 400.

churches, and are found in the throng, among weavers male and female', he wrote.[61]

On the means of detection, analysis and punishment, Bernard had little to offer. He quoted St Paul's injunction in the epistle to Titus to avoid heretics after the first and second admonition, believed that the Devil had caused members of the Cathar elite to accept burning and gave an ambiguous judgement on the precipitate burnings in Cologne. 'Their zeal we approve,' he commented, 'but we do not advise the imitation of their action, because faith is to be produced by persuasion, not imposed by force', and then added, 'Although it would, without doubt, be better that they should be coerced by the sword of him "who beareth not the sword in vain" than that they should be allowed to draw away many other persons into their error.'[62] In practice, a distinction between heretics who quietly sustained their views and those who proselytized was hardly meaningful; most wished for recruits and wanted to save the victims of Satan.

On detection, Bernard recommended that where suspect men and women were sharing accommodation, they should be presented with the alternative of Catholic monastic vows and separate living. If the alternative be not accepted, he warns 'they will be most justly expelled from the Church.'[63]

In 1145 Bernard conducted a preaching mission in the South of France and scored a spectacular success at Albi, where the papal legate had been derided, preaching to an overflowing congregation. His main target, Henry the Monk, was trounced and at the end of his sermon he asked those who accepted orthodoxy to raise their right hands 'as a sign of Catholic unity': all did so. It was effective revivalism by the most inspiring preacher of the age, backed by the obvious evidence of his ascetic life, by miracles of healing demonstrating, in Moore's words, 'that he had better access to the springs of divine support', by the power of personality and his ability to end conflicts.[64] Henry did not dare to confront him and his support declined.

In most places Bernard was successful, but at the village of Verfeil to the east of Toulouse he met resistance. Although he healed the son of a heretic and was heard by the people in the church, his words were drowned by the deliberate clashing of armour on the part of the knights when he tried to continue his discourse outside: it was a reminder that in the South heresy and anticlericalism had struck deep roots. Bernard cursed the village, later reflecting that the whole region was 'a land of many heresies' 'in need of a great deal of preaching'.[65]

Popes came to feel a special responsibility for Languedoc, a factor which helps to explain how it became the crucible for developments in the handling of heresy. There was no effective overriding authority. The absence of

[61]   Ibid., p. 397.
[62]   Ibid., p. 407.
[63]   Ibid., p. 408.
[64]   E. Griffe, *Les Débuts de l'aventure Cathare en Languedoc (1140–1190)* (Paris, 1969) (initial volume of series on history of Catharism in Languedoc with strong sense of locality), pp. 40–9; Moore, *Origins*, p. 275.
[65]   Moore, *Origins*, p. 113.

defined feudal tenures and widespread partible inheritance creating a class
of impoverished nobles preying on Church revenues, the lack of effective
central authority and the ravages of mercenaries all worked against the
interests of the Church. Popes had long been accustomed to hearing
appeals from churchmen in Languedoc for help against usurping secular
powers; in the twelfth century it became common for them to denounce
both the savage proceedings of mercenaries and the threat of heresy.

The early heretical movements in this area appear to have been of an
evangelical, anticlerical cast. Both Peter of Bruys and Henry the Monk
found listeners in their far-flung preaching campaigns. Bernard's biographer identifies another group in Toulouse which he calls Arians, who have
sometimes been identified as Cathars but the evidence is scant.[66]

It is most likely that the first Cathars to penetrate Languedoc appealed, as
in the Rhineland, by presenting themselves as a poor Church demanding
little in the way of support and exploiting pre-existing tensions over lands,
tithes and rents between churchmen and nobles.[67] No Anselm of
Alessandria recorded the earliest memories of Cathars in this area and the
tradition of their first apostles has disappeared. But a clue as to the nature
of their appeal was given some hundred years later by Federico Visconti,
archbishop of Pisa, preaching in commemoration of St Dominic on his feast
day, tapping a precious and otherwise lost source, the oral reminiscences of
Pisan merchants who transported wool and textiles from Northern France
overland to the Mediterranean ports for shipment to Italy.[68] Early Cathars,
he recalled, successfully influenced the anarchic nobles of the mountain
fortresses which lay athwart the route to the coast whence they were accustomed to prey on the caravans, exacting bruising tolls from the merchants.
The influence of the perfect so played on these rough warriors that they
greatly reduced their depradations. They could not influence them to
abandon sexual laxity altogether, but they persuaded them against adultery
with local married women, so cutting back the internecine warfare of
mountain families. Outside the mountain lands, the more peaccable were
impressed by this early success of the Cathar elite and disposed to accept
their message. It may be that only an entirely fresh religious force deploying
the enthusiasm of pioneers unstained by the long history of lay–clerical
quarrels could have had such an impact in an unpromising environment.

Naturally, the Cathars benefited from these anti-authoritarian attitudes
endemic in the South which held back repression and gave the pioneers
one of the most valuable of all commodities for a religious movement – time,

---

[66] 'weavers and Arians': see *PL* CLXXXV, col. 411, Griffe, *Débuts*, pp. 33–7; R. I.
Moore, 'St Bernard's mission to the Languedoc in 1145', *BIHR* XLVII (1974), pp. 1–4
believes they were not Cathars; Hamilton does not exclude this (*BHL*, p. 45); *GRK* III,
pp. 438–51 is sceptical. 'Arian' was initially a generalized term for the heterodox.
[67] Griffe's working hypothesis, *Débuts*, pp. 166–208.
[68] A. Vauchez, 'Les origines de l'hérésie cathare en Languedoc, d'après un sermon
de l'archevêque de Pise Federico Visconti (1277)', *Società, istituzioni, spiritualità: studi
in onore di Cinzio Violante* II (Spoleto, 1994), pp. 1023–36. I owe this reference to Dr R.
Panarelli.

free of interference, to develop contacts, build family links and capture enthusiasts for the rank of perfect.

In 1165 a Council was held at Lombers, a castle near Albi. A distinguished gathering, which included the Catholic bishops of Albi and Lodève, the archbishop of Narbonne, the viscount of Béziers, in whose lands Lombers lay, and Constance, countess of Toulouse, assembled to hear what was to all intents and purposes a quasi-legal pleading in which leading Cathars presented their case: no doubt Catholic authority intended that it should be an open demonstration that heresy was being preached which should lead to action by the secular powers backing the Church. Nothing of the kind happened. The 'Good Men' would not recognize the authority of the Old Testament and compelled the orthodox to cite against them texts only from the New. They pleaded that they themselves observed the standards laid down by apostolic authority and that their opponents did not. 'They said also', the record runs, 'that Paul stated in his Epistle what kind of bishops and priests were to be ordained in the churches and that if the men ordained were not such as Paul had specified, they were not bishops and priests but ravening wolves ... desirous of being called rabbis and masters ... wearers of albs and gleaming raiment, displaying bejewelled gold rings.'[69] On morality, the Good Men scored. When the bishops attempted to draw them out on their beliefs, they declined to respond, and, as orthodoxy made progress in debate, appealed to the people and made an orthodox-sounding declaration. They then revealed something of their unorthodoxy by refusing to swear to it, pleading the texts prohibiting oaths. It was thus felt that they had said enough for adjudication to be made against them, but no repression followed and they were free to continue their evangelization. It was a humbling experience for the bishops who had to endure public debate where there was no popular will to eliminate heresy, of the kind so vividly displayed at Cologne in Everwin's day, and where secular authority lacked the power or the will to listen to churchmen's pleas to take action.

Over decades, ecclesiastical authority generally had moved towards the exaction of fiercer physical penalties for obdurate heresy. The crusading movement had accustomed them to the use of 'holy violence' against enemies of Christianity. Churchmen who saw Cathars as a recrudescence of ancient Manichaeism could not be unaware that the penalty then had been burning. The hardening of attitude is demonstrated in the ambiguity of Bernard's attitude to physical punishment in contrast to Wazo's. Another straw in the wind is the decision of a Council at Rheims in 1157 aimed explicitly at the 'sect of the Manichees' decreeing life imprisonment for their *majores*, i.e. the perfect, and branding for followers.[70] Yet for those parts of Languedoc in which the attitudes revealed at Lombers prevailed,

---

[69]   Analysis, Griffe, *Débuts*, pp. 59–67; text, Bouquet XIV, pp. 431–4; trans. *WEH*, pp. 190–4; Moore, *Birth*, pp. 94–8; quotation, *WEH*, p. 191; discussion *GRK* III, pp. 389–98 (arguing against identification with Catharism, especially on doctrinal points, but time, place, title 'Good Men' are sufficient for a Cathar identification).
[70]   Moore, *Origins*, pp. 250–5, discussing change of climate; also his *The Formation of a Persecuting Society* (Oxford, 1987).

such developments were irrelevant. Meridional freedom, coupled with local factors favouring heresy and the weaknesses of bishops and secular powers, allowed a rapid development of Catharism.

As Catharism spread, names for the new heresy proliferated. Ekbert gives us a list. 'These are they which our Germany vulgarly [*vulgo*] calls "Cathars", Flanders "Piphles", France "Texerant" from the practice of weaving.'[71] These names were clearly popular and, by implication, hostile. 'Piphles' is hard to pin down; 'weaver' is pejorative. Weaving was amongst the *inhonesta mercimonia* which, in the thirteenth century, possibly earlier, was forbidden to Catholic priests. It sometimes took place in cellars to mitigate the nuisance of noise or enable work to go on night and day. This link with cellars and with one of the less reputable industrial activities heightened the general association of heresy with the margins of society and with dark and hidden places.[72]

Unfortunately, Ekbert muddied the waters by indulging in a flight of learning, in which he explained how the 'first masters' of Catharism assumed the title of 'Catharists, that is, cleansers' (*purgatores*) and 'Cathars, that is the pure'.[73] By 'first masters', as Patschovsky explains, he meant, not the first preachers of the Cathar heresy in the West, but the antique heretics from whom he was at pains to show that the Catharism of his day derived.[74] Another passage reads, 'and these had their origin from certain disciples of Manicheus, who were formerly called Catharists.'[75] Could Cathar preachers in the Rhineland have picked up, preserved and used a Greek term (*katharos*, pure) from forerunners in Byzantium? Would it then have been reproduced by Ekbert as the popular description of his time? Improbable.[76] What Ekbert in fact had done was to look in the classic catalogue, Augustine's *De heresibus* and use his learning to back his theology of ancient descent. A much more natural, hostile and popular origin lies in the current of superstition that linked all heresies to the service of Satan and his obscene rites. A generation later, Alan of Lille, searching in his *De fide Catholica* for derivations of the name, probably hit the nail on the head in the last of his three conjectures when he wrote, 'Or they are said to be Cathars from the cat, because, as it is said, they kiss the posterior of the cat, in whose form, as they say, Lucifer appears to them.'[77] Unconsciously,

[71]   *PL* CXCV, col. 16.
[72]   J. Lestocquoy, 'Inhonesta mercimonia', *Mélanges Louis Halphen* (Paris, 1951), p. 413, cited with discussion, Fichtenau, *Ketzer*, pp. 95–6.
[73]   *PL* CXCV, col. 16.
[74]   Patschovsky, 'Der Ketzer ...', p. 332, n. 50.
[75]   *PL* CXCV, col. 18.
[76]   But H. Grundmann, *Ketzergeschichte des Mittelalters, Die Kirche in ihrer Geschichte*, ed. K. D. Schmidt and E. Wolf II G Pt I (Göttingen, 1963) (succinct summary with bibliography), p. 24, Borst, *Katharer*, pp. 94, 240, Lambert, *Medieval Heresy*, 2nd edn, p. 58, have all believed it. Patschovsky is, however, convincing. Case also well presented by J. Duvernoy, *Le Catharisme: I La religion des Cathares* (Toulouse, 1976) (*JDR*), pp. 302–4, discussion Alan of Lille; pp. 297–311 (nomenclature); comment, Fichtenau, *Ketzer*, pp. 85–6; see *WEH*, no. 20, n. 2, pp. 687–8.
[77]   *PL* CCX, col. 366; Patschovsky, 'Der Ketzer ...', p. 331.

Ekbert bowdlerized the term he heard in Germany, not from the heretics themselves, but from their enemics. Like 'Texerant', but with more force, Cathar expressed the suspicion and distaste of Catholics at a popular level. Heretics were servants of Satan, deceived by his ministers. From this assumption it was easy to take the further step and assume that they actually worshipped him or his emissaries.

A generation after Alan of Lille, that grim persecutor of heretics Conrad of Marburg is witness that the tradition of kissing the cat, as the centrepoint of an elaborate, obscene ritual before an incestuous orgy engaged in by secret, heretical gatherings, was still living in Germany in his day.[78] 'Cathar' as a term for the new heresy became widely used and has supplanted all others in the vocabulary of the historian. But it had a dark origin and is a reminder that, side by side with the attempts to preach down Catharism and begin to wrestle with the beliefs and arguments of its supporters, there remained on the Catholic side a rich vein of prejudice and irrational fear, weakening attempts at reasoned investigation and refutation and spurring on the use of force, even to the death penalty, against the servants of Satan.

[78]   Patschovsky, 'Der Ketzer ...', p. 317; text and ref. below, p. 121.

3

The Wise Man from the East

As Mark's preaching progressed and communities of Cathars sprang into being in Northern and Central Italy, a certain Nicetas of Constantinople appeared in the West and confronted Mark and his followers. The Western sources that report on his activities do not know quite what to make of him: they call him Papa Nicetas, using the Latin for pope.[1] One source also calls him a bishop.[2] Whether he really was a bishop of a dualist church in the East or simply, as some have suggested, a talented individual with a charismatic personality cashing in on the perennial Cathar weakness for romantic Eastern connections,[3] we shall never know. Most probably his title was derived from the usual Byzantine designation 'papas' for a priest or monk. However, for the duration of his visit, he acted like a pope, with a supreme and discretionary authority.

Nicetas's message was simple. Mark's status and that of his followers was insecure. There was a flaw in the *ordo* of Bulgaria, the tradition derived from the East through which Mark received his status. Nicetas created such doubts in the minds of Mark and his associates that they decided to leave the *ordo* of Bulgaria and accept from Nicetas his *ordo*, that of Drugunthia. This decision would have involved a ceremony at the hands of Nicetas, conferring afresh on Mark the *consolamentum* and/or consecration as bishop, and very likely, reconsoling with the authentic *consolamentum* of Drugunthia the rest of the perfect who made up the Italian Church.

From Italy, Nicetas, invited by the Cathar community of Toulouse, passed over the Alps into Languedoc, taking with him Mark and leading members of his Church. At a great Council in 1167 at the village of S. Félix de Caraman in the Lauragais south of Toulouse, in the heartland of Languedocian Catharism, there assembled the most imposing international

---

[1] *De heresi catharorum in Lombardia*, ed. A. Dondaine, in 'La hiérarchie Cathare en Italie', *AFP* XIX (1949), pp. 280–312 (*DHC*) at p. 306, l. 5; *TDH*, p. 309, l. 6; table of sources, *GRK* III, pp. 456–71.

[2] '*episcopus illorum de Constantinopolim*', *AFP* XX (1950), p. 309, ll. 6–7.

[3] A hint in this direction in Fichtenau, *Ketzer*, pp. 152–3.

gathering ever recorded in the history of the Cathars.[4] Robert d'Epernon, bishop of the Northern French, was there with leading representatives of his Church, and the bishop of Albi, hitherto the only bishop of the fast-growing communities of Languedoc, together with the delegates of the other communities associated with Carcassonne, Toulouse and either Agen or the Val d'Aran[5] in the Pyrenees, and what the sources describe as 'a great multitude of men and women', that is, of *perfecti* and *perfectae* of the South of France.

Although the single source which describes Nicetas's visit gives no direct information on his reasons for crossing the Alps, it is a good working hypothesis that he was responding to an invitation from the Cathars of Toulouse, an especially fast-growing Church, to preside over a major territorial division, which they saw to be in Toulouse's interest, splitting up the one sprawling diocese of Albi into four by creating new bishoprics for Toulouse, Carcassonne and either Agen or Val d'Aran and carefully delimiting the territorial jurisdiction of Toulouse and Carcassonne. No doubt they had heard of Nicetas's momentous visit to Lombardy and wished to use the prestige of an Eastern leader to carry out a major reorganization of Languedocian Catharism in a peaceful and orderly fashion.

In the event, whether intended or not, the reorganization went well beyond questions of territory and jurisdiction and involved a change of *ordo* to that of Drugunthia, on exactly the same lines as had occurred in Italy. Either the personality and eloquence of Nicetas carried the day, as one may presume they did in Lombardy, or the Cathars of Northern and Southern France were already aware of the authenticity of his *ordo* and were prepared to accept the change. The multitude of the perfect then received the *consolamentum* from the hands of Nicetas and he presided, as desired, over the division of dioceses and conferred the episcopate on candidates who had been elected by the perfect of their Churches. Most significantly, he also conferred the *consolamentum* and the episcopate on the pre-existing bishops of Albi and of the Northern French, who thus by implication acknowledged that their original *ordo* was flawed. The source says that Nicetas also conferred the *consolamentum* and episcopate on Mark at S. Félix at this time, so that he would be bishop of the Church of Lombardy. This is unlikely.[6]

---

[4]   One source: *Les Actes du Concile Albigeoise de Saint Félix de Caraman*, ed. A. Dondaine, *Miscellanea Giovanni Mercati* v (*Studi et Testi* cxxv) (Rome, 1946), pp. 324–55 (*Act. Fel.*); B. Hamilton, 'The Cathar Council of S. Félix reconsidered', *AFP* xlviii (1978), pp. 23–53 (text pp. 51–3) supersedes earlier work; P. Jimenez, 'Relire la Charte de Niquinta, (1) Origine et problématique de la charte', *Heresis* xxii (1994), pp. 1–26, (2) 'Sens et portée de la charte', *Heresis* xxii (1994), pp. 1–28 (text pp. 27–8).

[5]   Agen for those who read '*agenensis*' instead of '*aranensis*' in the text on the titles of Churches; Agen still has priority, but Jimenez makes a spirited case for Val d'Aran (*Heresis* xxii, pp. 15–20).

[6]   Here I agree with Hamilton, *AFP* xlviii, pp. 31–2; Moore, *Origins*, 2nd edn, p. 213, n. 20: see Moore's narrative, pp. 205–15. I have not accepted the view of A. Brenon in *Le vrai visage du Catharisme* (Portet-sur-Garonne, 1988), p. 108 that Mark was 'only the most influential member of the Council' or her interpretation (p. 109), seeing

Mark's presence, together with leading followers, bolstered Nicetas's prestige and visibly supported the sense of unity of the great gathering, but it is hardly conceivable that Mark did not receive his reconsoling and/or episcopate from Nicetas in the presence of his Church back in Italy. We must postulate a confusion in the source.

Nicetas also addressed the perfect of the Church of Toulouse. Three sentences, probably a seventeenth-century summary of the record of Nicetas's sermon, have come down to us, providing a blurred record of the words of what must have been one of the commanding personalities of Cathar history.[7] He evidently touched on two themes of great potency among Cathars, namely the paradigm of Scripture and the prestige of the Eastern dualist Churches from which the Western Cathars knew they had derived their faith. He spoke of the seven Churches of Asia in the Apocalypse and of the existing Eastern Churches which he clearly saw as in some way echoing them, alluded to the customs of the primitive Church which bound the beliefs and practices of the Eastern believers of his day and drew from the patterns of the past an injunction to mutual peace among Churches, based on a division of territory mutually agreed. It was a scripturally based prelude to the business of delimiting new dioceses. Nicetas reflected on the peace which the Eastern Churches had among themselves because of the delimiting of their jurisdictions and, in passing, named them, proceeding as one might expect from a man whose home was in Constantinople, from the Great City in a swathe round the Balkans, using Eastern names in cases where the West had an alternative.[8] The Church of Constantinople he described as *Ecclesia romana*, that is the New Rome, and to the Church on the Adriatic, known in the West as Sclavonia, he gave the Byzantine name Dalmatia.[9] The sonorous roll-call of names no doubt

---

reconsoling as born only of the desire to multiply *consolamenta* as a source of greater security. The massive international character of the Council and the universal reconsoling argues that the participants were rejecting the old *ordo* and the old episcopate.

[7] All commentators amend the text: on reasons for corruptions, Hamilton, *AFP* XLVIII, pp. 26–9, 51. I accept the following emendations: (a) *Ep[iscopus] E[cclesiae]* between '*Marchus*' and '*Lombardiae*' in list of bishops. (*GRK* III, p. 536); (b) '*Ecclesia Romana*' instead of '*Ecclesia Romanae*' in the list of Eastern Churches (Hamilton, *AFP* XLVIII, p. 37); (c) '*sicut pergit ad Tortosam*' instead of '*sicut pergit apud Tolosam*' in the account of boundaries (Hamilton, *AFP* XLVIII, p. 41); (d) '*q*' in the colophon to read '*qui*' instead of '*que*', as assumed by Dondaine (Hamilton, *AFP* XLVIII, p. 28); (e) MCCXXII instead of MCCXXXII in the colophon (ibid). I do not accept Hamilton's tentative emendation of MCLXVII to MCLXXVI for the opening date of Besse's document (*AFP* XLVIII, p. 30): Hamilton is influenced by *TDH*'s dating of the origins of the Lombard Cathars to 1174 (*AFP* XX, p. 319; *WEH*, p. 371). *TDH* is not reliable on time and I prefer arguments for 1167 in Rottenwöhrer, *GRK* III, pp. 517–22; Jimenez, *Heresis* XXII, pp. 20–4.

[8] D. Obolensky, 'Papas Nicetas: a Byzantine dualist in the land of the Cathars', *Harvard Ukrainian Studies* VII (1983), pp. 489–500 at p. 493.

[9] On place names, F. Šanjek, 'Le rassemblement hérétique de Saint-Félix-de-Caraman (1167) et les églises Cathares au XIIe siecle', *RHE* LXVII (1972), pp. 767–99;

impressed the listening perfect, as it was intended to – '*Ecclesia Romana, et Drogometiae et Melenguiae, et Bulgariae et Dalmatiae*'. A faulty transcription has produced 'Drogometia' for 'Dragovitsa', the Drugunthia of an Italian source on Nicetas's doings in Lombardy, an important Church variously located in Thrace, Macedonia or in the region of the river Dragowitsa, south-east of Sofia. Melenguia is likely to have been situated in the land of the Slav tribe of the Milinguii in the Peloponnese, while Bulgaria was the place of origin of Bogomilism, and Dalmatia a more recent mission land for dualists, probably from Constantinople. These Churches, Nicetas said, had their precise limits, did nothing to the detriment of each other and had peace among themselves. 'Do thou likewise', he said.

They proceeded to. Evidently territorial division was a sensitive matter, to be taken seriously. The source records the setting up of a commission for the delimitation of the new dioceses of Toulouse and Carcassonne consisting of eight delegates from each side, who put down their decisions in a written agreement, following the limits of the Catholic diocese and archbishopric of Narbonne and passing over the Pyrenees as far south as Lerida. The line from Lerida to Tortosa on the coast formed the southern-most boundary of the diocese of Toulouse. It was an optimistic agreement, for although there was already a Catalan Cathar presence, it was unlikely to have been a substantial one, with numerous areas where there was no Cathar presence at all. The delegates of S. Félix were looking forwards to a missionizing future, on both sides of the Pyrenees.[10]

The agreement kept peace for more than a generation after 1167. In 1223 Pierre Isarn, newly elected bishop of Carcassonne, took advantage of a certain diminution of pressure from the Catholics in the aftermath of the disaster of the Albigensian Crusade, which had killed many perfect and had surely destroyed Cathar records, to set about organizing his diocese, recalling its territorial limits and the context of the decisions taken in 1167. His own archive may well have been destroyed. It is plausible to think that he employed the good offices of his confère of Toulouse to recover needful documentation for his purpose from the Toulouse archive, as the material he used has a certain Toulousan orientation. His agent, Pierre Polhan, copied out three documents: the record of the council at S. Félix de Caraman, possibly preserved as part of a history of Catharism designed for the instruction and edification of candidate perfect,[11] the sermon delivered by Nicetas to the Church of Toulouse and finally the detail of the boundary commission's ruling and the names of the sixteen assessors. The documents kept Nicetas's memory green, recalled the unified decision-making of the past as a pattern for Isarn's day and recorded the practical details of the diocesan boundaries.

Rottenwöhrer (*GRK* III, pp. 478–83) despairs of secure identifications; Hamilton (*AFP* XLVIII, p. 38) makes the case for the Orthodox bishopric of Dragovet as the source for Drogometia.

[10]   Comment, Jimenez, *Heresis* XXIII, p. 25.

[11]   Hamilton's hypothesis: a key point is the appearance of the opening phrase '*in diebus illis*' (*AFP* XLVIII, pp. 30–1).

But Isarn had little time to exercise his office. He was burnt in 1226. Problems of jurisdiction, which probably sparked off the recopying of the documents and later led to the summoning of a Cathar Council at Pieusse in 1226, were resolved by decision of the bishop of Toulouse, Guilhabert de Castres. He met the uncertainties of the perfect of the Razès, who did not know whether they belonged to the diocese of Toulouse or Carcassonne, by setting up a new diocese of the Razès for them in the same year.[12] Polhan's copy of the three documents fell into the hands of the antiquary Guillaume Besse, who published excerpts from it in 1660, while promising a full edition.[13] He never provided one and the original of Polhan's copying has disappeared. Hamilton's brilliant reconstruction of the documentary history of this strange fragment of evidence has restored it to the small but crucial canon of Cathar writings.

After his sermon and the setting up of the boundary commission, Nicetas disappears from history. He had had a remarkable success: he had persuaded all the Cathars of Northern and Central Italy and France to do what he wanted, and when he set sail for Constantinople, he left behind him four bishoprics in the South of France, one in the North and one more in Lombardy, all of which had accepted his *ordo* of Dragovitsa or Drugunthia.

He did not long outlive his triumph. After his death in the East, another visitor, Petracius of the Church of Bulgaria, arrived in Lombardy with companions to report that Simon, a bishop of Drugunthia from whom the origin of the *ordo* taken by Nicetas proceeded, had been discovered with a woman and had been guilty of other moral lapses – in other words had made a 'bad end'.[14] In Cathar theology, the fall of a bishop automatically brought about the fall of all whom he had consoled. His breach of morality invalidated not only his own *consolamentum*, but the *consolamentum* of all on whom he had laid his hands in solemn ceremony. This may have had a certain inner logic, whereby Cathars argued that if a perfect after receiving the *consolamentum* sinned, he had never been worthy of it and lacked the impeccability that should be characteristic of a candidate receiving the Holy Spirit. It created a lasting tension among the perfect, left to wonder whether the bishop who had consoled them had committed some secret sin and they had all forfeited their key to salvation.[15] This time there was no unified response to the disquieting news. Some believed Petracius, others did not. Accounts differ in detail.

In one version, Mark was still alive when the news came, and the story was that it was Nicetas himself who had made a bad end. Mark set off to take

---

[12] Hamilton assembles the background, *AFP* XLVIII, pp.49–50.

[13] Ibid., p. 30; Jimenez, *Heresis* XXII, pp. 10–11.

[14] '*fuit inventus in conclavi cum quadam, et … alia contra rationem fecerat*' *DHC* in *AFP* XIX, p. 306. *DHC*, subtly analysed by Paolini in *BHL*, pp. 88–90, stressing legal background, is generally preferred for events to *TDH* (faults discussed above, pp. 35–6).

[15] B. Hamilton, 'The Cathar Churches and the Seven Churches of Asia', in *Byzantium and the West c.850 – c.1200*, ed. J. D. Howard-Johnston (Amsterdam, 1988), pp. 269–95 at p. 279; F. Šanjek, 'Raynerius Sacconi O.P. Summa de Catharis', *AFP* XLIV (1974), pp. 31–60 at p. 49; *WEH*, p. 336.

ship to Bulgaria in order to receive once more a valid *consolamentum* and episcopal consecration, was dissuaded by a Cathar deacon living in southern Italy, suffered the affliction of a prison sentence and returned, still unconsoled, to Lombardy. In a vivid passage, the author of this version, the inquisitor Anselm of Alessandria, described how Mark's faithful follower, John Judeus, contrived to find his way down to the prison and by some means succeeded in receiving episcopal consecration from the hands of the captive Mark.[16] In another version, Mark was already dead when Petracius arrived and it was Judeus who had to meet the new challenge as bishop.[17] In either case the problem was the same: how to decide which was the authentic *ordo* and how to come to right judgement on the moral lapses of an Eastern bishop. Nicetas had sensitized the Lombard Cathars. Unity began to founder as one group remained faithful to Judeus and the *ordo* descended from Nicetas, while another group broke away and elected as bishop Peter of Florence.

This state of affairs lasted some years, till wiser heads who sorrowed over the divisions in their ranks decided on a plan to restore unity by despatching delegates from both the rival obediences to travel over the Alps and seek a decision from a Cathar bishop, most probably the bishop of the Northern French. Unity, lost through disturbances in the East, should be regained by a judgement arrived at in the West. The bishop adjudicated that both bishops and their followers should meet and lots be cast; whosoever was successful, whether Judeus or Peter of Florence, should accept the verdict and with his followers submit to the successful candidate, who would then seal the new unity by going to Bulgaria to receive a valid episcopal consecration and on his return reconsoling all the perfect. It was a decision which maintained the reverence for the Eastern dualists as the source of orders, by implication rejected the *ordo* brought by Nicetas and made use of the New Testament precedent to meet a difficulty, adopting the drawing of lots to find a bishop as the surviving apostles in Acts drew lots to find a successor to Judas.[18]

It broke down on the obstinacy of Peter of Florence, who refused to submit himself to the drawing of lots. It was deemed that by this decision he had by right (*de jure*)[19] forfeited his claim to be bishop, yielding it necessarily to Judeus. His followers deposed him and Judeus ruled. But still, because some of Peter's party disliked John Judeus, they would not submit to him and it became necessary to adopt another plan to achieve unity. Some of the wiser heads besought Judeus with prayers to resign in view of the animosity felt by some towards him so as to open the way for the selection of a universally acceptable candidate. Judeus saw that he could not preside in tranquillity and, wishing to restore the Cathars to unity, did what was required.

[16]   *TDH, AFP* xx, p. 309; G. Gonnet, 'Sur la présence cathare dans le sud de l'Italie vers la fin du XIIe siècle', *Heresis* xv (1990), pp. 45–9.
[17]   *DHC, AFP* xix, p. 306.
[18]   Acts 1:21–6.
[19]   *AFP* xix, p. 307, l. 8.

The delegates met in Council at Mosio in the countryside between Mantua and Cremona and adopted a more sophisticated procedure. The delegates should be required to choose a candidate from the opposing party, the followers of Judeus agreeing on a name from Peter of Florence's party, and vice versa. Two candidates emerged, Garattus from the Judeus party and John de Judice from Peter's. Lots were drawn and Garattus was successful. It seemed that the schism was at an end; a time was set for Garattus to decide on his travelling companions and for money to be collected for his expenses on the journey to Bulgaria to be consecrated bishop. But before the time was up, two witnesses gave evidence and Garattus was found guilty of reprehensible contact with a woman.[20] Very many Church members felt that because of this he was unworthy of the office of bishop and they were no longer bound by the promise of obedience they had made under the conditions of Mosio. It was the moment of fatal breakdown. Various groups chose their own candidates and despatched them to find in the East the authentic *consolamentum* and episcopal orders. One congregation at Desenzano, clearly adherents of the *ordo* of Nicetas, elected Johannes Bellus as their bishop and sent him to Drugunthia for consecration. Another formed at Mantua and sent a candidate to the Eastern Church of Sclavonia, identical with the Dalmatia listed by Nicetas in his sermon at Toulouse: another at Vicenza chose similarly and sent to Sclavonia, perhaps because it appeared to be a compromise between the clashing claims of Bulgaria and Drugunthia. Churches at Florence and in the Val del Spoleto similarly elected their own bishops: in these latter two cases a strong factor may well have been regional patriotism.

Garattus claimed that the new bishops were usurping his office but he was unable to stem the tide of factionalism. Asked by some Milanese Cathars to be their bishop in accord with the agreement at Mosio, he declined, being aware of the degree to which he had lost support and suggested instead that John Judeus, who had resigned in order to bring unity, was more worthy. Yet Judeus was reluctant to take up office again, so delegates were once more sent off across the mountains to consult the adjudicating bishop, who deplored the schism and sent word to Judeus that he should act in accord with the common decision of the past, go to Bulgaria for consecration and assume the episcopate in Lombardy over all who were willing to accept him. This was done. Judeus ruled till his death, then a certain Joseph, who was succeeded at last by Garattus. Patience had its reward.

Garattus still argued that he was rightfully bishop over all and that the usurping bishops were bound by their promise to obey him as the successful compromise candidate at Mosio unless he should release them from their promise. Evidently a certain residual unity in ritual practices remained, at least among some of the Churches, but even this was repudiated by Garattus. He made peace with Caloiannes, the bishop of Mantua, and absolved him; he was willing, in consequence, to join with him in the rite of

---

[20] '*duobus testibus astantibus reprehensibilis, causa unius mulieris, habitus est*', AFP XIX, p. 307, ll. 35–6; wording suggests lesser offence than that of Simon, see above n. 14.

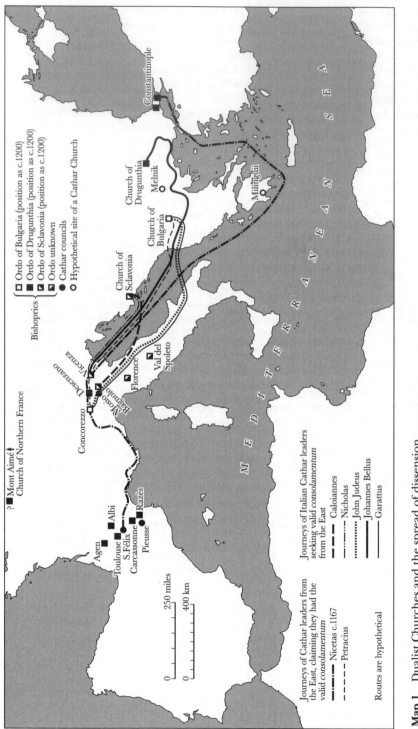

Map 1 Dualist Churches and the spread of dissension

Source: M. D. Lambert, *Medieval Heresy*, 2nd edn (Oxford, Cambridge, Mass., 1992), p. 127

Bishoprics
- ☐ Ordo of Bulgaria (position as c.1200)
- ■ Ordo of Drugunthia (position as c.1200)
- ◩ Ordo of Sclavonia (position as c.1200)
- ◪ Ordo unknown
- ● Cathar councils
- ○ Hypothetical site of a Cathar Church

Journeys of Cathar leaders from the East, claiming they had the valid *consolamentum*
- ▬▬ Nicetas c.1167
- ▬ ▬ Petracius

Journeys of Italian Cathar leaders seeking valid *consolamentum* from the East
- ▬▬ Caloiannes
- ▬·▬ Nicholas
- ·········· John Judeus
- ▬▬▬ Johannes Bellus
- ——— Garattus

Routes are hypothetical

Church of Northern France

Mont Aimé

Agen
Albi
Toulouse
S. Félix
Carcassonne
Razès
Pieusse

Concorezzo
Desenzano
Mosio
Bagnolo
Vicenza
Florence
Val del Spoleto

Church of Sclavonia
Church of Bulgaria
Church of Drugunthia

Melnik
Milinguii

Constantinople

MEDITERRANEAN SEA

the delivery of the prayer or the giving and receiving of the *melioramentum*, but with no other bishop and his flock.

Via the escalation of scandal and personal rivalry in the years following Nicetas's momentous journey, the one spring-time Cathar Church of Northern and Central Italy of Mark's day had broken up into six (see map 1): Concorezzo, the village outside Milan of Mark the Gravedigger, where he made his first converts; Desenzano near Lake Garda; Vicenza (or the March of Treviso); Bagnolo near Mantua, sometimes known as the Church of Mantua; Florence; and the Val del Spoleto. The wiser heads, the *sapientes* of the source, presumably men of wider vision and training, had worked hard to restore unity, skilfully using electoral devices and mediation, and had been aided by the sense of responsibility of one bishop, John Judeus, but all to no avail. Dissension came from the East via Nicetas and Petracius, who sowed the fatal seed of doubt about the validity of their orders. The hypersensitivity of the Cathars about their *consolamentum* and the moral standards of bishops, and the corroding effects of the doctrine of the 'bad end', swamped the will to unity in a combination of heightened rigorism, fear of loss of status and personal and territorial rivalries. Sexual peccadillos, rather than other lapses, stud the narratives which have come down to us. Accusations of sexual faults are notoriously hard to refute and can easily be 'managed' by ambitious power-seekers. Though he wrote a hundred years after the event, on the basis of oral evidence drawn from his experience of interrogations, and may well be mistaken on details of the breakdown of Cathar unity, Anselm of Alessandria none the less conveys effectively the atmosphere of suspicion in which reputations could be broken. He describes how Nicholas of the March of Treviso, who wanted to become a bishop himself, exploited the anxieties of individual perfect by asking them about the fate of Mark. 'Do you think he came to a good end or not?' he would say and then when, as they normally did, they replied affirmatively, he would go on, 'John Judeus says that Lord Mark came to an evil end and for that reason he wants to cross the sea to be reconsoled.'[21] Such corrosive comments undermined the leaders and opened the way to newcomers. Nicholas himself in the end secured a bishopric in his native region by such means.

Italians had a reputation for being quarrelsome; some perfect were primadonnas; the disunities of the Cathars in Italy to some degree mirrored the disunities of the burgeoning city states. The contacts with the East and the heavy expenses incurred by congregations to send their candidates, with companions, to distant sites to acquire an authentic *ordo* reinforced the splits as supporters who had spent money creating their bishops were thereafter reluctant to surrender their painfully acquired independence. Thus the coming of Nicetas and Petracius with the attendant events broke the Cathar unity in Italy in a highly visible fashion and left the rival Churches disputing, in friction, with only a marginal, superficial unity among some of them surviving. They passed out of history, weakened by Catholic pressures

---

[21] *TDH, AFP* xx, p. 309, l. 25–30; *WEH*, p. 170.

and competition, or coerced by inquisitors, with their splits still unhealed at the end of the thirteenth century.

Personal and regional rivalries and fears about the *consolamentum* were reinforced by doctrinal divisions, which appear to follow hard on the heels of the moral disputes. Borst comments: 'From organisational structuring came dogmatic division.' [22] This may even have been latent from the coming of Nicetas. The *De heresi catharorum*, the best source on the rise of disunity, composed between 1200 and 1214 by a Catholic observer some forty years after the events, a man who had perhaps been a perfect himself before his conversion, deploying some knowledge of the law and its terminology, says simply that Nicetas 'began to declaim against the *ordo* of Bulgaria, which Mark had' (*cepit causari ordinem bulgarie, quem Marcus habebat*).[23] At this point he does not mention a moral lapse as invalidating the *ordo* and it may be that a doctrinal difference lay behind Nicetas's objection to the *ordo* of Bulgaria – no details are otherwise given.[24]

Even if doctrine was not an issue at the outset, it soon became one and both the author of the *De heresi* and and Anselm of Alessandria proceed from a narrative of the origins of the Italian schism among the Cathars to an analysis of the differing doctrines of the rival Churches as they knew them in their own time. Sacconi, the master of Anselm, who had worked with him on inquisitorial duties and was himself an ex-perfect, wrote a *Summa* on Cathars and Waldensians c.1250, in which he devotes much space to analysis of the doctrinal divisions between the Churches.[25] For all the Catholic observers there was nothing surprising about these differences: unity and order was a mark of Catholicism, and confusion, disunity and incoherence, the work of Satan, was a mark of heresy, and in showing up these flaws, the treatise writers and observers were demonstrating the true character of heretical teaching.

For the Cathars, by contrast, the divisions continued to be a source of regret. The most intense differences were those between adherents of Concorezzo and Desenzano; in Sacconi's time, despite tensions and problems, the other Churches recognized one another, but not these two.[26] Salvo Burci, a layman of Piacenza who wrote the *Liber supra stella*, an informative and hortatory work on heresy, in 1235 witnesses to the intensity of the rivalry: 'each damns the other to the death', he said, 'the Albanenses [supporters of Desenzano] maintaining against the Concorezzenses that they themselves are the Church of God, that the Concorezzenses were once associated with them, having broken away from us; the Concorezzenses in return making a counteraccustion of like nature.' Yet, he goes on to say, the two sides 'have met together many times ... to discuss how they might agree

---

[22]   Borst, *Katharer*, p. 101.
[23]   *AFP* XIX, p. 306, l. 6–7; *WEH*, p. 161; on use of *ordo* and other terminology, Lambert, *Medieval Heresy*, 2nd edn, p. 126, n. 88; Paolini, *BHL*, pp. 88–90 is illuminating; see *GRK* III, pp. 537–8, 542–3.
[24]   Comment, Hamilton, *AFP* XLVIII, p. 47, n. 95.
[25]   Šanjek, *AFP* XLIV (1974), p. 49; *WEH*, pp. 329–46.
[26]   Šanjek, *AFP* XLIV (1974), p. 59; *WEH*, p. 345.

on one faith ... seeking to find a compromise in their teaching'. The cause of those anxious journeyings and conferences lay apparently in the disquiet of the believer class within the Churches, who were scandalized by the differences; some, indeed, he observes, went back to Catholicism because of this disunity. It was all in vain, 'For each sought mastery for their group', he explained, 'but violent quarrels persisted within both parties and every individual is sorely affected by the great discord. Whence it is obvious that they are not the Church of God ... .'[27]

A major reason why Concorezzo and Desenzano could not agree lay in the depth of their doctrinal differences. This cannot have been true before the schism between the Churches was finalized, at the time when some of the *sapientes* went to plead with Judeus to resign, for they argued that the unity candidate to emerge after the drawing of lots should exercise his episcopal authority over all Cathars 'without reservation';[28] this is inconceivable if a major doctrinal issue at that stage divided the disputing churches. but it was undeniably the case later. Desenzano became the stronghold of the unbending radical dualists, who believed in the existence from eternity of two principles – one good, the other evil. Concorezzo's supporters, in the tradition of Mark and the *ordo* of Bulgaria, as moderate dualists stood much closer to orthodoxy, would not accept an eternal evil principle and believed that there was only one good God, almighty and eternal, Lucifer being a fallen angel who 'with God's acquiescence'[29] separated the elements which God had made and created heaven and earth and a body for Adam.

The importance of evil in the world and the anxious search for escape from it lay near the heart of Cathar teaching, and major differences about the origins and place of evil were bound to divide the perfect as they gained

[27] Ilarino da Milano, 'Il "Liber supra stella" del piacentino Salvo Burci contra i Catari e altre correnti ereticali', *Aevum* XVI (1942), pp. 272–319, XVII (1943), pp. 90 146, XIX (1945), pp. 218–341 at p 309; *WEH*, pp. 270–1; discussion *GRK* III, pp. 525–8.

[28] Borst, *Katharer*, p. 101, n. 11, correcting *AFP* XIX, p. 307, l. 17.

[29] *AFP* XIX, p. 310, l. 22; *WEH*, p 165; full analysis of Cathar doctrine, *GRK* IV, *Glaube und Theologie der Katharer*. In Duvernoy's view (*JDR*, pp. 50, 58, 83, 329–47, *Heresis* VIII (1987), p. 58B) Catholic apologists exaggerated and misunderstood Cathar disunities. Certainly they were malevolent, made errors, did not always penetrate Cathar thought and were impatient of fluctuating scriptural exegesis. But Rottenwöhrer rightly argues that the flaws are not sufficient to lead to radical distrust of these sources (*GRK* III, pp. 528–9). If polemic had been as gravely flawed as Duvernoy claims, it would have been bound to fail in its effect (note E. Vacandard's comment, cited *GRK* IV (1), p. 25). The seriousness of some divisions and the effects they had on believers emerge from Salvo Burci (above n. 27): they are not just intellectual disputes among the few. In Languedoc, Durand of Huesca's witness (below, n. 35) cannot be undermined by the gratuitous argument (*JDR*, p. 345) that his information derived from his journey to Rome, rather than Languedocian experience, or that the crucial passage has been interpolated. An argument for tolerance/indifference on the doctrinal divisions in Languedoc, which Duvernoy derives from an interrogation in Doat 25 (see *Byzantinobulgarica* VI (1980), p. 142) rests on a misreading of '*in vulgari*' as '*in Bulgaria*' (*GRK* III, p. 529); analysis of research, *GRK* IV (1), pp. 22–7.

instruction in the secrets of their movements. Believers, with whom the perfect exercised a certain 'economy' in imparting doctrine, knew less of such matters and were more inclined to be distressed at the evidence of disunity. Doctrine came to matter more in the increasingly sophisticated and educated society of Northern and Central Italy.

Signs that the Cathars were affected by rising standards of education emerge from the very narratives of their disputes, especially from the *De heresi* with its stories of delegates, conferences, electoral devices and binding agreements[30] – already they had moved on from the monarchical government of Mark and his simple instruction. A counter-Church had developed, and with an increasing sophistication came, inevitably, an increasing concern with the bases of belief. Western Europe was a mission field for Eastern dualists and the proximity of Italy to the Balkans and Constantinople for a time kept an effective connection in being.

The journeys of Nicetas and Petracius in one direction, the abortive journey of Mark, and the journeys of the candidate-bishops in the other, witness to the reality of these links, as does the arrival in Concorezzo towards the end of the century of an Eastern apocryphon, the Interrogation of John, or Secret Supper, destined for the hands of Nazarius,[31] once *filius major* to Garattus and his successor as bishop of the Church of Concorezzo. Doctrinal differences between Eastern Churches came to be perpetuated in the West. Nicetas told his hearers that the Churches of the East lived in peace with each other: in the light of his own denunciation of the *ordo* of Bulgaria and Petracius's story of the lapse of the leader from whom Nicetas's *ordo* was derived, this sounds disingenuous. There was competition between these Churches and it is reasonable to think that it was a competition about right belief. Nicetas is described as belonging to the *ordo* of Dragovitsa/Drugunthia but also to the Church of Constantinople; it sounds like a description of a territorial church, located in one spot but belonging to a denomination whose beliefs were enshrined in doctrinal formularies.

How ancient the doctrinal divisions were is impossible to say. Paulicians were radical dualists: they had a separate origin from Bogomils and quite lacked the distinction between perfect and believers. At some stage, however, the Bogomils underwent some Paulician influence: this affected their understanding of their history and gave them a tradition which linked them to the early Christian centuries. Paulicians as individual converts to Bogomilism carried over something of their history, traditions and texts; they may also have influenced their hosts in the direction of radical dualist beliefs.[32]

---

[30]   Paolini, *BHL*, p. 89.

[31]   Lambert, *Medieval Heresy*, 2nd edn, p. 121; *WEH*, p. 456; both require correction in the light of Duvernoy's criticism (*JDR*, p. 35, n. 47). The apocryphon was brought *to* and not *by* Nazarius from Bulgaria.

[32]   Hamilton, 'The Cathar Churches ...'; comment, A. Brenon, *Heresis* XII (1989), pp. 156–8, unconvinced by article as a whole, yet seen as stimulating, throwing 'flying footbridges between sources'; *GRK* III, pp. 546–7 rejects Hamilton's identification of Nicetas's seven Churches with Paulician Churches.

Alternatively, at Dragovitsa a spontaneous mutation of doctrine may have taken place, perhaps only a short while before Nicetas's time. *De heresi catharorum* says that it was from Simon, bishop of Drugunthia, that the origin of the order of Nicetas sprang (*a quo origo suscepti ordinis a nicheta processerat*).[33] The phrase has commonly been taken to mean that Simon was the bishop who consoled Nicetas and from whom he derived the orders which entitled him to reconsole the perfect and bishops of the West, and it was Simon's conduct that invalidated the *ordo* and, in consequence, all Nicetas's ritual acts in the West. The point must stand. But did *origo* have a deeper meaning and imply, further, that Simon was personally responsible for a profound mutation of belief within his Church, carrying it from moderate to radical dualism?[34] It is far from inconceivable: later Italian Cathar history shows how leading individuals could strike out on lines of their own and carry other perfect with them.

Dualism was not a fixed body of doctrines. There was no ultimate doctrinal authority and the nature of Cathar life fostered movements of doctrine, sometimes quite far reaching. The tragedy of Italian Catharism was that no one interpretation of evil prevailed after Nicetas: the wavering, divided response to Petracius broke unity, at first apparently on an ethical issue, then doctrinal differences widened the splits and made them permanent.

The response of Southern France in the aftermath of Nicetas's journey was very different from that of Italy. His visit was clearly seen by Pierre Isarn, when he sponsored the copying of the record of S. Félix, as a source of strength for Catharism. All the emphasis of the documentation is on unity and territorial organization. Tensions did arise in Languedoc which faintly parallel the conflicts over shades of dualism, but they occurred a great deal less frequently and at a lower level, never issuing in the formation of rival Churches. In his polemical *Liber contra manicheos* of 1222–3, Durand of Huesca, a convert from Waldensianism, pointed to the existence of three currents of opinion among the Cathars of Languedoc in his day – those of the Greek heretics or, as he says elsewhere, Greek Manichees, the Bulgarians and the 'Drogoveti'; these, he said, were in dissidence and condemned each other. Durand knew Italy and had worked there, seeking recruits for his congregation of converted Waldensians, but the passage in the *Liber* makes it plain that these conflicting currents of opinion were to be found in the dioceses of Carcassonne, Toulouse and Albi:[35] his statement is a proof that the Languedocian Cathars were also influenced by the Eastern Churches and their conflicts, but clearly that influence never had the decisive role which it had in Italy.

The Languedocian Cathars were not free of troubles. In 1206, for example, a Council was assembled at Mirepoix and drew six hundred perfect, according to the witness of one defendant, to resolve some

---

[33]   *AFP* XIX, p. 306, l. 12–13.
[34]   Rottenwöhrer's suggestion, *GRK* III, pp. 565–6. See also *GRK* IV (3), pp. 282–4.
[35]   ed. C. Thouzellier, *Une somme anti-Cathare: le Liber contra Manicheos de Durand de Huesca* (Louvain, 1964), pp. 138, 210; *GRK* III, p. 525.

internal problems;[36] other details are lacking and the absence of information on any fall-out from it suggests that, whatever the difficulty, the Council settled it. Doctrinal unity by and large held firm; a form of radical dualism, Albigensian 'two-principle' doctrine, broadly prevailed.[37] Moderate dualism, described as a new heresy which had recently appeared in Languedoc, entered the region early in the thirteenth century, according to the anti-Cathar treatise, the *Manifestatio heresis albigensium*, composed 1206–14 and most probably before the Albigensian Crusade.[38] It did not win many adherents and remained marginal in the doctrinal history of the South. Some core of truth may lie behind an excited letter of 1223 to French bishops from a papal legate, Conrad, cardinal bishop of Porto, about an anti-pope in Eastern Europe in the region of Bosnia, Croatia and Dalmatia who had made Bartholomew of Carcassonne his vicar in Languedoc.[39] Bartholomew had allegedly displaced Vigouroux de la Bacone from his bishopric. Although the anti-pope was a chimera and Bartholomew, as traceable in the records, an insignificant Cathar, it is possible that the story was sparked off by some influence from the moderate dualist Church of Dalmatia/Sclavonia beginning to play on the Cathars of the South. But if a split in the ranks on doctrinal grounds threatened, it was very soon checked. One case from 1225 is recorded in which a sick man from Castelnaudary in the Toulouse diocese, among a group of hostages held at Narbonne, refused the *consolamentum* at the hands of two perfect, in the words of the inquisition record, 'because they were not of the faith of the heretics of Toulouse'.[40] But this, amongst the profuse record of administrations of the *consolamentum* in Languedoc, was extremely rare. The Cathar dioceses of Southern France were always able to contain their tensions and deviations and retained their territorial structure. The contrast with Northern Italy could hardly be greater: it forms a curious parallel with the political development of these lands – unification in France, a breakdown into quarrelling cities in Italy.

There were reasons for the contrasting situation of the Cathars in Languedoc. Petracius, with his insidious doubts, never crossed the Alps. Languedoc was less vulnerable to the Eastern conflicts. The intellectual level was generally lower at the outset than in Lombardy and development was cut short by the trauma of the Albigensian Crusade.[41] Effective persecution came later to Italy and their perfect had for longer the opportunity to debate and reflect on the bases of their truth.

---

[36]   *JDR*, p. 343.

[37]   *GRK* IV (2), p. 15.

[38]   A. Dondaine, 'Durand de Huesca et la polémique anti-Cathare', *AFP* XXIX (1959), pp. 268–71 at p. 271; *WEH*, pp. 231–5 at p. 234. Datings, *GRK* I (2), p. 262.

[39]   J-D. Mansi, *Sacrorum Conciliorum … collectio* XXII, col. 204, cited Hamilton, *AFP* XLVIII, p. 44; Y. Dossat, 'Un évêque cathare originaire de l'Agenais, Vigouroux de la Bacone', *BPH* Année 1965 (Paris, 1968), pp. 623–39; *GRK* III, pp. 539–42. Evidence for moderate dualism, *GRK* IV (2), pp. 413–19.

[40]   *GRK* III, p. 527. MS 609 fols 250v–251r.

[41]   I owe comment to Dr Y. Hagman and Mlle P. Jimenez.

Northern French Catharism has an obscure history: it was persecuted more vigorously at an earlier stage, and records of its life are very scanty. It fits uneasily into the patterns of doctrinal development. The bishop, as we learn from the record of S. Félix, accepted the *ordo* of Nicetas and presumably jettisoned the *ordo* he already had. As Rottenwöhrer has shown, the bishoprics of the South remained attached to a form of radical dualism while the North, it seems, did not. Hamilton argues that when the Italians in their disputes sought an adjudicator – a bishop 'over the mountains', as the *De heresi* reports[42] – they turned not to the Southern French but to the bishop in the North from whom they had derived their faith. A notary from the North had led the first Cathar mission into Italy and so, when they looked to the North, they were turning back to their roots. Yet the bishop who twice heard appeals from them consistently recommended the *ordo* of Bulgaria, which we know to have been moderate dualist, rather than the *ordo* of Nicetas.[43] Presumably the Church of the Northern French was able to make doctrinal transitions in quite a short time and without tensions. More one cannot say.

Nicetas himself is obscure. Our sources do not mention that he arrived in Lombardy with companions. Petracius is described as bringing an entourage; the arrangements for Garattus's journey to Bulgaria assume that for a weighty mission some companions are needful. It is not clear what commission Nicetas had from his own Church: Anselm of Alessandria calls him 'bishop of the heretics in Constantinople';[44] the *De heresi* simply calls him 'a man called Papa Nicheta'. We know that there were heretical Churches of the Latins and of the Greeks in Constantinople: to which of these did he belong? He has a Greek name: in what language did he address the perfect in Lombardy and at S. Félix? Nicetas is a mystery and is likely always to remain so.

---

[42]   *AFP* XIX, p. 306, l. 24.

[43]   Here I follow Hamilton's interpretation (*AFP* XLVIII, p. 33) in preference to Moore (*Origins*, 2nd edn, pp. 207, 215), who believes it to have been a bishop from Languedoc (see also comment, p. 307, n. 21). In either case, a change of doctrinal allegiance from Nicetas's radical to Bulgaria's moderate dualism must be postulated. Radical dualism remained dominant in Languedoc (see above n. 37): it is unlikely that a bishop there changed his allegiance. I turn therefore in preference to the bishop of the Northern French for the postulated change. To seek counsel from the mother Church of the Italian Cathars is a likely procedure for the Church in Lombardy. Only one bishop is involved; in Languedoc there were four. Problems of tact could arise in choosing between them.

[44]   *AFP* XIX, p. 306, l. 4.

4

The Growth of Catharism

Languedoc

Leading aristocrats

Catharism continued to strengthen in the years following the open debate at Lombers: when Nicetas presided over the council at S. Félix de Caraman in the Lauragais, where the count of Toulouse's power was frail,[1] delegates came and went with impunity. In 1177, Raymond V, count of Toulouse, appealing for aid to the chapter-general of the Cistercians, denounced the family discord created by heresy, the corruption of the clergy, the damage to churches, the rejection of the sacraments, of the doctrines of creation and resurrection of the body and the acceptance of the heretical belief in two principles, complaining that leading men ('*nobiliores*') were infected and that a great multitude followed them. It was powerful rhetoric and not insincere; yet Raymond cannot have been unaware that accusations of heresy would embarrass his chief rival, Roger Trencavel, viscount of Albi, Carcassonne and the Razès, then building an enclave in Raymond's lands and could be used as a stick with which to beat the rebellious inhabitants of Toulouse.[2]

The appeal brought a legatine mission to Toulouse, Henri de Marcy, abbot of Clairvaux, other prelates and the papal legate. They succeeded in inducing Pierre Maurand, a wealthy merchant, to make a public confession of errors, punished with a harsh penance of exile and the destruction of the fortifications of his town house: there is a suspicion that his emergence as a prime target for the mission's zeal owed something to social tensions in Toulouse and to his successful career as a businessman.[3]

Henri de Marcy and an English bishop attempted to secure from Roger Trencavel release of the Catholic bishop of Albi, reportedly imprisoned by heretics. The truth probably was that Guilhem Peyre de Brens, Roger's

[1] J. Duvernoy, *Le Catharisme*. II *L'histoire des Cathares* (Toulouse, 1979) (*JDH*), p. 215.
[2] *WHC*, p. 52; Griffe, *Débuts*, pp. 84–90.
[3] Political background, events, *JDH*, pp. 219–29; J. H. Mundy, 'Un usurier malheureux', *AM* LXVIII (1956), pp. 217–25.

seneschal, inherited from his father and an obstinate patron of Cathars, was pursuing a private quarrel with the bishop and the viscount was unwilling to interfere.[4] No doubt a prime aim was to induce Roger II to reject heresy and take action against it, but Roger avoided a meeting and was excommunicated. The abbot and his group met Roger's viscountess and then at Castres two veterans of Nicetas's great Council: Bernard Raymond, chosen by the perfect as bishop of the Cathar Church of Toulouse, consoled and consecrated by Nicetas and Raymond de Baimiac, probably one of the commissaries elected by the Church of Toulouse to decide on the diocesan boundaries, now Bernard Raymond's *filius major*.[5] They went under safe conduct to Toulouse and were interrogated by the papal legate Peter of Pavia and other prelates in the cathedral church of St Etienne.

It was a curious scene. The two Cathar hierarchs read out a script in the vernacular expounding their beliefs; some of their words appeared to conceal heresy and they were asked to expose their beliefs in Latin. This they were unable to do, to the legate's contempt. But, none the less, their profession of faith appeared to be Catholic. Then in the church of S. Jacques, in front of a great crowd which included the count, challenged to state anew their beliefs, their adherence to Catholicism and whether they had ever preached to the contrary, they agreed to do so and promptly faced an outcry from the count and others claiming that they were lying and had preached heresy. The pair refused an oath, pleading the text of Matthew. Before the excited crowd, the legate renewed their excommunication and received an oath from the count and other great men not to favour heretics. None the less, the safe conduct of the two was honoured. Perhaps the Cathars had expected open, equal debate instead of interrogation and condemnation: perhaps they feared the crowd and so lied. It was like the Lombers episode. Authority at this time lacked the power and confidence to proceed to a condemnation and had to be content with words. The two Cathar leaders remained safely in their refuge in Lavaur, only 35 km from Toulouse, but in 1181 Henri de Marcy, who had become legate to France, contrived to mount a minor expedition against the castrum. Skirmishing alone was enough and the castrum surrendered. The two openly confessed their heresy, were reconciled and rewarded by becoming canons in Toulouse, conceivably having to make some payment in lieu of penance to aid the endowment of their prebends. It was a startlingly easy solution.[6] The seat of the bishopric appears to have been moved for safety from Lavaur to S. Paul Cap de Joux on the marches of the Cathar bishopric of Albi under the control of the Trencavel dynasty and another bishop was elected; thus the Cathar cause was only slightly damaged.

Raymond V had also appealed to Louis VII, but Louis was in no condition to intervene and Raymond could not safely act on his own. His county had

---

[4] Griffe, *Débuts*, p. 101 is illuminating.
[5] Hamilton, *AFP* XLVIII (1978), pp. 51–3; *JDH*, pp. 224–6.
[6] *WHC*, pp. 85–6; 'payment', *JDH*, p. 218; Brenon, *Visage*, p. 112, detects contradictions within the abjuration; Griffe, *Débuts*, pp. 126–8 gives perspective. I owe gifts and advice to Dr Brenon.

never wholly recovered from Count Raymond IV's decision to go on the First Crusade and settle in the East and the region was distracted by the conflicting claims of three great powers: the Capetian kings of France, the Angevin kings of England and the counts of Barcelona and their heirs, the kings of Aragon. There was much warfare. The Church denounced the use of mercenaries – who featured alongside heretics as abuses to be eliminated – vainly, because the lack of defined feudal tenure of the kind familiar in Northern France robbed great men of the sinews of war: without a sufficient following of their own, the repeated use of mercenary forces, with concomitant distress and loss of overall control, was necessary. Action against heretics inevitably took second place to internecine struggles for power.

The Trencavel dynasty had a complicity with heresy. Lavaur had been held by Roger II with prominent heretics evidently living there in security. A sorrowful anecdote related by the chronicler Guillaume de Puylaurens in which the bishop of Béziers was crudely defied by a dying pro-Cathar relative, who insisted on his burial place being among the '*Bonosii*', that is, Bosnians, by which he meant Cathars, very probably refers to Guilhem Peyre de Brens, Roger's seneschal.[7] When Roger II died in 1194, he left as tutor to his young son and regent Bertrand de Saissac, a well-known adherent of Catharism; the Catholic bishop of Béziers obtained from him an oath not to introduce heretics, both Cathars and Waldensians, into the city and bishopric. But Bertrand demonstrated his contempt for Church law when he responded to an election held without his knowledge by the monks of S. Mary, Alet by exhuming the late abbot and placing the corpse in the abbatial chair to preside over a fresh election, so forcing the monks to choose a candidate who had his approval.[8]

The comital house of Foix had the deepest involvement. Berengar of Lavelanet, forty years later, recalled participating in a glittering occasion in 1204 at Fanjeaux, when Esclarmonde, widowed sister of the count of Foix came to be consoled by Guilhabert de Castres, *filius major* to the bishop of Toulouse, together with three other noblewomen, including Aude of the de Tonneins, the principal dynasty of the nobility of the Lauragais and widow of a great officer of the Trencavel dynasty, Isarn-Bernard senior of Fanjeaux. Berengar recalled the names of fifty-six notables of Fanjeaux, witnesses at the consoling, in addition the count of Foix himself. Guilhabert had close connections with the aristocracy and was known as a preacher. Esclarmonde, who went back to the South to preside over a house of perfect women at Pamiers, had evidently come to Fanjeaux because she had chosen Guilhabert to console her – much as a great Parisienne of the seventeenth century might vie with her contemporaries for the most fashionable confessor of the day. In 1206, the count's wife, Philippa, also retired to the South, to Dun to preside over a house of perfect women. Raymond-Roger never gave formal reverence to perfect, but was far gone in anticlericalism,

[7]   Ibid., pp. 148–50.
[8]   *WHC*, p. 72.

probably the starting-point for his Cathar sympathies, put into practice by the womenfolk of his dynasty.[9]

The death of Raymond V of Toulouse in 1194 and the succession of his young heir Raymond VI did nothing for the Catholic cause. The new count never wholly deserted the faith of his dynasty, made donations to abbeys and died a Catholic, but was complacent towards Cathars, moved perhaps by a secret attraction and a curiosity mingled with sympathy.[10] His outlook differed from that of his father and he was guilty of violently anticlerical acts, imprisoning the abbots of Moissac and Montauban, pillaging churches and chasing away from their bishoprics the bishops of Vaidon and Agen. When events in 1215 compelled him to surrender his stronghold at Toulouse, he took refuge with the pro-Cathar family of the Roaix, surely an indication of this true sympathies. This pro-Cathar constellation of power remained broadly intact until the summoning of the Albigensian Crusade against heresy after the murder of Pierre de Castelnau in 1208.

The reaction of churchmen

Henri de Marcy, presiding over a diocesan council, imposed an orthodox profession of faith on the merchant of Lyons, Valdes, who had been converted to a life of renunciation, had commissioned vernacular translations of Scripture and the Fathers and wished to serve the Church in observing Christ's commands at the Sending of the Seventy, maintaining a life of poverty and preaching. The profession of faith was prophylactic: in effect, Valdes was to be warned of the dangers of Catharism and required to abjure dualistic tenets. It revealed the continuing preoccupation with the grumbling Cathar problem. Valdes accepted the profession, but in the event was not to be held in obedience: he and many of his followers, determined to preach, broke with authority when permission to do so was withheld, and were excommunicated. They maintained, nevertheless, a genuine hostility to Catharism and spoke against it.[11]

One of the most capable of Valdes's adherents, the convert priest Durand of Huesca, composed a *Liber antiheresis*, a Latin manual designed to equip the more educated members of the Waldensian movement to argue both

[9]   M. Roquebert, 'Un exemple de Catharisme ordinaire: Fanjeaux', *Europe et Occitanie: les pays Cathares, Collection Heresis* v (Arques, 1995) (*EO*), pp. 169–211 at pp. 176–81 (illuminating); on Esclarmonde, A. Brenon, *Les Femmes Cathares* (Paris, 1992) (*BF*) (vivid account of Occitanian women, with special knowlege of inquisition sources: review, M. D. Lambert, *Cristianesimo nella Storia* xv (1994), pp. 212–16), p. 139; J. Duvernoy, 'Guilhabert de Castres', *CEC* xxxiv (1967), pp. 33–42; summary, *JDH*, pp. 265–6, translation of original evidence, p. 237, Philippa, pp. 156, 237, genealogy of house of Foix, p. 160. I owe advice to M. Roquebert.
[10]   M. Roquebert, *L'Epopée Cathare I: l'invasion* (Toulouse, 1970), p. 138.
[11]   A. Dondaine, 'Aux origines de Valdéisme: une profession de foi de Valdès', *AFP* xvi (1946), pp. 191–235.

with Cathars and with Catholic opponents.[12] He attacked the Cathars from local knowledge, pinpointing the weaknesses of the believer class and rejecting dualism. Both he and Valdes never gave up the ultimate hope of reconciliation with Rome, and Durand himself returned to Catholicism after participating in a debate at Pamiers in 1207.[13] He and those like him saw Catharism as an enemy and would have been happy to act as auxiliaries; but collective reconciliation never came and the Waldensians were generally treated as a hostile sect. Moreover, they were not numerous in the Languedocian heartlands of Catharism; greater concentrations lay in northern Languedoc or in the Rhône valley. In Quercy, considerable numbers of both Waldensians and Cathars were to be found side by side in the thirteenth century: there were open debates between the two groups in Montauban in an atmosphere in which Church authority plainly felt unable to repress heresy at all.[14]

The fruit of reconciliation after long conflict between Barbarossa and the papacy, the Bull *Ad abolendam* of 1184 denounced freely a variety of sects. It envisaged Italy and its problems as much or more than Languedoc: it was an early attempt to view heresy from an international angle. Above all, it aimed to put teeth into the episcopal obligation to pursue heresy – a proceeding not generally effective in Languedoc, where bishops, often uninterested or of mediocre calibre, lacked the vital support of the secular arm. It systematized existing arrangements, making widespread use of oaths from the secular powers, to respond to the Church's demands to act against heretics, and from individuals in parishes, 'synodal witnesses', to declare the presence of heresy. Bishops or their representatives were to visit once or twice a year the parishes where heresy had been reported and to impose the oath. Proof positive of the presence of heresy was not necessary; a suspicion alone was sufficient.[15]

The episcopate of Languedoc was the object of a devastating judgement by Innocent III, who called them 'blind creatures, dumb dogs who no longer bark', and acted ruthlessly on this in the course of his pontificate: by 1213 he had succeeded in removing from office the archbishop of Auch, the bishops of Fréjus, Carcassonne, Béziers, Viviers, Toulouse, Valence, Rodez and, the object of his greatest hostility, Berengar, archbishop of Narbonne.[16] Berengar ruled a province which, until Toulouse was made an archbishopric in 1317, extended from the Rhône to the Garonne. A predecessor, Pons, who reigned from 1162 to 1181, though he legislated against

---

[12]   C. Thouzellier, *Catharisme et Valdéisme en Languedoc à la fin du XIIe siècle et au début du XIIIe siècle* (Paris, 1966) (thorough textual analysis).

[13]   Griffe, *Débuts*, pp. 258–61.

[14]   M. Schneider, *Europäisches Waldensertum im 13. und 14. Jahrhundert* (Berlin, New York, 1981), pp. 8–19.

[15]   H. Maisonneuve, *Etudes sur les origines de l'inquisition* (Paris, 1960) (legislative aspect) pp. 151–6; comment, A. Kolmer, *Ad Capiendas Vulpes: Die Ketzerbekämpfung im Südfrankreich in der ersten Hälfte des 13. Jahrhunderts und die Ausbildung des Inquisitionsverfahrens* (Bonn, 1982) (precise, detailed investigation of legislation and events), p. 29, n. 21.

[16]   *WHC*, p. 66; comment, Griffe, *Débuts*, p. 142.

heresy, seems to have taken no action; he was extravagant with the possessions of the archbishopric and the losses were not made good under his
successor. Berengar, archbishop in 1190, a son of a count of Barcelona and
nephew to the king of Aragon, had an aristocratic disdain for his canonical
obligations. He never visited within his province, was evidently wholly uninterested in the heresy problem, did not observe *Ad abolendam* and saw his
prime duty to lie in undoing the effects of Pons's follies on the possessions
of the archbishopric. To canonical irregularities he was permissive.
Innocent finally deposed him in 1212.[17]

Quite independently of Berengar's idiosyncracies, problems of jurisdiction in Narbonne itself would have inhibited the pursuit of heretics, there
being constant and bitter rivalry between its viscounts and archbishops,
from which the citizens profited. The archbishop's negative attitude had
its importance, but the underlying factors working against vigorous
action to repress heresy went beyond personalities. Guilhem Peyre of Albi
(1185–1227), whose reign straddled the epoch of substantial growth of
Catharism and the crusades mounted against it, was a bishop of personal
calibre who made headway against his viscounts and increased the
privileges of his bishopric, yet even he found it politic not to proceed
directly against heresy. He was a shrewd strategist who needed his '*prud-
hommes*' and was unwilling to alienate his townsmen; he might debate
against heretics, but no more.[18]

By contrast, relations between bishops, aristocrats and rulers in Northern
France or England, though scarred by periodic disputes, had an underlying
sense of solidarity as members of a ruling class and a unity against heresy
which was lacking in the South.[19] Bishops there, intimately linked to great
aristocratic houses, were often locked in local disputes, and the poverty of
their sees led easily to undue preoccupation with temporal issues. There was
more individualism and families of high birth produced both heretics and
leading ecclesiastics.

Development in the South had taken place in a rhythm different from the
North. The magnificent churches of the pilgrimage route to St James of
Compostella were a reminder of traditional orthodox practices. The
crusading zeal which led Raymond IV to abandon his lands for the uncertainties of the First Crusade had not disappeared; Raymond VI, dying and
no longer able to speak, bore witness to the residual force of that tradition
as he clung to the habit which a Hospitaller priest flung over him as a sign of
the order's will to secure his burial.[20] Raymond no doubt also remembered
that Pierre de Faucon, Hospitaller prior of Saint Gilles, had travelled to
Rome in 1208 to plead for a lifting of his excommunication. After his death
the order remained faithful to his memory. The papacy was adamant in

[17] R. W. Emery, *Heresy and Inquisition in Narbonne* (New York, 1941).
[18] J. L. Biget et al., *Histoire d'Albi* (Toulouse, 1983).
[19] M. Barber, 'Women and Catharism', *Reading Medieval Studies* III (1977), pp 45–62
at p. 52; reprinted in *Crusaders and Heretics 12th–14th Centuries* (Aldershot, 1995).
[20] H. J. A. Sire, *The Knights of Malta* (New Haven, London, 1994), p. 118.

refusing Christian burial, but the order kept his body for years in a coffin above ground in the precincts of their house at Toulouse.

The South's attitude to nunneries left a gap for Cathar women perfect to fill, as religious houses for women developed very late in comparison with lands north of the Loire. Foundations made after 1100 were often modest in size and there were no such foundations at all in the twelfth century in the lands between the Aude and the Ariège. Those with wealth to bestow tended to value women's role in the continuance of a family line above their aspirations to the monastic life, as is indicated by the provisions of a will from the diocese of Maguelonne in which a father left one thousand sous melgoriens to a daughter taking the veil and five thousand to one getting married.[21] The fast-developing schools of Northern France, which did so much for the study of Scripture and theology, subjects which armed the clergy against heresy, had no equivalent in the South. Though it had its own intellectual achievements, especially in Roman law and medicine, it lagged behind in theology: there was no development of canon law such as burgeoned in the North. The South had its own, often somewhat archaic, religious tradition. Its great abbeys continued to recruit monks and Cistercians were able to win affiliations and secure new foundations. But it had weaknesses and had lagged behind developments elsewhere.

The election of Fulk of Marseilles, troubadour, then Cistercian abbot of Thoronet, as bishop of Toulouse in 1206, with his dynamic Catholicism, his personal poverty and preaching power and his deliberate campaigning within Toulouse against both usury and heresy, creating the Whites, a fraternity battling for the Church with its roots in the Bourg of Toulouse, revealed dramatically what had hitherto been lacking in the Southern episcopate. The patron of S. Dominic and a force behind the development of Dominican friars, Fulk, was the one contemporary churchman who by his personal abnegation and obvious lack of self-seeking or family objectives could match the Cathar perfect on their own ground. He describes the deplorable state of the finances of the bishopric on his entry to office. There were pitiable reserves in the treasury and he at first was so overwhelmed by creditors that he dared not let out his mules but watered them from the palace wells.[22]

Enforced poverty, the result of past conflicts and anticlerical pressures, spiritually valueless since it had not been voluntarily embraced, dogged the Church. Griffe, brooding on the factors which facilitated the growth of the Cathars in the South, puts his finger on usurpation of tithes as of prime importance.[23] The Gregorian reform movement put pressure on those who had usurped tithes in the past. Slowly, reluctantly and with the making of bargains advantageous to their families, certain lords in the twelfth century restored tithes – but, even then, not necessarily for the support of a

---

[21]   *CF* XXIII, passim, esp. articles by E. Magnou-Nortier, P. R. Gaussin, maps by Gaussin, pp. 301, 303, 310, 319, 327; Maguelonne episode, Magnou-Nortier, pp. 333–40 at p. 337.

[22]   B. Bolton, 'Fulk of Toulouse: the escape that failed', *SCH* XII, pp. 83–93.

[23]   Griffe, *Débuts*, pp. 166–208.

parish church, but for a monastery or chapter. In many small places, the petty lords of the countryside maintained their hold. Often they needed to: partible inheritance relentlessly subdivided holdings and rights within the co-heirs of a *lignage*, pushed members of the rural nobility into poverty and made them impervious to reforming ideas involving economic sacrifice. A country priesthood was often compelled to live on a pittance, with much of the normal tithe income in effect confiscated; standards and morale were low. A Council at Avignon in 1209 condemned clergy who were 'indistinguishable from laymen in conduct'. It was known that priests sometimes preferred to conceal their tonsures to avoid recognition: 'if the clergy went out in public', Guillaume de Puylaurens said, 'they hid their timid tonsures by bringing over their hair from the back of the head.'[24] The villages of Languedoc were not unique: as revealed dramatically in the register of the thirteenth-century bishop Eudes Rigaud of Rouen, priests in the villages of Normandy were ignorant and uxorious, yet there was no concomitant heresy in their parishes. Yves Dossat has argued that within the clergy of the Cathar-infiltrated areas in Languedoc there were redeeming elements and that historians have unduly blackened the reputation of the Catholic clergy as a whole.[25]

All this may well be true: what these investigations do is to throw into focus the constellation of factors, over and beyond the low standards of certain country clergy, which created a Cathar menace. Complacency or weakness at the top of society; chronic warfare and lawlessness; the unwillingness or inability to prosecute heretics and check the spread of heresy; a predisposition to heresy on the part of an impoverished rural nobility; anticlericalism and the problem of usurpation of tithes – all these worked together and were fused and made effective by a limited band of dedicated perfect, missionaries and preachers, often anonymous and unsung.

Petty nobility

The rural setting was important. The effects of partible inheritance over time were dramatic.[26] When Guillaume de Puylaurens wished to point the moral of his tale of the knights of Verfeil impiously clashing their arms and preventing St Bernard of Clairvaux preaching orthodoxy, he went on to say that the principal lord Isarn Nablat ended in penury at Toulouse and that this was a judgement of God on him and those like him. But he gives a clue as to why this happened when he mentions that there were a 'hundred' noble houses in Verfeil.[27] The poverty of many of these petty nobles was a direct consequence of partible inheritance, and the spoliation of

---

[24] *Chronica magistri Guillelmi de Podio Laurenti*, ed. J. Duvernoy (Paris, 1976), pp. 24–5; M. Barber, 'Catharism and the Occitan nobility: the lordships of Cabaret, Minerve and Termes', *The Ideals of Knighthood* III, pp. 1–19 at pp. 12–13.
[25] Y. Dossat, 'Le clergé méridional à la veille de la croisade albigeoise', *RHL* I (1944), pp. 263–78.
[26] J. L. Biget, 'Notes sur le systeme féodal en Languedoc et son ouverture à l'hérésie', *Heresis* XI (1988), pp. 7–16 (preliminary sketch).
[27] Griffe, *Débuts*, pp. 197–200.

churches, usurping of Church lands and revenues and favour to Cathars a not unnatural accompaniment to these circumstances. Jordan of Saxony, Dominican master-general in the thirteenth century, complained that parents put daughters into houses of perfect women so that they would no longer be a burden to their families; no doubt the proceeding was established well before his time, as soon as the Cathars were able to form their religious communities.[28] Cathar preachers were able to give a comforting justification for the withholding of tithes, since they taught that the Catholic Church was the evil Church of Satan, mired in the world of matter, and it was a duty not to support it.[29]

Impoverishment took the rural nobility down to the level of the villagers and diffused Cathar influence more readily and spontaneously.[30] Nobility still had a certain prestige, demonstrated in the bourgeois interest shown in the South for the aristocratic theme of courtly love. Clearly, chance and personalities played a role: to a limited degree, troubadour patrons and the vogue for Catharism coexisted geographically, but, though having anti-clerical traits in common, they had very different roots and courtly love had strong support in areas such as Limousin, where Catharism did not penetrate. Once sympathy for Catharism was established within a *lignage* it could travel both horizontally through family connections and downwards through lines of dependency. Verfeil, Lombers, Fanjeaux were all centres of Catharism and were all places where multiple inheritance and a proliferation of nobles occurred; at Fanjeaux in 1209, for example, there were fifty co-seigneurs.

In certain villages where the leading lights of the locality favoured Catharism, before the Crusade broke the pattern of life, Cathar preachers could speak freely and publicly, and small communities of perfect men or women existed, which provided advice and arbitration and acted as focus for the rituals of the movement.[31] They offered the facilities of an established Church. In towns, this was never the case. There Cathars were a minority. However, a meridional toleration tended to have its effect everywhere: heretics were left in a freedom which did not exist in Northern Europe. Families who protected Cathars had houses in towns and possessions in the countryside as well, with family and dependents in both. So, for example, the Lamothe sisters, in flight before persecution in the Crusade epoch, received vital support from believers in Toulouse, in the Lantarès, where Alaman de Roaix and Pons Saquet could offer them concealment in the countryside.[32] Similarly, Saix de Montesquieu, knight of Puylaurens in

[28]   G. Koch, *Frauenfrage und Ketzertum im Mittelalter* (Berlin, 1962) (Marxist work, not wholly conventional; on statistics outdated by M. Hanssler), p. 28.
[29]   Brenon, *Visage*, p. 42.
[30]   Ibid., p. 191.
[31]   A. Brenon, 'La maison Cathare', *EO*, pp. 213–32; E. Griffe, *Le Languedoc Cathare de 1190 à 1210* (Paris, 1971), passim; balanced exposition on courtly love and Catharism, Brenon, *Visage*, pp. 197–204.
[32]   Arnaude de Lamothe's confession of 1244 is a major source. I owe a direct translation from Doat 23 fols 2v–49v (part full, part summarized) to the kindness of Mr A. Murray, University College, Oxford. Partial text, Koch, *Frauenfrage*, pp. 186–200; dramatized account *BF*, pp. 13–58; Lantarès refuge, p. 44.

the country, also kept a house in Toulouse and used it to give a year's refuge to his sister Berengaria, a perfect. Conversely, the deacon Guillaume Salomon, who was active in Toulouse, used the house of Huc Isarn for delivering sermons; influences and personalities passed readily to and fro between the two milleux.[33]

The geography of heresy

A small but influential body of support within towns had to be reckoned with. Biget assesses Cathar support in Albi at only 10–12 per cent of the population and reflects that the habit of labelling Cathar heresy in Languedoc 'Albigensian' may well have a literary origin in the report of Geoffrey of Auxerre, companion to St Bernard on his preaching tour of 1145, who described Albi as 'contaminated' above all others in the region. Geoffrey had no intimate knowledge of Languedoc and the 'contamination' may well have been the result, not of Catharism, but of the preaching of Henry the Monk.[34] Bishop Guilhem's reluctance to take open proceedings against the Cathars implies that they had influence despite their minority status. In Toulouse, Bishop Fulk took a different attitude: he battled openly against the heresy, drawing support from the Bourg and from reactions against usury. His deliberate policy of creating a lay fraternity reveals that there, too, despite their limited numbers, Cathars were seen as antagonists of some weight.

A curious piece of evidence comes from the tragic siege of Béziers in 1209 at the opening of the Crusade, when its bishop produced a roll (now known as the Domairon roll) with names of two hundred and twenty-four heretics, which again suggests that the number of Cathars there was small as well. Four were marked VAL, presumably Waldensians: the assumption is that the remainder were known Cathars and may well have included, over and above Béziers citizens, refugees from the region. Not all were perfect; the record refers to one of the named going to hear the preaching of the heretics – at most, he could only have been a believer.[35]

The matrix of the Catharism of Languedoc lay within the lands of the count of Toulouse, the Trencavel viscounts of Albi, Béziers and Carcassonne and the count of Foix. Feudal geography set the scene. The heads of these great houses were unable or unwilling to persecute heresy. This opened the door to the Cathar missionary and gave him that most precious of commodities, time – time to build a circle of supporters, to instruct, to find candidates for the *consolamentum* and to obtain patrons.

Anne Brenon's map (see map 2) plots the hierarchical structure of the Catharism of the thirteenth century: the bishoprics of Toulouse, Albi and

---

[33] Berengaria, Doat 24, fols 125r–v; Salomon, *JDR*, pp. 256, 276, 284; on Lantarés and Lamothe sisters, M. Roquebert, 'Le Catharisme comme tradition dans la "Familia" languedocienne', *CF* XX, pp. 221–38 at p. 225.

[34] Biget, *Albi*, p. 56; see Griffe, *Débuts*, pp. 40–2.

[35] *JDH*, p. 235n.

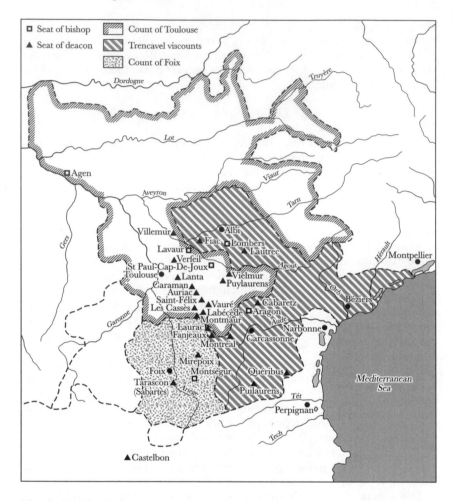

Map 2   Cathar bishoprics and deaconries in Languedoc
Source: A. Brenon, *Le vrai visage du Catharisme* (Portet-sur-Garonne, 1988), p. 119

Carcassonne as agreed in the Council of S. Félix in 1167, along with that of Agen (assuming that '*aranensis*' be corrected to '*agenensis*') and the last foundation, Razès, agreed by the Council of Pieusse in 1226, together with the web of deaconries that underpinned the bishoprics, whose office-holders supervised the houses of the perfect, heard their ritual confessions and disseminated Cathar belief. This whole structure is set within the boundaries of the great landholdings, with one possible exception – the community of Agen. If the perfect of the Agenais were sufficiently numerous and influential in 1167 to obtain a bishopric, then the basis of their Church was laid down while Agen was still part of the Duchy of Aquitaine and under the Angevin dynasty which was not reluctant to persecute; only in 1196 did Agen pass to the count of Toulouse as dowry with Jeanne, sister of Richard Coeur de Lion when she married Raymond V. Agen apart, the inference from the map is clear: the great landholders of the South made the Catharism of Languedoc possible.

Agen was an outlier, its adherents found mainly along the line of the Garonne as far as Marmande to the north. The river formed a barrier. To the west, Gascony remained apparently untouched as there are no records of trials or pursuits at all. The vernacular of the region, albeit not a major barrier to communication among the Occitanians, none the less may have provided some deterrent to Cathar missionaries. Farther west and south, in the basin of the Adour, the Basque imprint was apparent; circumstances differed so greatly from those in the county of Toulouse that Cathar infiltration would be unlikely.[36]

Nearer to the Garonne, the circumstances of life more closely resembled those of Languedoc but with the important qualification that its violent anticlericalism was lacking. Cistercian abbeys here still had considerable influence. A reading of the cartulary of Berdoues reveals village notables and Cistercian houses about 1200 living 'in a material and spiritual symbiosis'.[37] If a Cathar influence slipped over the river, ecclesiastical authority seems not to have recognized it – or perhaps not even wanted to.[38] Directly to the north of Toulouse a Cathar presence existed in Quercy with a scattering of deaconries and some houses of the perfect but faded out at the level of Gourdon and Cahors.[39]

A linguistic as well as a geographical barrier, the Rhône was even less permeable than the Garonne; Cathars were never reported to its east. Thus the heartland of the movement lay within the quadrilateral formed by Toulouse, Albi, Carcassonne and Foix, above all in the Lauragais, site of a natural line of communication for invaders, travellers and missionaries between Aquitaine and the Narbonnaise, dominated by its hill-top villages and castles where the nobility were most touched by the heresy. Laurac, once the capital of the Lauragais, Fanjeaux and Montréal were fortresses of Catharism where the old faith was despised; to the north of this formidable trio lay S. Félix, the site of Nicetas's Council.[40]

The complacency of the great lords was, however, not the sole factor working for Catharism. The Trencavel dynasty was heavily implicated but the heresy was by no means spread equally across its territories, fading away in the east. At Béziers, support was relatively thin. In the plain of the Biterrois lay prosperous villages with lords who were active in donations for parish churches and charitable purposes. To the north, Servian lay near the outer limit of Catharism not far from the noble houses in the sphere of Montpellier, which, was strongly orthodox; its lord Stephen married Navarra,

[36] B. Cursente, 'La Gascogne refractaire à l'heresie: une société differente?', *EO*, pp. 131–47.

[37] Ibid., p. 145.

[38] A gentle suggestion of Cursente, p. 147.

[39] Brenon, *Visage*, p. 120.

[40] M. H. Vicaire, 'Saint Dominique à Prouille, Montréal et Fanjeaux', *CF* I, pp. 15–33 at pp. 17-23.

daughter of one of the great matriarchs of the heresy, Blanche of Laurac. She influenced her husband to give Cathars refuge in his castles and allow them to preach publicly and give sustained instruction. But in 1210 Stephen recanted; his wife left, became a perfect and died peacefully at Montségur in 1234. Heresy at Servian was a short-lived phenomenon.[41]

In the mountains, on the most spectacular and defensible castle sites, the will of the great houses counted for remarkably little; geography kept these minor lords in semi-independence whatever their formal tenurial links. At Cabaret north of Carcassonne, at Minerve to the east in the precipitous terrain of the Black Mountain area and at Termes in a similarly rugged landscape in the Corbières, Cathar lords, bounded by horizontal links of family and self-interest, could defy the outside world. Authority was well aware of the problems of siege among the precipices and of these lords' skills in ambush and guerrilla warfare; consequently, once Catharism had established itself it lived on, spreading among the dependents of the lords, who repeatedly gave refuge to the perfect. When Raymond de Termes, for example, beaten by dysentery rather than a Crusade army, surrendered his castle in 1210, Pierre de Vaux de Cernay calculated that it was thirty years or more since Catholic sacraments were administered in the castle chapel.[42]

For all the support given by the comital house, there was evidently no body of perfect men and women in Foix sufficient to justify setting up a bishopric; high patronage was not enough to bring a major Cathar community into being, although it did lead to the instituting of houses of perfect women at Pamiers and Dun, and Raymond Agulher functioned as deacon of Tarascon before the Crusade. Again, initially at an aristocratic level, some influence radiated across the Pyrenees into Catalonia, but in general the Spanish peninsula was little affected.[43]

The Cathar centre of gravity shifted further to the south in the course of the thirteenth century under pressure from persecution. The high peak, Montségur, a curious outlier of the Pyrenees, was a vantage point from which almost all the Cathar heartland could be surveyed.[44] But it was only developed as a prime centre by Guilhabert de Castres responding to the new and more deletorious situation after the surrender of Southern forces

[41]   M. Bourin, 'Tensions sociales et diffusion du Catharisme en Languedoc orientale au XIIIe siècle', *EO*, pp. 105–30, with doubts on identification of Blanche's daughter at Servian, pp. 121–3, 124; C. Amado, 'Faible impact de l'hérésie dans le Languedoc central méditerranean: le paradoxe biterrois (1170–1209)', *EO*, pp. 83–103; Servian, pp. 92–5; *BF*, p. 181; Griffe, *Languedoc*, for most thorough exposition of distribution of heresy before Crusade; 'sustained instruction', my interpretation of Griffe, p. 26.
[42]   Pierre des Vaux de Cernay, *Hystoria Albigensis*, ed. P. Guebin and E. Lyon, 3 vols (Paris, 1926–39), I, pp. 182–3, 185–7; Barber, 'Catharism and the Occitan nobility'; on the Corbières, Brenon, *Visage*, p. 120. M. Costen, *The Cathars and the Albigensian Crusade* (Manchester, New York, 1997) (concise survey: esp. clear on role of nobility).
[43]   A. Cazenave, 'Les Cathares en Catalogne et Sabarthès après les registres d'Inquisition: la hiérarchie Cathare en Sabarthès après Montségur', *BPH Année 1969* (Paris, 1972), pp. 387–436.
[44]   *BF*, p. 123.

in the Treaty of Paris in 1229. (It is marked as a see because he made it his base.) A further shift southwards took place after Montségur fell; Catharism only became strong in the lands of Foix in its last years.[45]

Along the Mediterranean littoral, Montpellier was a Cathar-free zone. Here the strength of the meridonal *lignage* had worked in the opposite direction to sustain orthodoxy and maintain links between pre-Catholic forces, the papacy itself, the bishoprics of Lodève, Béziers and Agde and the abbey of Aniane. The counts were a successful dynasty of the eleventh and twelfth centuries, ruling at a point which was a natural staging post on the Domitian Way, used in the twelfth century by legates and pilgrims. Guilhem VIII (1172–1202) was the patron of the Catholic controversialist Alan of Lille; amongst the families with which he was intimately linked were the Montpeyroux who gave bishops Gaucelm to Lodève and Pierre to Agde. Because of his scriptural knowledge, Gaucelm was chosen to lead the interrogation of heretics at the Council of Lombers. After Count Guilhem's death, Montpellier passed via his daughter Marie to the kings of Aragon and remained under their rule a strongpoint of orthodoxy.[46]

Narbonne was more equivocal. A small number of prosecutions for heresy in the thirteenth century were recorded; some confiscations, perhaps for heresy as well as rebellion, occurred but were not recorded. Given its geographical position and commercial links with areas affected by Catharism, it seems unlikely that the heresy had so small a hold there as the records suggest; more likely, neither archbishop nor viscount wanted to introduce complications into the already awkward jurisdictional situation. On the other hand, reticence about heresy would have been difficult to sustain had Narbonne in reality had a strong Cathar presence. At Perpignan to the south, the map is again blank.

The Cathars seem to have been weak along the coastline. If heresy had entered the South directly, perhaps via Constantinople from the Balkans or commercial links to Italy, it would have been natural to expect the missionaries to have left their mark on or near the sea ports. It was not so; the deaconries and bishoprics lay inland and their distribution, running southwards from the line of Marmande, Gourdon or Cahors, may suggest an entering overland rather than from the Mediterranean. Trade routes were means of entry not only for merchants but for Cathar perfect set on missionary action.

The attractions of Catharism

The ethical appeal of the perfect was the first factor in building up a Cathar presence. The evidence of the sermon of Federico Visconti, archbishop of Pisa, recording the impact of early Cathars on the mountain lords, restraining them from banditry, points in this direction, as does the subsequent inquisition evidence of the dedicated lives of numbers of perfect, perhaps especially women perfect. The recollections of Cathars

---

[45] Brenon, *Visage*, p. 120; for Guilhabert, below pp. 135, 136, 138, 140–1.
[46] Amado, in *EO*, pp. 86–9.

interrogated in the 1240s reveals a world about the turn of the century in which reverence for the perfect and an awareness of their abstemious lives was part of their background.

Such early memories throw into focus whole societies in which heretics spoke freely and the young were unobtrusively initiated stage by stage into heretical beliefs and practices. In certain families, sometimes in whole villages, heresy rather than orthodoxy had become the norm. In his confession of 1245, the knight Bernard Mir Acezat remembered a time in the village of Saint-Martin-la-lande in the Lauragais when there were as many as ten houses of perfect, who moved about with freedom. They gave him nuts to eat and taught him to genuflect, that is perform the *melioramentum*, acknowledging their unique status: he was being taken into the very first stage of complicity. Later, he became squire to Aymeric, the wealthy lord of Laurac and Montréal, whose widowed mother Blanche presided over a community of perfect women at Laurac.[47] Childhood experience and contact with a great Cathar family made him a believer.

Arnaude de Lamothe, captured and recanting in 1243, made a full confession in the following year, revealing a first contact with heresy with her mother, elder sister and her uncle's widow before the Crusade when she was about seven or eight, listening in their home in Montauban in Quercy to perfect women who visited them; she saw her mother and aunt give the *melioramentum* after the preaching. Then a deacon and a male perfect, probably a relative, Bernard de Lamothe came and preached and took the two sisters to a house of perfect women at Villemur, where they were trained in their way of life and, after three years, still before the coming of the crusaders, consoled in the deacon's house at Villemur.[48]

Pierre de Gramazie learnt his heresy through working in a workshop of the perfect in Fanjeaux, where he had heard their preaching and adored them; these perfect had to engage in physical work to gain a living. This was common enough; certainly at the end of Cathar history the perfect felt obliged to work, in accord with the Pauline text, and something of this feeling may have prevailed earlier. Bernard de Villeneuve learnt both heresy and sewing from two perfect with whom he lived for a year at Laurac.[49]

Bernard Oth, lord of Niort in the pays de Sault in the Razès, came to heresy in approximately 1205–6: when about four or five years old he was entrusted to his grandmother Blanche of Laurac and his aunt Mabilia, who lived in a small community of perfect women. There he ate bread blessed by them and witnessed the coming and going of Blanche's aristocratic relatives and contacts and the regular ritual exchanges in the giving of the *melioramentum*. Heretical ritual and respect for the perfect thus became a part of his mental furniture from his earliest days.[50]

[47]   Griffe, *Languedoc*, p. 126, n. 43; *BF*, p. 143.
[48]   Koch, *Frauenfrage*, pp. 186–7.
[49]   Griffe, *Languedoc*, p. 189.
[50]   Ibid., pp. 148–9. W. L. Wakefield, 'The family of Niort in the Albigensian Crusade and before the Inquisition', *Names* XVIII (1970), pp. 97–117, 286–303; updated version at Potsdam College, State University of New York. Professor Wakefield has given generous help.

Guillelme Martine remembered a blend of hospitality and instruction when as a young girl she went to the heretics and received bread and nuts. In their confessions, the son, daughter and grandson recalled the career of Furneria, wife of Gillaume-Roger, brother of Pierre-Roger of Mirepoix, who was consoled, lived at Mirepoix with other perfect women, then moved to Lavelanet in the Ariège; she returned to her husband's house at Mirepoix but only to take her daughter back with her. Though still young, the daughter was consoled in 1208, sharing the rigours of their life for three and a half years. But in the end she left and married. When the Crusade shook the old security, Furneria did not return to married life, but fled to Montségur.[51]

Whatever the importance of anticlericalism in providing an ambience in which heresy could thrive in Languedoc, and whatever the role of quarrels over tithes and lands, at the heart of the earliest recollections of the Cathars who came before inquisitors in the 1240s are the perfect, men and women, instructing, praying, receiving the *melioramentum*, giving hospitality.

The ceremony of consoling in its simplicity and confidence drew support. Arnaude de Lamothe remembered the details when she and her sister Peirona accompanied by the perfect women who had welcomed and trained them went to the deacon's house in Villemur.[52] He and one other perfect asked them first if 'they wished to give themselves to God and the Gospel'; secondly, if they would promise 'not to eat, meat, eggs or cheese or any fat except vegetable oil or fish; not to take any oath, nor to lie, not to satisfy any bodily desire – all this for the rest of their lives'. Here was an appeal to self-immolation and idealism, comparable to that of a nun, answered in this case by teenage girls, continuing a life with older women companions which they had already experienced and which they were evidently freely choosing. As always, the ceremony took place in a private house, in ordinary surroundings and not amidst the grandeur of an abbey church. The two girls believed they were giving themselves to 'God and the Gospel', a gospel understood to consist in a radical simplicity in which all the apparatus of worship in the medieval Church was cut away and the baptism of John, administered in water, was superseded, replaced by a ceremony not imposed on infants without the use of reason but only those of an age to understand what was happening, in which candidates made a free choice and the 'baptism of the Spirit' was administered by the laying on of hands. Arnaude and her sister went on to promise – as the inquisitorial summary describes it – 'not to abandon the heretical sect through fear of fire or water or other kind of death'. Then 'the male heretics placed their hands and a book on the heads of the witness and her sister, and read from the book and made the two girls say the *Pater Noster* in the heretical way', that is, substituting 'supersubstantial bread' for the 'daily bread' of the orthodox version. The book was a gospel or New Testament, the inspired book of the Cathar Church in contradistinction to the Old Testament, in

---

[51] Griffe, *Languedoc*, pp. 148–9.
[52] I follow hereafter Murray's translation (above n. 32). For consoling, Doat 25, fols 4r–5v, Koch, *Frauenfrage*, pp. 187–8.

whole or in part inspired by Jehovah, an evil god or spirit, whose world, given over to evil, was the world of matter.

In the ritual of the *consolamentum*, which we have in a Provençal [53] vernacular version, the Cathars call their Church simply the Church of God. Here, before the solemn laying on of hands, the elder exhorted the candidate, recalling one after another the scriptural texts on the necessity of baptism and on the practice of the laying on of hands in Acts and, key text for Cathars, the words of John the Baptist, 'I baptize you with water but he that shall come after me is mightier than I ... He shall baptize you in the Holy Spirit and fire', and of Jesus as cited by Luke in Acts, 'For John truly baptized with water; but you shall be baptized with the Holy Spirit not many days hence.' [54]

The clear implication was that the Catholic Church was the Church of John the Baptist; the true Church of God administered its baptism by the laying on of hands. The elder concludes the first part of his exhortation by saying, 'This holy baptism, by which the Holy Spirit is given, the Church of God has preserved from the apostles until this time and it has passed from Good Men to Good Men until the present moment and it will continue to do so until the end of the world.' [55] In other words, the candidate was entering into the tradition of the apostles and following the apostolic way of life. The tradition of the medieval Church was a false one, the way of Satan. Text after text of the ritual reinforced the powerful message of the authenticity of the Cathar teaching and the way of life of the consoled. There followed more citations on the necessity of keeping the commandments and precepts of Jesus and on the power given to the Church of God, that is, the perfect, to forgive sins, to bind and loose, heal, cast out devils, speak with tongues.

Except for the crucial rejection of baptism by water, its replacement by the laying on of hands and the restriction of membership of the Church to the consoled, the sequence of texts and exhortations calling for a holy way of life, not stealing, killing or lying, blessing persecutors, was orthodox. At one point, where the elder picked his texts on the rejection of the world, of concupiscence and 'the spotted garment which is carnal',[56] he plainly intended to justify the renunciation of all sexual contacts and the eating of meat – not *per se* unorthodox, but heretical when taken in conjunction with the belief that all matter was evil, the creation of Satan or an evil god.

There was nothing obvious in this sermon to alert a candidate or onlooker to the heresy implicit in the proceedings; the solemn and powerful sequence of texts reinforced trust in the perfect, and fanned idealism. In the ritual, the candidate responded to the words, 'you must keep the commandments of God and hate this world' by saying 'I have this

---

[53]   L. Clédat, *Le Nouveau Testament traduit au XIIIe siècle en langue Provençal, suivi d'un rituel Cathare* (Paris, 1887); *WEH*, pp. 483–94.
[54]   John 1: 26–7; Matt. 3: 11; Acts 1: 5.
[55]   *WEH*, p. 488.
[56]   Jude 1: 23.

will. Pray God for me to give me His strength':[57] the elder then proceeded to the consoling ceremony itself.

In Arnaude's confession, after the two girls had said the paternoster, the two heretics genuflected often, prayed and gave them the 'peace', kissing first a book, then the shoulder, the male perfect kissing each other on the cheeks. Though so young, they had the Spirit and were entitled to the *melioramentum*, which they were at once given, solemnly recognizing the status the sisters had attained, though no male could kiss a female.[58] 'Many heretics of both sexes were there', the confession runs, 'it was a major occasion.'

They returned to the community of perfect women and lived there for a year, 'eating, praying, fasting and blessing bread from month to month' and 'apparelling' and 'adoring' and 'doing everything else that heretics of either sex normally do'. The 'apparelling' was a monthly confession of faults largely of a ritual character, concerning minor breaches of the way of life. As in a well-run community of nuns, the regular performance of set duties in a body of women with a common purpose had its own attraction: the life took them over.

Then came the crusaders and the community began to wander, till at length, 'terrified of persecution', the two sisters gave up, went home, ate meat and were reconciled by the bishop of Cahors. They did not marry and, some ten years later, again influenced by Bernard de Lamothe, then *filius major* to the Cathar bishop of Toulouse, entered the nunnery at Linars in Quercy, which had been infiltrated by perfect women[59] and thence were taken to the house of a believer and his wife at Lavaur, where they were reconsoled. Reawakened by Bernard de Lamothe, individual inclination, the power of the consoling and role of the perfect carried them back to active Catharism. Perhaps their mother was the most important influence of all. Sick, her family grown, she too joined the Linars sisterhood and was consoled with her daughters. Family background was the key. Bernard de Lamothe was an influence; the mother and aunt had been present when the girls first met Cathars; family tradition and early, evidently happy, experience carried them ultimately over the fear of persecution and death, the pressure of reconciliation to Catholicism and the will to independence which regularly carried some teenage converts away from the life of the perfect.

The formidable matriarch, Blanche de Laurac, was another, though rather different, example of a mother's influence sustaining the faith.[60] She held power in a way which Arnaude's mother did not, for she was the widow of Sicard de Laurac, one of the most powerful men in the region and commanded the resources to endow an informal convent of Cathar perfect in her own home. Nobles and their connections visited; the deacon Bernard

[57] *WEH*, p. 490.
[58] Koch, *Frauenfrage*, pp. 122–33, with observations on implications of ritual.
[59] *BF*, p. 26, correcting R. Abels and E. Harrison, 'The participation of women in Languedocian Catharism', *MS* XLI (1979), pp. 215–51, at p. 229.
[60] Griffe, *Languedoc*, pp. 108–13; on Blanche and her house, *BF*, ch. 12.

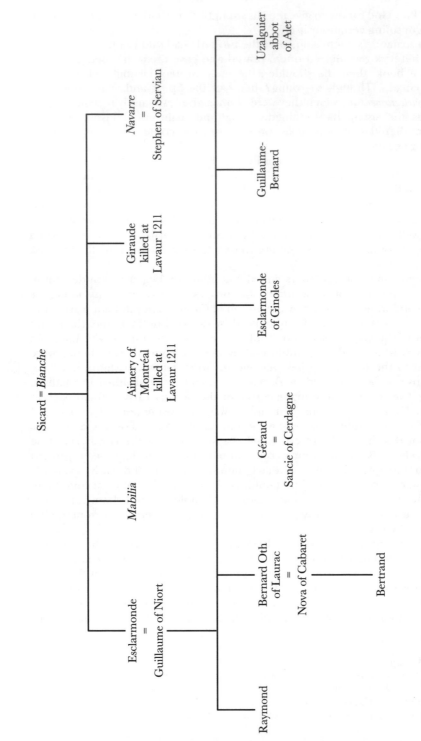

Figure 2 The descendants of Blanche of Laurac. Perfect shown in italics.

Source: Duvernoy, *Histoire*, p. 238

Raymond resided in Laurac, carried out ritual functions and preached; all her children were believers or sympathizers and her daughter Mabilia was consoled. Catharism was thus diffused both through family education and through lines of blood and dependency. In his lifetime, Sicard was a bene- factor of the Cistercian abbey of Boulbonne; how far his Cathar sympathies had then extended is unclear. Blanche's religious views dominated the settlement: official status had in practice moved from the Church at Laurac to Cathar deacons and perfect. Testifying in 1245, the widow Na Gauzio said that at the turn of the century, she had seen many perfect living publicly in Laurac, where the whole population gave them the ritual adoration and heard their preaching.[61]

At the Cathar strongpoint of Fanjeaux, a major role appears to have been played by another matriarch, Guillelme de Tonneins, who lived in a community of perfect women; her granddaughter testified to visiting about 1193 and being given bread, wine, nuts and fruit. Catharism in Fanjeaux was of long standing: Bernard Gasc as an old man remembered living with his mother near a house of perfect and visiting them in 1175. Guillelme was one of those who anchored the faith in the leading nobility, helping to create a *lignage* of wealth and power which produced active patrons and men and women perfect in every generation. One son-in-law was a high officer of the viscount of Carcassonne and a man of considerable wealth; another, Pierre-Roger de Mirepoix le Vieux, was the principal co-seigneur of Mirepoix and father of the defender of Montségur in the great siege of 1243–4.[62]

Visits to houses of perfect women, the welcome given to children, the contact with relatives play a recurrent role in the earliest recollections of veteran Cathars and lead historians to be inclined to give a special role to the dedicated women who, having had children, retired to their homes and gathered friends and relatives round them to form mini- communities, aided by the extreme flexibility of the organizational side of the perfect's life. The ritual and dietary requirements were rigid; by contrast, the assembling of little groups of perfect men and women was marked by simplicity and ease of management. Groups formed at the will of individuals, sometimes supported on a widow's endowment or other forms of inherited wealth, sometimes by their own labours. For celibates without continuing family obligations, their austere way of life was not costly. Movement was not restricted and thus their influence could be diffused among the uncommitted population. Family influence radiated out from the communities and they acted as support points for the deacons who presided over the monthly confession of faults, preached and exhorted. In town or country, where there was Cathar patronage and support, an informal, fluid network of communities of perfect came into being, acting as a focus for Cathar preaching and observance and having the flexibility and accessibility of the beguinages of the late Middle Ages.

---

[61]   Griffe, *Languedoc*, p. 113, n. 13.
[62]   Roquebert in *EO*, pp. 175–8, 182.

Obedience, territorial links, loyalty to a dynasty or employer carried Catharism down the ranks of society and committed a class of dependents to the faith of the uppermost layers. Jourdain de Roquefort, lord of Montgey, scion of an established Cathar family, son of a believer killed fighting on the South French side in the Albigensian Crusade, with lands in the Black Mountain and the eastern Lauragais, could anticipate that his men would be supporters of his faith. In fact, in the inquisition sources his bayles of Vaure and Montgey and his miller and dependent Guillaume Guibert can be observed playing an active part in the support and protection of the perfect; no doubt their adherence to Catharism was underpinned by idealism and respect for the hard lives of the perfect, but their faith took off in the first instance from their dependence on Jourdain and his *lignage*. Another of Jourdain's men, Pierre Grimaud, pleaded before the inquisition that he had acted in favour of the Cathar cause under compulsion, that is, as a dependent of a great Cathar family, '*quasi coactus*'. This was not accepted as mitigation and he was condemned to perpetual imprisonment in 1247.[63] Yet his plea may not have been simply a ruse: a dependent was expected to share in and serve the ideology of his master.

Another example of dependency and its effects is the case of the miller Guillaume Garnier, devoted aide to the Lamothe sisters in the Lantarès in the 1230s and dependent of the Auriol family near Lanta; his allegiance and his economic dependence exposed him to Catharism and carried him into a fervent devotion. When Arnaude's sister died, he buried her in the forest; finally, he fled to Montségur, became a sergeant in the garrison, volunteered at the end to be consoled and thereby condemned himself wittingly to be burned when the fortress fell.[64] Dependency provided a context for such idealism on the part of the few, and for a broader, less dramatic, allegiance for the many.

The beginnings of counter-argument

Decades of relative tranquillity in the later twelfth century in certain regions allowed a build-up of blocks of dependency and family interest resistant to persuasion. The Catholic Church grew increasingly aware of the hostile force which confronted it. MS 47 of the Bibliothèque Municipale d'Albi, an archaic form of polemical material from the cockpit of Languedoc dating from a time between the meeting of Barbarossa and the pope at Verona in 1184 and the Albigensian Crusade, provides a glimpse of an attempt to grapple with Catharism through biblical knowledge.[65] The author assumes that heretics will easily be met with and discussions take place. He knows the difference between Cathars and Waldensians and

---

[63]   Roquebert, 'Le catharisme comme tradition ...', *passim* and p. 224 (convincing account of effects of dependency).

[64]   Below, p. 169.

[65]   R. Manselli, 'Una "Summa auctoritatum" antiereticale (MS 47 della Bibliothèque Municipale di Albi)', in *Atti della Accademia Nazionale dei Lincei*, 8th ser., XXVIII (1985), pp. 321–97.

concentrates his fire on the more dangerous, the '*boni homines*', whom he describes as Manichaeans.

A simple *summa auctoritatum*, the compilation collects New Testament texts with which to confute heretical teaching – awkwardly disposed, since the texts are put in on stray spaces or blank folios in a miscellaneous codex containing the Song of Songs, the Acts of the Apostles and excerpts from Church Fathers. The collection is battle equipment for face-to-face confrontation, pebbles for the sling of a clerical David against the Goliath of Catharism. The author has faith that truth will confute error and that the superior biblical understanding of a properly equipped churchman will demonstrate the falsity of the Cathar use of Scripture. The process of compilation has the side-effect of building knowledge of Cathar teaching, though there is much that he does not know. He is inclined to take his opponent on to the ground where he himself is best equipped and, all unconsciously, obscure the importance of Cathar myths and apocrypha, which, as they were not readily divulged in the earliest stages of initiation, are not well known to him. Here is a dogged orthodox opponent grappling against his own reconstruction of Cathar theology with scriptural weapons, often soundly chosen, but failing to understand that Catharism generally attracted untrained minds, whose emotions were stirred by the contrast between the rigorous, ascetic perfect and a relaxed local clergy of limited training, and who were drawn to their vivid metaphors and narratives. Such converts were not easily susceptible to logical, Scripture-based argument.

Yet the massing of texts had a certain persuasive force. Churchmen in these decades still had a touching faith in persuasion, and, despite the disorderly fashion in which it was set out, the text collection was designed to underpin that process. It has an importance in the history of the Church's counter-attack against the Cathars, for summaries of this simple pattern were forerunners of the polemical, anti-heretical treatises of the thirteenth century, powerful, scholastic constructions rising from such humble foundations.

Italy

The long conflict with Barbarossa, his expeditions, lawyers and anti-popes, the encouragement of violence and the distracting effects on churchmen, gave free play to all forms of religious dissidence in Northern and Central Italy. It was the spring-time of Italian Catharism. Preaching and private missionizing could be carried on virtually unchecked. The Life of St Galdinus, Archbishop of Milan 1166–76 gives a clue as to what was happening when it records how 'the holy man set himself to combat that deadly plague and by many discourses and much preaching ... recalled the people ... and, by instructing them in the fundamentals of the Catholic faith in so far as he was able ... advanced his cause by both word and example.'[66] The example was important, a contrast to the preoccupation

---

[66] *WEH*, p. 151.

with wealth and power that stained the record of too many contemporary prelates. None the less, there is no word of judicial action. The canon law was evidently powerless; the archbishop was constrained to oppose Catharism by preaching alone. There is no reason to doubt his personal impact but, without the exercise of legal constraints, his actions had limited long-term effect. A generation later, Jacques de Vitry called Milan 'a pit of heretics'.[67]

A similar picture of the freedom of the discontented to launch attacks on the teaching of the Church and on the conduct of churchmen with impunity emerges from the text written between 1177 and 1185 of Vacarius the canonist's refutation of the heresy of his friend Speroni, once consul in Piacenza, who had been involved in prolonged conflict with the papacy over the rights of the monastery of St Giulia in Piacenza and initiated a movement in his native city rejecting priesthood and sacraments *per se* in favour of a quietist, personal union with God.[68]

Vacarius's tone, recalling how he and Speroni shared lodgings as students, and his reasoned debating style, firm but compassionate with no allusion to the physical penalties for heresy, implies the freedom of action Speroni and his followers had had to diffuse their beliefs. Partly perhaps because of its quietism, Speroni's movement seems not to have sparked off a crisis, and, though still requiring refutation in 1235, apparently faded out finally without publicity. None the less, both its emergence in the 1170s and its continuing existence is symptomatic of the absence of ecclesiastical control over religious opinion and also of a strain of radicalism in Lombardy which gave a platform to the outright challenge to orthodoxy represented by Catharism.

Arnold of Brescia was long dead and his direct following dispersed, but his spirit lived on in a profound anticlericalism which became part of the mental furniture of communal leaders, both a weapon and an inspiring force in the long series of struggles between bishops and municipalities over lands and rights. Part of the inheritance from Arnold, and ultimately from the current of thought set in motion by the Pataria, was the diffusion of the conviction that the contemporary Church had betrayed the gospel and that its priesthood, mired in the pursuit of money and power, was no longer a channel of grace and the sacraments it administered were invalid.[69]

It forms part of the background of a number of different challenges to Church leaders. It was characteristic, for example, that when Waldensianism crossed the Alps, it grew more radical, appointing ministers for the sacraments on a permanent rather than an *ad hoc* basis, so creating a Counter-Church, in contrast to the more conciliatory spirit of Valdes. The radicalism abroad in the cities of Northern and Central Italy, which so affected the Waldensians and split their movement in 1205, fostered the cause of the Cathars when they stigmatized the Church as a Church of Satan and preached uncompromising opposition based on their own distinctive

---

[67]   *Lettres de Jacques de Vitry*, ed. R. C. B. Huygens (Leiden, 1960), pp. 72–3.
[68]   Lambert, *Medieval Heresy*, 2nd edn, pp. 77–8; *WEH*, pp. 152–8.
[69]   Vauchez, 'Moviment religiosi ...', p. 321.

doctrines. Despite the distortions involved, their exaltation of the New Testament and rejection of the Old appealed to the widespread desire for a return to the apostolic age, as also the claim of the perfect, the Good Men, to be the true heirs of the apostles in contradistinction to the Catholic priesthood. The asceticism of the perfect, the simplicity of their meeting places and rejection of church buildings meant that their organization was cheap to uphold. Catharism needed little in the way of material goods and benefactions, pointing a contrast to the needs of leading churchmen and the buildings and shrines of Catholicism – all the more poignant as material possessions and rights lay at the centre of the conflicts with the Church in the cities. It was common among the heretics in Italy to believe that the Church had been corrupted when Pope Sylvester received possessions through the Donation of Constantine – it was a feature of the Italian rather than the Southern French scene and a sign of the importance of the poverty/possession issue in Italian consciousness.[70] The image of the poor Church of the apostolic age as a pattern for the twelfth-century Church, fruit of the reform agitation against simony in the Gregorian reforms, for a time aided the Cathar appeal, even though an observance of poverty was not an intrinsic part of the obligatory way of life of the perfect.[71] The currents of thought in the later twelfth century ran in directions favourable to the unfolding Cathar movement.

Not till the end of the long conflict with Barbarossa could churchmen begin to turn their attention intensively to the problem of heresy: the decisions of the Third Lateran Council of 1179 marked a beginning, followed by the Bull *Ad abolendam* of 1184, fruit of the final settlement between the pope and emperor, and issued with Barbarossa's support. By that time much ground had been won by the heresies, probably by Catharism most of all. Galdinus had been an exception in grappling with the problem: his *Life* is explicit that the target of his counter-preaching was the Cathars. Everywhere bishops, battling over secular issues in their cities, were inclined in sweeping style to call opponents heretics because of their opposition to episcopal authority and possessions; on the other hand, the figures for the numbers of perfect in Italy, given by Sacconi, the Dominican inquisitor and former perfect, in mid-thirteenth century when the movement had passed its peak, are solid evidence that Catharism in the affected areas of Northern and Central Italy mustered a substantial membership.[72] It is reasonable to think that the bases for this powerful numerical presence were laid at the time of maximum opportunity for religious dissent, in the 1160s and following decades.

Supra-national though it was, *Ad abolendam* had a special eye for the Italian scene; it marked a step forward in the Church's response to the challenge of dissent, yet passing in review the different names for heretics, it

[70]   R. Manselli, *L'Eresia del Male* (Naples, 1963) p. 182, n. 56; G. Gonnet, 'La donazione di Costantino in Dante e presso gli eretici medievali', *Il grano e le zizzanie* I (Rome, 1992), pp. 91–121.
[71]   Paolini, 'Esiti ereticali ...', pp. 127–86 at pp. 140–2.
[72]   Below, pp. 209–11.

gave no means of identifying a heresy and distinguishing one from another, and it relied on the episcopal pursuit of heresy, still an uncertain business, to make sanctions effective. Thus this Bull introduced no major change in Italy in the balance of advantage between ecclesiastical authority and heresy, and Catharism continued to profit.

Galdinus, however, is the likely spur to one major breakthrough in this period – the conversion of Bonacursus, a doctor or magister of the Cathars, who made a public confession in Milan of the doctrines which he repudiated.[73] It was the first crack in the solid front hitherto presented by leading Cathars in Italy and a first check obtained by persuasion rather than force in the upward movement of the Cathars. Bonacursus subsequently wrote, or contributed to, the *Manifestatio heresis catarorum*, providing thereby an account of Cathar beliefs followed by a summary of scriptural authorities for use against Cathars and then refutations of the heresies of the Arnoldists and the Passagini. Ilarino the editor inclines to believe that these sections were tacked on to a version of Bonacursus's declaration after the Bull of 1184. He contrasts the tone of the section on the Cathars, 'a shout of alarm', revealing to the public doctrines hitherto unknown, with the comparatively tranquil language of the prologue to the passage on the Passagini, when the tempestuous emotions of the first baring of his own former beliefs have passed; on internal evidence, he argues for a composition in stages between the end of Galdinus's episcopate in 1176 and 1190.

Bonacursus's service to the Church which he now publicly embraced was to reveal in detail from his own intimate knowledge the myths of the Cathars, their exotic interpretations, especially of the Old Testament, the profound challenge to orthodoxy represented, for example, by the belief that Jesus was an angel concealed as a man, and the divisions between radical and moderate dualists. As the inner secrets of Catharism were reserved to the most committed followers and revealed cautiously, Bonacursus's statements were a shock to superficial auditors, who knew Cathar preachers primarily as devout, ascetic figures who spoke to them of the renunciation of the world in familiar, scriptural language and denounced the sins of the clergy. With Bonacursus's treatise, a pattern of controversy was set, with Catholic controversialists dwelling on the most *outré* features of Catharism and the extent of their inner divisions, which they tended to exaggerate, and Cathar preachers flaying clerical failings and pointing to the moral superiority of the perfect.

The *Manifestatio* was a simple, practical treatise, designed to provide ammunition for denunciation of Cathars, Arnoldists and Passagini, containing a *summa auctoritatum* for the preacher or missioner, a working aid to follow up and give effect to *Ad abolendam*, subsequently overtaken in Italy by more profound, detailed works giving a depth of information on Cathar teaching which Bonacursus lacks. But the *Manifestatio* has the distinction of being the first known example of an Italian anti-Cathar tractate –

---

[73]   Ilarino da Milano, ' "La manifestatio heresis catarorum quam fecit Bonacursus" secondo il Cod. Ottob. Lat. 136 della Biblioteca Vaticana', *Eresie medioevali, scritti minori* (Rimini, 1983), pp. 154–203; *WEH*, pp. 170–3.

the starting-point of a genre of writing which distinguishes the Italian scene from that of Languedoc, where such works are much rarer.

Slowly a counter-attack began to develop. But there was a long way to go. Heresy in general in Italy had moved far and fast since Arnold of Brescia's day; still more since the first intimations of heresy in the eleventh century, when it appears to have been the product of the country rather than the town. The Catharism of the later twelfth century was emphatically an urban product, gaining its foothold through the battles waged by the communes against the Church, by disorder, and by the fluidity of the Italian scene.[74]

Concorezzo, though near Milan, was a small place but became the seat of a bishopric because of its personal associations with Mark the Gravedigger and the beginnings of Italian Catharism. Desenzano near Lake Garda, the seat of radical dualists, may have become a bishopric because of personal links of which we know nothing or simply because it was more out of the way and less liable to attract the attention of heresy-hunters. Other bishoprics were based in Vicenza and Florence: that of Mantua was transferred to Bagnolo in the countryside perhaps for reasons of security or because their second bishop originated in the locality.[75] Cathar bishops and teachers were itinerant and the bishoprics lacked the territoriality of the Languedoc Cathars: they often covered large areas and, because of the splits created in the time of Nicetas and Petracius, had a denominational rather than territorial character.

Nevertheless, the growth points lay in the Italian cities, where a long battle was fought between the heretics, their patrons and the Catholic clergy: Northern and Central Italian Cathars rarely recruited peasants. Where sources enable us to pinpoint occupations, Cathars tend to come from trades active in urban settings: weavers, though in less significant numbers than elsewhere in the Cathar world, tailors, blacksmiths, leather workers, millers, innkeepers, carters, pedlars.[76] At a higher level, Cathars made inroads amongst the bourgeoisie of the towns, proprietors of land and houses in town and country, merchants and moneylenders and amongst the urban nobility of feudal background, sometimes with substantial holdings and with houses and castles in the *contado* where refuges could be provided for perfect and their sympathizers under pressure. A wide range of Italian society was touched by this heresy, pre-eminent among all others, but it included very few marginal elements. Its profound rejection of the visible world seems to have had no special attraction for the poorest. Revolutionary as Catharism was in doctrine, it was far from revolutionary in social and economic matters and the poor were not likely to see it as a vehicle for changes which would better their lot.

The flux of Italian society aided the diffusion of Catharism in part because Church structures did not keep pace with a burgeoning population, in part because the very movement of individuals – whether merchants

---

[74]   Violante, 'Hérésies urbaines ...', p. 180.
[75]   Ibid.
[76]   I follow closely Violante, ibid., p. 185.

or pedlars in pursuit of business, urban patriciates passing to and from their country settlements, reformers moving from monastery to hermitage or to one of stricter regime or itinerant preachers – over time created an instability and rootlessness which left sections of the populace unusually open to new religious initiatives.[77] The set forms of Church life no longer seemed adequate in a fast-changing world and the itinerant character of the Cathar elite seemed better to match a society itself in movement. Till the itineracy of the friars in the thirteenth century, the Church was at a disadvantage.

The early history of Italian Catharism can probably never be written in depth since the volume of early reminiscences elicited by inquisitors in Languedoc does not exist in Italy, where inquisitors became effective only later and records are much less extensive. There are not the details of family, class and occupation which make Languedoc the best field for investigation of the socioeconomic factors in the spread of Catharism. More close analysis of the inner history of cities may win clues: Merlo, reflecting on Vicenza, believes that it can hardly be a coincidence that this city, which lost two bishops to assassination within twenty years, developed as a Cathar centre with bishopric and advances the generalization that heresy in Italy found favourable circumstances for its expansion in particular conjunctions of events – when ecclesiastical power was challenged and contradictions in the upper levels of society exploded in destructive conflicts.[78] Both he and Vauchez, surveying Italian heresy in the high middle ages, concur in finding a vital key in the failure of the popular religious enthusiasm of the day to find an outlet in contemporary, orthodox institutional Church life.[79]

Other Lands

Outside these prime expansion areas in Italy and Languedoc, facts are hard to come by. There certainly was a presence in northern Europe: an '*episcopus Franciae*' was present at the Council of S. Félix de Caraman, most probably a bishop in the same succession, to whom the anxious Italians sent for counsel on the best means of healing their growing schism, thereby reverting for support to the Church of their origin.[80] The Northern French Church had status and a missionary past but did not grow sufficiently to require territorial subdivision on the lines of Toulouse. Some historians have believed that one of its strong points, perhaps even the seat of its bishopric, lay at the bourgade of Mont-Aimé, today a wood-crowned incline above a surrounding plain in the bishopric of Châlons-sur-Marne,[81]

---

[77] Perceptive comments, ibid., pp. 186–7.
[78] G. G. Merlo, 'Un contributo sulla storia ereticale a Vicenza nel duecento', *Ricerche di storia sociale e religiosa* XXXIX (1991), pp. 201–9 at pp. 208–9.
[79] Vauchez, 'Movimenti religiosi …', pp. 320–2; attractions of Catharism, pp. 323–6.
[80] Above, pp. 46, 59.
[81] *JDH*, p. 125.

alluded to in the mysterious letter of appeal from the Church of Liège to a pope in the 1140s. This would indicate the presence of another focus of Catharism in the North running parallel to the Rhineland group described by Everwin of Steinfeld. The clergy of Liège saw Mont-Aimé as a source of a 'heresy which appears to have overflowed various regions of the land',[82] a tradition recognized in mass burnings at this site in 1239.

In their letter, the clergy had felt unable to characterize the heresy under one name, but they and the local population were clear about the need for action, the populace seeking to burn suspects, the clergy seeking proper judgement and having recourse to the pope. The picture is one of solid defence of orthodoxy by clergy and people, the factor which explains the inability of Catharism under the North French episcopate and in northern Europe generally to make progress.

England was a particularly decisive example. A party of immigrant missionaries, arrived from Flanders or the Rhineland, were rounded up, brought before a Council in Oxford presided over by Henry II in 1166, branded and turned adrift in the winter to die. Their beliefs were anti-sacerdotal, rejecting the sacraments including matrimony, but the bald account gives no mention of distinction between adherents as in the Liège letter. They may or may not have been Cathars, but the implication was the same: where clergy and secular power were united and authority effectively wielded, heresy could be put down. 'Pious harshness', the chronicler William of Newburgh observed, 'purged the kingdom of that pestilence' and 'preserved it from ever again intruding'.[83]

By and large, in northern Europe hostility checked expansion and the element of despair at the widespread toleration of heresy which marks the sources for Languedoc and the sense of crisis which emerges in Italy is lacking. There is fear of 'pestilence' or 'poison' and its insidious penetration, but it is coupled with a determination to act and a confidence that action can be taken. So Catharism appears only sporadically in the north, but it showed resilience and a readiness to accept martyrdom, and even the Northern French bishopric, shadowy as its history is, contrived to continue, its last-known office-holder being observed by a perfect from Languedoc c.1271–2, living peacefully in exile at a refuge at Sirmione, a peninsula jutting into Lake Garda;[84] an evacuation of the hierarchy to safer sites in Northern Italy may have taken place after the great burning of Mont-Aimé in 1239.[85] The bishop was finally arrested in 1289 and the order given that he should be taken back to France.[86]

The will to persecute did not prevent the emergence of heretical groups in Burgundy, Champagne and Flanders, in Nevers, Vézelay, Auxerre,

---

[82] *WEH*, p. 140; see below, pp. 122–4.
[83] *WEH*, pp. 245–7, quotation, p. 247; Russell, *Dissent and Reform*, pp. 224–6; H. E. Hilpert, 'Die Insel der Gläubigen? Über die verspätete Ankunft der Inquisition im *regnum Angliae*', in *Die Anfänge der Inquisition im Mittelalter*, ed. P. Segl (Cologne, Wiemar, Vienna, 1993), pp. 253–68.
[84] *JDH*, p. 190.
[85] Borst, *Katharer*, p. 231.
[86] *JDH*, p. 128.

Troyes, Besançon, Metz, Rheims, near Soissons, Rouen and Arras, witnessed in chronicles and other sources in the twelfth century.[87] Sometimes the information is insufficient for a Cathar identification, means of detection crude and archaic; uncertainty of procedure is recurrent, coupled with unwillingness to let suspects free.

Full descriptions of the beliefs of heretics are rare, which makes more noteworthy the discovery of part of a sermon (no. 46) in a MS collection of St Vaast, datable to c.1200, anonymous but possibly by a canon of Saint-Pierre du Castel, Arras, preaching to a lay congregation and denouncing the heresies of the 'Bougres'.[88] Arras had been the scene of a full-scale investigation in 1183 after the discovery and imprisonment of four suspects. After Christmas, the highest authorities, ecclesiastical and secular, the count of Flanders and the archbishop of Rheims, arrived to take the matter further, whereupon a whole community of heretics was uncovered, nobles, non-nobles, clergy, knights, peasants, widows and married women and subjected to the ordeal by water and the hot iron: many were cleared, others burnt.

Sermon 43 alludes, by way of edification, to a master of the Bougres of Arras in the past, who was subjected to the ordeal of the hot iron before the high altar of the church, let out a great cry and said that his heretical belief was worthless. It is tempting to see in this a reference to the struggle to gain convictions in 1184 and to surmise that remnants had survived, making needful a warning to the faithful.

Sermon 46 also alluded to the Bougres of La Charité-sur-Loire,[89] which was an important focus for Catharism from 1198 until the assault by the leading inquisitor Robert le Bougre in 1233.[90] The preacher's purpose was to associate the heretics he denounced with those of La Charité: they shared the same name and beliefs and were thus one more of the foxes tied together by Samson, fired and thrown into the standing corn of the Philistines. These heretics were unmistakably Cathar for their rejection of the Church's sacraments flowed from a profound rejection of creation, repudiating the Old Testament, believing that the law of Moses was given by the Devil, denying the resurrection of the body; there was an elite class of the 'perfect' who claimed to administer the Holy Spirit by the laying on of hands and who would not eat meat, eggs or cheese. The preacher included the obligatory reference of controversialists to Mani, commented suspiciously on the prayers 'murmured' by the perfect among their believers in contrast to the *Gloria Patri* and the paternoster said with full voice, and expanded on the quality of the well-prepared vegetables, fish of every kind, fruit and wine not watered, which they consumed and which clearly in his mind vitiated their asceticism: they hid themselves in lay clothing, but were wolves, he said.

---

[87]   Borst, *Katharer*, p. 103.
[88]   B. Delmaire, 'Un sermon arrageois inédit sur les "Bougres" du nord de la France', *Heresis* XVII (1991), pp. 1–15, text, pp. 11–15.
[89]   I accept Delmaire's reading of MS, ibid., p. 7.
[90]   Below, p. 122.

Largely commonplaces of controversy, these are in fact only decorations on his precise report of heretical tenets, which is not stylized and which leaves no doubt that the heretics were Cathars. The report is also of interest because it provides an early example of the term 'Bougre', an abuse word derived from Bulgar, Bulgaria being known in the twelfth century as a source of Cathar heresy; later it took on the pejorative sense of sodomite.[91] It was applied to the inquisitor Robert, recalling his Cathar origins, and given to some of his victims by Philippe Mouske, the thirteenth-century rhyming chronicler.

The 'Bougres' of La Charité-sur-Loire were the object of intense investigation about the beginning of the thirteenth century, a group including adherents of wealth and standing, resilient to pressure.[92] The bishop of Auxerre was tenacious in pursuit, the suspects resourceful in avoiding definitive condemnation. The matter passed to Innocent III, who dealt with the case with skill and restraint but with no full uprooting of the heresy; after the death of the zealous bishop, Innocent, referring to heresiarchs called 'consolers', complained in 1208 that La Charité was a Babylon infected with heresy,[93] still so when Robert le Bougre set about purging it in 1233.[94]

There were odd cross-currents in the locality: a dean of Nevers was accused of heresy and deprived of office though not of his revenues; an abbot was accused of stercoranism and Origenism; a knight, a familiar of the count of Nevers, known as an oppressor of the Church, was burnt for heresy; and a nephew, Guillaume, archdeacon of Nevers, falling under suspicion, escaped to refuge in Languedoc, where he openly joined the Cathars, took the name Thierry, defended their cause in the debate of 1206 with Bishop Diego of Osma and St Dominic and gave instruction in the heresy under the protection of the lord of Servian in the Biterrois.[95]

The inadequacy of the chronicles precludes investigation of the factors at work in these cases, but hint at possible tensions between the bishop and people of La Charité, at conflict over usury, the possible use of heresy either positively to stimulate depredations against the Church or to give justification for them. The case remains an intriguing might-have-been of Cathar history.

In Germany, the story of Catharism, which can be followed sporadically from Everwin of Steinfeld to Conrad of Marburg in 1231–3,[96] tails away for the rest of the thirteenth century and cannot be followed in any detail. A blind fanatic, Conrad burnt suspects in droves, making away with innocent Catholics as well as genuine Cathars. A stray confession of a certain Burchard, incorporated in a composite work on enemies of the Church, the Passau Anonymous of 1260–6 or earlier, gives a clue on the state of the

---

[91] *JDR*, pp. 309–11 (with interesting speculations).
[92] *JDH*, pp. 139–43 (La Charité heresy Cathar).
[93] Thouzellier, *Catharisme*, p. 150.
[94] *GRK* III, pp. 349–57 (Nivernais generally), but *JDR* is right to see La Charité as Cathar (evidence of sermons).
[95] *JDH*, pp. 140–1.
[96] Below, pp. 117–22, with full refs.

movement probably about the time of Conrad's persecution. Where Burchard made his confession remains unknown; he learnt Catharism originally, he said, from his father in Liège twenty-four years previously, since when he claimed to have had no further contact with Cathars apart from his parents, his twin brother William and Henry, a barber. He gave a bare, sober account of basic Cathar tenets, in outline authentic. Like many a suspect, he may have wished to play down his participation and shield his contacts; or his confession was indeed a fair indication of a movement that had dwindled and passed into a shadow-world of a few families and individuals.

The confession of Lepzet, also in the Passau Anonymous and clearly datable to Conrad's pursuits, includes information about the worship of Lucifer, the expectation among Cathars that he, unjustly deprived of heaven by the good God, would return in glory, and refers to obscene initiation rites. Cathar belief in the creation of a visible world by a fallen leader of the angels or an evil principle had been perverted by their enemies into a crude Luciferanism. Slander was not new: the story of the kissing of a cat – the origin of the term 'Cathar' – goes back a generation earlier. But Conrad gave this type of slanderous material wide publicity.[97]

Both Burchard and Lepzet allude to a form of ritual suicide, Burchard citing it as hearsay from his father speaking of a 'martydom' for the sick, who were then suffocated with a cushion, and Lepzet speaking of a choice placed before a member of martyrdom through strangulation or euthanasia after the *consolamentum* through the refusal of food and drink, this latter being subsequently known as the *endura*.[98] It is hard to touch firm ground in the overheated atmosphere of reportage in Conrad of Marburg's era, but, on the face of it, the confessions give a first fragment of evidence for the *endura*.

Stories of Luciferanism reached other sources. Berthold of Regensburg, one of the greatest of all preachers in German-speaking lands, included references to the slander as well as attacks on authentic Cathar beliefs in his vigorous, challenging and rhetorical style. He lumped heresies together, attacking Waldensians as well as Cathars, stigmatizing failures to report heresy as a mortal sin, ridiculing the Cathar teaching on a 'false' crucifixion, which made Christ into a 'simulator' and constantly reverting to scriptural texts and allusions to demonstrate, for example, the reality of the creation by God. A tolerant eclecticism and a sense of live and let live is plainly one of his targets: faith, he says, must not be mixed with disbelief, but remain like the pure, clear water of baptism.[99]

Together with standard *topoi* about secrecy, hypocrisy and the influence of demons on heretics, comes the slander that Cathars adored the Devil, and the derivation of the term 'Cathar' from *cattus*,[100] but none the less this is

---

[97]   *GRK* IV (3), pp. 200–12 on Burchard and Lepzet; Catharism in Germany, Patschovsky, *DA* XXXVII, pp. 651–65, whom I follow (see below, p. 118 n. 18).

[98]   Below, p. 122.

[99]   A. E. Schönbach, *Studien zur Geschichte der altdeutschen Predigt, 3 Stück: Das Wirken Bertholds von Regensburg gegen die Ketzer* (Vienna, 1904), 'simulator', p. 4; water of baptism, p. 14.

[100]   Ibid., p. 31.

only a strand in his broad brush denunciation of main-line Cathar beliefs, given with a vitality and perception that argues for personal contact or knowledge from those who did have contact with a living Catharism. Berthold, who lived on until 1272, is evidence that Cathars had survived Conrad's epoch, though doubtless greatly diminished in numbers and influence compared with the Waldensians.

There is evidence of a Cathar presence in the Duchy of Austria. It is plain that the vernacular poet, Der Stricker, active broadly between 1220 and 1250 and with connections to Lower Austria, knew Cathar doctrine, attacked it and enjoined the Catholic practices of confession, penance, communion and the mass on the lines of the pastoral movement which flowed from the Fourth Lateran Council.[101] Certain verses have been interpreted as attacks on the Cathar doctrine of a fictive crucifixion and the *consolamentum.* The poet's *Klage,* a long poem denouncing political and spiritual evils of the day, includes alleged Luciferan doctrine and accusations of immorality based on the worship of Satan seen as the partner of God. That slander was now firmly settled in Catholic sources; the implication is that the Cathar movement was still alive.[102] This is supported by some heretical statements included in the Passau Anonymous such as the belief that a woman dying in childbirth would be damned. The Anonymous was at pains to copy out pre-existing material on Catharism as, for example, Sacconi. Although he includes no actual confessions, Segl none the less argues for a surviving Catharism. Its trail runs faint: Luciferanism and some Cathar sentiments derived from an inquisition at Krems in the early fourteenth century are the last traces.[103]

---

[101] P. Segl, *Ketzer in Österreich: Untersuchungen über Häresie und Inquisition im Herzogtum Österreich im 13. und beginnenden 14. Jahrhundert* (Paderborn, Munich, Vienna, Zürich, 1984); Der Stricker, pp. 137–52.

[102] Segl, *Ketzer in Österreich,* p. 152 corrects A. Patschovsky, *Der Passauer Anonymus* (Stuttgart, 1968), p. 98.

[103] Segl, *Ketzer in Österreich,* pp. 228–31.

5

Innocent III, Heresy and Reform

To the problem of heresy Innocent came prepared. He recognized its growth to be one of the major perils confronting the Church, together with the loss of Jerusalem and the rise of Saracen power in the Holy Land, and the territorial threat of the Hohenstaufen in Italy. His Bull of 25 March 1199, *Vergentis in senium*, directed to the clergy, consuls and people of Viterbo in the papal Patrimony, aimed to shock the fautors of heresy into compliance and was the first major piece of law-making against heresy since *Ad abolendam* in 1184. Ever the most capable of stage-managers, Innocent demonstrated the importance he attached to the decretal by putting it at the beginning of the register of the second year of his pontificate.[1] In a real sense, he was, in Ranke's phrase, 'the heir to Henry VI'. Henry's early death, the vacancy in the Empire and the disputed succession which followed provided both challenge and opportunity to Innocent. Determination to recover papal authority over the Patrimony and build the nucleus of a papal state, to prevent the Hohenstaufen inheritance of the Regno and Empire being held by one man and to secure an amenable candidate for the imperial throne, all intertwined and interacted with the struggle against heresy.

In 1199, the initiative lay with the papacy. *Vergentis* was designed to apply pressure by hard, material punishment against 'defenders, receivers, fautors and believers of heretics'; those who remained recalcitrant after exhortation were deemed to be subject to *infamia*.[2] They lost civil rights of election and of holding civil office; if clergy, of holding benefices; if lawyers, of exercising office as judges, advocates or notaries. Possessions were to be confiscated and the rights of heirs removed. The deprivation of rights of inheritance is particularly harsh, punitive rather than medicinal. Innocent

---

[1] H. G. Walther, 'Ziel und Mittel päpslicher Ketzerpolitik in der Lombardei und im Kirchenstaat', in *Anfänge*, ed. Segl (colloquy at Bayreuth University 1992, with up-to-date bibliography, precise discussions), pp. 103–30 at p. 114.
[2] Summary on *Vergentis*, L. Kolmer '… *ad terrorem multorum*: Die Anfänge der Inquisition in Frankreich', in *Anfänge*, ed. Segl, pp. 77–102 at pp. 83–5; implications, O. Capitani, 'La repressione antiereticale', *Storia dell' Italia medievale* (Rome, Bari, 1987), pp. 677–8.

justified it by an appeal to the precedent of the crime of *lèse-majesté* in imperial law, having in mind the *Lex quisquis* of 397 with its arbitrary and draconian penalties against those guilty of conspiracy, or even thinking of conspiracy against the emperor.[3] If such penalties were to be applied for the crime of treason against the civil power, he argued, how much more were they appropriate to those guilty of *lèse-majesté* in matters of belief.

Vergentis brought to an end earlier discussions by decretists on the relevance of antique imperial legislation to the twelfth-century problem of heresy. Most significantly, Huguccio, a powerful influence on Innocent, had argued for its use and had drawn a comparison between a thief who stole Church goods – like a heretic – and a thief who stole property of the State. The penalty for the former should be greater than that for the latter. Others argued similarly, even supporting the rightfulness of imposing confiscation of goods of innocent children on the analogy of *lèse-majesté*. Innocent thus in 1199 brought to fruition earlier discussions by professional canonists, made them effective in practice and gave official sanction to the concept of the injured majesty of Christ.[4]

The commune of Viterbo, where there had long been a Cathar presence, was in conflict with the commune of Rome. The pope backed Rome. Viterbo defied him. Both spiritual and territorial issues were in play and *Vergentis* could be used as a means of breaking down the autonomy of the city – *ratione peccati*, by reason of the sin of heresy. Viterbo had a key role in the pope's plan for the recovery of his authority and the build-up of an effective papal state, it and Orvieto being among the cities which in 1189 Henry VI had promised to return to papal control.[5]

At Orvieto, conflict arose over the city's determination to take the fortress of Acquapendente; the pope was determined to prevent this and imposed an interdict. Orvieto yielded to the interdict and Innocent sent in an agent of his own, Pietro Parenzo, a courageous and impetuous young man of the Roman senatorial nobility, who became *podestà* and proceeded vigorously to apply the confiscation penalties of *Vergentis* to heretics and, probably, their fautors, who had had freedom of action during the interdict and the bishop's absence. A 'council' of Cathars from neighbouring towns had been held, presided over by a certain Petrus Lombardus from Viterbo: there were even, it was said, plans for ejecting the Catholics and making the city a

---

[3] L. Kolmer, 'Christus als beleidigte Majestät: von der Lex "Quisquis" (397) bis zur Dekretale "Vergentis" (1199)', in *Papsttum, Kirche and Recht*, ed. K. Modek (Tübingen, 1991), pp. 1–13.

[4] Ibid., p. 12.

[5] On Viterbo and Orvieto, D. M. Webb, 'The Pope and the cities: anticlericalism and heresy in Innocent III's Italy', *SCH* Subsidia IX, pp. 135–52 at pp. 139–41; rise of Catharism in Orvieto, J. M. Henderson, 'Piety and heresy in medieval Orvieto: the religious life of the laity c.1150–1350', unpublished PhD thesis, University of Edinburgh, 1990, pp. 38–45 (I am grateful to Rev. Dr Mary Henderson for generous permission to use her thesis); M. Maccarrone, 'L'eresia ad Orvieto e l'envoi del rettore Pietro', *Studi su Innocenzo III* (Padua, 1972), pp. 30–48; Walther (*Anfänge*) illuminates the relation between legislation and papal lands; survey, C. Morris, *Papal Monarchy: the Western Church from 1050 to 1250* (Oxford, 1989), pp. 417–51.

stronghold of heresy. The heresy party felt strong enough to challenge Parenzo as he set about fining, confiscating and pulling down palaces. In the *Legenda* written shortly after his death by a canon of Orvieto, the young *podestà* was aware that he was in mortal danger and when he returned to Rome for Easter 1199, Innocent, encouraging him to stand fast, gave him the plenary indulgence normally offered to crusaders. Back in Orvieto in May, he was betrayed by his servant, seized, taken out of the city, made to eat dirt in a parody of the mass and killed when he declined the Cathars' demands to rescind his measures. The *Legenda* puts Parenzo into a framework consciously recalling Christ's passion from the triumphal entry into the city to the betrayal by a servant after a final meal.[6] The true Parenzo may well have had less of the saint and more of the politician in him than the *Legenda* allows. His courage and his refusal to yield to threats none the less sparked off an important reaction. In a blaze of feeling, his body was taken to the cathedral; miracles proliferated; his brother, Parenzo di Parenzo became *podestà*; heretics and their protectors were repressed.

Vergentis was first applied in the papal lands but its language makes plain that Innocent also envisaged its use outside, where the work of confiscation was to be carried out by the secular powers. So its provisions were recommended to the king of Hungary in 1200 against protectors of heresy in the lands of his vassal Ban Kulin of Bosnia, and a cardinal legate was given the task in the same year of making *Vergentis* effective in Languedoc.[7] The full effects of the edict were to be felt later. In the meantime, the arrangements in *Vergentis* for imposing *infamia* on possibly orthodox descendants gave grounds for disquiet.[8] In the intensity of his passion against heresy, Innocent had outrun justice and later at Viterbo, then at Faenza, he modified them.

Events at Viterbo followed a course not unlike that which prevailed in Orvieto: excommunications and interdict were imposed and Innocent called on the people to reject the leaders of the commune: if the latter protected heresy, they were *ipso facto* incapacitated from holding office under his Bull. When in June 1207 all adult inhabitants of Viterbo took an oath to observe the statutes, including measures against heresy, and Innocent himself came to an assembly held in September to regulate the affairs of the whole Patrimony, the measures of confiscation were quietly adapted. Total disinheriting of heirs was abandoned and the modification prevailed in the canon *Excommunicamus* of the Fourth Lateran Council, which summed up Innocent's heresy legislation. Innocent felt specially responsible for putting down heresy in his own lands, lest he should be exposed to the reproach, 'Physician, heal thyself.'[9]

---

[6]   Henderson, *Piety*, pp. 32–3.
[7]   Walther, *Anfänge*, p. 117.
[8]   Ibid., pp. 118–20; juristic background, O. Hageneder, 'Der Häresiebegriff bei den Juristen des 12. und 13. Jahrhunderts', in *Concept of Heresy*, ed. W. Lourdaux and D. Verhelst, pp. 42–103; P. D. Diehl, 'Overcoming reluctance to persecute heresy', in *Christendom and its Discontents*, ed. S. L. Waugh and P. D. Diehl (Cambridge, 1996), pp. 47–66; effects on politics, p. 53.
[9]   Ibid., p. 54, n. 39; quotation, Webb, in *SCH* Subsidia IX, p. 141.

In Northern and Central Italy generally, territorial and doctrinal issues intertwined. Heresy was a stick with which to belabour ecclesiastical opponents; or, it might be, temporal grievances against the Church provided a seed-ground for heretical teaching, in which the simplicity and apparent clarity of Cathar preaching and practice was an attraction in contrast to the stale complexities of battles over land, rights and offices between churchmen and communal leaders. Bishops, including those of high character, were tenacious in resistance to inroads on ecclesiastical authority and wealth: Bishop Lanfranc at Pavia saw in an apparently harmless request for the clergy to make a substantial contribution to the defence of the city a pretext for trampling on ecclesiastical liberty.[10]

Northern and Central Italy

Innocent's actions towards the Italian cities were as much concerned with political and jurisdictional controversies as with heresy. As temporal lord in the papal state which he was engaged in rebuilding within a new constitutional framework, Innocent saw clearly that political supremacy and the authority to repress heresy effectively went together: outside, the situation was more complex. His overriding interest lay in maintaining territorial security in Central Italy for the papacy and obtaining from the Welf–Hohenstaufen dispute an emperor who would respect the rights and needs of the Church and papacy and would himself be ready to act against heresy. Disappointed, Innocent moved from the Welf Otto of Brunswick to the young Hohenstaufen candidate, Frederick, who then reigned as Frederick II. Milan was not prepared to move against Otto as the pope desired: there must be a suspicion that Innocent's most forceful complaint to Milan in 1212 about their protection of heresy owed its timing at least to the city's opposition in that year to the advance of Frederick's army *en route* to claim his rights in Germany. He reproached them, 'Not only do you not capture the aforementioned little foxes, you favour and defend them to the extent that with you they are changed from little foxes to lions, from locusts to horses ready for war ...'[11] He included the veiled threat of a crusade against them as against the Albigensians in the South of France; but the political and military situation in Italy made such an anti-heresy crusade inconceivable. Innocent could not afford to take whole-scale action against Cathars and other heretics in Italy; if one city appeared particularly recalcitrant on any issue, he could only use hostile cities in the vicinity to act as counterweights, favouring, for example, Pavia or Cremona against Milan. Allies were liable to be demanding, as Cremona was, requesting territorial gains in return for its support.

A pope, however, had advantages. It was in his discretion to suppress a bishopric or institute a new one. Innocent used this power to appeal over the heads of hostile city leaders to civic pride, as in Piacenza and Milan, where he threatened to alter the cities' ecclesiastical status and remove their

[10]   Ibid., p. 136.
[11]   Ibid., p. 150.

right to have either archbishop or bishop. A reward for the men of Viterbo for accepting anti-heretical statutes in 1207 was the confirmation of cathedral status for their church. Saints, relics, miracles and canonizations also had a part to play. In Florence, with its long Cathar tradition and its record of missionary enterprise to Orvieto and Viterbo, the relic of St Philip, brought from Jerusalem and placed by the bishop elect in the baptistry, wrought its first miracle, he explains, 'so that the upholders of the orthodox faith may rejoice and the damnable troop of heretics tremble.'[12] In Cremona, the canonization of the devout Guelf merchant Homobonus in a Ghibelline city might have been expected via the play of local patriotism to make Cremona less hostile to the Guelf cause, less inclined to patronize heresy and more sympathetic to their bishop. It exerted influence on an indifferent business community, for it demonstrated that the conduct of a merchant could be sanctified. Homobonus, who had worked for reconciliation with the Ghibellines, provided a model pattern of peace-making in politics coupled with aloofness from the heretics.[13]

Innocent became aware that interdict could be a two-edged sword: it had failed at Orvieto and he may have had this in mind when he wrote to the bishop of Ferrara in time of interdict in 1208 permitting him to baptize and confirm and to preach sometimes. When he lifted an interdict in Bergamo in 1210 he confessed that 'because of the withdrawal of divine service, certain people became disaffected and hardened of heart, and the followers of heretical depravity put forward their false dogmas with greater confidence.'[14] He was cautious towards Treviso which, he wrote, was 'called a sink of heretics',[15] where interdict had been imposed for the murder of its bishop. Yet he was willing to allow relaxation should it in the long run open the way to action against heretics.

Innocent was aware of the degree to which heresy prospered because of the failings of the clergy. In a letter to the people of Treviso, he referred bluntly to 'the excesses of the clergy, whose evil example disturbs you'.[16] He was slow to act against the bishop there and, indeed, never did depose him although his failings were part of the problem, but he was ready to stigmatize the Lombard clergy for their faults, checked abuse of the appellate jurisdiction of the papacy by local clergy and imposed reforming constitutions on unsatisfactory clergy at Verona. Yet such measures could only scratch at the problem of clerical abuse; a pope could threaten, advise and exhort but in the last resort he was dependent on local bishops and clergy and their supporters. Reform had to be a long-term business.

Innocent's actions against heresy were sporadic, sparked off by local appeals and abuses or by the involvement of cities with heretical populations in disputes over territory and rights involving papal interests.

---

[12]   Ibid., p. 142; removal of episcopal status, pp. 144, 150–1; relic at Florence, p. 142.
[13]   On Homobonus, B. Bolton, *The Medieval Reformation* (London, 1983), pp. 102–3.
[14]   Webb, in *SCH* Subsidia IX, p. 148.
[15]   Ibid., p. 149.
[16]   Ibid.

Anticlericalism, Ghibelline traditions and local disputes with the clergy went hand in hand with the support of heresy. Innocent cannot have been unaware that communes and their officers embarked on anticlerical campaigns because of jealousy of what they saw as an excess of ecclesiastical rights and a desire to tap clerical wealth, and that heresy rode on the back of such sentiments. The bishops and clergy were by no means always in the right and Innocent recognized this. Overall, however, his assumption was that territorial stability and the securing of rights of churches and the papacy in both political and ecclesiastical spheres, provided the right basis for the repression of heresy. Authority was to be supported and it was the task of the bishop to see that heresy was put down.

Innocent intervened in the complexities of Italian politics where he felt he could and should. He was concerned to have anti-heresy legislation accepted into municipal statutes, to encourage the election of leaders who would make use of *Vergentis* to uproot support for heretics and to aid hard-pressed members of the episcopate. All his efforts outside the papal states were over-shadowed by his lack of real power; in spite of their magniloquent claims to pastoral wisdom, Innocent's letters, while revealing evidence of his powers of prudent decision-making, cannot wholly conceal the degree to which a wily politician had constantly to adapt his proceedings to the realities of power.

Attitudes to heresy and reform

Innocent detested heresy, and especially Catharism. It was an enemy to be destroyed. The pope had understood better than his predecessors the sincere zeal and the yearning for reform that lay behind heretical move-ments in the twelfth century, and looked to find a place within the Church for those representatives of movements such as the Humiliati and the Waldensians, who were willing to accept authority and repudiate heresy, allowing them to continue within Catholicism the essentials of their way of life.[17] He was not disposed *tout court* to reject the use of vernacular transla-tions of Scripture, provided that its exposition remained under lawful control.[18] The principles to be followed, as he explained to the bishop of Verona entrusted with the examination of the Humiliati, were those of the prudent farmer who takes precautions lest in his labour he uproots wheat together with tares.[19] He was recommending to an episcopate more inclined to a crudely disciplinary approach an even-handed justice which distin-guished between the genuinely heretical and noxious, which should be destroyed, and innocent enthusiasm, which could be welcomed. Those rescued for orthodoxy were expected to work against the heresies they had abandoned. Reconciled Humiliati were to seek to confute the error into

[17]   B. Bolton, 'Innocent's treatment of the Humiliati', *SCH* VIII, pp. 73–82; M. Maccarrone, 'Riforma e sviluppo della vita religiosa con Innocenzo III', *RSCI* XVI (1962), pp. 29–72; summary, Lambert, *Medieval Heresy*, 2nd edn, pp. 91–100.
[18]   L. E. Boyle, 'Innocent III and vernacular versions of Scripture', *SCH* Subsidia IV, pp. 97–107.
[19]   *PL* CCXIV, cols 788–9; H. Grundmann, *Religiöse Bewegungen im Mittelalter* (2nd edn, Hildesheim, 1961; 1st edn, 1935) (*RB*), p. 74.

which they had once fallen: the Poor Catholics, reconciled Waldensians, were expected to be prepared to act as spies or *agents provocateurs* with regard to Cathars.[20] The sensitive distinctions which Innocent employed to find a place in the Church for former heretics applied to evangelical movements only, not to Cathars. Writing to Treviso in 1207, Innocent patiently expounded what Cathars believed, their teaching on marriage and creation: this was heresy and it had to be put down.[21]

Innocent was not a gentle man: he rejoiced uninhibitedly over military triumphs, and when he used such terms as '*exterminare*' and '*animadversio debita*' (due penalty) for the treatment of heretics, his meaning was not restricted simply to canonical sanctions or the expulsion from cities – he had in mind the death penalty, once imposed by Bishop Riccardo in Orvieto and also used by King Philip Augustus in France.[22]

Crusade within Christendom had made its appearance fleetingly in 1199 when Innocent was grappling (as regent and suzerain for the young Frederick II in Sicily) with the Hohenstaufen leader, Markward of Anweiler. In a letter to the Sicilian people, he described Markward as another Saladin, allied to Saracens; the Holy Land could best be relieved by the defence of South Italy against him, so resistance to Markward should be rewarded by the indulgences available to crusaders for the Holy Land. It was a desperate gambit by Innocent, who lacked influence in the South and could not get troops together.[23] No more is heard of the indulgence proposal; none the less, it showed the pope ready to use the crusade mechanism when *in extremis* within Europe.

Languedoc

In practice, the South of France was the field where crusade could be deployed. The needs of Languedoc imposed themselves as soon as Innocent became pope. In April 1198, he gave wide-ranging commissions to Cistercians both to preach and to ensure that spiritual and secular weapons were used against heretics and fautors. In June 1200, he entrusted cardinal John of St Paul with the duty of applying *Vergentis*. Commissions were renewed; the two Cistercians were replaced by others including in 1203 Ralph of Fontfroide and Pierre de Castelnau, once a litigious archdeacon of Maguelonne who had taken the Cistercian habit at Poblet, a man of the South; and, in 1204, a third monk, Arnaud Amaury, also once abbot of Poblet and then of Cîteaux.[24] Cistercians still appeared at the end of the century a *corps d'élite*, men of devotion and resolution, with a long record of

[20]   Capitani,'La repressione', p. 685.
[21]   Webb, in *SCH* Subsidia IX, p. 149.
[22]   Capitani, 'La repressione …', pp. 676, 678, 692–4, 700–1; criticism of Fliche, p. 691; Morris, *Papal Monarchy*, p. 420; Maisonneuve, *Etudes*, p. 123.
[23]   E. Kennan, 'Innocent III and the first political crusade', *Traditio* XXVII (1971), pp. 231–49.
[24]   Fullest account of legates, C. M. Dutton, 'Aspects of the institutional history of the Albigensian Crusades, 1198–1229', unpublished PhD thesis, University of London, 1993, chs. 1, 2, with tables showing all activities, pp. 126–35 (I am grateful to

fidelity to the papacy. Around them hung still the aura of St Bernard's preaching power; it was natural that Innocent should turn to them in his long attempt to reform the region. The phrase which he used repeatedly was '*negotium pacis et fidei*' (the enterprise of peace and faith); only after his death, as the problem of heresy came to dominate all others, was the order of the words reversed to become 'the enterprise of faith and peace'.[25] A first aim was to create peace in the Midi – as in the Christian world, the vineyard of the Lord, as he loved to say[26] – which was the essential platform for repression of heresy and clerical reform. In the heartland of Cathar heresy, Innocent had little success in peace-making, he was seeking to breathe life into the ancient institution of the Peace of God, at one time so potent a weapon against internecine warfare;[27] his legates were using oath-taking in order to settle differences, secure the expulsion of mercenaries and obtain action against heretics, pre-eminently Cathars.

Some success was achieved with the acceptance of statutes hostile to heretics at Montpellier, Arles and Carcassonne. At Toulouse, matters went better than expected and the consuls swore an oath to repudiate heresy, but only in return for a concession of civil liberty, which pleased the municipality but involved the infringement of the rights of Raymond VI. A public debate was held at Carcassonne in 1204 under Peter II of Aragon, in which heretics, legates and other Catholics participated: the proceedings may well have clarified the distinctions between heresy and orthodoxy, but did not issue in any repression. These were meagre results for the years of endeavour.[28]

Only in eastern Provence via Pierre de Castelnau and Arnaud Amaury did Innocent score a victory. In 1207, a 'peace of the legates' was agreed, sworn to by the leading magnates of the area, including Peter of Aragon: it lasted with minor infractions for some six years. The unwillingness of Raymond VI, as count of Toulouse and marquis of Provence, to take the oath and join in the peace precipitated a breakdown of relations between him and Pierre de Castelnau. Friction had long existed. When, in 1198, Innocent had recommended his first Cistercian legates to a series of archbishops in the South and neighbouring areas, they had found little welcome. Leading churchmen often resented the exercise of a distant papal authority by Innocent's agents, as did the higher nobility, and legates were received coldly. One ground for the split between Pierre and Raymond lay

---

Dr Claire Dutton for generous permission to use her thesis); events, J. Sumption, *The Albigensian Crusade* (London, 1978) (vivid account, shrewd on war and personalities, weak on heresy and repression, chs 1–3, 25 are better unread, see review W. L. Wakefield, *CHR* LXIV (1978), pp. 667–9); *WHC* provides political realism.

[25]   M. H. Vicaire, 'L'affaire de paix et de foi du Midi de la France', *CF* IV, pp. 102–27; on use of terms, Segl, *Anfänge*, p. 4, n. 10.

[26]   B. Bolton, 'Philip Augustus and John: two sons in Innocent's vineyard', *SCH* Subsidia IX, pp. 113–34 at pp. 113–14. I owe help to Dr Bolton.

[27]   See Vicaire, in *CF* IV, p. 125: Peace of God had lost spiritual force and was to be shored up by juridical means.

[28]   *WHC*, p. 88.

in Raymond's continuing use of mercenaries, a problem which remained largely unresolved. Pierre excommunicated Raymond and Innocent confirmed his decision, listing in the Bull of May 1207 his grounds, which ranged from Raymond's maintenance of Aragonese who ravaged the land and his confiscation of the patrimony of the bishop of Carpentras, to the protecting and receiving of heretics.[29]

Peace, the problem of *routiers*, anticlericalism and attacks on Church property and the toleration of heresy were interconnected, both in the minds of the pope and legates and in reality. Despite the fact that Pierre and Arnaud were both men of the South, neither pope nor legates appear to have understood the complexities of meridional politics and the degree to which disorder had become endemic and was linked to the institutional peculiarities of the region. It was near inevitable that Raymond should feel obliged to use mercenaries, given the weakness of his authority and the absence of the feudal tenures which in Northern France knit together the interests of lord and vassal and facilitated the raising of armies.

The count was constantly enjoined to repress heresy in his lands, but this was a task unusually difficult for him given the prevailing contempt for churchmen among the leading laity and the meridional tradition of toleration. Catharism was well embedded in certain families and regions and Raymond lacked the resources and authority to challenge it even if he had had the will to do so. His quarrels with churchmen were over lands and rights, it should be noted, rather than doctrine, and were often dictated by strategic considerations. Gregorian reform had not made the headway in his lands that it had elsewhere and Raymond was unsympathetic to reform ideals; yet the evidence suggests that, disordered as his private life was and oppressive as he might be to churchmen, his piety was conventional, issuing in a substantial number of benefactions. But, to the legates, Raymond appeared evasive and untrustworthy.

At a month's remove by the communications of the time from the flow of events, Innocent was dependent on the information he received from his legates. His choices were not fortunate: the early ones left little mark, Pierre and Arnaud were men of power, well able to act, but unsubtle and unable to appreciate the problems of their opponents. The quality of the local episcopate soon came under scrutiny and Innocent backed his legates in decisions made to remove them. By 1212, when the archbishop of Narbonne was finally removed, most of the episcopate had been replaced.[30] Though not unjustified, the legates' manner of proceeding alienated opinion.

Scant progress had been made by preaching and the legates had grown disheartened, when in 1206 a chance meeting with two Castilian churchmen, Bishop Diego of Osma and his subprior, the canon Dominic de Guzman, offered new hope; they suggested wandering preaching in poverty on the apostolic pattern of the Sending of the Seventy. It meant meeting Cathars and Waldensians on their own ground and abandoning the way of power. Innocent gave support and a preaching campaign was pursued at

[29]   Vicaire, in *CF* IV, pp. 111–15; Roquebert, *L'Epopée* I.
[30]   *WHC*, pp. 65–8.

various times between 1206 and 1208 by legates, other Cistercians and Diego and Dominic. There were signs that this type of ascetic preaching by men of knowledge and resolution represented a way forward. The work became methodical: territory was divided up among preachers; rest-points with provisions were set up. The echo of Jesus's commands at the Sending of the Seventy was strong. Speaking of the preaching tours, the chronicler Pierre de Vaux de Cernay used the same phrase as the Vulgate of Luke 9, '*circuibant per castella*' (they went from village to village).[31]

Preaching was interspersed with formal debates with heretics, with exchanges of written lists of authorities. After debate at Montréal, there was a substantial number of conversions of Cathars; there was success at Servian. At Pamiers, Diego and Dominic achieved conversions of Waldensians, among them most notably Durand of Huesca, subsequently leader of the orthodox Poor Catholics. Arbiters from both sides were sometimes used. At Montréal, Dominic recorded a page of authorities supporting the orthodox side of the argument, which was handed over to the Cathars. They put it in the fire: three times the fire rejected it. A knight who was already wavering, witnessed an event he saw as a form of judgement by ordeal, giving the verdict of heaven. His fellow Cathars wished to suppress knowledge of the affair, but the knight proclaimed it and went over to the Catholics. The campaign faded in 1207 and Diego returned to his diocese in September. Dominic, however, worked on, using a base at Fanjeaux in the heart of Cathar country and giving attention to his hospice-nunnery at Prouille nearby, founded in 1206 to keep the daughters of the poor nobility of the region out of the hands of the Cathars and to provide a refuge for converted Cathar women.[32]

Apostolic poverty and the use of reasoned argument were the keynotes of Dominic's approach. He attracted companions, influenced the Cistercians and was supported by Bishop Fulk of Toulouse. But heresy was deeply embedded and however effective the preaching and debating, much time was needed before it could have full impact. Though Innocent supported the preaching movement, he remained pragmatic, willing to support a variety of initiatives. Preaching, force, oath-taking were not fenced off from each other.[33] Innocent was nothing if not versatile: English delegates in Rome concur in receiving an impression of a 'brilliant, quick-witted man with a rough tongue'.[34] From an early stage, he attempted to bring force and diplomacy to bear by appealing to the natural champion King Philip Augustus either to intervene directly or to put pressure on his vassal Raymond VI. Preoccupied with the conflict with the king of England, Philip refused. Peter II of Aragon, with his territorial interests in Languedoc and his record of legislation against heretics in Aragon, could well have appeared a suitable instrument: but Innocent would have been aware that

[31] Luke 9: 6.
[32] M. H. Vicaire, *St Dominic and his Times*, trans. K. Pond (New York, 1965); *CF* I; for Durand, detailed account, Thouzellier, *Catharisme*, 3rd part.
[33] Vicaire, in *CF* IV, pp. 105–6.
[34] C. R. Cheney, *Innocent III and England* (Stuttgart, 1976), p. 7.

had he used Peter he would have antagonized Philip.[35] A suitable champion could not be found. However, in November 1207, in the aftermath of the excommunication of Raymond in May, the pope again raised the possibility of an expedition from the North to be led or directed by Philip.[36] The news of this *démarche* alarmed Raymond. He decided to treat with the legate, but the negotiations were unsatisfactory and Pierre and Raymond parted with angry words. In January 1208, Pierre was assassinated by an officer of the count. There is no evidence that he had given orders for Pierre to be killed, but his unwisdom in failing immediately to express his sorrow or to hunt down the murderer led the pope to assume the worst.

It was shattering news. The Navarrese ambassador described how, on hearing it, the pope sank his head in his hands and went away to pray at the shrine of St Peter below the high altar. Sensitive as he was to the vital role of the papacy in directing the Church, the murder of his legate appeared a gross, deliberate affront and a sign that the situation in the South of France was out of control. Raymond was 'vacillating and wily but not stupid',[37] nor was he a Cathar. But in the face of the dark picture given by his agents of Cathar-dominated lands and after many disappointments, the pope could not judge the situation calmly. He renewed the excommunication and wrote yet again to Philip, who declined to act directly. Legates, meanwhile, were ordered to preach crusade with indulgences as for the Holy Land; they made the fateful decision that forty days' service would qualify.[38]

The Albigensian Crusade

Raymond warded off the imminent threat by professing repentance, accepting terms and submitting to a humiliating penance in which he appeared naked before the cathedral church of Toulouse, gave an oath of obedience and, absolved by the papal legate, was drawn by him with blows into the church.[39] He joined the army as crusader for the minimum forty days, perhaps in his cunning way hoping to gain by an attack on his rival, the 24-year-old Raymond-Roger, viscount of Béziers, who had declined to join with Raymond in submission. He in turn was probably influenced by the intense rivalry with the house of St Gilles and the unfulfilled hope of aid from Peter of Aragon.

In July 1209, the army moved against one of the viscount's principal cities, Béziers; Raymond-Roger felt he could not defend it in person and asked the citizens to stand fast while he rode on to Carcassonne.[40] The people of

[35]   *WHC*, p. 91; see Dutton, 'Aspects …', p. 65 on the crucial role of the king of France; opposition began to melt when Louis VIII took the cross in 1226. Honorius III wished Philip to participate, just as Innocent did, Dutton, 'Aspects …', p. 206.
[36]   Not a crusade proper, as Dutton, 'Aspects …,' pp. 29–31.
[37]   *WHC*, p. 93.
[38]   Dutton, 'Aspects …', pp. 93–4, 96.
[39]   On significance of this, Fichtenau, *Ketzer*, p. 140.
[40]   Narrative, J. Berlioz, '*Tuez-les tous, Dieu reconnaître les siens': la croisade contre les Albigeois vue par Césaire de Heisterbach* (Portet-sur-Garonne, 1994) (thorough analysis,

Béziers had an unusual inner solidarity: in 1205, the bishop had declined to impose abjuration of heresy on the consuls and now he went ahead to warn them of the size of the approaching army and to offer terms promising lives and property in exchange for the surrender of a list of known heretics, over two hundred strong. The citizens declined and launched a sortie; then, against the odds, an unplanned counter-attack by some footsoldiers broke through the defences. Amaury, as legate and spiritual leader accompanying the army, was asked what should be done with the inhabitants and replied in a tradition reported by the Cistercian chronicler, Cesarius of Heisterbach: 'Massacre them for the Lord knows his own.'[41] Cesarius liked to give his sources and it may be significant that in this case he introduces the *mot* with the words 'he is reported to have said',[42] on the other hand, Amaury's words incorporate a quotation from the second epistle of Paul to Timothy dealing with the question of heresy, which the *Glossa Ordinaria* treated as a reference to predestination.[43] This makes it a little more likely that these words from the mouth of an educated member of the hierarchy were authentic. A curious dialogue in Gervase of Tilbury between a ghost and a priest of this epoch casts light on the attitudes of some clergy. Speaking from the omniscience of the other world, the ghost reported that the death and massacre of Albigensians was pleasing to God and that the good who had not polluted their faith with heresy had none the less sinned by tolerance.[44] Béziers was tolerant: it would not surrender its heretics either in 1205 or 1209. It was a proud city with a will to independence, resisting a crusade whose strength they tragically underestimated.

Massacre followed. Many were burned in the cathedral where the roof collapsed. The infantry who took the town were unlikely to have known anything of the parley between the bishop and the citizens: they assumed they had taken a stronghold wholly given over to heresy. In fact, it is likely that little more than 10 per cent of the population were either heretics or sympathizers.[45] By custom, declining terms exposed defenders to the possibility of sack and massacre; but the few hours of action on 22 July in no way resembled the long drawn-out sieges which roused blood-lust in victory. The massacre, though not planned, had its effect. Narbonne submitted shortly after and smaller points where resistance could have held up the army were deserted as it marched on to Carcassonne. There the effects of heat and disease and the awareness of what Béziers had suffered undermined

---

intriguing bibliography, black humour), p. 119; Sumption, *Albigensian Crusade*, pp. 90–4; M. Bourin, *Histoire de Béziers* (Toulouse, 1986), pp. 95–101.

[41] '*Caedite eos. Novit enim Dominus qui sunt eius*', *Dialogus miraculorum*, ed. J. Strange (Cologne, 1851, reissue, Cologne, 1922) I, p. 302; Berlioz, *Tuez-les tous*, pp. 71–83. '*Caedere*' is stronger than '*necare*' as Berlioz notes, p. 76. Arnaud Amaury as spiritual leader, Dutton, 'Aspects …', pp. 92–6; list of heretics, C. Amado, in *EO*, pp. 83–103 at pp. 98–101.

[42] '*fertur dixisse*'.

[43] 2 Tim 2: 19, with ref. back to Num. 16: 5; *Glossa Ordinaria*; Berlioz, *Tuez-les tous*, p. 80.

[44] Berlioz, *Tuez-les tous*, pp. 88–98; text, p. 94; see also p. 109, n. 6.

[45] *WHC*, p. 76; Bourin, *Béziers*.

morale. When surrender had been agreed, Raymond-Roger, who headed the garrison, was granted safe-conduct: this was not honoured and he was placed in confinement to die, probably, of dysentery. The ruthlessness of the crusading leadership led to further surrenders.

There followed years of campaigning, first to recover the lands of the Trencavel, then to move on to Toulouse and settle the problem of Raymond. The exigencies of warfare and politics threw up a first-class military leader in a baron of the Ile de France, Simon de Montfort who was elected successor to Raymond-Roger after the fall of Carcassonne.[46] His eye for terrain and his sense of tactical opportunities repeatedly won successes for the Albigensian Crusade and his ferocity against turncoats helped to preserve the momentum of campaigning when his forces suddenly shrank as those who had completed their forty days went home, leaving only a small nucleus to fight. Amaury of Montréal, who had once yielded to Simon, rebelled in 1211 and held Lavaur against him: when he and his ninety knights were forced to surrender, they were all executed on the spot and, after maltreatment from the soldiers, Amaury's sister was thrown down a well and stoned to death. Heretics captured as the town fell were burned outside in a collective holocaust.[47]

Simon used terror deliberately: he was executing as rebels those whom he considered to be insurgents against him in his role as viscount of Carcassonne.[48] At Bram, in a theatrical horror, a garrison who resisted him all had their eyes put out and were left under the leadership of one one-eyed man to find their own way to Cabaret.[49] Though terror made up to some extent for deficiencies in size, it still could not at a stroke subdue the region or winkle out heresy. The sudden blow leading to acceptance of orthodoxy and the opening of effective repression of heresy overall yet eluded the crusaders. Innocent had not reckoned with a long war. He may well have believed that an expedition that was little more than an armed progress would cowe opposition.[50]

The army had eliminated Raymond-Roger and threat alone reduced Raymond VI to an ostensible submission, yet the existence of determined meridional lesser nobles, in a hard terrain within accessible strongholds capable of holding out in long sieges, caused war to drag on. Bitterness created by a savage civil war stiffened local feeling against crusaders. Behind

---

[46]   Y. Dossat, 'Simon de Monfort', *CF* IV, pp. 281–302; sidelights on Countess Alice, M. Zerner, 'L'épouse de Simon de Montfort et la croisade albigeoise', *Femmes–Marriages–Lignages XIIe-XIVe Siècles: Mélanges offerts à Georges Duby* (Brussels, 1992), pp. 449–70. See also J. Shirley, *The Song of the Cathar Wars* (Aldershot, Vermont, USA, 1996) (first English translation of Provençal poem on Crusade, with intro., maps).

[47]   Sumption, *Albigensian Crusade*, pp. 129–33.

[48]   See Dossat, 'Simon de Montfort'.

[49]   Sumption, *Albigensian Crusade*, p. 111.

[50]   Dutton, 'Aspects ...', clarifies problem of sustaining a series of campaigns (see esp. chs 4–6; detail on recruits, service, finance), asks key question (pp. 223–5) why did Crusade do as well as it did? A defeat such as Montgey was rare. Part flaws in meridional armies and leadership, part more meridional support for Simon than sometimes supposed (Dr Dutton in correspondence).

the conflicts over lands and rights lay the fundamental clash between a canon law which gave legitimacy to crusade and a feudal law which did not.

The logic of war, Simon's ambition and Amaury's determination in guiding the campaigns were leading to a wholesale dispossession of land-holders. Amaury had no confidence in Raymond's submission: though he pleaded for the right to defend himself and early in 1210 visited Innocent in Rome to make his case, the churchmen on the spot and the papal legates insisted on his guilt. He was again excommunicated: requests to clear his name were rejected and his territory left open to attack. As it became apparent that, abetted by the legates, Simon de Montfort intended to take Raymond's lands, Peter of Aragon, concerned for his own rights and the secure continuance of the expansion of his own house, intervened diplomatically on Raymond's side. A split emerged between Innocent, still profoundly unsympathetic to Raymond, yet as a canonist sensitive to the accusation that Raymond had not been given a fair hearing, and Arnaud Amaury, hostile to Raymond, radical in temperament and convinced that only a drastic change of landholding in the South would open the way to satisfactory repression of heresy. The views of the legates prevailed. Peter then intervened militarily and was killed at the battle of Muret in the summer of 1213. Simon's keen eye for tactical advantage, Peter's impetuosity and Raymond's inaction contributed to a remarkable victory.[51]

Peter was a Catholic sovereign, fresh from victory over the Moors at Las Navas da Tolosa, to which Amaury had himself taken troops: his presence on the Southern side in the civil war demonstrated how far the resistance to the Crusade was motivated, not by defence of heresy but of lands, rights and the meridional way of life based on the bonds of loyalty between nobility and their followers. Peter would not have appeared to Southerners as an alien figure, as Simon did; there were natural links of language and culture between them. When in his Statutes of Pamiers, Simon revealed his intentions of developing a principality ruled according to the conventions of his own land, an Occitanian patriotism began to emerge.[52]

Northern sources, such as Pierre de Vaux de Cernay, show how the differences between North and South easily led crusaders to condemn as tainted with heresy the Southern nobility as a whole. Simon de Montfort's own piety was beyond reproach: he was assiduous in attendance at mass and maintained long and friendly contact with St Dominic. He was the athlete of Christ, convinced of the righteousness of his cause, unwilling to tolerate any suspicion of heresy: those who came before him and were unwilling to recant were summarily burned. Clergy moved about in the crusading army. The archdeacon of Paris was assiduous in organizing the sinews of war, even supervising the making of a way over a ravine at the siege of Termes. Two brothers, bishops of Orléans and Auxerre, joined the Crusade. Mass was regularly celebrated. Crusaders on certain occasions went barefoot.[53]

---

[51] Set piece on Muret, M. Roquebert, *L'Epopée Cathare II: 1213–1216. Muret ou la dépossession*, (Toulouse, 1977), pp. 187–236. See *L'Epopée* I, pp. 18–19 for clash of feudal and canon law.

[52] As Roquebert clarifies in *L'Epopée* I.

[53] M. H. Vicaire, 'Les clercs de la croisade', *CF* IV, pp. 260–80.

Together with the disruptive effect on Church life, the conflict worked in some measure against Catholicism. War inhibited other means of combatting heresy. St Dominic continued his preaching and rescue work on a small scale, aided by Innocent; he received support from Bishop Fulk of Toulouse and in 1215 was given a charter to preach with his companions in the diocese of Toulouse and receive a portion of its revenues. But his position was precarious, as was that of Fulk, who had successfully formed a White Confraternity of leading citizens to battle against both usury and heresy, but lost support when he insisted on sending its members to aid Simon in his attack on Lavaur in 1211. Furthermore, he asked Raymond VI to leave Toulouse as interdict was valid wherever Raymond resided and Fulk wanted to ordain priests. Raymond reacted by requiring him to leave: he could no longer carry the citizens with him and spent long years in uneasy exile.[54]

The Crusade fell on the Cathars like a thunderclap. Simon's *ad hoc* burnings cut down the number of the most devoted perfect, who refused conversion to escape the pyre; Pierre de Vaux de Cernay depicts Amaury's dilemma at the negotiations for surrender. 'He passionately desired to see God's enemies die, but as a monk and a priest he did not dare to strike the blow himself.'[55] In the event, some 140 declined the offer of their lives in return for conversion and were burned; few yielded. Double or more that number were burned after Lavaur surrendered and there were lesser collective burnings, sixty or more at Les Cassès.[56]

In these episodes, the Cathar Church lost idealists whom it could ill afford to forfeit. Where they could, the perfect fled from cities to fortresses in the countryside which they hoped would be impregnable: such an assembling together explains the batches brought to the pyre – the most committed and the most vulnerable to betrayal. Others evaded disaster. Furneria of Mirepoix fled to Montségur, a fortress not touched by the Crusade; three sisters from Castelnaudary fled to Cremona. Pockets remained untouched: at Caraman, Lanta and Verfeil around 1215 few died without receiving the *consolamentum* and a house of perfect men at Miraval took in a knight mortally wounded fighting against the crusaders. Some recanted: on recovery after receiving the *consolamentum* in 1206, Bernard Blanc de Laurac was received by Bishop Fulk and a brother of the Catholic bishop of Carcassonne, a perfect at the time of the arrival of the Crusade, also abandoned his faith.[57]

But an essential nucleus survived. Houses of perfect women, displaced for fear of the crusaders, reopened on more secure ground; so Fabrissa de Mazerolles installed herself with relatives at Gaja-la-Selve and held reunions of supporters.[58] The *filius major* to the Cathar bishop of Toulouse, Guilhabert

[54]   Mundy, *Repression*, introduction, pp. 24–5; Morris, *Papal Monarchy*, p. 447.
[55]   Sumption, *Albigensian Crusade*, pp. 117–18 (free trans.) from Pierre de Vaux de Cernay; Vicaire, in CF IV, p. 267 (portrait of Arnaud Amaury, pp. 265–8). English translation in preparation, W. A. Sibly and M. D. Sibly, *The History of the Albigensian Crusade* (Woodbridge, forthcoming).
[56]   WHC, pp. 98–9; Sumption, *Albigensian Crusade*, p. 113.
[57]   Griffe, *Languedoc*, pp. 148–9.
[58]   Roquebert, *L'Epopée*, I, p. 295.

de Castres, found refuge at Montségur, held by a determined fautor, Raymond de Pereille, its magnificent defensive position attracting other leaders such as Gaucelin, a Cathar bishop, Bertrand Marty, subsequently bishop, and Jean Cambiaire, made *filius major* in 1229.[59] The freedom of the past had gone: Guilhabert's presence was a vivid illustration of the insecurity forced on the Cathars, for years earlier he had been one of the protagonists in open debate with Dominic and Catholics at Montréal, free to speak and to come and go as he pleased. Resentment at the suffering and dispossession brought by the Crusade ensured the continuance of fautors, and an Occitanian patriotism, loyalty to Raymond VI and family links with heresy prevented a break-up of its structure. The *consolamentum* was still administered and many were still able and willing to protect the heretics. The believer class was still in being, even in lands occupied by the crusaders.

The existence of a residual strength among the perfect is revealed by the actions of their hierarchy. In 1226, the Cathar bishop of Toulouse, Bernard de Lamothe, summoned a council attended by a hundred perfect and set up a new bishopric for the Razès.[60] So Innocent was foiled in his principal purpose in Langedoc: he had damaged Catharism but was very far from eliminating it.

Bosnia

At the rim of Western Christendom, Innocent could only expect spasmodic influence. In an excited letter to Innocent, Vukan of Zeta and Montenegro accused his neighbour, Ban Kulin of Bosnia of favouring heresy, claiming that ten thousand subjects had been affected. Bosnia was a backward land, superficially Christianized, a refuge for Cathars fleeing from repression launched by Bernard, archbishop of Split.[61] Innocent wrote to the archbishop and to Kulin's suzerain, Emeric king of Hungary, urging him to put pressure on Kulin, and at the turn of the year 1202–3 sent his chaplain, John de Casamaris, to investigate. Kulin protested his innocence. He may well have been slandered: a stone recording his building of a church in commemoration of a victory is incised with six crosses, which would have been unlikely had he been an adherent of Catharism, though possibly neither he nor his churchmen would have understood where the boundary between heresy and orthodoxy lay.[62]

As a result of the legate's enquiry, seven men referred to as 'priors', evidently the superiors of quasi-monastic communities, made promises, first in the presence of Kulin and the legate in Bosnia at Bilino Polje on 8 April 1203, then twenty-two days later on an island off Csepel in the Danube

---

[59]   Ibid., pp. 301–5; clarifies early role of Montségur.
[60]   Above, p. 49.
[61]   Below, ch. 12 *passim*; events, J. V. A. Fine, *The Bosnian Church: a New Interpretation* (Boulder, Colorado, 1975) (FBC), pp. 121–34, Vukan's motive, p. 124; summary account, Lambert, *Medieval Heresy*, 1st edn, pp. 142–50.
[62]   *FBC*, pp. 121–2.

south of Budapest in the presence of Kulin, Emeric and Hungarian churchmen. They submitted themselves to the discipline and authority of the Roman Church, promising to have altars and crosses and books of the New and Old Testaments, to see that their priests said mass and heard confessions and kept the feasts of the Church. Men and women were to be separated in dining and sleeping accommodation. They agreed to drop the title of Christian as opprobrious to other, presumably non-monastic, Christians.

The legate was acting as Innocent wished, bringing enthusiasts and quasi-monastic groups under authority. The 'brothers' at Bilino Polje were not treated as heretics but they promised that they would not in the future receive any person to live with them whom they knew certainly to be a 'Manichaean' or an adherent of another heresy. The submission was prophylactic. The legate urged the appointment of a Latin bishop and the setting up of three or four new dioceses. Emeric reported to the pope the measures he had taken to influence Kulin's son and two leading Bosnians against heresy. Hungary was established as the natural supporter of orthodoxy, and Innocent demonstrated his abiding concern with the uprooting of heresy and the establishment of Catholic authority at the very limits of the Western Church's jurisdiction.

The Fourth Lateran Council

This, the greatest of all medieval Councils, was designed to sum up Innocent's plans to forward reform and the crusade to the Holy Land, to continue the battle against heresy and provide a legitimate framework for future action.[63] Albeit not named, Catharism was the principal target of the dogmatic definitions contained in the first of the canons issued at the last session of the Council, held on 30 November 1215. The definition of transubstantiation, the affirmation of the necessity of baptism and the legitimacy of marriage cut directly at the Cathar rejection of matter and all sexual intercourse and their pejorative, sceptical attitude to the mass. The statements of faith functioned as checklist for the presence of heresy, an improvement on the loose listing of names of heretics in *Ad abolendam*; obstinate denial was a clear-cut ground for conviction. The essence of heresy hereafter lay in obstinate deviation from the definitions of the Church. The pursuit of heresy remained in the hands of the bishops and the procedures of *Ad abolendam* continued.

Canon 3, *Excommunicamus*, detailed what was to be done with heretics and fautors, giving the Council's authority to the provisions of *Vergentis in senium*, albeit with a modification of the penalties announced in 1191 for the innocent heirs of the guilty: their disinheriting was quietly dropped. The achievement of *Vergentis* in providing effective means of putting pressure on powerful fautors remained, as did the use of crusade indulgence applicable to the Holy Land for those who fought against heresy at home.

[63]   B. Bolton, 'A show with a meaning: Innocent III's approach to the Fourth Lateran Council, 1215', *Medieval History* I (1991), pp. 53–67.

On the awkward matter of Raymond VI and his lands,[64] Innocent at the Council sought a compromise: Trencavel lands to Simon but the rest of Languedoc to Raymond. There was ferocious debate. Come to appeal to the fathers of the Council, the count and his young son waited outside, probably in the Lateran cloister. Angered by the tumult, the pope walked in the garden of his palace.[65] His very success in replacing the tainted, inert bishops of Languedoc worked to his detriment, and despite dissentient voices, the episcopate had their way. Most were determined supporters of Simon and the Council backed them. Innocent had to concur. Raymond lost the lands occupied by the crusaders.

At another point, also, the episcopate seems to have asserted its wishes – in the canon prohibiting the founding of new orders, apparently a check by the conservative elements to Innocent's innovative measures.[66] The Dominican experiment survived, for Dominic was himself a canon regular and his group of preachers could fairly be termed a reformed group of canons. It is unlikely that Innocent could possibly have foreseen the massive importance of Dominic's order for the conquest of heresy. Brilliant and responsive, he showed a continued care for Dominic, but he is likely to have placed greater hopes in the Humiliati who had some 150 houses and whose work was praised by Jacques de Vitry.

Still less is he likely to have invested hopes in the significance for the future of St Francis of Assisi and his band of companions, who were advised by their bishop to go to the pope in 1210 for permission to carry on their way of life of extreme poverty combined with wandering preaching based on the Sending of the Seventy in Matthew 10.[67] His reaction was one of pastoral caution: he doubted whether the way of life was not too hard to be sustained. St Francis's original Rule consisted largely of scriptural texts to be observed literally throughout life. In the traditional account, the pope's doubts were conquered by a cardinal's objecting that if the pope and Sacred College refused to accept Francis's proposals as demanding too much of mankind, they were in peril of declaring the gospel to be too hard. Innocent accepted Francis's proposals with a certain subtlety, giving in the first instance only an oral permission to proceed, recognizing in them a penitential brotherhood and meeting their will to preach by a fine distinction between *praedicato*, full dogmatic preaching reserved to the priesthood and the trained, and *admonitio*, moral exhortation open to lay persons and consequently to the new foundation. His response brought forth fruit a hundredfold.

Tenacity and a highly professional use of canon law similarly marked Innocent's handling of offending churchmen.[68] The major problem

---

[64] Innocent was uneasy about Raymond losing his rights and instructed his legate Peter of Benevento to avoid a definitive settlement before the Council (Dutton, 'Aspects …', pp. 102–6).

[65] Bolton, 'A show with a meaning …', p. 60.

[66] Point clarified, Maccarrone, in *RSCI* xvi (1962), pp. 29–72.

[67] On early Franciscans, D. Knowles, *Religious Orders in England* I (Cambridge, 1950), pp. 114–26; generally, C. H. Lawrence, *The Friars* (London, New York, 1994).

[68] For what follows, W. Trusen, 'Von den Anfängen des Inquisitionsprozesses zum Verfahren bei der *Inquisitio haereticae pravitatis*', in *Anfänge* ed. Segl, pp. 39–76; and

was the higher clergy. The cumbersome procedure of *accusatio* let the unscrupulous go free and was therefore rarely used: if the accusation failed, the accuser faced the same penalties as the accused would have done and, given the powers of a great ecclesiastical magnate without conscience to suborn witnesses or manipulate evidence, it was dangerously easy for it to fail. The alternative, *infamatio*, also had grave weaknesses, since in this ancient procedure the suspect could purge himself by oath-helpers. To find such helpers was not difficult for a powerful offender, even when there were manifest faults and the *infamatio* of the suspect apparent. It could upon occasion bring suspicion wholly unjustly, as Innocent found in the affair of the bishop of Fünfkirchen, an innocent man accused of incest by his enemies.

From the first, Innocent displayed a deep passion for correcting the sins of the clergy, above all those in high office. His *Licet Heli* of 1199 recalled the punishment of God on the priest Eli, who fell and broke his neck in consequence of his failure to discipline his unworthy sons, and a series of letters and decisions flayed the sins of prelates. Through his own decisions, case by case, he adapted the *infamatio* so as to diminish the role of the oath-purgation and developed a partial substitute, *inquisitio famae*, a procedure of inquiry designed to set in motion an inquisition of fact to bring forward evidence to support or refute suspicion.

A stage in development is marked by a case from the province of Narbonne, that of the bishop of Agde in 1205, where Innocent used delegates to investigate the facts after the bishop had been provisionally removed from office. The decretal *Qualiter et quando* in the following year set out a procedure for delegates investigating a bishop, and in 1212 Innocent adapted it so as to provide safeguards for those under investigation, who were henceforth entitled to the names and statements of witnesses against them. Oaths of purgation still had a subsidiary role, but the more rational proceeding of inquisition now occupied the foreground. It was a disciplinary proceeding designed to detect and convict erring clergy; it had as yet no implications for the pursuit of heresy. Nevertheless, it developed within canon law an *inquisitio* procedure that, in other hands and under other circumstances, went on to form one of the powerful weapons of ecclesiastical authority.

Modern research has come to see Innocent less exclusively as a jurist and more of a pastoral figure influenced by the theological attitudes of the Paris school. His decree at the Lateran requiring a minimal confession and communion from the laity was a milestone in pastoral care with long-term effects for heretics. More than any previous pope, Innocent tried to grapple decisively with the long-lasting problem of Catharism embedded in regions of Languedoc: his ultimate solution, the Crusade, broke many lives. It opened the way for major changes which facilitated effective

---

'Der Inquisitionsprozess. Seine historischen Grundlagen und frühe Formen', *ZRGKA* cv (1988), pp. 168–230. I am grateful to Professor Trusen for photocopies and help.

pursuit of heresy, but it did not eliminate the Cathars. Crusading could not provide the swift, surgical solution that Innocent envisaged. A month after his death in 1216, the fall of Beaucaire to the forces of Raymond's heir signalled a renewal of campaigning and opened a new phase of war threatening Simon de Montfort's supremacy. As his repeated attempts to bring Philip Augustus into the field show, Innocent desired action from a sovereign to overawe the defenders of heresy, but he had to make do with a heterogeneous and fluctuating army of aristocrats and individual knights. The emotional shock of the legate's murder, anti-heresy sentiment and support for crusading brought in substantial numbers and stimulated effective planning and recruitment, but the weaknesses of campaigning on the forty-day basis could not be overcome even by the skill of Simon, a commander of genius, nor could it provide the stable financial and military power to sustain the wholesale revision of land structure which flowed from the campaign. Neither Innocent nor his successors seem to have considered as a solution to the Albigensian military problem the attracting and subsidizing of substantial numbers of pro-Catholic settlers.

In Italy matters never proceeded to extremes and the pope, scion of a Campagna family, was dealing with political situations which he understood. He threatened crusade but never used it, and only limited progress was made against the Cathars. What remained for his successor was the outline of a policy of putting pressure on cities to incorporate anti-heresy statutes and supporting enthusiasts of the stamp of Pietro Parenzo who would use political muscle against heretics and their defenders. The success of the mendicant friars came after his death and owed most to the heroic skills and sanctity of their founders and the devotion of early followers; yet their initiation owed much to Innocent's welcome for innovations and, in the case of Francis, readiness to take risks.

The Fourth Lateran Council vividly set out a programme of reform for the whole Church. Splendidly stage-managed, it was designed to impress the assembled delegates with the central needs of the time. Significantly, on the first day of the plenary session, Innocent put on the bishop of Agde to talk about heresy in the lands most affected by Catharism. Perhaps this was his most significant achievement: that he compelled ecclesiastical authorities, who had for so long denounced heresy without finding a means of dealing with it, to face the menace squarely, presenting them with lines of action. He pointed the way to a two-pronged approach, making a place in the Church for enthusiasts who had strayed and were ready to return, while using the full vigour of the law to act against the recalcitrant.

6

The First Inquisitors

Neither of Innocent's successors, Honorius III (1216–27) and Gregory IX (1227–41), shared his remarkable subtlety and flexibility, and their pontificates witnessed the breakdown of Innocent's favourite scheme for a long-term settlement of the problems of the Regno and Empire: the selection of the young Frederick Hohenstaufen as the papal candidate who would be amenable to direction and would end the menace of hostile control of the imperial lands in Northern Italy and the kingdom of the South. Frederick proved a menace in his own right: the problem began to cast a shadow over Honorius and, after some vicissitudes, became the major preoccupation of the last years of Gregory, displacing the pope's concern with heresy.

In the lands where it struck root, Catharism proved extraordinarily resilient. Swift solutions proved impracticable. Yet Honorius, with his quiet calibre, is not to be underestimated. He held the line inherited from Innocent, in unpropitious circumstances: under him the friars spread and developed – the crucial agents for the overthrow of Catharism.[1] Gregory, a powerful and emotional personality, receptive to a variety of expedients to tame heresy, responded enthusiastically to news of success in the field and made major blunders in his eagerness to put down Catharism. Like Innocent, he combined profound understanding of canon law with pastoral zeal, but his major contribution to the fight against heretics lay in the development of purpose-built inquisitorial procedures. Under him, an accelerated form of proceeding, originally devised by Innocent III to deal with sinning prelates,[2] came into its own as the weapon *par excellence* against the heretics. The friar-inquisitor, equipped with full powers both to pursue and to judge, began to make his appearance, fruit of a series of experimental commissions granted by Gregory, principally to Dominicans, in his restless search for means of action against heretics. Inquisitors with special commissions and overriding powers, often but not necessarily friars, sometimes complemented the actions of

---

[1]   See Morris, *Papal Monarchy*, pp. 562–4. I owe comment to Dr Claire Dutton.
[2]   Above, pp. 109–10.

bishops, who never lost their authority to put heresy down, and sometimes rivalled them.

The innovation began to prove its worth. From the earliest days, wide-ranging commissions and streamlined procedures opened the way to blunders and abuses of justice, but their practical effectiveness was plain. Inquisition changed the circumstances in which the Church fought against heresy.

Honorius III

Honorius III had the task of grappling with Innocent's legacy; he lacked the steely quality of Innocent and was too easily managed by the emperor Frederick II, to whom he showed the indulgence of a quondam tutor. But he accepted Innocent's priorities – of securing the papal position in Italy against the menace of Hohenstaufen power, of recovering Jerusalem, of pressing on with reform and of destroying heresy – and brought to his task tenacity and high abilities as an administrator. Under his rule, the mendicant friars established their bases and began an extraordinary expansion, above all in towns. In consultation with the Franciscan leadership, their cardinal protector Ugolino of Ostia provided the nascent order with the *Regulata bullata* in 1223, which retained much of the radical idealism of the founder, while adapting his vision to the practical needs of lesser men;[3] the Dominicans broke out from the confines of Languedoc and became an international order with a general authorization to preach and a special vocation to teach the faith.

Honorius supervised the incorporation of Innocent's anti-heresy legislation into imperial law. Canon 3 of the Fourth Lateran Council was accepted by Frederick II in 1220, following his coronation by Honorius. On the other hand, the election of his son Henry to be successor as emperor, although he was already crowned ruler of the Regno, breached Innocent's intention to separate Empire and Regno in the interest of papal independence and authority; Frederick's solemn declaration that the Empire had no rights over the Regno was only a form of words, the papacity tacitly accepting that one of the Innocent's most firmly held objectives had been shouldered aside. Side by side with the heresy legislation, Frederick issued laws binding the leadership of the Italian communes to respect the liberty of the Church, and proclaiming penalties for failure to do so. He was, in fact, proposing an alliance of papacy, Empire and bishops to reduce the independence of the usurping communes. The material sword, which Frederick readily put at the disposal of the Church in its action against heresy, was at the same time a tool to carve a way into overly independent cities for imperial authority.[4]

---

[3]   R. B. Brooke, *Early Franciscan Government* (Cambridge, 1959), pp. 69–70.
[4]   Comment, K. V. Selge, 'Die Ketzerpolitik Friedrichs II', *Probleme um Friedrich II, Vorträge und Forschungen* XVI, ed. J. Fleckenstein (Sigmaringen, 1974), pp. 309–43 at p. 331, G. Miccoli, 'La repressione', in *La storia religiosa*, ed. G. Einaudi, at p. 709; perspective, Morris, *Papal Monarchy*, pp. 559–68; also F. Giunta, 'Die Politik Friedrichs II gegen die Ketzer', in *Stupor Mundi*, ed. G. Wolf (Darmstadt, 1966), pp. 289–95.

In any case, in his willingness to accept papal legislation against heretics, Frederick was in full accord with his grandfather Barbarossa or his own Welf rival Otto IV. Emperors saw the repression of heresy as their duty and, provided there were no other major tensions with the papacy to complicate matters, were ready to carry it through. Frederick, most intellectual of emperors, could not fail to be aware of the role of anti-heresy legislation in the edicts of his classical predecessors, both Christian and pagan, whom he emulated. A Constitution of 287 against Manichees, for example, imposed confiscation of goods and work in the mines for supporters and death for leaders; in 297 Diocletian burnt them. Although Christians in the early centuries advocated charitable treatment of religious deviants amongst them, Augustine's experience and that of his fellow bishops in North Africa of the Donatist heresy caused a shift towards the use of force, and the excesses of the Circumcellions led the Council of Carthage in 410 to petition the emperor to revoke his edict of tolerance. Thus Christian emperors became persecutors. Edicts imposing penalties for heresy subsequently became part of Justinian's code. So, when Frederick accepted anti-heretical legislation, he was following the ample precedent of the imperial past.[5]

In 1224 he went further and issued a Constitution at Catania imposing the penalty of burning for recalcitrant heretics in Lombardy after due examination by the bishop, with the alternative of tearing out the tongue if it was felt more desirable to allow the victim life. Frederick's reputation as a free-thinker is undeserved: he was a conventional believer, following imperial precedent in harsh treatment of heretics. However, apart from the burning of heretics by a *podestà* at Rimini in the presence of the emperor in 1226, in practice little happened in that decade.[6]

In Italy, the most significant event was the legation of Ugolino to Lombardy and Tuscany, following closely on Frederick's coronation, when, apart from his edict on heresy, he also received the insignia of a crusader and promised to go on crusade before August 1221.[7] Preparation for crusade, the gathering of troops and money, the creation of the peace necessary for contingents to set out, the defence of ecclesiastical rights and lands and giving effect to Frederick's edict were all bound up together. In a whirlwind tour between the end of March and October 1221, Ugolino acted for the emperor no less than the pope in this phase of reconciliation, endeavouring to induce the cities to incorporate the imperial legislation against heresy in their statutes and thereby enforce the aid of the secular arm for churchmen putting down heresy. With considerable skill, exploiting local circumstances, Ugolino obtained money and promises of men for the crusade, but it seems that only in three cases, Mantua, Bergamo and Piacenza, did he get what he wanted, the insertion of the edicts. It was

[5]   Survey, Selge, 'Die Ketzerpolitik Friedrichs II'; Maisonneuve, *Etudes*, pp. 36–40.
[6]   Selge, 'Die Ketzerpolitik Friedrichs II', pp. 329–30.
[7]   C. Thouzellier, 'La légation en Lombardie du cardinal Hugolin (1221): un épisode de la cinquième croisade', *RHE* XLV (1950), pp. 508–42; Miccoli 'La repressione', pp. 711–14.

not that the cities were positive supporters of heresy but that they were distracted by inner feuds and outer conflicts and by the tensions between communes and bishops. The leadership did not see repression of heresy as a matter of high priority and were reluctant to take action that would reinforce episcopal power, while the bishops themselves felt too weak to make strong demands and, where they could influence townsmen, were content with expulsions of heretics and the imposition of fines for non-compliance, penalties weaker than those in Church law.[8] For Ugolino, the legation can only have been instructive; through it one of the shrewdest minds in the Sacred College had direct experience of the powerful hindrances in the way of putting down heresy.

Tensions between pope and emperor had grown before the end of Honorius's reign. A passionate supporter of a crusade to recover Jerusalem, Honorius made sacrifices in order to persuade Frederick to lead it, but in vain. Frederick saw crusading as an emperor's duty, following the tradition of Conrad and Barbarossa, and had first taken the cross as a young man in 1215,[9] but the problems of government led him repeatedly to put off his participation. Ugolino, elected to succeed as Gregory IX in 1227, was less sympathetic and excommunicated the emperor for not fulfilling his vow. It was the harbinger of a long, bitter conflict of papacy and Empire.

In Languedoc, the powers of the papacy to influence events were strictly limited. The balance began to tilt to the meridional side after Beaucaire invited in Raymond VI's son and attacked Simon de Montfort's garrison in 1216; later, Toulouse rose and in 1218 Simon was killed by a stone from a catapult while fighting off a counter-attack. When he could, Honorius preferred to treat the Albigensian war as a local campaign, allowing Southern bishops to issue indulgences and trying to enlist local support for Simon's cause. Unlike Innocent, he had a real rather than potential crusade to support during 1217–21, when the Fifth Crusade attacked Egypt, and he wished to husband resources. But after Simon's death, he was willing to issue general indulgences to aid his son Amaury to keep the crusading army in being, and in 1221, via his legate Conrad of Urach, vainly attempted to found a crusading order for Languedoc like the Templars or the Spanish orders. Like Innocent, his enduring aim was to induce Philip Augustus to enter the field and in this he failed.[10] Amaury de Montfort lacked his father's genius and was compelled, first, to negotiate truces and finally, to abandon his claims. At last, in 1226, Philip's successor Louis VIII assembled a substantial royal army and Southern resistance began to crumble. Louis's early death could not rescue Raymond VII and in 1229 the weary sequence of campaigns initiated by Innocent III ended in the Peace of Paris, a compromise which still allowed Raymond for his lifetime some two-thirds of the lands of his father against concessions and indemnities, the delivery

[8]   Miccoli's comment, 'La repressione', p. 714.
[9]   H. M. Schaller, 'Die Frömmigkeit Friedrichs II', *DA* II (1995), pp. 493–513 (decisive exposition). I am indebted to the author for his kindness.
[10]   On Honorius's actions, Dutton, 'Aspects ...', pp. 47–54; projected order, pp. 230–2; events, *WHC*, pp. 114–29.

to royal custody of his daughter Jeanne to be married to a brother of the king, a promise of support for the Church and the dismissal of mercenaries. The way was open for effective persecution of heresy, but was by no means guaranteed.

Gregory IX, Conrad of Marburg and the rise of the inquisition

Gregory IX was a distinguished canon lawyer and had wide experience of diplomacy and the battle against heresy before he took office. He also had an unusually deep sense of the ravages of Satan and his ministers in the world, and was convinced that, together with other evils, heresy advanced because of the influence of the Devil. He tightened legislation. In Languedoc, his legate Cardinal Romanus worked with Blanche of Castile, regent for the young Louis IX, to bring the Albigensian campaigns to an end and followed it up with a Council at Toulouse designed to ensure both that peace endured and that heretics were finally repressed. Via the decisions of the local Councils in Languedoc, a form of police team had evolved over the years, turning the old passive synodal witnesses of *Ad abolendam*, dependent on periodic visitations, into more active groups who had a continuing duty to watch for evidence of heretical activity and report it, not to an occasional synod, but directly to the appropriate authorities. The Council confirmed this arrangement and added to the lay teams the local priest – in every locality a priest and three laymen were to undertake this duty. After the Council, Romanus held a legatine *inquisitio*, in which he and other prelates present interrogated suspects, received confessions and imposed penances. Romanus made one significant ruling: that suspects were not entitled to know the names of their accusers for fear of reprisal.[11]

After Cathars were detected in Rome in February 1231, and burnt if recalcitrant or sent into harsh imprisonment in the monasteries of Monte Cassino and Cava if repentant, Gregory issued new statutes which built on the legislation of Innocent III but sharpened the punishments.[12] 'Condign punishment' for the obdurate meant the death penalty; those who abjured, but only after capture, were to suffer perpetual imprisonment. The obligation to denounce heretics was imposed on all under pain of excommunication. Those who believed the errors of heretics (the more marginal supporters) were adjudged to be heretics and treated accordingly. An edict of the senator Annibaldo Annibaldi followed the lines of *Vergentis* and arranged for the goods of convicted heretics to be divided into three parts, the first portion to be split between those who denounced and those who captured the heretics, the second to be paid to the senator and the third to be used to repair the walls of Rome. The edict referred to 'inquirers'

---

[11]   Kolmer, *Ad Capiendas* (detailed analysis of development of inquisition procedures, review, J. H. Mundy, *Speculum* LIX (1987), pp. 401–2), pp. 64–79. On development from old synodal witnesses, Kolmer (pp. 67–9) corrects Maisonneuve. J. L. Biget, 'I Catari di fronte agli inquisitori in Languedoc, 1230–1310', in *La Parola all' accusato*, ed. J-C. M. Vigueur and A. P. Bagliani (Palermo, 1991), pp. 235–51 analyses procedure, with special reference to the episode at Albi 1286–7.

[12]   Miccoli, 'La repressione', p. 717.

(*inquisitores*) nominated by the Church with the duty of discovering heretics, an obvious parallel to the anti-heresy groups of the Council of Toulouse. Both Gregory IX's statutes and the edict of Annibaldi were put in the papal Register and sent for publication in their dioceses to the bishops of Italy and Germany.

Between 1227 and 1232 the pope issued a number of commissions to the Dominicans, often, but not always, linked to heresy.[13] Plainly he had a high regard for the friars; equally plainly he was eager to second their mission to the people, while simultaneously casting round for some means to make truly efficient the pursuit, capture and judgement of heretics. These various functions are treated separately. A Bull of April 1227, praising the order for its work of evangelization against heretics 'and other death-dealing plagues',[14] urged the bishop of Olmütz to encourage the faithful to hear the Dominicans' sermons and confess to them; in May the Bull was addressed to all the priests of the order and to the episcopate in general. An order of June 1227 to the prior of Santa Maria Novella, Florence, by contrast, placed its emphasis on repression: the prior, together with another Dominican and a Florentine canon, were required to capture the Cathar heresiarch Philip and his followers and hold them in close confinement until they were ready publicly to abjure their errors; thereafter, the commission had authority to receive them back into the Church. The pope's order presumably envisaged an element of persuasion in leading Philip and his circle to repentance: the major factor, however, was likely to be the pressure of imprisonment. A missive of 1223, addressed to the Dominicans of Würzburg, described the friars as 'experienced doctors of the soul'[15] and called on their skill and devotion to work on those in Germany who had been prompted by the Devil to engage in homosexual practices, and to persuade them to continence or marriage. Heresy was frequently alluded to, as Gregory urged the brothers through persuasion to break the barriers which Satan had erected against salvation and 'sweep away the whole stain of heretical depravity'. The brothers had a general role to play as shock troops of Catholicism: the homosexuality and the heresy which they were to put down were, in this rhetorical phrase, linked equally as breaches of the divine order.

Ille humani generis of November 1231[16] came closest of all to being a true inquisition commission. It ordered prior Burkard and his fellow Dominican Theodoric of the house at Regensburg to deliver a general sermon, of a particularly solemn character, in the presence of assembled prelates, clergy and people against the 'lethal poisons' disseminated by the Devil through his ministers against the faith. The sermon was to be followed by a diligent search for heretics by the friars and 'reliable persons'. In this Bull, friars

---

[13]   Surveyed, P. Segl, 'Gregor IX, die Regensburger Dominikaner und die Anfänge der "Inquisition" in Deutschland', in *Regensburg, Bayern und Europa, Festschrift für Kurt Reindel ...*, ed. L. Kolmer and P. Segl (Regensburg, 1995), pp. 307–19. I am grateful to Professor Segl for an offprint.

[14]   Ibid., p. 317.

[15]   Ibid., p. 318.

[16]   Trans. E. Peters, *Heresy and Authority in Medieval Europe* (London, 1980), pp. 196–8.

were expected to exhort, persuade, seek helpers and pursue heretics: in sum, to carry out most of the functions of classic inquisitors, even including the imposing of penances on those who repented, but still omitting one vital aspect – the function of hearing evidence and then passing judgement.[17] That remained in other hands.

The Regensburg Bull was the forerunner of a series of similar orders to friars elsewhere. These were years of experiment, in which Gregory was feeling his way forward, adopting expedients as suitable occasions and personnel offered. Given the original Dominican vocation to preach against heresy, their training and their elite status, it was natural for him to lean heavily on them.

A mandate issued by Gregory in 1227 to Conrad of Marburg, a secular priest with a long and effective career as crusade preacher, belongs to the same early, experimental phase of Gregory's attack on heresy.[18] It may even have been initiated by Conrad himself, recognizing in the new pope a kindred spirit who shared his own deep hostility to heresy. The pope commended Conrad's care in the investigating of heresy in Germany and ordered him to make use of helpers in the work so that the tares in the field of the lord might be uprooted by the appropriate authorities. Conrad was, at this stage, an 'inquirer' but not a judge. Pursuit of heresy and preaching against it may have seemed two sides of the coin: judgement lay in the hands of the bishops.

Conrad of Marburg was a formidable personality, a rigorous ascetic with powers of eloquence and a command over uneducated audiences, who was given a position of trust by the Landgrave of Thuringia when he joined Frederick II's crusade, and as confessor and spiritual adviser exerted sway over the Landgrave's wife Elizabeth.[19] When the pope wrote again on 11 October 1231, it was to praise his zeal and his achievement in uprooting from the field of the Lord 'not only heretics but also many heresiarchs' and release him from obligations to examine and decide on controversial issues not linked to heresy, which could distract him from his task, to enjoin him to choose 'co-adjutors', to call on the secular arm where necessary and to

[17] Kolmer, *Ad Capendias*, p. 111 defines a 'true' inquisitorial commission. The inquisitor alone and independently both investigates and reaches a final judgement. *Ille humani generis* fails this test, as Segl argues in 'Gregor IX', pp. 309, 314–16. Segl's conclusion is supported in preference to D. Kurze, 'Anfänge der Inquisition in Deutschland', in *Anfänge*, ed. Segl, pp. 131–93 at pp. 155, 158, and A. Patschovsky, 'Zur Ketzerverfolgung Konrads von Marburg', *DA* xxxvii (1981), pp. 641–93 at p. 645.
[18] Kurze, 'Anfänge der Inquisition ...', pp. 147–9; on the significance of Conrad's proceedings, Kurze is preferable to Patschovsky, 'Zur Ketzerverfolgung ...', pp. 665–90. Patschovsky provides an account of events and sources and is illuminating on *Vox in Rama* and Luciferans, *DA* xxxvii, pp. 651–65.
[19] A. Patschovsky, 'Konrad von Marburg und die Ketzer seiner Zeit', *Sankt Elisabeth, Fürstin, Dienerin, Heilige*, ed. Philipps Univ. Marburg (Sigmaringen, 1981), pp. 70–7; 'Konrad von Marburg, Inquisitor', *Neue Deutsche Biographie* xii (Berlin, 1980), pp. 544–6; character, Kolmer, *Ad Capiendas*, p. 118, Kurze, 'Anfänge der Inquisition ...', p. 184, n. 190.

impose at his discretion excommunication and interdict on fautors of heresy. Further clauses empowered him to reconcile to the Church those who abjured, give indulgences to those who heard Conrad's preaching or aided him in the attack on heresy, with a plenary indulgence for those who died in this task, and recommended for Conrad's inspection Gregory's new statutes on heresy.[20]

The context of the new commission helps to explain its content. Gregory's first conflict with Frederick II was over, settled by the Peace of San Germano in 1230, and the pope was eager to take advantage of the peace to drive forward against heresy. Henry VII, acting for Frederick in Germany, gave full support and the archbishops of Trier and Mainz, cited by Gregory in the letter as the sources of his information on the proliferation of heresy, were evidently putting their weight behind the campaigns against heretics. It is likely that they were acting with, and in support of, Conrad, and that the 'glorious' things which Gregory had heard about Conrad's work emanated from them. Bishop Conrad II of Hildesheim, who, like Conrad, had had a successful early career as a crusade preacher, also had a zeal for the uprooting of heresy and was a lasting supporter of Conrad's efforts.[21] Conrad acted with the backing of the episcopate: Gregory, enthusiastic about the progress made in Germany, was eager to remove obstacles in the way of a zealous preacher and 'inquirer' with a rare talent of appealing to the people.

The result was disaster. In the period of less than two years before he was murdered on 30 July 1233, borne up by the passion of the uneducated masses who followed him, Conrad initiated a reign of terror. Accompanied by two helpers, Conrad Tors, a Dominican, and a layman called John, ill omened because he had only one eye and one hand,[22] Conrad roved, seeking out heretics and accepting the flimsiest of evidence to make a conviction. The secular arm lay at his disposal. Those he convicted were burnt. Those who abjured had their heads shaved – a sign of heresy visible to all like the mark of Cain. The accused had, in effect, the narrowest of choices – between confessing, even to the most improbable practices or tenets, or denying their complicity and facing the fire. There were many victims, some falling to motives of revenge by malicious neighbours or, the chronicler tells us, to the desire of actual heretics to draw into condemnation innocent Catholics. A remark of Conrad promising 'martyrdom' to those who continued to assert their innocence and were burnt, shows that he was aware that his headlong action might convict the innocent.[23] The scale of the disaster is hinted at by the figure of some fifty men who achieved rehabilitation after Conrad's death, though under his regime they had confessed: they included a count of Solms.

[20]   Revised edn, Kurze, 'Anfänge der Inquisition ...', pp. 190–3, comment, pp. 131–2, 149–56.
[21]   Ibid., pp. 179–85.
[22]   Patschovsky's comment, in *DA* XXXVII, p. 648.
[23]   Ibid., pp. 667–8.

Conrad met his match when he pressed on with a charge of heresy against Count Henry II of Sayn, who insisted on his right of trial in the court of King Henry VI. Traditional procedure of *accusatio* defeated Conrad: his witnesses failed, withdrew or were shown to be enemies of the count, who made his purgation successfully. Conrad's higher ecclesiastical allies, the archbishops of Trier and Mainz, turned against him and wrote to complain to the pope. Undeterred, Conrad set off to call crusade against those who would not acknowledge his tribunal and was murdered on the road, together with a Franciscan companion. With his death, followed probably by that of Conrad Tors and John, the storm subsided.

Gregory's wide commission to Conrad in 1231 was used for a campaign in which guilty and innocent perished together. Strictly speaking, it was a true inquisitorial commission, or was used as such by Conrad, in that he acted not only as inquirer but as judge as well, making life and death decisions without any right of appeal. Gregory was reported in 1234 as regretting that he had granted Conrad so much power, which had caused such *confusio*.[24] But he did not repudiate him and he condemned his murderers. In a letter to Gregory of 1234, the archbishop of Mainz and a Dominican, Bernard, once a papal penitentiary, criticized Conrad's procedures and their effects, reported how justice had been done in the aftermath and sent to the pope those who had accused the innocent, leaving him to decide what should be done in their case as well as in that of the innocent dead and of schoolboys who had taken part in the burning of heretics – an action that was normally an obstacle to receiving ecclesiastical orders.[25]

The net effect of Conrad's campaign was to blot out from the sources information about the pursuit of heretics by other authorities, the Dominicans or the bishops, the disturbance over Conrad being so great as to obscure all else in the minds of contemporaries. Conrad killed Waldensians and probably accelerated the demise of a German Catharism which was already frail.[26] It was a horrifying albeit isolated, episode in German Church history. After it, the pursuit of heresy through the decisions of king, bishops and aristocrats was damped down and the first sweeping and passionate phase of Gregory's heresy policy in Germany came to an end.

Its most lasting effect, however, was on the mind of the pope, and through him on the inquisitors of the future. Conrad's arbitrary exaction of confessions led him easily to the construction of an artificial heresy, that of the Luciferans. The slander that heretics worshipped demons or the Devil and engaged in promiscuous or unnatural sexual practices was not new – it appeared in chroniclers' accounts of heresy at Orléans in 1022, was repeated in other contexts and was known to Alan of Lille a generation

---

[24]   Kurze, 'Anfänge der Inquisition …', pp. 167–8.
[25]   Ibid., pp. 171–2; p. 172, n. 144 notes the strange legalism with which ecclesiastical authority in effect burnt heretics via the secular arm, yet might refuse priest's orders to a candidate who had marginally participated in a burning by throwing wood on the pyre.
[26]   Patschovsky's conclusion, in *DA* XXXIII, pp. 664–5.

before Conrad's campaign. But Conrad gave the tradition renewed vitality and transmitted it, revitalized, to Gregory, who issued a Bull, *Vox in Rama*, denouncing the sect in June 1233.[27] It is easy to see how a notion of the worship of Lucifer could emerge from a limited knowledge of actual Cathar beliefs and rites. Cathars did believe in a creation, or ordering, of the world by Lucifer and believed that their souls were angels fallen from heaven with him; from a belief in a devilish creation, it was an easy step to credit Cathars with worship of the creator of this world. Imagination and a dark tradition of obscenities practised by marginal groups, which went back to Roman slanders against Christians, soon filled any gap in knowledge of the actual worship that Satan demanded and which the Cathars allegedly gave him.

In the Bull of 1233, sent to Conrad of Marburg but clearly the fruit of his tumultuous investigations, to the emperor, to his son King Henry VII and to the archbishop of Mainz and other bishops including Bishop Conrad, the pope described the practices of these worshippers of Satan: the appearance of a monstrous toad to a novice entering the sect, and then of an ice-cold, pale man, followed by a banquet and the appearance of a black cat, whose hind quarters were kissed by most of those present. After the kissing came a ritual exchange, as reported by Gregory, in which the words '*parce nobis*', a fragment of the genuine Cathar ritual of the *melioramentum*, were embedded, then the extinguishing of the lights followed by a promiscuous and sometimes homosexual orgy. These heretics, Gregory explained, believed that the Lord had done evil in casting out Lucifer, and that he would ultimately return to glory 'when the Lord has fallen from power' and that his followers would then be rewarded with eternal glory. There was a logic behind the exposition for all its lurid embellishments, for it was widely accepted that the heretic, by his abandonment of true belief, became part of the world of Satan. In *Vox in Rama*, Gregory described how, after the novice had kissed the ice-cold, pallid man, 'every remnant of faith in the Catholic Church that lingers in the novice's heart leaves him.'[28] If the heretic belonged to Satan, then it was logical to expect that he would wish to worship Satan and his demons: from this inference followed the construction by orthodox chroniclers and inquisitors of a framework of worship which inverted, with its obscene rites, that of the Catholic Church.

To Gregory, the rituals and orgies were literal truth; the language of his Bull conveys a more than conventional emotion of sorrow and horror over the growth of this sect in Germany and issued in a clarion call to action to arrest the spread of the sickness, applying fire and sword to wounds which would not respond to lighter medicines, and promising the Holy Land indulgence to those who took up the cross against the heretics. The pope's

---

[27]   *Vox in Rama*, ed. K. Rodenberg, *MGH, Epistolae saeculi XIII*, I (Berlin, 1883), no. 537, pp. 423–5, trans. E. Peters, *The Magician, the Witch and the Law* (Hassocks, 1978), pp. 156–7. For Gregory's attitudes to crusading and Satanic influences, R. Kohn, 'Die Verketzerung der Stedinger durch die Bremer Fastensynode', *Bremisches Jahrbuch* LVII (1979), pp. 15–85. There is no link to Conrad of Marburg.
[28]   Peters, *Magician*, p. 157; *MGH*, p. 433; on sources for notion of Luciferans, Patschovsky, in *DA* XXXVII, pp. 651–65; survey, Cohn, *Europe's Inner Demons*, pp. 16–31.

commitment against Luciferans explains why he did not throw Conrad over: if Conrad had engaged in excesses, he had none the less uncovered and pursued a dangerous sect. Conrad's methods of extorting confessions readily provided 'evidence' of the existence of an imaginary heresy, born of a distorted understanding of Catharism: the accused, threatened with the fire if they did not submit, were prepared to admit to anything that Conrad and his helpers might suggest.

However, Luciferanism was not solely the fruit of Conrad's methods of investigation: a woman suspect called Lucardi confessed to Luciferanism in the court of the archbishop of Trier, where there is no evidence of the use of methods of extracting information comparable with those of Conrad.[29] Clearly there was a nucleus of belief in Devil worship in Germany: Conrad gave it massive publicity and, through his influence on Gregory IX, ensured that the papacy gave the belief its full confirmation. *Vox in Rama* added Luciferanism to the list of heresies to be combatted by inquisitors.[30]

Another and notorious early inquisitor, Robert le Bougre, operated over a wide swathe of territory in both France and the Empire, beginning in 1232 in Franche-Comté, continuing in La Charité-sur-Loire in the Nivernais in 1233 for some eleven or twelve months; as part of a general reaction of the episcopate against friar-led inquisition, he was suspended in 1234–5, then in 1236 engaged in an anti-heretical sweep of two to three months ranging from Champagne into Flanders, which issued in burnings at, for example, Cambrai in February and Douai in March; finally in the spring of 1239 he played a part in the interrogation of suspects and the burning of between 180 and 187 heretics at the dramatic site of Mont Aimé in Champagne.[31] Robert claimed to Gregory that he had achieved dramatic results in preaching against heresy in La Charité-sur-Loire, leading heretics to come to him voluntarily with wooden collars or chains round their necks, offering to give evidence about their fellow sectaries, including close relatives; impressed, Gregory responded on 19 April with a commission to Robert to judge as well as preach in La Charité and neighbouring regions. He emphasized to Robert the insidious perils of heresy and the dangers of feigned conversion; of the dangers of procedural irregularities and injustice he said nothing.[32]

---

[29]   Patschovsky, in *DA* XXXVII, pp. 661–2; see *GRK* I (1), pp. 146–7; I (2), pp. 434–8.

[30]   Patschovsky, 'Der Ketzer …', pp. 317–34. The author develops the idea of the necessity of giving devilish attributes to heretics, given the assumptions of this period. One would like to ask, none the less, how far this development takes place outside German-speaking lands.

[31]   Major revision recasts sequence of events, G. Despy, 'Les débuts de l'Inquisition dans les anciens Pays-Bas au XIIIe siècle', *Problèmes d'histoire du Christianisme: Hommage à Jean Hadot* IX (1980), pp. 71–104, correcting classic article, C. H. Haskins, 'Robert le Bougre and the beginnings of the Inquisition in Northern France', *Studies in Medieval Culture* (Oxford, 1929), pp. 193–244. See comment on unused material in Thomas of Capua, P. Segl, 'Einrichtung und Wirkungsweise der *inquisitio haereticae pravitatis* im mittelalterlichen Europa. Zur Einführung', in *Anfänge*, ed. Segl, pp. 1–38 at p. 27, n. 120 (see also for general bibliography).

[32]   *Gaudemus in Domino* (19 April 1233), T. Ripoll, ed. A. Bremond, *Bullarium Ordinis FF. Praedicatorum I 1215–1280* (Rome, 1729), pp. 45–6.

Map 3 The sees of the bishops at the great burning of 1239
Source: G. Despy, 'Les débuts de l'Inquisition dans les anciens Pays-Bas au XIIIe siècle', *Problèmes d'histoire du Christianisme: hommage à Jean Hadot* IX (1980), p. 85

Reputedly a former Cathar himself – hence his title – Robert established a reputation among a series of chroniclers for ferocious and arbitrary procedures. One reported that he could detect heretics by speech and gesture alone; another wrote of a certain little writing, a *cartula*, which, placed on the head of a suspect, caused that person to say whatever Robert desired. He did not act alone: in Franche-Comté there was his fellow

Dominican, prior of the convent at Besançon and another friar. In 1236, travelling from Peronne in France to Cambrai in the Empire, he was given an escort provided jointly by the king of France and the bishop of Cambrai, also a prince of the Empire, leading to the supposition that an exceptionally unpopular inquisitor needed an exceptional escort. But the joint provision could have been simply a matter of diplomatic protocol as he travelled between jurisdictions.

At the great burning of 1239 there was present the king of Navarre, the count of Champagne and no fewer than sixteen bishops, principally of the Archbishopric of Rheims but also from those of Sens, Lyons and Trier; the presence of bishops is also recorded at other burnings. In other words, Robert was acting with the concurrence or active support of the secular and spiritual powers. The very wide geographical spread of bishops who attended the holocaust at Mont Aimé implies that the victims also were drawn from their sees, the whole designed to be a major spectacle to spread terror – a kind of raid on heresy conducted not simply by Robert but by the bishops pre-eminently within the far-flung Archbishopric of Rheims to gather together the suspects for interrogation and execution. Mont Aimé is unlikely to have been any longer a fortress of heresy, but was chosen because of its past association. It was not a natural strongpoint but was set in a landscape with lords who were not substantially sympathetic to, or tolerant of, Catharism. The analogy is not with Montségur, still a Cathar stronghold when it was overwhelmed by a royal army in 1243, but with the castle of Gattedo in Lombardy, once a Cathar refuge, where in 1254 Innocent IV grubbed up the bones of heretic bishops and burned them, demonstrating the Church's triumphant recovery after the killing of Peter of Verona.

The chronicle accounts of Robert le Bougre are weak, with legendary overtones: from them it is impossible to gain a clear, detailed picture of the beliefs of those who suffered, and something must be allowed for an anti-Dominican bias. It may be that the magical *cartula* represented the popular fear and hostility in a semi-literate society for the written evidence, the fruit of interrogation on which suspects were convicted, and that the story retailed by Matthew Paris (and one other) that his arbitrary behaviour led to his deposition and life imprisonment is a legend.[33]

Some historians may prefer the rival accounts that leave him to pass the evening of his days in peace at St Victor, Paris or Clairvaux. Evidence from the reputable Gerard of Fracheto, on the other hand, of a friar whom he does not name, an inquisitor held 'in such renown that almost the whole of

[33]   Revisions on escort and mass burnings from Despy 'Les débuts ...'; *cartula* interpretation H. Grundmann, 'Ketzervehöre des Spätmittelalters als quellenkritisches Problem', *DA* XXI (1965), pp. 519–75 at p. 520, *Ausgewählte Aufsätze* I, pp. 364–416 at p. 365; for Gattedo, see below, p. 124; site of Mont Aimé *JDH*, p. 125: it is common to acknowledge Mont Aimé as a Cathar centre and to argue that Cathars were the principal target both of the clergy of Liège's letter to the pope (above pp. 16–17) and of the great burning at the site in 1239. Despy notes the imprecision of the sources and is not convinced.

France trembled before him',[34] who became insolent, would not listen to his elders and was condemned to imprisonment, sits uncomfortably well to Robert's case. He was unmistakably a remarkably zealous inquisitor, who covered much territory. Re-examination of the chronology of his life makes it unlikely that he was suspended as an individual from duty in 1234–5 because of his excesses, and analysis of the Mont Aimé episode should surely acquit him of personally amassing the great harvest of victims in 1239. There is no case for aligning him *tout court* with the wild Conrad of Marburg. None the less, there is a sinister note of triumphalism in his correspondence with Gregory IX about his own work in La Charité-sur-Loire, procedures remained highly fluid in these years and the position of inquisitor was only too easily abused. Acquittal of Robert as an arbitrary, wilful inquisitor is not yet justified: a verdict of not proven best fits the existing evidence.

Inquisitors in the South of France

In the South, Gregory's experiments with agents to pursue and judge bore fruit. His commission to Conrad of Marburg ended in confusion and injustice, and there remains the suspicion that that given to Robert le Bougre was scarred by arbitrary proceedings. Here, by contrast, Gregory's grants of authority to Dominicans were the basis for the formation of long-lasting tribunals which did much to roll up Catharism. He intended that the Dominicans, whom the provincials were to appoint for the task of pursuing heresy in April 1233, should have full powers and should make judgements. They were the inquisitors and were to work in cooperation with the episcopate, whose powers were to be in no way diminished. Under pressure from pope and king, Raymond VII issued in the same month statutes to assist prosecutions, and Gregory appointed a new papal legate with special responsibility for the heresy issue. Dominican inquisitors were appointed for the dioceses of Toulouse, Cahors and Albi. It is at this point, in the spring of 1233 in Languedoc, that we may fairly speak of the birth of the inquisition as historians understand it, emerging almost casually from the series of initiatives taken by Gregory since his accession.[35]

The machinery for action to take advantage of the new political climate following the Peace of Paris was all in place, but the friars found themselves cramped by local hostility. The consuls in Toulouse objected to accusations of heresy and Arnold Dominic, a key witness who betrayed former associates, was murdered; uproar followed the burning of the corpses of exhumed heretics. At Albi, Arnold Catalan was beaten and his clothes torn; in the

[34] Gerard of Fracheto, *Vitae fratrum Ordinis Praedicatorum*, ed. B. M. Reichert (Rome, Stuttgart, 1897), p. 292; trans. Haskins, *Studies in Medieval Culture*, p. 227 noting (n. 2) that though Robert's name is not in the Reichert MSS, Echard had seen it.
[35] For this and what follows, Kolmer, *Ad Capiendas*, pp. 127–45; *WHC*, pp. 130–52; trans. Pelhisson, pp. 207–36; earlier work, Y. Dossat, *Les Crises de l'Inquisition Toulousaine au XIIIe siècle 1233–73* (Bordeaux, 1959).

bourg at Narbonne, the Dominican Ferrier, an inquisitor appointed by the archbishop, met stiff opposition over an attempted arrest complicated by local tensions, which led to the sacking of the Dominican convent in 1235. A concentration of effort on the exhuming and burning of corpses was symptomatic of the friars' weaknesses, for where the dead were concerned, problems of evidence and the vulnerability of witnesses were less acute.[36] The dragging of bodies through the street was a vivid, if offensive, demonstration that the sin of heresy had its effects beyond the grave and it was an open threat to relatives who had complicity with heresy and whose turn was yet to come.

Raymond VII supported the pursuit of heretics in early years. He seized nineteen in 1232, and one of his bayles, Mancip of Gaillac, went to Montségur to demand its surrender, naturally in vain, and later arrested a Cathar deacon and three other perfect; another bayle from Lavant brought heretics to Toulouse for trial and burning. But Raymond changed his attitude to inquisitors in 1235.

The consuls of Toulouse thwarted inquisitors. Alaman de Roaix, one of the wealthiest citizens who had initially been penanced by Romanus but continued in active support of the Cathars, was left free to walk the street despite his contumacy in failing to appear before William Arnold and Stephen of St Thibéry, who excommunicated him in 1237. The friars appointed lacked local knowledge and were unaware of the enmities sometimes responsible for tainted evidence. They were inexperienced in cross-examination, and subsequent evidence against some of those they interrogated shows that they did not succeed in penetrating defendants' guard. There were conspiracies of silence and Cathar supporters worked to give guarantees of orthodoxy for accused sectaries.[37]

There were irregularities caused by the friars' passionate zeal to come to grips with the heresy and their wish to work speedily. At this stage, they remained on good terms with the episcopate, who took their own measures against heresy. The two jurisdictions worked successfully side by side and there were no outrages on the scale of those associated with Conrad, probably because provincials were responsible for appointing suitable candidates as inquisitors and could with some success avoid giving power to distorted personalities. But, contrary to Gregory's wishes, the friars were inclined to skip the seeking of counsel from other clergy before giving judgement and in a case in 1234 were guilty of sharp practice in their handling of the affair of two suspect sisters, who were subjected to a doubtful horse-trading deal over the appeal they launched against their treatment. They were promised their peace if they withdrew their appeal, and, when they did so, were promptly sentenced to confinement for life in an abbey.[38] Romanus's rule that the names of witnesses should not be divulged was observed and weighted the balance of inquisitorial proceedings versus all defendants. Raymond VII, who had his own motives for

---

[36]   Clarified by Kolmer, *Ad Capiendas*, pp. 129–30.
[37]   Helpful summary, ibid., pp. 147–8.
[38]   Ibid., pp. 131–2.

protesting, complained to Gregory in 1234 that the friars were not keeping to the rules. Gregory was unwilling to check a promising campaign, but required his legates to investigate abuses. They made a concession to Raymond by restricting the jurisdiction of the inquisitor Peter Seila, whom he accused of enmity. The appointment of the Franciscan, Stephen of St Thibéry in 1236 may have been intended to prevent Dominicans keeping decision-making, in effect, exclusively within the confines of their order and imperilling objectivity.

In Toulouse, the opposition succeeded in expelling, late in 1235, first the inquisitor William Arnold and then the whole convent, the friars remaining in exile for months. Finally in 1238 Gregory halted the work of the tribunal at Toulouse. The understanding with Frederick began to crumble and as conflict grew so it pushed the battle against heresy further down the list of the pope's priorities. Gregory was determined to detach Raymond from alliance with Frederick and was aware of the count's hostility to the friars' proceedings. At the same time, reports of frictions and appeals to Rome caused the pope anxiety about the objectivity of the Dominican inquisition; for the moment he allowed the friars only to complete the investigations they had begun, with participation by legates, and otherwise left the pursuit and judgement of heretics to the episcopate.

There was a balance of success and failure. The chronicler William Pelhisson, who lived through these events, described with enthusiasm how the friars were inundated with confessions on Good Friday 1235.[39] In the following year the inquisitors seemed to be on the verge of a breakthrough when a perfect, a veteran of many years, confessed his heresy and began giving names of his associates. Still the results were comparatively disappointing; exhumings might create terror as well as anger, but overall there were fewer convictions of the living than the friars would have wished. Catharism, whether in town or country, had not been broken.

The nature of inquisitorial procedure

The potential injustices of inquisitional proceedings, in which the names of witnesses were withheld, accusations were summarized and no defence advocates were allowed, emerged even when a select group of friars rather than self-recommended individuals were in charge. Officially, appeals were not allowed, though they did occur; in any case, appeals to Rome were expensive and beyond the means of poorer defendants. In effect, the chances in law of reversing a faulty judgement were feeble and the potential effects of mis-judgement serious. The participation of counsellors in final judgement was only an imperfect check on malpractice. A guilty verdict had profound consequences for the life and possessions of individuals and families, carrying with it possible penalties of death, imprisonment, confiscation of goods, public disrepute, onerous penances and pilgrimages.

There were obvious dangers when one person or group of persons was responsible for all the stages of a case from the preliminary investigation to

---

[39]   *WHC*, pp. 216–17.

the final judgement. By the 1230s the distinction between manifest heretics and those who were suspect was already an ancient one, since it had emerged both in *Ad abolendam* and in the canon *Excommunicamus* of the Fourth Lateran Council. Its origins and continual survival in inquisitorial procedure was linked to the ancient *accusatio* procedure and to the oath of purgation. It was too useful to inquisitors to be abandoned, but its effect in practice was that from the outset a defendant who appeared before an inquisition tribunal carried the burden of proof. He or she was suspect or would not have been required to appear; on that defendant, then, fell the obligation to demonstrate that the suspicion was ill founded, resting on malice or misunderstanding or the evidence of an enemy. In truth, the flaws in *inquisitio* proceedings, stripped of safeguards for the sake of efficient prosecution, were built-in defects, inherent in the procedure itself. At all times, a defendant was heavily dependent on the conscience and good judgement of individual inquisitors.[40]

The earliest years of the predominantly Dominican inquisition in Languedoc were formative. Though the friars made mistakes, they were forging an efficient instrument of repression. The initial *sermo generalis* officially launching an inquiry provided both a personal appeal to the populace, a menace and a body of information. Auditors were informed of the dangers of heresy, of the penalties attached to it and of the tenets of orthodoxy. The time of grace which followed, when those who confessed to complicity in heresy could expect to receive much lighter penances than would otherwise be the case, encouraged witnesses to come forward. Pastoral action, preaching and inviting confessions led onto and fed the legal examinations: '*persuasio*' and '*coercitio*' coexisted and fed each other.

Documents were kept, but not as yet registered; only later was the necessity of a register and the advantages of information understood as a prime weapon against backsliders. Experience, nevertheless, began to build up and a notary was used in 1237.[41] As a rule Dominicans provided good agents of repression from an order destined by its founder to preach against heresy, with a theological training and supported by their communities. The irregularities and failures in the conflict with local Cathars in the early years of the most important tribunal at Toulouse should not blur the achievements of the early friar inquisitors as pioneers in development.

Friars and inquisitors in Italy

In Italy Dominican intervention was important, but was not at first apparently based on commissions which gave powers of judgement on the pattern which prevailed in Languedoc.[42] In Milan in 1229 the *podestà* appointed a

---

[40]   See survey of inquisitorial procedure, B. Hamilton, *The Medieval Inquisition* (London, 1981).

[41]   Kolmer, *Ad Capiendas*, p. 143.

[42]   Walther, 'Ziele und Mittel päpstlicher Ketzerpolitik ...' in *Anfänge*, ed. Segl, pp. 103–30, esp. pp. 121–8 (with bibliography); comment, Segl, 'Einrichtung', in *Anfänge*, pp. 1–38 at pp. 27–31, noting role of temporal policy in papal activities against heresy in Papal States.

commission of twelve members to pursue heretics, which included two Franciscans and two Dominicans, but it remained subject to the decisions of the archbishop's court. Gregory sent Dominicans to a series of dioceses, recommending them as helpers in the struggle against heretics. As late as 1237, Gregory's organization of the Dominican pursuit of heretics in Italy still had at its base the formulae of *Ille humani generis* and did not provide the friars with an independent jurisdiction. Both Franciscans and Dominicans preached against heresy: revivalist campaigns strengthened orthodox forces in the city. Lay associations – sometimes pre-dating the friars, sometimes brought into being by the friars' endeavours – were a focus for fervour and provided an alternative to Catharism, with an active role for the membership under clerical leadership; certain of the associations were directed against the heretics and provided auxiliaries for the fight against unorthodoxy.[43] Progress was made, albeit slowly and with setbacks, in the insertion of anti-heretical statutes in municipal legislation.

When the pope despatched the Dominican Roland of Cremona to Piacenza in 1234 to contest the influence of a *podestà* who was a fautor of heretics, the move almost ended in disaster. Roland was assailed by armed men when he attempted to preach and barely escaped with his life; a companion was mortally wounded. Although the *podestà* was forced out, he took up residence in a castle near Lodi where he continued to receive heretics: the situation remained volatile. Guala, a Dominican who became bishop of Brescia in 1230, did good service in cowing heresy and became a papal legate. But the decisive factor was the attitude of the municipal leadership of the individual city which was influenced, not only by regional factors, but by local and general political considerations, family conflicts and allegiances and by its relationship with the bishop. Politics was confused and volatile and it was less easy for the papacy in Italy to impose a policy than in Languedoc. For a few years a window of opportunity opened, as the emperor and the pope were reconciled at the Peace of San Germano in 1230, when Frederick renewed anti-heretical legislation and even showed a willingness to pursue heretics in the Regno. But a wariness remained on the papal side: Gregory shied away from a full cooperation with the emperor in the pursuit of heretics in Northern Italy for fear of the consequences of giving Frederick too much scope in a sensitive region.[44]

In 1233 a Dominican, John of Vicenza, had a meteoric career as a revivalist preacher, beginning in Bologna, then working at Padua and in the March of Treviso and profiting by the mass movement of repentance, the Alleluia of 1233, built on a widespread revulsion against the internecine conflicts of Italy; even the grim tyrant Ezzelino da Romano, who, if not a Cathar, gave tacit toleration to Catharism, felt it expedient not to stand aside.[45] In the emotional months when John held his auditors in the hollow of his hand, heretics were burned over three days in the old Roman

---

[43]   See below, p. 177, n. 17.
[44]   Miccoli, 'La repressione', p. 719.
[45]   A. Thompson, *Revival Preachers and Politics in Thirteenth Century Italy: the Great Devotion of 1233* (Oxford, 1992).

amphitheatre at Verona. John's power disappeared almost as rapidly as it had grown up, but the mass burning had long-term effects. It struck fear into the hearts of Italian Cathars. It demonstrated that they were not immune to the actions of friars and bishops and papal legislation. Another Dominican, Gerard of Modena, reinforced statutes against heresy at Parma and other cities; in Milan more stringent laws against heresy were put on the statute book under the influence of Peter of Verona in 1233. At Monza and Vercelli Franciscans were responsible for anti-heresy laws. The Alleluia was a spontaneous movement which began as a local initiative with friars preaching in the Veneto and spread beyond all expectations; it aided the papal drive against heresy, though its aim was peacemaking and the repression of factionalism.

Some Italian cities long maintained their resistance to adopting anti-heresy legislation imposed from outside. At Genoa a *podestà* refused to show the statute book to the bishop of Tortona and it was not until 1256 at least that the city would accept laws against heresy. The *Liber supra stella* of Salvo Burci of Piacenza, written in 1235, is at pains to justify the temporal punishment of heresy. Moneta of Cremona, in his massive *summa* against the heretics of 1241, includes a passage arguing for it 'for the instruction of the unlearned in the Church'.[46] The justifications are a sign that the punishment of heresy met resistance. In the major centres of population the friars had established themselves by the mid-1230s; both Franciscans and Dominicans preached against heresy and carried on a peaceful pastoral mission, whether anti-heresy statutes were received in their cities or not. They stood apart from ancient quarrels over land and rights between the municipalities and their bishops, which so often fostered heresy, and their lack of wealth and their disinterestedness differentiated them from traditional clergy. They were often allied with the *popolo* and the new forces in the communes.[47] Their influence against heresy continued to work when Gregory IX became distracted by the renewed and more intense conflict with Frederick II. Cooperation between pope and emperor came to an end; Frederick felt that the friars as agents of the papacy were his enemies and would not allow them into the Regno. There were cities where little progress in eradicating heresy could be made: municipal governments were too hostile. The advances of Catharism in the first half of the thirteenth century had been worrying, and as the renewed conflict with Frederick developed, Gregory had to tread more carefully, for he needed the cities' alliance. Effective counter-action certainly began to develop in Italy in the 1230s and the Alleluia marked a step downward for all heretics; none the less Catharism had still not lost its function and Catholic counter-attack was patchy. The battle with the Cathars was far from won.

---

[46]   Diehl, 'Overcoming reluctance ...', pp. 47–8; D. M. Webb, 'The possibility of toleration: Marsiglio and the city states of Italy', *SCH* XXI (1984), pp. 99–113.

[47]   Perspective, Vauchez, 'Movimenti religiosi ...', pp. 311–46; G. Barone, 'Gli ordini mendicanti', in *Storia dell' Italia religiosa*, I: *L'Antichità' e il Medioevo*, ed. G. de Rosa, T. Gregory and A. Vauchez (Rome, Bari, 1993), pp. 347–73.

7

The Cathars of Languedoc

The course of events

It must have seemed in the early years of the Albigensian Crusade that Catharism was going to be destroyed in short order. Tragic and terrifying events, compounded by de Montfort's own terror tactics, spread alarm far and wide, the disaster of Muret and death of Peter of Aragon removed the hope of a major external intervention in favour of the cause of the old Southern houses and the fortunes of Raymond VI reached a nadir at the Fourth Lateran Council when his county was declared forfeit.

Yet, though Simon received the title of count, thus brusquely succeeding Raymond, and was accepted as such by King Philip, he still had no more substantial backing in his enterprise than the adventurers and former crusaders who had settled in Languedoc as his vassals. Philip stood aloof. The rising at Beaucaire in favour of Raymond's son, which Simon could not repress, then broke the de Montfort reputation for invincibility. A decisive turn of fortune in favour of Raymond occurred in 1218 when Simon was killed at Toulouse. The city stood firm against an abortive intervention in 1219 by French royal forces under Philip's son Louis and territory began to fall to Raymond VI and then to his son who succeeded him in 1222. By 1225 Raymond VII had recovered much of his land and the Trencavel heir had been installed once again at Carcassonne.

But the Southern revival did not last. Louis, now King Louis VIII, intervened again in 1226 and the appearance of a serious royal force in the field led to a series of defections; the ravaging carried out by Humbert of Beaujeu after Louis's death finally convinced Raymond VII in 1229 of the need to surrender both to the Church and to the royal power and to make what terms he could.[1] Nevertheless, the swing of fortune to Raymond VI and VII and the period of negotiation which preceded the arrival of Louis VIII's army, though ultimately ineffectual, changed the climate in which the Cathar Churches operated. Mass slaughter of perfect was over. Individuals

---

[1] E. Griffe, *Les Cathares et l'Inquisition (1229–1329)* (Paris, 1980), pp. 7–9 on implications of agreement, and comital power.

and small groups could be picked off, even members of the hierarchy, as in the case of Picrre Isarn, bishop of Carcassonne, who was captured and taken to Caunes to be burned in the presence of Louis VIII.[2] The old pre-Crusade freedom could never return.

Yet there was a lifting of spirits and a restoration of activity. Some of the perfect had not fled to refuges in the early years of the Crusade but slipped underground [3] or engaged in a calculated conversion, as Arnaude and Peirona de Lamothe seem to have done, no doubt under the influence of their mother Austorgue, being reconciled to the Catholic Church by the bishop of Cahors c.1212.[4] Perfect in the field could expect to be fiercely dealt with, but those who abandoned their errors in such private transactions as that engaged in by the Lamothe sisters were treated mercifully. They came quietly back to Catharism. In 1224 Arnaude records a preaching by Bernard de Lamothe in the home of Joanna of Avignon, another woman who had supposedly repented of her Catharism, together with her sister Peirona, two other sisters, their mother and three other women. Little seemed to have changed: all adored the visiting perfect, and subsequently Arnaude and Peirona went to the nunnery at Linars and were reconsoled. Perhaps the illness of Austorgue caused them to turn back to Catharism, but the greater security of the 1220s must have been a significant factor.[5] No doubt there were other such cases as Cathars came out of obscurity and communities were reformed. Houses were reoccupied or built; Guilhabert de Castres with his brother and fellow perfect Isarn, after taking refuge in the Pays de Sault, dominated by the Niorts, seem to have spent much of the years 1211–19 at the fortress of Montségur not far away. In 1219, however, he kept a house at Dun which lay under the protection of the Countess Philippa of Foix, with her community of perfect women, and in 1221 felt assured enough to engage in discussions with the count of Palhars and other men of note at Mirepoix. He moved about the Cathar countryside in the 1220s protected by powerful patrons, including at Castelnaudary in 1225 the bayle of the count of Toulouse; the most significant sign that easier times had come lay in his decision to build a house at Fanjeaux and live there.[6]

Fanjeaux's liberation was the fruit of the successes of the count of Toulouse: under de Montfort, who kept the lordship in his own hands, the village as a Cathar centre had suffered heavily. The perfect and leading Cathars had fled before the Crusade, often taking refuge at Montségur, and certain possessions were given to Simon's companions, who in turn gave a proportion for the endowment of the Catholic nunnery at Prouille. As the tide of conquest swung back and the counts of Toulouse resumed power, the perfect and their patrons returned; lands were reclaimed, with the exception of the gifts to Prouille, which appear to have been respected;

[2]   *JDH*, p. 260.
[3]   Y. Dossat, 'Les Cathares d'après les documents de l'inquisition', *CF* III, pp. 71–104, periodizing, pp. 72–7.
[4]   Murray, transl. Doat 25 fol. 7r.
[5]   Ibid., fol. 7v et seq.
[6]   Duvernoy, in *CEC* XXXIV, p. 34; Roquebert, in *EO*, p. 187.

houses of perfect re-opened and Guilhabert preached almost as freely as in the days before the Crusade. A leather workshop trained apprentices and inculcated Catharism; some went on to be consoled. Perfect passed through and preached in the communities or in the houses of believers and patrons; perhaps as many as a hundred believers were in or near Fanjeaux in the years 1221–9.[7]

Other villages in the Lauragais, not as dominated by Cathars as Fanjeaux, had a less dramatic history, where the perfect lived on in 'islands of quiet' having returned from Montségur to which refuge they had earlier fled. Men perfect engaged in manual labour, planting gardens at Avignonet or labouring in the fields at Auriac, Cambiac and Le Mas: women perfect sometimes gleaned after them or span yarn.[8] A pragmatic toleration often enough prevailed after the Crusade had passed, or in places where its influence was only indirectly felt; if perfect were good workers, it was in the interest of landholders to employ them and parish clergy might also welcome an absence of friction. Greater freedom eased the economic conditions for perfect as they could more easily take jobs or join in communal enterprises and were consequently less dependent on alms. When a Cathar workshop opened in Cordes in 1224, it was an opportunity for the perfect Sicard de Figueiras to mingle preaching with weaving.[9]

Le Mas was a prosperous place, where support for Catharism was aided by the adherence of a ruling house of moderate wealth and power, which in 1245 included five brothers and a widowed sister, children of Garsen who had been burned; she had once lived as a perfect in her house together with her daughter Galharda, also subsequently burned; a grandson, Odo of Quiriès, was consoled there before he died, as was a sick daughter-in-law, Fauressa, who later recovered and abandoned her Catharism.[10] Clearly, Garsen was another matriarch like Blanche of Laurac, diffusing her faith among her children. She, her daughter and others fled the village in the Crusade epoch, then returned about 1220 before going on to Montségur. Investigations by inquisitors suggest that, though Catharism in Le Mas had deep roots going back to 1185 and numbered leading personnel among its adherents, it captured only a minority of the inhabitants, perhaps a quarter or at most a third.[11] The Crusade seems not to have had a major impact, for there is no record of members of the ruling class being involved in the fighting and no confiscations are known; perfect were still sometimes seen in the years of intense fighting elsewhere in Languedoc and, though the

---

[7]   Roquebert, in *EO*, pp. 183–90.
[8]   I follow closely unpublished work of Professor W. L. Wakefield (WLW), based especially on Toulouse MS 609, where he has unrivalled knowledge. Return from Montségur, MS 609 fol. 106r; manual labour, Doat 24 fols 21r–22r, MS 609 57v, 66v.
[9]   *JDH*, p. 261; comment, M. Becamel, 'Le Catharisme dans le diocèse d'Albi', *CF* III, pp. 237–52 at pp. 246–7.
[10] W. L. Wakefield, 'Heretics and inquisitors: the case of Le Mas-Saintes-Puelles', *CHR* LXIX (1983), pp. 209–26, genealogy, p. 211; G. Šemkov, 'Le contexte socio-économique du Catharisme au Mas-Saintes-Puelles dans la première moitié du 13e siècle', *Heresis* II (1984), pp. 35–53.
[11] Calculation of W. L. Wakefield, in *CHR* LXIX, p. 212.

Cathar presence had certainly weakened in Le Mas, inhabitants were still drawn to Catharism during the whole period between 1210 and 1229 and adherents were active enough to ensure that Guilhem de Malhorgas, on falling ill about 1226, was consoled by perfect who came from Laurac.

With the return of a greater freedom for Cathar membership, came something of the old willingness to debate issues of faith or even to fraternize:[12] Cathars and Waldensians debated in Quercy and Waldensians' offers of service as doctors were widely accepted. An argument about matrimony and the salvation of children between an Avignon notary and the Cathar deacon William Ricard ended in a shared meal of figs and grapes in which they were joined by the men of Lagarde. On the other hand, in about 1227, so far from debating peacefully, some of the populace reacted violently when Cathars preached in the public square and there followed 'a great brawl of Catholics and heretics'. In Le Mas, when Bernard Bofilh argued for the Cathars against Arnald Pitrell, the debate became so heated that Arnald's mother feared for her son's safety and called him away.[13]

The events of the Crusade, the fighting and the burnings, inevitably raised tensions. In Toulouse, the cause of the town's rights and sentiment for Raymond VI unified opinion on the Cathar side against the Crusade cause. After a conflict over an interdict with Raymond, Bishop Fulk was compelled to leave and thereafter spent years in bitter exile from the episcopal residence, his life bound up with crusading forces.[14] When in 1227 Louis VIII's troops were besieging Labécède and defenders shouted down at him from the walls saying that he was not their bishop but the bishop of devils, he replied in sardonic agreement, 'Right. They are the devils and I am their bishop.'[15] The Confraternity of the Whites, whom he had once led in reaction against usury and heresy in the Bourg of Toulouse, disintegrated, splitting up between those who followed the bishop into exile and those who remained to fight the crusaders.

None the less, a meridional tolerance and unwillingness to draw sharp lines between heresy and orthodoxy still resurfaced in various places. Na Cavaers, a co-seigneur of Fanjeaux, a woman of wealth and education and devoted Cathar believer, who attended preachings and consolings in the 1220s, and was friendly enough with Guilhabert de Castres to give him a present of an eel, yet continued her mother's tradition of making donations to Prouille and ended her days as a nun there. Was her final decision and the gifts she made a prophylactic against the effects of the pressures of persecution, which intensified in the 1230s and 1240s, or was there always a genuine duality of allegiance in her mind, however illogical?[16] Strange and sudden choices were made by Cathar sympathizers in cases where there was

[12]   WLW citing Doat 25 fol. 316r.
[13]   W. L. Wakefield, 'Heretics as physicians in the thirteenth century', *Speculum* LVII (1982), pp. 328–31.
[14]   Mundy, *Repression*, p. 24.
[15]   Ibid.
[16]   S. Nelli, 'Na Cavaers, coseigneur de Fanjeaux, la dame qui jouait le double jeu', *Heresis* VI (1986), pp. 26–34.

no obvious material gain. Guilhem de Malhorgas in Le Mas, whom his friends plainly thought a proper candidate for the death-bed *consolamentum*, on recovering decided to become a Cistercian.[17]

In contrast to the relationship of unremitting hostility which existed between friars and perfect, that with monks and nuns held a certain ambiguity. Linars is a case of a nunnery which seems to have been taken over by women perfect. Older religious houses were deeply embedded in society and their inmates intimately connected to families with heretical members and throughout the period of toleration, and well beyond, abbots, priors and monks showed themselves accommodating to heretics: Dominicans and Franciscans, newcomers on the scene, had no such inhibitions.[18] The most remarkable case of fraternization between monks and heretics occurred at the abbey of Sorèze, where Guilhabert Alzieu and other monks were regularly in the company of the perfect. Their complaisance was of long standing for Guilhabert had even used his influence with Arnaud Amaury to obtain letters of reconciliation for the Cathar deacon Bofils. Rixende Baussane, a perfect who resided in the area, was on excellent terms both with the monks and parish priest of Sorèze, attended mass and made an offering, as her young nephew who lived with her later recalled. This genial symbiosis of the faiths was only cut short by the arrival of an unsympathetic priest in 1242.[19]

Catharism had struck such deep roots in parts of Languedoc, and so benefited from an instinctive, easy-going toleration characteristic of the region, that a long, hard campaign in the most affected regions was required before it could be dislodged. Duvernoy, pre-eminent historian of the inquisition in Languedoc, argues that the mental climate in the South was hostile to the dramatic and the sacred and was marked by a certain ironic indifference among the mass of the population, not so much the fruit of the presence of Catharism as a precondition for its toleration – and so its subsequent growth.[20] When pressure to put heresy down – often enough urged on by newcomers in Church and State from the North – flagged, as it did in the 1220s, such sentiments resurfaced and Catharism could breathe again. It was its last age of comparative freedom.

A core of organization survived the ferocious years, including some key members of the hierarchy. The Church of Toulouse was less affected than any other and had retained its bishop, Gaucelin, a *filius major*, Guilhabert de Castres and a series of deacons. Carcassonne suffered more, though its bishop, Bernard de Simorre escaped death. Of Albi and Agen we know little. In Albi, since the orthodox bishop, Guilhem Peyre, maintained his prudent caution towards Cathars, little information is available: it seems to

[17]   *JDR*, p. 167.
[18]   Dossat, in *CF* III, pp. 93–5; reflections on common lines between Catholic and Cathar attitudes, pp. 100–2. Heresy could penetrate Cistercian houses (nature unknown): D. Baker, 'Heresy and learning in early Cistercianism', *SCH* IX, pp. 93–107 at pp. 98–101; *JDH*, pp. 269–70.
[19]   Dossat, in *CF* III, pp. 97–100.
[20]   *JDH*, p. 197.

have been a bishopric with less support than Toulouse, which was clearly pre-eminent among the Cathars in the 1220s. Toulouse had a solid body of perfect who lived on in the Lauragais: support for Cathars had been strengthened by the shared patriotisms of the sieges of Toulouse and the calibre of their leadership, especially that of Guilhabert de Castres.[21]

There is evidence that the Cathars of Carcassone revived as the crusading tide ebbed. In Hamilton's plausible hypothesis, Pierre Isarn, as successor bishop in 1223, was seeking advice from the senior and more powerful diocese of Toulouse on the nature of his diocesan boundaries, reaching back to the decisions of Nicetas and the Council of S. Félix de Caraman to clarify them.[22] No Church with its back to the wall would have felt able to spend time on a historical and jurisdictional investigation of this kind. At the Council of Pieusse in 1226 a witness remembered up to a hundred of the perfect being assembled with members of the hierarchy. The lord of Pieusse, whose wife had been consoled, also attended and no doubt gave the Council his protection. The perfect of the Razès had complained that it was not convenient for them to have recourse for their needs to the perfect and hierarchy of the Toulousain or the Carcassès and asked for a bishop of their own.[23] The problem was handled with tact, as a candidate from the diocese of Carcassone, Benoît de Termes, was chosen and there ordained by the bishop of Toulouse. The impression given is of a Church handling its affairs with sophistication in comparative security.

Yet 1226 was the year in which the shadow of defeat fell across the prospects of Raymond VII and the cause of meridional independence. Louis VIII, who had been ceded all Simon de Montfort's rights by Amaury, moved with a substantial army and besieged Avignon: it was a clear signal that the Capetian monarchy had entered the field in earnest and led the more labile of Cathar patrons to consider making their peace with Church and monarchy. Bernard Oth of Niort, grandson of Blanche of Laurac, who had a long history of complicity with Catharism and had once rescued Guilhabert de Castres from Castelnaudary when it was besieged by Amaury de Montfort, wavered. He wrote to the king offering negotiations on behalf of himself, his father and brothers and assisted in the capturing of perfect at Laurac. But he soon reverted to his habitual role as Cathar patron, held the fortress at Cabaret for a month in 1228 or 1229 against royal troops and, before its surrender, ensured that his father-in-law, the lord of Cabaret, escorted two perfect men to safety. But his brief switch to submission, orthodoxy and persecution was a straw in the wind and it later stood him in good stead when he and his family were accused of heresy, for both an archdeacon and a Hospitaller of Pexiora witnessed to his support of the Catholic Church.[24]

[21]   Ibid., pp. 263, 225–6.
[22]   *AFP* XLVIII, p. 43.
[23]   *JDH*, pp. 262–3.
[24]   Wakefield's interpretation, in *Names* XVIII, see esp. pp. 105–6.

Olivier de Termes also briefly submitted to royal power in the aftermath of Louis's intervention, reverted to support Raymond VII and finally in 1228, with his brother, submitted to royal commissioners, promising fidelity to the king and aid against his enemies and those of 'Holy Church'. Olivier more than once went back on his promises, secure in the remote fortress of Quéribus or others in the Corbières, but was ultimately forced into submission without reservations to Church and king.[25] In this he was typical of a number of Southern nobles who had fought the crusaders or were tainted patrons of heresy: they engaged in a long fighting retreat against Northern French power and orthodoxy in the hope of salvaging all they could of land and independence. They aided the survival of the Cathars but were unable to prevent defeat.

Such submissions, coupled with the ravaging of Humbert de Beaujeu, led Raymond VII to accept terms at the Peace of Paris in 1229 which contemporaries believed too harsh, but Raymond was entitled to believe that he had come a long way from the nadir of the fortunes of the house of St Gilles in 1215. Like his vassals, he may well have thought the situation could in the long run be managed to his advantage: in the event, the childlessness of his daughter Jeanne's marriage to Louis IX's brother Alphonse of Poitiers carried even Toulouse itself into the hands of the French monarchy. A similar calculation may have influenced his submission to the Church, with the drama of public penance; he may have thought also that, despite the implications of his promise to aid the pursuit of heretics, he could at least mitigate persecution and muffle its effects on the nobility and dependents who had fought for him and his father. The stern, unbending figure of Cardinal Romanus, who in his first legation of 1225–7 had ensured that war would continue and Raymond not be allowed to escape with a compromise, in his second, of 1228–30, pressed home the Church's advantage and in the Church Council of Toulouse in 1229 set the conditions for effective prosecution of heresy. The instituting of inquisitional proceedings in 1233 and the use of friars as inquisitors subsequently gave full force to Romanus's arrangements.[26]

Duvernoy believes that the perfect were warned of the likely effects of the Treaty of Paris: three days after the treaty, a party of them left Gourdon, wept over by believers. Guilhabert de Castres at S Paul Cap-de-Joux, re-established as his episcopal residence after 1228, gave the word to his patron to move him out together with the deacon of the Lantarès and others: they wandered on through temporary hiding places in the countryside till they and others in flight reached a refuge in the depth of the Corbières.[27] Arnaude de Lamothe, Peirona and their mother were already on the move; her confession describes how the party transferred 'when the king of France came to Avignon', that is, in 1226.[28] There followed a

---

[25] A. Peal, 'Olivier de Termes and the Occitanian nobility in the thirteenth century', *Reading Medieval Studies* XII (1986), pp. 109–29.
[26] Dutton, 'Aspects ...', pp. 120–5.
[27] *JDH*, pp. 268–9.
[28] Murray transl. Doat 25 fols 13v–14v.

number of short stays of two to four months in various houses in Toulouse. Then there was a significant development as they were taken by night to the countryside where they occupied various sites for a few days at a time, ending with a stay of three years on an estate in Lanta owned by Ponce Saquet of Toulouse. It is plain what was happening: patrons with land and houses in the country were smuggling them out to places where their dependents could be relied on to keep silent. Even there, more secrecy was needed: in Lanta, Arnaude says, they went first to 'a shed' belonging to Ponce Saquet.[29]

The movement was all downhill. From being a little group who could live with care under the perfection of good patrons in town or country, Arnaude and her sister were becoming hunted fugitives. Elsewhere perfect took to hideaways in the Lauragais or to the heights of the Cabardès: Fanjeaux began to evacuate and its refugees formed a nucleus for the garrison of Montségur.

Still, events in the 1230s left hope for the perfect and their supporters. Popular tumults such as the manhandling of Arnold Catalan at Albi when he tried to exhume the corpse of a condemned woman, the rebellion of the Bourg at Narbonne with the pillaging of the Dominican convent, and the expulsion of the friars from Toulouse, showed the feeling against persecution and no doubt led some to believe they might yet win through. Family solidarities, neighbourly feeling for those who, though tainted with heresy, had long lived together in peace, operated against the zealous churchmen and inquisitors. Bishop Fulk, asking a knight why he did not expel heretics, received the classic answer: 'We cannot. We have been reared in their midst. We have relatives among them and we see them living lives of perfection.' The cooperation of secular authorities was necessary for the arrest and pursuit of suspects and this was not always forthcoming. Bayles and other officials could be bribed. At some date no longer ascertainable from the source, two sisters of Guilhabert de Castres, both perfect, were arrested, then released on payment of nine thousand sous. Evasion was sometimes quietly facilitated. Clergy did not necessarily welcome the disruptions and emotions released by arrests and pursuits. Raymond at first cooperated but, as we have seen, in 1234 complained about the actions of inquisitors; in 1238, diplomatic necessities in his battle with Frederick II led Gregory IX to suspend the work of the inquisitors at Toulouse. Bernard Oth of the Niort dynasty, who with his relative Guillaume, was finally condemned for heresy in 1236, escaped sentence of death because of the reaction of his neighbours, French lords who had acquired land nearby and who feared regional war.[30]

While the flow of politics and self-interest inhibited the steady development of repression, enthusiasts on either side joined battle. The spirit of the

[29]   Ibid., fol. 19r (boaria).
[30]   *WHC*, pp. 74–5 (reply to Fulk), pp. 143–6 (Narbonne), pp. 146–9 (Toulouse), pp. 226–8 (Albi); Duvernoy, in *CEC* XXXIV (1967), pp. 33–42; Wakefield, in *Names* XVIII, p. 115; see also Kolmer, *Ad Capiendas*, pp. 101–2, Wakefield's interpretation of events 1232–6 preferred.

Dominicans is revealed in a story told by Guillaume de Pelhisson, historian of their convent at Toulouse, who related how the Bishop Raymond du Fauga, himself one of the friars, got wind of a consoling which had taken place in a house close by the convent, just as the friars had come from the mass for St Dominic's day and were washing their hands in preparation for their meal. He slipped quickly into the house and the Cathar supporter, whose consoled mother-in-law lay in a high fever, could only warn her that 'the Lord Bishop was coming'. She seems to have assumed he meant the Cathar bishop and when Raymond spoke to her 'about contempt for the world and earthly things' revealed her heresy. She declined to recant, was carried out on her bed and burnt forthwith in the count's meadow; the son-in-law was arrested. Bishop and friars returned to the convent and, in their pleasure at the confounding of heresy 'giving thanks to God and the Blessed Dominic, ate with rejoicing what had been prepared for them'.[31]

The case of Jean Teisseire from the Bourg of Toulouse showed the magnetism which Catharism could exert in the most adverse circumstances. When Jean's heresy was investigated, he protested his innocence 'I have a wife and I sleep with her. I have sons, I eat meat and I lie and swear and I am a faithful Christian', but was convicted by witnesses. He was to be burnt, but so many defended his cause and made an outcry that execution was delayed. In the bishop's prison, while still protesting his innocence, he fell in with perfect awaiting trial and was so influenced by them that he was consoled, acknowledged his Catharism after all and, refusing to recant, was burnt with the rest.[32]

The bishop and friars on one side, Jean Teisseire and the perfect on the other – these were the passionate enthusiasts, undeterred by manhandling, threats and death. Between them were the many of ordinary clay who would be influenced by politics and economics and for these the massive series of confiscations revealed to us by a document issued by Philip III of France in 1279 granting amnesty to some two hundred and seventy-eight citizens of Toulouse and returning property formerly confiscated for unspecified offences but presumably for heresy, contumacy or rebellion, bears witness to the pressure to which many tainted families had been subjected. Evidently, side by side with the battles over individual cases, the imprisonments, the escapes and the acts of defiance which run through chronicle and inquisition material, there was a steady work of convicting and punishing, leading to substantial loss of ownership and economic detriment for individuals. Although the orthodox in a family could take up where the heretical were forced to leave off, confiscations dealt sharp and immediate blows at existing patrons. Philip III's diploma witnesses to the wisdom of the monarch and his advisers in rescinding past punishments when the climate of thought in Languedoc had changed and Toulouse had surrendered its independence *vis à vis* royal power. But it also shows the degree to which certain wealthy and patrician groups, even including former consuls in

---

[31]   *WHC*, pp. 215–6 (trans. Pelhisson).
[32]   Ibid., pp. 212–14.

Toulouse, had patronized heresy.[33] After 1229 the forces of orthodoxy drew on their victory in the long wars and began to crack the bases of Cathar patronage. In the aftermath of 1229, synods were still pre-eminently concerned with the repression of heresy and the support of bishops, their officers and inquisitors; not till mid-century could they concern themselves with the pastoral activity and reform of morals which had been a preoccupation of synods north of the Loire some thirty years earlier.[34]

Peaceful instruction by Dominicans was hampered by their involvement in inquisitorial proceedings; nevertheless, as elsewhere, the friars, both Dominican and Franciscan, raised standards of preaching and gained recruits. Dominican statutes insisted that novices should be able to preach in the vernacular of their locality, so when the numbers of Dominican convents in Languedoc rose in regular progression from two in 1215 to twelve in 1231, seventeen in 1242 and twenty-four in 1252, they were swelling with local recruits familiar with the people of the region and their customs. The diffusion of auricular confession, following on the decree of the Fourth Lateran, set new standards for pastoral care and moral teaching especially among more educated town dwellers. Mundy has drawn attention to the varied charitable foundations in Toulouse and the Toulousain, an outlet for idealism with a strong practical emphasis, dealing with concerns not generally met by the Cathars.[35]

Guilhabert de Castres, the leading figure in these years, was not deceived about the darkening of the prospects for Catharism after the Peace of Paris. He saw further, beyond the immediate problems of persecution, probably, than some of his colleagues and in 1232, together with an assembly of some thirty perfect and a gathering of knights, summoned Raimond Pereille, lord of Montségur to meet him. Raimond escorted the party to the fortress, stopping overnight on the way and making a fire for Guilhabert, now an old man who felt the cold. Guilhabert persuaded Raimond to make a stronghold for Catharism so that the Church would 'be able to have its seat and its head there, and to send from thence and defend its preachers'.[36]

As a young man, Raimond had acceded to a similar request from a Cathar deacon at Mirepoix sometime before 1204 to refurbish the *castrum*; in the

---

[33]   Mundy, *Repression*, argues (a) these were condemnations for heresy; (b) 70 per cent were condemned before 1237; (c) 'backbone' of heresy in wealthier patrons broken before 1240. P. Hordern, in *EHR* CIII (1988), pp. 477–8 does not believe (a) and (b) adequately proved, so suspends judgement on (c). I believe Mundy probably right on (a), follow Hordern on (b) and am consequently cautious on (c). See J. L. Biget, *Annales* XLII (1987), pp. 137–40; W. L. Wakefield, *CHR* LXIII (1987), pp. 328 –9. *Repression* is a major but problematic work.

[34]   R. Foreville, 'Les statuts synodaux et renouveau pastoral du XIIIe siècle dans le Midi de la France', *CF* VI, pp. 119–50 at pp. 136–7.

[35]   M. H. Vicaire, 'L'action de l'enseignement et de la prédication des Mendiants vis à vis des Cathares', *CF* XX, pp. 277–304; 'L'action de St Dominique sur la vie regulière des femmes en Languedoc', *CF* XXIII, pp. 217–40; J. H. Mundy, 'Charity and social work in Toulouse, 1100 and 1250', *Traditio* XXII (1966), pp. 203–87.

[36]   *JDH*, pp. 271–2, quotation, p. 272 from Doat 22 fols. 226r–227r.

years of greater security it had remained a strongpoint for Raimond's family and some perfect and was a place of pilgrimage. It lay in a convenient position at the frontiers of the lands of Toulouse and Foix. Now it assumed a new importance. It looked wellnigh impregnable, since its height, its rocky crags and the lack of any approach route except from the south-west, meant that it could only be taken by a substantial army after a long siege. From this date it grew as a mission centre from which leaders could travel down, comfort the perfect, carry out ritual functions, console and preach. Under pressure, the *faidit* knights and their families assembled there. Raimond invited his cousin to join him and gave him his daughter in marriage.

A community perhaps four to five hundred strong grew up in this mountain refuge, not only in the fortress but in a village scattered round it at the summit with its own defences, workshops, housing for artisans and their families, devoted to Catharism but not consoled, plus numerous communities of male and female perfect who worked to support themselves and serve the village. It had no peasants and no cultivable land close by, and was dependent on levies and collections and the sale of goods; in time of intense need, as in 1233–4 and again in the winter of 1241–2, urgent collections were made in their support. It had an effective garrison under Pierre Roger and spiritual leadership under Guilhabert de Castres who reinforced the hierarchy of the Church by consecrating at Montségur a certain Teuto as bishop of Agen, Vigouroux de la Bacone as *filius major* and Jean Cambiaire as *filius major* for Toulouse.

Montségur was unique. Only Cathars and Cathar sympathizers lived there and it developed in consequence an intense inner life. Pilgrims came, sometimes the ill and aged to be consoled, sometimes relatives visiting perfect who had chosen to live there, sometimes sympathizers staying for instruction and inspiration, bringing provisions for their stay. Guilhabert probably died a natural death on the sacred mountain which his vision had helped to create: his last known act was the consoling of Arnaud Dejean in 1240 or 1241. His decision of 1232 created a remarkable focus for Cathar belief and practice, but it also gathered in one spot many of the most devoted supporters of the faith vulnerable to a determined and well-equipped besieging force.[37]

The perfect and their supporters

Everywhere in the Cathar world, the perfect occupied centre stage. They alone were the Church; only their prayers were efficacious. In contrast, the believers who attended them, witnessed their breaking of bread and listened to their sermons were perpetual postulants. The ritual exchange of the *melioramentum* had a peculiar pathos. Still in the power of Satan, the

---

[37]   M. Roquebert *L'Epopée Cathare* IV: *Mourir à Montségur* (Toulouse, 1989) (stresses Montségur as '*un clan familial*' with strong mutual obligations); Brenon, *Visage*, pp. 249–69; *JDH*, pp. 271–2 (Cathar bishops); Duvernoy, in *CEC* XXXIV (1969), p. 39 (Guilhabert's death).

believer could not pray to God; instead, he or she had to beg the perfect to utter the prayer. Abasement on the knees, with the palms on the ground or perhaps stretched out on a bench, dramatically emphasized the gulf between the perfect who saved and the earth-bound believer. In the most solemn form of the ceremony, three profound inclinations of the head on to the hands, so far as to kiss them, was accompanied by 'Bless us' (*benedicite*), 'Lord', or 'good Christian' or 'good lady', 'the blessing of God and your own', 'Pray God for us' and on the third inclination, 'Lord, pray God for this sinner that he deliver him from an evil death and lead him to a good end.' The perfect responded affirmatively to the first and second prayers and to the third at greater length alluding to the *consolamentum*: 'God be prayed that God will make you a good Christian and lead you to a good end.' [38]

The ritual exchange was an act of faith. Honors, wife of Giraud de Castelnau, a witness in the great enquiry of 1245–6, remembered on the occasion when the perfect were present that the lady of the house in Toulouse enjoined her to give the *melioramentum* and showed her how to do it, though the perfect told her not to perform the rite unless she believed in their status. [39]

The *apparellamentum* was a monthly rite, a collective confession of faults by the perfect, gathered for the ceremony presided over by a deacon or, on certain special occasions, the bishop. Touring his jurisdiction to hear this collective confession was one of the prime duties of a deacon, who was always male; no doubt it was an opportunity for pastoral care, as he could be expected to inquire into the welfare of a community of perfect, and for picking up information on security and possible dangers, or on economic problems.

An Occitanian version of the *apparellamentum*, described as the service ('*lo servisi*'), has survived. In the presence of a deacon or other members of the hierarchy, the assembled company of perfect say together, 'We have come before God and before you and before the order of the Holy Church to receive the Service, pardon and penance for all our sins ...' In beautiful phrases, they go on to lament and ask pardon for a series of offences, some of a kind familiar to any monk – distraction, malice and idle words – others in language tinged with implications of dualism as when they say, 'For many are our sins wherein we offend every day, night and day ... voluntarily and involuntarily, and more by our will which evil spirits arouse in us in the flesh in which we are clothed', going on to speak of putting aside 'every desire of the flesh and every impurity'. The rite concludes with a powerful plea, unmistakably Cathar, 'O Lord, judge and condemn the imperfections of the

---

[38]   Y. Hagman, *Catharism: a Medieval Echo of Manichaeism or of Primitive Christianity?* (originally PhD thesis, History of Religions, Lund, 1988), esp. pp. 74–85. Fullest account of rituals, *GRK* II (1), *Der Kult, die religiöse Praxis, die Kritik am Kult und Sakramenten der Katholischen Kirche, Der Kult* (Bad Honnef, 1982), pp. 1–447; *meliora-mentum*, pp. 4–38; significance, pp. 35–7, noting Catholic misunderstanding implicit in inquisitorial term '*adoratio*', p. 36; J. Guiraud, *Histoire de l'inquisition* I (Paris, 1935), p. 183; evidence of low abasement, Doat 24 fol. 136v (WLW).
[39]   WLW using MS 609 fol. 90v.

flesh. Have no pity on the flesh, born of corruption, but show mercy to the spirit, which is imprisoned. Direct for us the days, the hours, the obeisances, the fasts, the prayers, and the preachings, as is the custom of good Christians, that we be not judged or condemned among felons at the Day of Judgement ...' [40]

Supporters were often present at the ritual and might hear a sermon from the presiding deacon. The occasion would reinforce reverence for the perfect, revealed in all their anxious care to avoid offences as they walked the tightrope of precise observances, fasts and abstinences, and increase awareness of the holiness of their Church, seen as line after line of perfect stretching back to the apostles; early in the rite the perfect recalled before God 'the salvation of all righteous, glorious Christians', 'blessed ancestors at rest' and 'brothers here present'.[41] It resembled the Catholic liturgy except that in place of the saints of the calendar there were the 'righteous, glorious Christians', the Cathars. Provided the perfect did not fall into such sins as required a re-consoling, the *apparellamentum* served as a means of purification from the infiltration of earthly desires and contacts, and a multitude of tiny infractions of the rules of the life they had accepted.

A later section of the same MS, best described as 'rules of conduct for various occasions', shows what this could mean.[42] It is concerned primarily with prescribing in detail prayers and procedures to follow when the perfect was out in the world away from the community house. A tender conscience is at work in this little *aide-mémoire*, a very precise and rigorist one. A deacon, perhaps a bishop, is concerned that a perfect should not pick up any personal belonging left lying in the road unless sure it can be returned to its owner, and gives advice on what to do if a perfect happens upon an animal or bird in a trap. A perfect should normally release an animal, which contained an imprisoned soul, but must always leave a recompense for the hunter deprived of his prey – if that is not available, the perfect must not interfere.[43] The prayer, i.e. the paternoster, features repeatedly: to be able to say it and address God as Father was the privilege to which a perfect attained only after the *consolamentum* and its arduous preliminaries. So he is told that if he is travelling on horseback he should say a 'Double', i.e. the paternoster sixteen times. It was a kind of talisman: perfect (described as Christians) should say the prayer 'when embarking in a boat, when entering a town, or when crossing a stream by a plank or a dangerous bridge'.[44] It was most intimately associated with eating and drinking, the regulations rigid. 'If a Christian wants to drink during the day, he should have prayed to God twice or more after eating. And if Christians drink after the evening Double, let them perform another

---

[40] *WEH*, pp. 484–5; comment, p. 466; *GRK* II (1), pp. 383–440; see also *JDR*, pp. 203–16.

[41] *WEH*, p. 484.

[42] Ibid., pp. 491–4; see *GRK* II (1), pp. 354–82.

[43] M. R. Harris, 'Le problème des bonshommes devant l'animal piégé dans le rituel Cathare Occitan', *Heresis* II (1984), pp. 15–19.

[44] *WEH*, p. 491; role of prayers, *GRK* II (1), p. 382.

Double.' In such minutiae lay ample opportunity for infractions and for burdened consciences.

The ethical targets of the perfect were high, as both the ritual of the *apparellamentum* and *consolamentum* demonstrates, but much emphasis in their way of life lay on the minutiae and punctilious observance of ritual, prayers and fasting: it was for this they seem especially to have been esteemed by their flock. Their common prayer ran, 'We go among worldly people, we mingle, talk and eat with them and thus we sin in many things so that we harm our brothers and our souls.'[45] Believers were edified by the spectacle of the perfect wrestling with the temptations of the flesh and accepting penance. The deacon imposed collective penances, often accompanied by a sermon; individuals may have been given penances of their own but information is lacking.

In days of relative freedom, quite large numbers of supporters would gather to the ritual of the *consolamentum* of a healthy candidate, hear the solemn injunctions to a high ethical and ascetic life; in the death-bed ceremonies, a small family group would witness the quiet, often secret, arrival of the perfect and the giving of their supreme gift, an assurance of salvation. The perfect had to arrive when death was imminent but the candidate still able to speak: even in days of toleration, this must have been difficult, involving journeying, perhaps by night, and interruption of routine. The devotion which perfect showed in administering the *consolamentum*, unmistakably mirrored in inquisition records, maintained respect for them.

On formal occasions, a perfect would preside at table to bless the meal, to bless, break and distribute bread on the pattern of Jesus in the gospels.[46] Arnaude de Lamothe, in training with her sister in the house of perfect at Villemur, remembered how meals were enfolded in the rituals of the perfect. 'She and her sister', the record runs, 'ate with the women at the same table, eating bread blessed by the heretics and other food put on the table. And whatever they ate, and when beginning each drink, they would each say "*Benedicite*" and the heretics answered "May God bless you".'[47] Whether within a community of perfect or with supporters at table, the constant duty of prayer, the performance of ritual, the sacred powers of the perfect were presented to the perfect themselves, to young postulants and to supporters in the world.

Formalities highlighted the unique position of the perfect, but other factors strengthened their appeal. Catharism was a fashion for a significant period of time amongst some members of the elite of this society[48] and it long retained its hold within the rural nobility; in consequence, it received its share of their wealth and could afford to use, buy and copy books. A

---

[45]   *WEH*, pp. 484–5. Psychology of perfect ably sketched, R. Manselli, 'Eglises et théologies Cathares', *CF* III, pp. 129–76.
[46]   Blessing of bread, *GRK* II (1), pp. 55–85 is indispensable; note correction of *JDR* at p. 85.
[47]   Murray, transl. Doat 23 fol. 3v.
[48]   'a distinguished way to make one's salvation', *JDH*, p. 135.

gospel book or a New Testament was an essential instrument for the administering of the *consolamentum*: in the Provençal ritual the ceremony proper opens with the candidate receiving the book from the hand of the elder, then listening to an exhortation heavily based on gospel texts and finally having the book placed on his head by the elder, while another perfect put his right hand on the candidate.[49] By promising to observe the way of life of the perfect, the candidate was accepting the standards set by the gospel as the Cathars understood it. A gospel book was equally essential for the consoling of the sick.

To read and expound Scripture was another of a perfect's duties, sometimes explicitly noted by believers in their evidence to inquisitors. A demonstration of the authority of the perfect in exposition occurred in the hall of a knight at Labécède about 1236–7, when in quasi-ritual fashion a scribe and notary read the text of the Passion, the perfect expounding: the presence of the notary, a profession growing in importance in the region, and apparently represented in Catharism in a proportion beyond normal statistical expectation, gave weight to the occasion.[50]

When the deacon Raymond Fort was apprehended by the sub-bayle of Caraman about 1240, two men who were with him escaped with his 'book', presumably a gospel used in consoling. It was entrusted to believers and returned to him when he managed to escape in Toulouse and return to his pastoral duties. Supporters arranged a collection to bribe both the bayle and sub-bayle not to take further action.[51] The book was plainly a valuable and essential item of equipment for a deacon, like a skilled craftsman's set of tools.

Books gave prestige. Probably a majority of the numerous references by witnesses to 'books of the heretics' were to the New Testament or books from it. But there were others. Arnald Faure had a 'book of medicine' which he left with a believer in Auriac.[52] Another supporter had 'many writings' about the warfare of God and Lucifer,[53] another a 'text of the heretics' paternoster', presumably with the Cathar reading 'supersubstantial bread'.[54] Durand of Huesca, in his *Contra Manicheos* of 1223–4, reproduced the text of a Cathar polemic which would otherwise be unknown to us.[55] A suspect believer in the inquisition held in Quercy 1241–2 kept a 'book of the heretics' which he was ready to lend out.[56] Another witness remembered seeing a cache containing the Old and New Testaments, the Prophets and three other works hidden in a grotto in the valley of the Lot near Vers in Quercy: no one can now say whether they were the books of one well-

[49] *WEH*, pp. 488–91.
[50] P. Biller, 'The Cathars of Languedoc and written materials', *BHL*, pp. 61–82 at pp. 75, 82.
[51] Wakefield, in *JMH* XII, p. 233.
[52] Biller, in *BHL*, p. 70.
[53] Ibid., p. 69; WLW.
[54] Biller, in *BHL*, p. 69.
[55] C. Thouzellier, *Un Traité Cathare inédit du début du XIIe siècle d'après le 'Liber contra manicheos' de Durand de Huesca* (Louvain, Paris, 1961).
[56] Biller, in *BHL*, p. 77.

equipped perfect or represented a group library.[57] Believers themselves owned books and safeguarded those of the perfect when they could not keep them.

The perfect gained respect because they evidently had a part in the world of books and learning: some were veterans of debate with Catholic churchmen, could handle Scripture and impress their hearers. The Occitanian ritual has Latin material in it, further impressing its hearers. Though the legate interrogating two perfect in Toulouse in 1178 scorned their ignorance of Latin and the necessity of treating doctrinal issues in the vernacular, it is unlikely to have been characteristic of the elite in the thirteenth century.[58] While the Languedocian perfect lacked the speculative brilliance and quarrelsomeness of the Cathar leadership in Italy, they were still able to hold their own in preaching and debate against Catholics, and convince followers of the rightfulness of their interpretation of Scripture. Hearers remembered their sermons – Arnaud Huc, the deacon, preaching about the fatted calf at Sorèze, Pons de Sainte Foy at Lanta talking to women supporters about Martha and Mary as symbols of hope.[59] At least until the friars' calibre of preaching began to have its effect, the perfect could match and excel in quality run-of-the-mill Catholic clergy.

The educating power of Cathars was a potential weapon in their hand: it was known that nobles handed over their daughters to the heretics to be brought up, when they were unable to look after them themselves.[60] At Le Mas about 1235 a boy whose mother was a warm believer was asked if he would come with them: they promised that they would make him a good scholar, no doubt assuming at the same time that they could make him a good perfect. His duty of herding cattle at first prevented him but he eventually went to join them. Firm believer as she was, his mother was not prepared to accept this, went to the house at Le Mas and, berating him, pulled him out by the hair.[61] The knight Maffre de Paulhac recalled accepting the *consolamentum* at the age of fourteen and staying four years in a house of the perfect, who wanted him to learn grammar and believed he would become 'a great pillar of the Church'.[62]

Unlike the stricter Catholic orders, such as the Carthusians, the perfect were not hidden away in remote places but were in constant contact with their faithful. Cistercians had sought desert places in their flight from the temptations of the world; St Bernard's dynamic personality and the needs of the Church had drawn them back into activity in preaching and intervening in the cause of reform. Even so, they returned from the rough and tumble to their monasteries and estates. This was never so for the perfect. Their

[57]   H. Blaquière and Y. Dossat, 'Les Cathares au jour le jour, confessions inédites de Cathares quercynois', *CF* III, pp. 259–98 at p. 284, comment, Dossat, in *CF* III, p. 89, Biller, in *BHL*, p. 71.
[58]   *WEH*, p. 197.
[59]   WLW using Doat 25, fols 269r–v, 314v.
[60]   Above, p. 68.
[61]   Wakefield, in *CHR* LXIX (1983),p. 217.
[62]   Brenon, in *EO*, p. 225.

communities were small, twenty at maximum, informal, generally based in households, rapidly instituted, dispersed, or re-formed, in easy, lasting contact with supporters and neighbours. As external pressures grew, places of refuge in remote and inaccessible places became more significant, but the original and natural milieu for the perfect was an ordinary house or workshop in town or village. The aristocratic houses which mattered so much for the prestige of Catharism were no doubt supported by the rents and income of estates or widows' portions, but the others had to support themselves.

The perfect combined rigidity in diet, fasting, the saying of prayers and the performance of ritual with flexibility in economic life. The Benedictine stress on stability of place as a key element in sustaining spiritual life was not significant in Catharism: persecution, the needs of families and the accidents of patronage meant that individual houses came and went in a locality, and communities moved when it was needful. The rituals required no separate room or structure, with images or shrines: Cathars scorned the setting aside of a building to act as a church in the Catholic fashion. The initiation of a community was thus a matter of the greatest simplicity and cheapness. An *ancianus* exercised authority in a house of perfect men, with an equivalent office for women; these officers would carry out the rite of blessing bread at meals.

The inquisitors recorded large numbers of houses in places where the religion had struck root – as many as fifty in Mirepoix, for example, a hundred at Villemur – and they provided an essential basis for its practice.[63] Sometimes the sexes were not rigidly segregated. Raymond de Pereille, lord of Montségur, kept his mother and mother-in-law, both *perfectae*, in his house for some thirty years.[64] The houses of the communities were so open that serious breaches of the ascetic way of life to which the perfect bound themselves could not long have been concealed. Working practices facilitated contact with the rank and file of believers or those casually interested. The perfect were their own advertisement.

The interpretation of perfect as dreamy contemplatives without active working lives has long been exploded; so too the belief that they used instruments of work in a largely symbolic fashion, as Gandhi did with his loom.[65] There were perfect who were weavers, tailors, shoemakers, barbers or dealers in skins.[66] At Hautpoul near Mazamet in the modern *département* of Tarn a house of five had workplaces constructed for them in the neighbouring woods.[67] At Fanjeaux weaving was strong, children bringing

[63]   Ibid., p. 233; Dossat, in *CF* III, pp. 72–3.
[64]   Brenon, in *EO*, pp. 217, 221.
[65]   J. Duvernoy, 'Les Albigeois dans la vie sociale et économique de leur temps', *Annales de l'Institut d'Etudes Occitanes, Actes du colloque de Toulouse de Septembre 1963*, pp. 64–72. The author asks me to note its early date; in fact, it transformed understanding of labour of perfect. See also *JDR*, p. 196.
[66]   Occupations as listed: WLW using MS 609 fols 180r, 166v, Doat 21, fol. 190v, MS 609 fols 99r, 150v, 153v, Doat 21 fol. 197r, Doat 23 fols 117r–18r, 257v–59v.
[67]   Duvernoy, 'Les Albigeois', p. 7, citing Doat 23 fol. 249b.

bobbins in exchange for nuts.[68] Some rented land,[69] others occupied humbler positions. Arnald of Villepinte and Bernard of Saint-Estève reaped grain for William of Le Mas in about 1225.[70] One witness remembered seeing two perfect stopping to pray in the course of their work among the vines of Guilhabert Alzeu.[71]

Perfectae also filled a variety of roles. Aristocratic women were not cut off from the personal contacts of their world: Blanche of Laurac gave hospitality to knights and squires of Aimery de Montréal, and Berbegueira of Loubens, wife of a knight of Puylaurens, continued to visit her friends among a small circle of perfect, the mother and sisters of Sicard of Puylaurens.[72] A *perfecta*, Lombarde of Villepinte, visiting at Fanjeaux as guest of an adherent, her son-in-law's brother, was occupied over a period of three weeks in little ceremonies, receiving the *melioramentum* and blessing bread. Sometimes it is impossible wholly to disentangle personal and family contacts and religious purposes. Children were brought up in these houses; sometimes a grandmother brought in a grandson or granddaughter, as a house with resources could provide an aristocratic upbringing not cut off from the world. Azalais du Cucuroux took in her granddaughter Ermessinde at Laurac when she was four and looked after her for six years; aunts looked after young nieces.[73] Houses of men might also include children to enable a consoled father to bring up his son.[74] Some houses could more fairly be described as hospices than organized communities.

Perfectae often moved from community house to community house; training might well exact movement, as in the case of Dulcie Faure of Villeneuve-la-Comtal, who left her husband about 1226 and at first took refuge with the perfect of her own village, then was escorted to a house directed by Blanche of Laurac in Castelnaudary where she stayed for a year, finally entering formal training after having stayed a further year in another community founded by Blanche, at Laurac itself. The implication is that Laurac was better equipped for the instruction of a neophyte.[75] A witness in 1245 remembered baking bread for three women who lived in a wood at La Guizole near Les Cassès and span wool to support themselves.[76] Even under pressure and forced to move or hide in out of the way places, women perfect were concerned to pay what they could or provide some return to the believers who supported them.

---

[68]   Roquebert, in *EO*, pp. 175, 176.

[69]   A. Roach, 'The Cathar economy', *Reading Medieval Studies* XII (1986), pp. 51–71 at pp. 60–1; review, M. Roquebert, *Heresis* IX (1987), pp. 123–4 (rejects Roach on consoling at Montségur).

[70]   I follow closely W. L. Wakefield, 'Heretics and inquisitors: the case of Auriac and Cambiac', *JMH* XII (1986), pp. 225–37.

[71]   *BF*, p. 206.

[72]   Brenon, in *EO*, p. 226; general background of women's role in society, J. H. Mundy, *Men and Women at Toulouse in the Age of the Cathars* (Toronto, 1990).

[73]   Roquebert, *L'Epopée* I, pp. 112–13; *BF*, pp. 134, 135.

[74]   WLW using MS 609 fol. 246r, Doat 22 fol. 40v.

[75]   *BF*, pp. 131–2.

[76]   *JDR*, p. 198.

Preaching or debating publicly was a very rare occurrence for women and was practised principally by members of the upper class, who had the confidence and the education to do it. The most famous case in the pre-Crusade era was Esclarmonde de Foix, who, according to Puylaurens, was told by a Cistercian at the debate at Pamiers in 1207, 'Go to your distaff, madam. It is not proper that you should speak at such a gathering.'[77] In over five thousand interrogations in MS 609, the record of the massive investigation in 1245–6, witnesses reported observing women perfect on 1,435 occasions but saw them preaching on only twelve. Three hundred and eighteen *perfectae* are named, of whom only eleven are known to have preached. In her long career, Arnaude de Lamothe admitted to preaching only during a stay of three weeks at Massac.[78]

Perfectae diffused Catharism in personal conversation. Pierre Magis, a building worker from the Montauban region, was led to believe that 'the heretics were good people' after he had eaten at the table of a *perfecta*, who took the opportunity to talk to him and other workers.[79] They catechized young girls and helped to bring up children in the faith; in formal communities older women would encourage and instruct young candidates for the *consolamentum*. Their expositions and conversations mattered greatly, but preaching proper remained a man's task. Except in a grave emergency, consoling also lay in the hands of men. Witnesses in MS 609 gave evidence of over 150 consolings: in none of these did a woman perform the rite.[80] As persecution grew, rank and file perfect were called in a little more often than in the absence of deacons – still men. Arnaude de Lamothe as a young candidate was not consoled in the house of the women perfect at Villemur where she was trained, but was taken to a deacon's house. Raimonde Jougla, whose stormy history included her father's throwing her naked out of his house, allegedly because of her Cathar tendencies, but in reality because he believed the story that she had become Guilhem de Gouzens's mistress, consorted with women perfect who were her friends, delayed her consoling but finally accepted it from a man in a knight's house at Laurac.[81]

Mothers influenced daughters, with varying success. If they were too young, they were likely to leave, perhaps because their personalities were not yet formed and they were yielding only to persuasion; perhaps, as Anne Brenon surmises, because the fasting and abstinence was too much for young appetites and the presence of older women oppressive; perhaps again because the true motive for placing them was economic. Na Comdors of Le Mas said that her mother forced her to be consoled when she was not yet ten. The very young often did not stay: in the conventional phrase,

---

[77]   *Chronica*, ed. J. Beyssier (Paris, 1904), p. 435, trans. Abels and Harrison, *MS* XLI (1979), pp. 227–8.
[78]   Ibid., p. 228 and n. 70; Murray transl. Doat 23 fol. 10r.
[79]   *BF*, p. 214.
[80]   Abels and Harrison, *MS* XLI, p. 227.
[81]   Ibid.; *BF*, pp. 265–7.

they 'ate meat and took a husband'; on the other hand, they might well remain believers.[82]

Houses had their own women superiors with a role comparable to that of a prioress in Catholicism. But this was as high as a *perfecta* could rise: the hierarchy of a Cathar diocese was recruited solely from *perfecti*. Women evidently had a crucial supporting role, but not a leading one. They aided the men with gifts of money and food, gave them accommodation, listened to their preaching, took the advice and orders of a male hierarchy, brought candidates to be consoled by men, made their *apparellamentum* in the presence of a male deacon.[83]

Motives for undertaking the *consolamentum* or becoming a believer varied greatly. Sometimes, as in the case of Arnaude de Lamothe, one can only surmise that a deep religious commitment was at work: servants said of Orbria, wife of Guilhem Sans, that she 'so loved the heretics that in order to listen to their sermons she had left her husband and wanted to have herself made a heretic', that is, be consoled.[84]

Some, though committed, shrank from the ultimate test of the fire: Raimonde Jougla confessed that it was this that made her draw back when her companions were burnt. Finas, brought up in a Cathar family at Rabastens and, at the time of her confession, wife of the pro-Cathar lord of Tauriac, took her Catharism cautiously. She was a frequenter of the perfect but on one occasion took a lettered adviser to look in their books to check on what they said. Fabrissa, daughter-in-law of the matriarch Garsende of Le Mas, was interested enough to leave her husband to join Garsende with a view to being consoled, but succumbed to her husband's persuasion and returned to him; one may suspect the driving force of an unhappy marriage kept some women in a perfect community. In about 1206 the young Audiart Ebrard was consoled: she stayed only a year and then took a husband. Some thirty years later she was given the relatively light penance of wearing yellow crosses on her clothing, which she had to admit she did her best to conceal. Hers had been a conversion without depth.[85]

Probably two emotions warred with each other, which have a broadly determining role for women generally: one was the satisfaction of the *perfecta*'s life, the sense of community, the purpose given to life by the strenuous fasting and prayer, the undoubted attraction of a leadership role on occasions when *perfecti* were not present, the status and reverence due to the perfect and the constant receiving of the *melioramentum* from all supporters. Most gave it, men and women, even if some aristocrats withheld it from her, as Bernard Oth, an idiosyncratic supporter seems to have done, admitting to giving the *melioramentum* only to his grandmother.[86]

Against this was the darker side of Cathar teaching. Women supporters in Cambiac learned to regret their attitude to Ermessende Viguier, a young,

[82]   *BF*, pp. 132–3, 180.
[83]   *JDR*, p. 265.
[84]   *BF*, p. 105.
[85]   *BF*, pp. 267 (Jougla), pp. 170–1 (Finas), pp. 130–1 (Ebrard).
[86]   See Doat 24 fols 83v–84v for Bernard's years with Blanche.

pregnant housewife, who was laughed at when she attended their gathering and told she was carrying a demon in her belly. She never forgot the insult and took a terrible revenge when, some twenty-three years later in 1245, she exposed a conspiracy of silence in the village to the parish priest. Her neighbours imprisoned her overnight in a wine tun to keep her silent before the inquisitors, saying to her son who held her hand, 'Boy, do you want to help this hag who wants to destroy us all?' It was of no avail: Ermessende had long been a determined enemy of Cathars and had quarrelled with her husband on the issue. The coarse laughter of the women was something more than village spite for it sprang directly from Cathar ideology.[87] When a *perfecta* visited a sympathizer, pregnant wife of a Toulouse merchant, she condoled with her, advising her to ask God to liberate her from the demon in her belly; another believer was warned that if she died while pregnant she could not be saved.[88] This paradox lay at the heart of Catharism. All the evidence shows that it spread through the family, was sustained by family links, that matriarchs played a major part in diffusing the faith and yet the core of belief was profoundly hostile to maternity and the family.

Statistics derived from MS 609 throw light on what was happening. The MS contains the names of 719 active perfect of whom 318 were women – slightly less than 45 per cent.[89] This is a high figure. In contemporary Catholicism, the nuns would certainly not have equalled or nearly equalled the total number of men professionally engaged in religious duties – priests, monks, friars, clerks. Attitudes to sexuality were thus not deterring women from entering the ranks of the perfect. Moreover, Catharism was exerting a pull on some women that Catholicism was not – partly, perhaps, because of the respect which women perfect enjoyed and the openness of their houses; partly because of the lack of provision for the monastic life for women in the Lauragais before the foundation of Prouille.

At the believer level the position was very different. Of 466 cases of believers and sympathizers within MS 609, only 125 were women, that is, only 26.8 per cent,[90] a clear indication that the anti-procreative ideology was repellent to the average woman. It is also a likely explanation for the greater appeal of Waldensianism which gave considerable scope to women and where, though celibacy was valued, the movement was not touched by the outright hostility of Catharism to sexuality. The record of the inquisition by Peter Seila in Quercy in 1241–2 included 646 names: of those who had clearly embraced Waldensianism or Catharism, the Waldensians had 52 per cent, the Cathars 30 per cent women.[91]

---

[87]   Wakefield, *JMH* XII, pp. 232, 233; ideology, originally Bogomil, Puech and Vaillant, *Traité*, p. 81.
[88]   Doat 22 fol. 57r, MS 609 fols. 117v, 239v.
[89]   Abels and Harrison, *MS* XLI, p. 225.
[90]   Ibid., p. 241.
[91]   Schneider, *Europäisches Waldensertum*, p. 12; survey, P. Segl, 'Die religiöse Frauenbewegung in Südfrankreich im 12. und 13. Jahrhundert zwischen Häresie und Orthodoxie', in *Religiöse Frauenbewegung und mystische Frömmigkeit im Mittelalter*, I, ed. P. Dinzelbacher and D. R. Bauer (Cologne, Vienna, 1988), pp. 91–116;

Loose talk about a preponderance of houses of women perfect has to be given up. In an unpublished judgement, W. L. Wakefield has argued that houses of *perfecti*, though less publicized in modern writing, were probably more numerous. Duvernoy's calculation of the numbers of *perfecti* and *perfectae* before 1245 points in the same direction.[92] If, as a result of modern scholarship, notions of a special appeal of Catharism to women must now be definitely abandoned, the anecdotal evidence of the resilience, courage and supporting power of those women who did become perfect or believers and their importance throughout Cathar history is unmistakable. But they worked with and through families. Evidence from an investigation at Auriac shows, for example, that of the fifty-three female believers there, thirty-eight had one or more relatives involved in Catharism and twenty-six attended meetings, preachings, consolings and the like accompanied by their husbands.[93]

Much as within Catholicism, levels of adherence varied and supporters could be ill instructed. A strange belt and braces approach to salvation led one dying woman to accept both the Catholic extreme unction and the Cathar *consolamentum*; another abandoned Catharism after one of the perfect told her that a candle she intended to light to the Virgin in church would be of more use in her own home.[94]

Catharism spread in an atmosphere of crude anticlericalism. At Le Mas, Bernard of Quiriès, of a heretical family, was accused of relieving himself on the tonsure of an acolyte during a dice game 'in opprobrium ... of the whole Catholic Church'; in 1235 the same man formed one of a group in an attack with swords and stones on the prior of Le Mas, who stole two horses and threatened to kill any monk who came out.[95] Bernard Oth's record as a believer has 'smudges', in Wakefield's phrase; his quarrel with Archbishop Peter Amiel of Narbonne was no doubt intensified by the inheritance of Cathar teaching and by Amiel's territorial policy, but it owed a great deal to Oth's aggressiveness and desire for land and in 1232 issued in theft, cattle raiding, burning of buildings and violence towards the archbishop. Oth's case also shows us how a believer could ruthlessly manipulate the position of the Cathars to his advantage. He determined to be rid of his wife Nova, at one time trying to force her to be consoled, and so frightening her that she left him altogether; at another offering Archbishop Amiel a deal whereby he would receive an annulment in return for the betrayal of Nova

---

comments, E. McLaughlin, 'Die Frau und mittelalterliche Häresie: ein Problem der Geschichte der Spiritualität', *Concilium* XII (1976), pp. 34–44; M. Hanssler, *Katharismus in Südfrankreich: Struktur der Sekte und inquisitorische Verfolgung in der zweiten Hälfte des 13. Jahrhunderts* (originally PhD thesis) University of Regensburg 1991, pp. 92–109, demonstrates exaggeration of numbers of houses in Koch, *Frauenfrage*, casts doubt on 'feminine emancipation' hypothesis; excellent statistics.

[92]   J. Duvernoy, 'La liturgie et l'église Cathare', *CEC* XXXIII (1967), pp. 3–16, XXXV (1967), pp. 17–30 at pp. 25–6.

[93]   Abels and Harrison, *MS* XLI, p. 245.

[94]   Ibid., p. 244.

[95]   Wakefield, in *CHR* LXIX, pp. 216, 217.

and other heretics who, he said, were constantly in his hall.[96] All was not idealism; there was light and shade within the Cathar community as there was in Catholicism.

The perfect depended in a casual, trusting manner on believers and sympathizers as protectors and guides. Ever eager to classify heretics and their offences, inquisitors knew a category of *ductores* and *receptores*. *Ductores* knew the ground, they could escort their charges by night, avoiding hostile neighbourhoods and the traps and ambushes of the enemy; *receptores* kept safe houses, fed and supported the perfect for minimal reward.[97] Sometimes guiding appeared to be a simple business transaction; those who were caught pleaded that they were unaware that their clients were heretics, more often they were sympathizers who might expect payment. Peter de Corneliano and his uncle escorted seven perfect on a journey for a fee of ten solidi, but when they refused to pay, Peter was turned off Catharism and refused to adore heretics for thirty-four years. In 1237 Arnaud Roger, a knight of Mirepoix, received financial reward for guiding and in 1238 was given a share in two pounds of pepper for helping with the guiding of eight heretics from Montségur.[98] Guillaume Garnier, a herdsman in the countryside round Lanta who worked for the pro-Cathar family of the Auriol, showed an extraordinary devotion to Arnaude de Lamothe and her sister, guiding them from one refuge to another, constructing cabins for them in the woods or putting up tents; he was utterly committed to the Cathar cause and financial reward seems to have played no part at all.[99]

The economic relationship of perfect and many sympathizers could hardly be called commercial, though perfect often wished to make some gift or give money for the services or food they received. Little tokens showed affection and gratitude – silk, a felt hat, underpants. So, in Gourdon, Arnaud Rectus was given a cup after he had shaved some heretics and given them wine; another sympathizer received a pair of scissors in return for substantial services in acting as a depository and donating food and shelter.[100]

Food was the most common contribution made by supporters – grain, flour, bread, ash-cakes, fish, cabbages, onions, chick peas, beans, raisins, figs, apples, cherries – all the more important as persecution grew more efficient and the perfect found it harder to earn for themselves. Fish provided a boost to the protein in the diet of the perfect, who are best described as fish-eating vegans, and could be valued as a delicacy. When Pons Faber of Villanova wished to lure two perfect into a trap, he gained their trust with the gift of a salted herring.[101]

---

[96]   Wakefield, in *Names* XVIII, pp. 106, 110.
[97]   Dossat, in *CF* III, pp. 89–90.
[98]   Roach, 'Cathar economy', pp. 62–3.
[99]   Roquebert, in *CF* XX, pp. 225–6.
[100]   *JDR*, p. 249 (silk, etc.), Roach, 'Cathar economy', p. 63 (cap, scissors).
[101]   Roach, 'Cathar economy', p. 64; examples of food from WLW unpublished analysis.

The *receptores* suffered the greater risk and inconvenience. They served out of affection and reverence; in return, they could expect little material but much spiritual reward in the perfects' blessing at meals and their lasting presence. Family connections tended to provide the most secure backing. An example of such devotion is the case of B. Remon, who had a sister who was a perfect: he escorted her and her companions from Toulouse to Montauban, paid the heavy sum of fifty solidi for their accommodation and later made her a tunic and cape. In hiding with a companion near Montolieu, Raimond Carabassa relied on his two sons to supply him with food. Pons Viguier of Saint-Paulet in the Lauragais, a poor labourer in a vineyard, gave pathetic witness to the power of filial sentiment when he told the inquisition how he twice took food to his mother after she had received the *consolamentum* but found he could do no more because he was too poor, saying, 'If I had had more, I would willingly have given her more, heretic as she was.' He remained a sympathizer, but his son became a perfect and was imprisoned in the Château Narbonnais in Toulouse, and, at the time of his confession in 1246, his wife had just left him to join, he believed, the perfect.[102]

In an emergency, Cathars could call on a wide support, as in the episode at Roquefort where the women of the village attacked a sergeant of the abbot of Sorèze who had come to arrest two women perfect with sticks and stones. In the ensuing confusion, the women escaped and the abbot was told that the disturbance had arisen because his sergeant had arrested two respectable married women in error. In another case a crowd covered up a consoling ceremony by hurling missiles at the priest's house, thus preventing him from intervening. Such actions could never have been sustained without a strong majority sentiment in favour of the Cathars.[103]

The sentiment had an economic base and had economic effects. On the one side, Cathars were generally more popular because, unlike the Catholics, they did not demand tithes. They were a cheap Church: offerings were voluntary, the more readily given because of the general respect in which the perfect were held. Here lay a likeness to the mendicant friars; though, in contrast to the regular practice of the Franciscans, for example, the Cathars did very little formal begging – it was simply understood that the perfect needed help. But in both cases, the success of the support system, formalized or not, rested on the assent, even enthusiasm, of the donors. The indications are that, while both the perfect and their sympathizers included those who were poor, in its heyday the Church as a whole was quite prosperous. The hierarchy commanded resources of money and manpower. Throughout his career Guilhabert de Castres moved in the best circles, conferring with men of power and escorted by Cathar chivalry. As the position of the Cathars improved in the 1220s, he could build a residence in Fanjeaux: when the threat of persecution grew, as it did in the 1230s, he did not need to flee to cabins in the woods as so many of his fellow perfect did, but was taken by *faidit* lords to their fortresses. At ease in the

---

[102]   Roach, 'Cathar economy', p. 64. (Remon, Carabassa); *BF*, pp. 176–7 (Viguier).
[103]   Hanssler, 'Katharismus', pp. 213–14 from Doat 26 fols 39v–40v.

world of power, he could command resources, at his will Montségur was refortified, and it is from Montségur that we have a glimpse of one way in which his economic power was sustained. About 1239, a dying man bequeathed a horse to the Cathars; Raimond Roger of Toulouse brought it to the bishop at Montségur. They had a meal, the horse was sold to Roger and the proceeds no doubt went to swell the coffers of the movement.[104]

Guilhabert's successor as bishop, Bertrand Marty, also had economic muscle: when he needed an escort in 1232, he lent Pierre Mazerolles two hundred sous, so enrolling him as one of the Cathars' regular escorts.[105] Deacons, the most mobile of all the Cathar leadership, never seem to have had difficulty in financing their journeyings. Anne Brenon argues that, as Catharism emerged from the darkest period of the Albigensian Crusade, deacons succeeded in deploying communities of perfect as part of a strategy of reconquest for the faith, which implies a certain control of the sinews of economic support for the community houses.[106] Cases are known where payment was made for enlargement.

Enemies reproached the Cathars with their wealth. Durand of Huesca derided them as 'mighty traders in acquiring this world's wealth, owning fields, vineyards, their own houses, workshops'. The evidence that they had sufficient resources to sustain and extend their work as a Church is unmistakable. Perfect 'rented and bought houses and had them repaired; they bought utensils, such as forceps and razors, contracted for construction of an apparatus to crush flax and a store chest for grain, rewarded their guides and even made gifts to their friends.'[107] It seems a far cry from the claims made by the Rhineland Cathars of the twelfth century observed by Everwin of Steinfeld to be the poor of Christ 'with no fixed abode fleeing from city to city like sheep from wolves':[108] the favour of a segment of Languedocian aristocracy, the hinge of their success, had modified their ideals.

But the essence of Catharism always lay in asceticism, fasting, celibacy and the renunciation of certain food rather than poverty. From the text of the poor wandering preachers in Matthew 10, the ideal of a series of transient movements of the twelfth century along with the Waldensians and subsequently the friars, the Cathars kept the notion of travelling two by two: like the Waldensians, they attached importance to this. Poverty, however, was transient, the fruit of persecution in Everwin's time, as it was to be again in the later, suffering years in Languedoc. Asceticism remained the unchallenged core of the Cathar appeal.

As further categories of Cathars, the inquisitors listed the *questores* and the *depositarii*; they give clues about the origins of the Cathars' reserves of wealth. The workshops in which the humbler perfect toiled are unlikely to

---

[104] Duvernoy, in *CEC* XXXIV, pp. 33–42, *passim*; aid by *faidits*, p. 40; horse, Roach, 'Cathar economy', p. 65.

[105] J. Duvernoy, 'Bertrand Marty', *CEC* XXXIX (1968), pp. 19–35; Brenon, in *EO*, pp. 220–3; *JDR*, pp. 236–7.

[106] Brenon, in *EO*, p. 220.

[107] WLW analysis; Durand's evidence, Paolini, 'Esiti ereticali ...', p. 160, n. 80.

[108] *WEH*, p. 129.

have done more than provide a livelihood; the small gifts of money and food which came from so many sympathizers plainly oiled the wheels, made life easier and were demonstrations of affection, raising morale. For the core of wealth sustaining the houses and the pastoral campaigning, we must look at the endowments of the higher born and above all the continued flow of bequests, often made at the death-beds of the consoled. The consoling of the dying marked the high point of a supporter's spiritual life. With the muttered words and the imposition of the book, the sick sympathizers received the supreme gift available to them, the rite which assured salvation. It was a moment for generosity. The Cathar Church made its dying supporters aware of the economic aspect: a standard question asked if anything was owed to the Church. Gifts at death were a heretical parallel to the burial fees and offerings customary in orthodoxy – but, it may well be, with a heightened significance. Some gifts were substantial: up to a thousand sous, a vineyard, a bed with its furnishings, though quite small sums, even one sou, were also accepted. More commonly, thirty, forty or fifty sous were given, perhaps with some cheese.[109]

In the case of the sick supporter, Esclarmonde, consoled in the cowshed of Alaman de Roaix at Lanta, the bequest included the small, precious objects of a woman who was not wealthy – a tunic, twenty-two denarii, a linen cloth, a gold coin, a winnowing fan, a cloak.[110] Sometimes there was haggling. Bernard Oth de Niort refused to honour his brother Raymond's bequest, perhaps out of meanness, perhaps because he hoped at the time to make peace with Louis VIII; when he lay wounded at Laurac in 1230, his friend Guilhabert de Castres rebuked him and forced him to give one thousand two hundred sous. According to another, more hostile account, he promised one thousand sous when he thought he was dying and, on recovering, gave only ten.[111] After five years' dispute, a widow gave a bed with furnishings in lieu of the fifty solidi bequeathed by her husband which a fellow executor had refused to honour, she having already given her fifty. The inquisitor's scribe's summary made the bequest sound like a fee agreed on at the death: 'it was given by Serena, widow of Atho Arnaud' he wrote, 'at the demand of the heretics for the heretication of the said Arnaud'.[112] Arnaud Daniel of Sorege in 1229 had a simple solution: he kept a cache of three hundred solidi and showed it to a friend whom he required to fetch the perfect for his consoling and immediately hand over the money.[113]

It was evidently part of a bishop's duties to ensure that bequests were honoured: in 1236 Bertrand Marty demanded, apparently in vain, that Guido Castillon, knight of Mirepoix, hand over a horse left by his brother Isarn when he was consoled at Castelbon. There were sanctions. In 1242, two perfect demanded of Pierre Fournier, a sick barber of Fanjeaux, that he fulfil the testamentary dispositions of his father and mother before he was

[109]   Roach, 'Cathar economy', pp. 55, 56.
[110]   Ibid., p. 54.
[111]   Ibid., p. 55; Wakefield, in *Names* XVIII, p. 299.
[112]   Roach, 'Cathar economy', p. 55 from Doat 24 fols 262v–263r.
[113]   Ibid., pp. 55–6.

consoled; they refused his offer of payment in kind and the encounter broke up with curses from Fournier.[114]

Depositarii acted for the perfect and their supporters, receiving money and legacies on behalf of the Church in informal arrangements based on friendship and trust. Ugo Rotland of Puylaurens was one such and in 1252 kept a pot containing six hundred solidi embedded under his threshold. Alaman de Roaix, pillar of Catharism in Toulouse, was accused in 1237 of having letters entitling him to collect money left to the Church in Cathar wills. Alaman was a man of substance and this was clearly a more formal arrangement.[115]

Questores was another term used by inquisitors for the treasures of the Church, regular collectors of money and gifts, who took offerings, hid reserves and, where necessary, changed money or turned petty coinage into something more substantial. Deacons probably exercised a supervisory role.[116]

Social needs were met by *ad hoc* collections. When Bertrand Marty was arrested by the bayle of Fanjeaux in 1233, a collection of three hundred sous was made in astonishingly short time, with contributions ranging from three to twenty-five sous per head; the bribe delivered, the prisoner was quietly set free in a wood.[117] When famine threatened Montségur, there was a widespread response.[118]

Cathars were accused by their enemies of practising usury. As revealed in the great inquisition of 1245–6, there was little sign of its practice in the countryside; in towns it may have been somewhat different. In general, major practitioners tended to be orthodox in belief, unwilling to draw attention to themselves by any doctrinal deviations. On the other hand, there was no reason why Cathars should reject the practice of usury and they were certainly not adherents of the moral reform of the Paris School of Robert de Courçon, to which Bishop Fulk of Toulouse belonged. It would have been surprising if some supporters holding reserves of Cathar wealth did not practise usury. There is likely to have been a good deal of slander in these charges and it is fair to assume that usury and banking do not account for Cathar reserves of wealth.[119]

Examination of the evidence for the economic life of the Cathars reveals the importance of their hierarchy. Bishops presided, took precedence at all ceremonies, at consoling, the breaking of bread, and were responsible for the appropriate action to be taken when a perfect fell and had to be reconsoled. In their hands lay the governance of their dioceses, the control

---

[114] Duvernoy, in *CEC* xxxix, p. 24 (Castillon); Dossat, in *CF* III, p. 91 (Fournier); full translation, *JDR*, p. 247.
[115] Roach, 'Cathar economy', pp. 58 (Rotland); p. 57 (Roaix).
[116] *JDR*, p. 250 (money); Roach, 'Cathar economy', pp. 57–8 (deacons).
[117] Duvernoy, in *CEC* xxxix, p. 24.
[118] Roach, 'Cathar economy', p. 65.
[119] Lambert, *Medieval Heresy*, 2nd edn, p. 110; shrewd analysis, *JDR*, pp. 252–4. Hanssler, *Katharismus*, pp. 110–28 argues against any major ethical distinction between Catholic clergy and perfect.

of the Cathar economy and the choice of tactics in the long battle with their Catholic enemies.

The Cathars evidently put a high valuation on their bishops, for they introduced the two additional ranks, *filius major*, elder son, and *filius minor*, younger son, in order to secure a smooth succession when a bishop died. The *filius major* became bishop at once: there were no uncertainties and none of the wrangles over succession which stud medieval Church history. Vacancies were unknown: the selection of a new *filius minor* created in effect the next bishop but one. Cathar attitudes to the succession of bishops mirrored their attitude to that of deacons – there is the same passion for security in the sequence of officers, witnessed by the episode in which a believer contrived to get into a prison in order to present Pons de Sainte Foy, deacon of Lanta, with a wax tablet on which he could write the name of his successor.[120] The superior will to unity of the Cathar Churches of Languedoc and, in contrast to Northern Italy, their relative lack of interest in doctrinal debate created an effective and continuous hierarchical structure based on agreed territorial divisions, punctiliously observed. This parallel to the structure of the Catholic Church was an aspect of the determined Cathar claim to be the one true Church in contradistinction to the Church of Satan.

The institution of the episcopate reinforced the role of natural leaders and gave further weight to the Cathar challenge: they seem to have been forceful personalities and none cracked under the pressures of persecution. Betrand Marty, for example, could have escaped from Montségur, did not and died with his flock. It was a feature of Cathar life evidently valued by the perfect, who accepted their commands and attended the Councils they summoned. But bishops appear to have played only a limited part in the epic phase of Cathar growth in Western Europe, and they certainly played no part at all in the hard-fought struggle for a Cathar revival in the Ariège at the turn of the thirteenth and fourteenth centuries. By then they had been driven out of existence.

Doctrine

In a largely oral society in which the symbolism of public acts and ceremonies had a major role, Catharism appears to be a religious movement held together by gestures which surrounded the perfect and emphasized their links to believers. Many had no wish to look beyond these ceremonies, the laying on of hands in the consoling, the blessings, the *melioramentum*. For them it was the life rather than doctrine which moved them. The preaching of the perfect incorporated scriptural texts and alluded to the events and personalities of the Bible, confidently using them together with highly coloured myths of Gnostic type to assert that the Cathar Church was indeed the Church of Christ and the Catholics the instruments of Satan. The believers accepted this and generally, especially before the counter-offensive of the Church had gathered momentum, lacked the instruction and perhaps the will to query the expositions of the perfect.

---

[120]   Dossat, in *CF* III, pp. 73–4.

The early inquisitors of Languedoc were primarily policemen: trained as preachers, the Dominicans deputed to hold inquisitions would certainly exercise their skill in the *sermo generalis*, but beyond this they were investigators demanding information, cross-examining, checking witness's statements against their evidence, seeking full confession. The questions dealt primarily with external acts and contacts, whereby membership of, or a merely superficial sympathy with, Catharism was revealed: to these were appended questions often of a standarized kind about beliefs. So the schedule of questions, which can be reconstructed from MS 609, included such queries as: Have you ever seen heretics (i.e. Cathar perfect)? When? Where? Who else was present? Did you and others adore them? Did you ever witness a *consolamentum*? Did you ever give them anything? This went on to: Did you believe they were good men, speakers of truth, friends of God, even though you knew the Church pursued them? Did you hear their errors about the creation of visible things? About the sacred Host? About baptism? About matrimony? About the resurrection of bodies? Did you believe these?[121] The emphasis was on a knowing disobedience to Church teaching and association with known heretics, and seems rarely to have included a probing of the bases of a witness's beliefs.

This stress on acts rather than doctrine sprang not only from the predilections of inquisitors and the needs of efficient police work, but from the intellectual landscape of the South, advanced in the study of law, comparatively weak in theology. Notoriously, the efforts made by ecclesiastical authority to remedy this deficiency, especially through the foundation of the University of Toulouse, were slow to take effect. The Dominicans and their opponents did battle pre-eminently on the field of rites, obedience and disobedience and ethics. On the Catholic side, there was a lack of the scholastic refutations of heresy which were such a feature of the Italian counter-attack on Catharism; no Languedocian Cathar seems to have been capable of writing an advanced defence of his faith comparable to the Italian *Liber de duobus principibus*. Inquisitorial procedures took precedence and the Cathars themselves seem to have been happy enough with their myths and their fluent and subtle management of Biblical texts. Intellectual development within Catharism which might in time have carried the leadership forward to the level more common in Northern Italy, in turn issuing in internal conflicts about doctrine, was cut short by persecution.[122]

A rare opportunity to glimpse the attitude of a Languedocian believer is afforded by the episode in which a Franciscan, William Garcias, engaged his relative Peter in conversation on belief in the common room of his convent in Toulouse in Lent 1247 while, all unknown to Peter, other friars were listening concealed either on a balcony or among the rafters, later to give evidence on his investigation.[123] Peter expressed his mind in pungent, some-

---

[121]   WLW, analysis, based on MS 609.
[122]   Learning, *CF* v. I owe comment on persecution to Dr Y. Hagman and Mlle P. Jimenez.
[123]   *WHC*, pp. 242–9; orig. Doat 22, C. Douais, *Documents pour servir à l'histoire de l'inquisition dans le Languedoc* II (Paris, 1900), pp. 90–114.

160   *The Cathars of Languedoc*

times apothegmatic, sentences in which positive features of Catharism were
bound up with an explosive hostility to Catholicism. He referred to his wife
as a nincompoop and said he had not had sexual intercourse with her since
Pentecost two years ago, that marriage was prostitution, and that there was
'no matrimony except that of the soul with God'.[124] The Roman Church was
a 'harlot who gives poison',[125] the law of Moses 'nothing but shadow and
vanity ... that God who gave that law was a scoundrel'.[126] A crucial text from
the first chapter of St John's gospel emerged: 'All things were made by him;
and without him was not anything made that was made.' In the Vulgate, the
term used is *nihil*, '*Sine ipso factum est nihil.*' Peter followed a tradition of
interpreting the *nihil* to mean visible things, turning John's poetic phrase
into support for their central tenet that the visible world was not the
creation of the good God. 'Visible things', he said, 'are "nothing".'[127]

Clearly, William was trying both to expose Peter's heresy and wean him
back to Catholicism with counter-arguments. But Peter was a committed
believer, of Cathar parents, whose mother had only been prevented from
receiving the *consolamentum* by a Catholic priest; he had in his house a
portion of vernacular Scripture which he used to buttress his views,
describing it as 'a Passion, written in Romance, as it actually occurred'.[128]
He had a clear understanding of the basic Cathar rejection of the whole
visible world and sexuality as evil, and the ability to gloss away counter-texts
which did not support dualism. William made no headway. When he
objected the Colossians text 'In Him were all things created in heaven and
earth, visible and invisible', Peter replied 'Visible to the heart and invisible
to the eyes of the flesh'. William showed him his hand and asked if flesh
would rise again; Peter struck a wooden post and said, 'Flesh will not rise
again except as a wooden post.'[129]

Positive Cathar belief intertwined with anticlericalism and rejection of
contemporary practices: chanting in church 'deceived simple people',[130]
alms for souls in purgatory was rejected, all preachers of crusade were
described as 'murderers',[131] and both the mass and Church ownership of
property repudiated as innovations dating only from Sylvester's time. Peter
said 'No miracle which can be seen by the eyes is anything ... neither the

124   *WHC,* p. 246.
125   Ibid.
126   Ibid., p. 243.
127   Ibid., John 1: 3; Rottenwöhrer convincingly resolves controversy over correct
interpretation of *nihil* in Cathar thought, *GRK* IV (2), pp. 48–60 (Garcias, p. 54),
backing C. Thouzellier *v.* R. Nelli and rejecting Nelli's reconstruction of a Cathar
philosophy. Summary of controversy without resolution, G. Gonnet, 'A propos du
"Nichil" ', *Heresis* II (1984) pp. 5–14. Compare Rottenwöhrer's *Unde Malum?*, pp.
378–84 with *JDR*, pp. 53–5. Garcias's statement is often echoed in inquisition
evidence, e.g. Doat 21 fol. 233r, 22 fol. 3r, 24 fol. 254r (WLW).
128   *WHC,* p. 246.
129   Ibid., p. 244, commenting on Col. 1: 16.
130   Ibid., p. 245.
131   Ibid.

Blessed Francis nor any other person performed a miracle.'[132] Confident, slogan-like statements and denunciations, backed by all the clarity – or apparent clarity – of a dualist cosmology, left him impervious to his Franciscan relative's argumentation.

Witnesses referred to Peter's belief in what they described as two gods, the one good and benign, creator of invisible and incorruptible things, the other evil and malign, creator of the visible and transitory. He was thus in the mainline radical dualist tradition of the Languedocian Cathars and was instructed enough to have adopted this doctrine. The dialogue was relatively crude, probably characteristic of the level of debate and understanding of the time.

Inquisition procedure in these early years was such that the Garcias debate is the fullest statement of belief drawn from a living witness in Languedoc before 1250. MS 609 has fragmentary utterances confirming the main lines of Peter's involuntary confession, with additional details and glimpses of confusions to which ordinary believers, only casually and informally instructed, were often subject. The two god proposition is there: 'All visible things were made by the wish and will of God but he himself did not make them.' 'The god of the Old Testament was malign: one should put faith only in the god who made a new heaven and a new earth.' Another witness described the dialogue between God and the Devil over the making of man: 'And God said to the Devil, He will be stronger than you or I, but make him from the slime of the sea.' The Devil did so and then God said, 'He is good, for he is neither too strong nor too weak. And God sent a soul to man.' Another described Christ as the bayle of God.[133]

Belief was plainly Docetist. Christ was not truly born of the Virgin but only concealed himself in her: thus Mary had no power of intercession. Another confession echoed Garcias on marriage as prostitution, but went on to add a dark statement about women dying in pregnancy who could not be saved, for unborn children were demons. Popular scepticism cohered with Cathar doctrine in the belief that the Host could not be the body of Christ, since if it were as large as a mountain, it would long ago have been eaten up. One witness had an idiosyncratic view of metempsychosis. He said bluntly that when the soul left the body of a man it entered the body of an ass to seek salvation, and that the soul of man passed through as many bodies as it could before it was saved. This is surely contrary to the logic of Cathar teaching, since every incarnation continued the soul's subjection to Satan: its true goal was to escape the chain of being, reach the body of a man or woman who would receive the *consolamentum* and so pass to heaven, discarding the material envelope in which the soul had been enclosed. The standard inquisitor's question about belief in a bodily resurrection was designed to tease out the heretical belief in the evil nature of the body.[134]

[132]   Ibid., p. 246.
[133]   WLW, analysis; *WHC*, p. 177; see also pp. 252–3.
[134]   WLW.

How far the inner secrets of Catharism were reserved for the perfect or candidate perfect is not always clear. Dulcia Faure implied that it was only after a considerable time in communities of women perfect, and after entering on a formal novitiate at Laurac, that she was instructed in dualism, which she told the inquisitor many years later she did not accept.[135] Though dualism in one form or another underpinned the structure of Catharism, its nature was not always clearly grasped by believers or youthful neophytes, and it could repel possible converts.

Perhaps the Cathar who told one witness that the Devil made the body of man and God gave it a soul and then 'the man leaped up and said to the Devil, "I do not belong to you" ',[136] best conveyed the emotions of those attracted to dualism in any age: sorrow at the condition of humanity, its fundamentally spiritual nature being chained to the diabolical, not merely, as in Catholic interpretation, by personal decisions, that is, sinful acts, but by 'matter, the animal, the sexual', coupled with a passionate wish to escape that diabolical nature by as total an abstention from the material world as possible and, in the case of Catharism, by the gesture of the laying on of hands in the *consolamentum*. The logic of the gesture itself being a part of the material world did not trouble contemporaries. 'I do not belong to you' was a cry from the heart; consoling was the way out.[137] How widespread these emotions were, it is now impossible to say: by this date Catharism was long established and had an institutional life of its own. But it seems reasonable to think that what we can call the 'dualist sentiment' had a role to play, predominantly among the perfect.

The most secure guide to Cathar academic teaching at this stage is provided by the extracts given verbatim by Durand of Huesca for the purpose of refutation from an anonymous polemical treatise of about 1220, based largely on scriptural texts and designed to defend Cathar faith, especially on creation and the salvation of God's people (the Cathars). A candidate for authorship has been named, but since, despite his long experience and contacts, Durand could not name the author, we are now unlikely to be able to do so. What is certain is that the author was a man equipped for learned debates, with a skill in the management of Biblical texts.[138] He was a radical dualist, believing in two principles. A good God has made the heaven, or heavens, where He dwells, and another, good earth in which the Cathars, who have escaped from the power of Satan, will dwell. In a doctrine comparable to that of the Italian Albanensians, Satan once interfered by force in the world of God and made the visible earth with its evil creatures,

---

[135]   *BF*, pp. 131–2.

[136]   Doat 25 fol. 7v.

[137]   I follow closely M. H. Vicaire's comment, *CF* VI, pp. 400–1 (background discussion).

[138]   C. Thouzellier, *Traité; WEH*, pp. 494–510, analysis of *Liber*, in Thouzellier, *Catharisme*, pp. 303–424. *Traité* discussed, *GRK* IV (2), pp. 17–66, with corrections of Duvernoy, Thouzellier; authorship, *GRK* IV (2), p. 26 supporting J. Duvernoy, 'Un traité Cathare au début du XIIIe siècle', *CEC* XIII (1962), pp. 22–54 at p. 27; C. Thouzellier, 'L'emploi de la Bible par les Cathares (XIIIe s.)', *The Bible and Medieval Culture*, ed. W. Lourdaux and D. Verhelst (Louvain, 1979), pp. 141–56.

demons and 'earthly men'. He made the Pharisees, body and soul. God's sphere is described as a complete world, a mirror of the earthly world but wholly good and eternal, the destination of God's people.

The radical antimony of good against evil runs through all the fragments of the unknown's work: he interprets the *omnia* and *nihil* of St John's gospel through a series of biblical citations. *Omnia* is discussed in relation to his concept of double creation: it may be used in biblical texts, and consequently in the author's treatise, to mean a creation of either God or Satan. By contrast, *nihil* refers solely to creation by Satan. He cites Paul in 1 Corinthians to support his interpretation, where Paul says, 'if I have not charity, I am nothing', together with Old Testament texts in order to reach his conclusion: 'If all the evil spirits and evil men and all things that are visible in this world are nothing, because they are without charity, therefore they were made without God.'[139] His translation of the '*Sine ipso factum est nihil*' must then read 'that which is made without God is nothing'. It is a forced exegesis, pushing biblical texts and concepts into his own all-embracing interpretation of the struggle between good and evil, oversimplifying the New Testament notion of the world; yet plainly the anonymous Cathar's exposition was no mere device to attract the unwary to his view, but sprang from a profound conviction that he and his fellow teachers held the key to the Scriptures and that the orthodox obfuscated the simple truth. So he writes,

> Further Paul says of the good creatures: 'For every creature of God is good.' If every creature of God is good, and the world, as some persons say, is God's creation with all that are therein, what reason is there that they should not be loved. For John forbids loving them. If the world ought not to be loved, and if those that are therein ought not to be loved, then it cannot be admitted that they are of God, for everything which is of God is good and therefore to be loved ... And is not all that is in the world the concupiscence of the flesh ...? O insensate *litterati*, who has fascinated you not to understand that: O full of all tricks and fraud, sons of the devil, enemies of the cross of Christ and of all justice, why do you not desist from resisting truth? O blind leaders of the blind, what can be plainer in holy Scriptures?[140]

Rejection of Catholic exposition as deceitful, distorting plain truth, was one factor which made the perfect resilient: they believed their own teaching was a sound, common-sense interpretation of the Bible, and were forearmed against that of their opponents.

Though standing in the mainstream of radical, two-principle dualism and resembling the Albanensian author of the *De duobus principibus* in his evident lack of interest in Cathar myths, the author is still an individualist, with doctrinal twists of his own.[141] Variety of opinion was a natural product of the

[139]   1 Cor. 12: 2; *WEH*, pp. 504–5.
[140]   Ibid., pp. 505–6.
[141]   *GRK* IV (2), pp. 26–66, *passim*.

perfect's sovereign power of interpretation: circles of believers cohered round a leader and repeated his views. But there were also confusions among the rank and file, the product of home-grown reflection on the preaching combined with local superstitions. There were regional differences. In Languedoc radical dualism was dominant: a moderate dualism emerged early in the thirteenth century, not before, and vanished from the sources after 1230 – possibly the fruits of contacts, not sustained, with the bishopric of the North French.[142]

A gulf yawned between radical dualism and the doctrines of the medieval Church. Taken as a whole, the dominant beliefs of Languedocian Catharism – with the two principles, two heavens and earths, the complications of transposing most biblical events to a 'heavenly' earth, Christ with a heavenly body, 'overshadowing' Mary, able with this body to pass with dry feet over the water, not part of the divine essence and not a true Saviour, but so to say a middleman for conveying the *consolamentum* to the chosen people of God, the Cathars, Mary as an angel, souls wandering through a series of bodies, human or, according to another school of thought, animal as well, even including snakes and hens, the grim picture of life on the visible, 'earthly' earth in the power of Satan, subject to the play of arbitrary chance rather than God's ordering, in effect a kind of hell – all this represented a far-reaching challenge to orthodoxy. It would perhaps be natural to expect such views to be those of a minority; it was not so. Radical dualism retained its dominance throughout the history of the Cathars in Languedoc.

By contrast, under the influence of Catholic controversialists, some Italian moderate dualists made revisions. Desiderius and his party, for example, moved closer to a Catholic Christology; at the same time, the Albanensian wing remained a stern minority.[143] Moderate dualism had little impact in Languedoc. Persecution inhibited persuasion and the context of the heresy was less sophisticated. There is no sign of any intellectual shift comparable to that of Desiderius. The implication must be that a tradition established in the Cathar Churches in Languedoc at their founding remained in place, modified and adapted by individual perfect, but subject to no fundamental change.

Through minute analysis, Rottenwöhrer has demonstrated that, by and large, both in Languedoc and Italy, controversialists did not falsify Cathar views, though capable of some distortions or simplifications: their evidence, the results of interrogations by inquisitors, and the Cathars' own works form an ensemble which is a fair guide to their doctrines. If there are eccentricities, they will more commonly spring from the Cathars themselves than from the blackguarding of hostile polemicists, and in Languedoc from a greater admixture of popular superstition.[144]

[142] Ibid., pp. 413–19, doctrines, pp. 419–28; Northern French hypothesis, p. 429.
[143] Below, pp. 194–207.
[144] *GRK* IV (2), p. 433 (tentative conclusion); D. Müller, *Albigenser – die wahre Kirche? Eine Untersuchung zum Kirchenverständnis der 'ecclesia Dei'* (originally PhD thesis, University of Würzburg); interesting aim to establish Cathars' self-view, but assumes

Languedocian Catharism was independent. Despite major likenesses, it did not lean on the Italian Albanensians and held doctrines of its own. That fact is a reminder of the independent nature of regional Churches in Catharism and the importance of geography. The Alps were an effective barrier.

The massacre of Avignonet and the fall of Montségur

From 1240, damaged by political and military events and the reckless actions of its patrons, Catharism slipped back. Raymond Trencavel, heir to the viscounty of Carcassonne and Béziers, who had never accepted dispossession, moved from his refuge in Aragon to raise rebellion in the ancient lands of his dynasty. Received with enthusiasm by some indigenous nobility, he went on to besiege Carcassonne; in the bourgs outside there was no effective resistance, and thirty-three clerics who had taken refuge in a church in the Bourg of Saint Vincent were killed. But the siege ended when a royal army approached, and the rebellion failed.

Cathars had seen hope in the rebellion. Their bishop Pierre Polhan was present at Salsigne near Cabaret when local men attempted to prevent the royal garrison aiding their colleagues at Carcassonne and again at Montréal, where retreating rebels were besieged by royal forces. Its failure damaged them by ruining petty nobles of the countryside who gave residual support and by facilitating the effective imposition of royal power in the Carcassès and the Razès. Royal power was unambiguous in support of the repression of heresy and the noose tightened.[145]

Raymond VII stood aloof from the revolt at this stage. He too aimed to undo the effects of the Albigensian Crusade, but by diplomatic means. He was aware that an important segment of his political support was sympathetic to the Cathars and this, rather than any personal complaisance to their beliefs, caused him to tread cautiously. A *rapprochement* with Gregory IX offered him the opportunity to have his childless marriage annulled to seek remarriage and a male heir, and hope thereby to upset the settlement of 1229 and secure Toulouse for his dynasty. It was not an *outré* hope since his daughter Jeanne and her husband Alphonse of Poitiers remained persistently childless and male inheritance could override other possibilities; moreover, Gregory needed Raymond on his side in the conflict with Frederick II and was prepared for concessions. Raymond, abandoning his alliance with Frederick, swore to support Gregory against him and made an alliance with Louis IX which included a promise to take Montségur.[146]

---

polemicists, inquisitors gravely distorted Cathar teaching. Here I prefer Rottenwöhrer, comments *GRK* IV (1), pp. 19–20, 131–2, (2), pp. 58–60 (nihil controversy), (3), pp. 295–6, 307–9, 333–4, fundamental discussion, pp. 372–8. *GRK* brings out great variability within Cathars' doctrines, not assimilated in Müller.

[145] Outline, *WHC*, pp. 153–67; *JDH*, pp. 280–1 (esp. Polhan); Griffe, *Inquisition*, pp. 68–74; full narrative, with political background, Roquebert, *L'Épopée* IV.

[146] M. Roquebert, *Montségur: les cendres de la liberté* (Toulouse, 1992) (well-written, fully documented description), p. 121. See also his *Les Cathares: de Montségur à Bélibaste, 1245–1321* (Paris, 1998).

Siege was attempted, but made little impact; only a substantial force effectively encircling the fortress and prepared to stay could hope to conquer it, and it is unlikely that Raymond's heart was in the action. Gregory died before the annulment was granted and a long interregnum foiled Raymond's hopes of remarriage. So when a conspiracy against Louis IX, led by Hugh count of La Marche and supported by Henry III of England, was hatched, Raymond was tempted to join and secure the over-throw of the Peace of Paris by force; he was backed by a number of Southern lords and by Raymond Trencavel. News of the conspiracy stirred hope once more among the Cathars of an end to royal and North French dominance and of liberation from investigation and punishment.

The long hiatus in the actions of the inquisitors based in Toulouse had ended in May 1241; Peter Seila carried out an inquisition in the region of Quercy, making effective use of the time of grace and receiving numbers of voluntary confessions.[147] Raymond continued to support episcopal prosecu-tion for heresy, but he objected to Dominican friars; his complaints went unheard. In the Lauragais the Dominican William Arnold accompanied the Franciscan Stephen of Saint-Thibéry on tour with a small entourage in 1241; by the end of May 1242, they had reached the village of Avignonet some twenty-five miles south-east of Toulouse and were quartered in the castle of Raymond VII's bayle Raymond of Alfaro.[148] Inquisitorial parties depended wholly on the support of the secular power for protection: it was the misfortune of the inquisitors and their assistants that in Raymond of Alfaro they had stumbled across a Cathar sympathizer, son of a Navarrese mercenary captain and an illegitimate half-sister of Raymond VII, who acted as informant and intermediary for a Cathar fighting force directed by Pierre-Roger of Mirepoix, who set out from Montségur, gathered support on the way and on 28 May was guided into the walled village to the castle. The door of the hall where the inquisitors were sleeping was axed, as were all inside, including the prior of Avignonet who had come on a visit. The military force was aware of the importance of inquisitorial registers: these were taken and sold. The news of the deaths was received with rejoicing among sympathizers. One pro-Cathar housewife, Austorga of Resengas, said to her husband, 'All is free'; he replied, 'All is dead.'[149] The husband was the wiser. Only the naïve could imagine that one killing would check the pursuit of heresy, and it is hard to accept that a shrewd political leader like Raymond should have allowed himself to support the assassination, for all his mistrust of the friars.[150]

In a curious parallel to the assassination of Pierre de Castelnau which precipitated the Albigensian Crusade, the assassination backfired: Raymond's rebellion collapsed as his allies were defeated or surrendered and in October 1242 he capitulated to Louis IX and had to accept that the

[147]   *WHC*, pp. 168–9.
[148]   For what follows, Y. Dossat, 'Le massacre d'Avignonet', *CF* VI, pp. 343–59.
[149]   WLW using Doat 24 fols 1r–7r.
[150]   WHC, p. 171 preferred to Roquebert, *Montségur*, pp. 123–4.

Figure 3   The Cathar fortress of Montségur

Photograph: J. L. Gasc

settlement of 1229 would never be undone by force. He moved towards a full reconciliation with the Church and ceased to blow hot and cold over the persecution of heresy. His bayles responded: there was firmer backing for investigation and punishment, and at the end of his life in 1249, Raymond himself was responsible for one of the great mass burnings when eighty accused were executed at Agen. Political interest, coupled with his own lack of personal sympathy for Catharism, in the end prevailed and Catharism lost even the half-hearted restraint on the pursuit of heresy which had marked Raymond's policy after 1235.

The most important casualty was Montségur and its powerful nucleus of perfect. It was known that the assassination had been organized from there and that fact provided the springboard to a decision to take the fortress and eliminate the major focus of the heresy. Led by the royal seneschal of Carcassonne with contingents from the archbishop of Narbonne and bishop of Albi, the army had the calibre and provisioning which alone could reduce Montségur. It fell after a siege lasting from the summer of 1243 to March 1244.

Catharism on the summit ended in a blaze of gallantry. About ninety-eight men formed the fighting force;[151] mastery of the terrain, a catapult and the precipitous crags kept a much larger force at bay; lines of communication were long kept open, albeit perilously. Pierre-Roger and his garrison hoped Raymond would in the end move to raise the siege and there were rumours that a force might be sent by the emperor. A Cathar bishop in Cremona sent in a fraternal letter offering asylum: it was refused. But a nocturnal climb by a royal force up the precipices below the Roc de la Tour surprised the garrison and gave a vital foothold high up the mountain, those who had ascended by night looking in horror by daylight at the heights they had scaled.

Reserves of money were evacuated: after concealment, probably finding their way to the Lombard Cathars. Pierre-Roger finally negotiated a fifteen-day truce before surrendering, having obtained an agreement with the seneschal which saved the lives of the garrison. Nothing could save the perfect: heresy was not negotiable. They were taken down the mountain and, when they declined to recant, were thrust with combustible material into a wooden palisade, probably formed of the remains of the wooden village in which the inhabitants of Montségur were housed. So two hundred or more were burnt, Bertrand Marty perishing with his flock. The canonical obligation to destroy the houses of heretics was thus fulfilled.[152]

Before the end, Montségur saw a remarkable flowering of Cathar faith.[153] Its attraction as a high place drew the relatives of the perfect for personal and social reasons, but also to hear preaching and receive blessing, to make a retreat, in illness to be consoled, or in health to join the perfect. Visitors included pilgrims from far afield and their numbers fluctuated, but the permanent population grew. On the eve of the siege there were over four hundred residents, including children, wives and mistresses, the garrison being composed of both sympathizers and mercenaries. While the siege went on, Bertrand Marty preached, garrison members visited the perfect, the *convenenza* was used to ensure the *consolamentum* could be administered to the dying even if they had lost the power of speech and, witnessed by sympathizers on very moving occasions, the mortally wounded were consoled. There was an intense devotion.

Anticipating their end, the perfect distributed their goods to the believers who were to survive – food, money, items of clothing. Bertrand Marty gave fifty doublets made by the perfect themselves to Pierre-Roger. On the last Sunday of the siege, 13 March, twenty-one believers and sympathizers who could have gone free, asked to be consoled. It was a death sentence. On the

---

[151]   Figures, Roquebert, *Montségur*, pp. 135–6, siege as whole, pp. 130–57; *JDH*, pp. 286–95.

[152]   Duvernoy concludes wood for execution came from village and rejects Dossat's hypothesis (*CF* VI, pp. 361–70) that burning was at Bram. Victims listed, Roquebert, *L'Epopée* IV, pp. 417–26.

[153]   M. Roquebert, 'Montségur, refuge ou quartier general?', *La Persécution du Catharisme XIIe–XIVe siècles, Collection Heresis* VI (Arques, 1996) (hereafter *Persécution*), pp. 159–92; 'Le Catharisme dans le "familia" ', *CF* XX, pp. 226–8.

following Thursday, 16 March, they were pushed into the enclosure with the rest. Some belonged to families heavily committed to the Cathar cause, such as Corba de Pereille, who, leaving behind husband and family, preferred to die with her mother Marquesia and daughter Esclarmonde. A wounded man, Guillaume de Lahille, son of a woman perfect, may have believed he could not survive, but preferred to die with his sister Bruna and his cousin India. He was of the nobility, but there were humbler sympathizers such as Guillaume Garnier, formerly a devoted supporter of Arnaude de Lamothe. Most remarkable of all among these volunteers were garrison members who appear to have been only mercenaries at the outset but had been converted by the preaching, the consolings and the presence of so many determined idealists on the mountain. The great days of Catharism in its heartland thus ended in both tragedy and glory, in an episode that demonstrated yet again the remarkable power of Catharism in the gravest adversity.

The fall of Montségur marks a *caesura* in Cathar history in Languedoc.[154] It was a fortress thought to be impregnable; the successful siege by Hugh of Arcis showed that there were no fortresses where Catharism could find security. However misguidedly, the garrison and the perfect they defended believed in the possibility of rescue from outside, through Raymond VII or Frederick II; that was shown to be illusory. The Cathars would have to survive, not by open defiance but by concealment. Rebels had to become fugitives.

Events in the early 1240s also mark a dividing line in the history of the pro-Cathar section of the nobility. After the failure of the Trencavel revolt, the assassination at Avignonet and the reaction which it provoked, the more shrewd and far-sighted came to see that the old cause of the South was lost. Members of the Niort family had been involved in the revolt: Géraud de Niort contrived to make peace with Louis IX and handed over the ancestral castle at Niort, which received a royal garrison and was destroyed in 1255. The family escaped major penalty from inquisitors, probably because Louis was disposed to be lenient to aristocrats who severed links with heresy. Raymond de Niort had intimate links with Catharism since he had married Marquesia, daughter of Pierre-Roger, military leader at Montségur, and was troubled by investigations. He contrived to avoid imprisonment, but the family as a whole lost its position because of complicity with heresy. Olivier de Termes, who had joined the Trencavel rebellion, made his peace with Church and king, joined Louis's crusade to Damietta, displaying in the Holy Land a military skill which he had learnt in war in Languedoc; he became a trusted royal supporter and so rescued his family lands.[155] Others, too tainted with heresy or too committed to Cathar beliefs, took to the *maquis* and joined the hunted life of the perfect, forming a class of *faidits* who recur in the confessions.

Arnaude de Lamothe's life as a perfect had ended before Montségur fell; its quality eroded because, through the need for secrecy and fear of

---

[154]   Comment, *BF*, p. 298.
[155]   Wakefield, in *Names* XVIII, pp. 295–303; Peal, *Reading Medieval Studies* XII, pp. 117–29.

betrayal, she could never feel securely settled in any one place. In a part of the forest at Lanta called Pierre-Belloc, she and her sister stayed in a little subterranean hideaway, being brought food and visited by adherents; her sister died, perhaps because of the underground damp. The rule that a perfect should have a companion was observed even under persecution, so a supporter brought a young girl called Jordana whom she in the crisis consoled alone. Peirona was buried in the forest and the two moved on to another estate, only to return briefly to the underground dwelling before moving on again through a sequence of refuges. Perfect sometimes joined them to hold an *apparellamentum*, when the women perfect gave the males the *melioramentum* and themselves received it from believers. The essentials of the life were maintained till their capture in 1243. There is no evidence of betrayal; their secret had been kept for many years by those who sheltered, fed and escorted them. They were taken to Toulouse, where, perhaps influenced by the obligation on the perfect to tell the truth, Arnaude made a full confession, giving a multitude of names, after a year's stay in prison. She is described as *conversa*, one who abjures. Strictly, she had relapsed, for she had renounced heresy in youth, but it seems likely that abjuration saved her life. It was the end of a long, devoted Cathar career.[156]

[156]   Murray transl. Doat 23 fols 18r–49v; Peirona's death, 22v–23r; Jordana's consoling, 23r. Wakefield believes she survived; source is silent.

8

The Battle for Souls in Italy

Catholic piety and the confraternities

St Dominic from the first intended to confute Catharism by the word, through preaching; St Francis, by contrast, intended his brothers to engage in moral exhortation rather than full dogmatic instruction, to preach by the example of their lives. Paul Sabatier believed Francis 'never consented to occupy himself with questions of doctrine'.[1] But he was well aware of heresy. In his Rule he requires care to be taken to examine the beliefs of postulants and in his Testament commands the brothers to take captive any who 'refuse to say the Office according to the Rule ... or ... are not true to the Catholic faith' and bring them to the Cardinal Protector.[2] He never mentioned Cathars explicitly but they were known in Assisi, there was a Cathar bishopric in the Val del Spoleto and it is easy to detect in his writings an emphasis which runs plainly counter to the Cathars.[3]

In Francis's letter to all the faithful, he stresses the importance of confession and communion, reverence to priests and the frequent visiting of churches – all abhorrent to Cathars.[4] Aware of Innocent III's prohibition of 'games' in churches, he gained permission from the pope to institute at Greccio the Christmas crib which gave new popularity to an ancient custom in desuetude and emphasized the reality of Christ's birth from a real woman, not from the 'overshadowing' of an angel: he talks explicitly about the Virgin's womb.[5] In the *Lives* he is shown contemplating with intense feeling the suffering of Christ. This Franciscan form of personal piety, with

---

[1]   P. Sabatier, *Vie de S. François d'Assise* (1894), trans. L. S. Houghton as *Life of St Francis of Assisi* (London, 1908), p. 41.
[2]   M. A. Habig, *St Francis of Assisi: Writings and Early Biographies* (Chicago, 1973), p. 69; Rule, p. 58.
[3]   K. Esser, 'Franziskus von Assisi und die Katharer seiner Zeit', *AFH* LI (1958), pp. 225–64 (fundamental).
[4]   Habig, *Writings*, pp. 93–9; rightful belief on Eucharist, Admonitions, (ch. 1), p. 78.
[5]   L. Gougaud, 'Le crèche de Noel avant Saint François d'Assise', *Revue des sciences religieuses* II (1922), pp. 26–34; on Virgin, Esser in *AFH* LI (1958), p. 251.

Figure 4 Giotto, *Franciscan Crib, the Hermitage of Greccio*, from the frescos of St Francis, Assisi

Photograph: Scala, Florence

its emphasis on the Holy Family and the Passion, albeit not new, for the theme was one developed by St Bernard and the Cistercians, nevertheless had great effect on popular religion through the enthusiasm for the Franciscan ideal and the rapid growth of the order and was always inimical to the Cathar worldview. Above all, the Canticle of Brother Sun, in its optimism, its acceptance of all creation, its praise of God for his creatures, its implicit allusions to Genesis, for Cathars the record of the evil Jehovah, and its joy in the interdependence of man and the natural world, was a potent response to Cathar belief in the evil nature of the visible and material.[6]

The battle between Catharism and Catholicism, long drawn-out in Italy, was more subtle and many-layered than in Languedoc. Largely because of political factors, neither crusade nor inquisitorial proceedings had the decisive role which they had in Southern France: peaceful competition was a more important strand in the conflict and in this Franciscan piety and preaching, alongside the Dominican power of dogmatic exposition and the development of lay confraternities, had an important role. General use of Franciscans as inquisitors did not occur before Innocent IV's reorganization in 1254; consequently they remained more popular than the Dominicans who were heavily involved in the use of force at an early date.

The cities were the cockpit of conflict.[7] Each side battled to discredit the other. A glimpse of this can be caught in two anecdotes related to St Francis. In one an attempt was made to expose him as a relaxed meat-eater, by implication inferior to the sternly ascetic, near-vegan perfect. As guest in a house in Alessandria, Francis, mindful of the biblical injunction 'eat what is set before you', joined the family in eating a capon and, when a beggar called, with characteristic generosity gave him a piece on some bread. Next day the pseudo-beggar sought to display the capon while Francis was preaching and expose him to ridicule, only to find that a miracle had taken place and the capon had turned into fish – thereby knocking the bottom out of the Cathar case, for fish, believed not to be a product of coition, was permitted to the perfect. Clearly well informed about Catharism, the crowd cried out against the beggar, who, discredited, begged Francis's pardon. The biographer, Thomas of Celano, calls the beggar a 'son of Belial'; a Cathar connection seems undeniable.[8]

In the second anecdote, Stephen of Bourbon names Francis's tempter as a certain '*paccharius sive manichaeus*' who tried to embarrass the saint and damage the priesthood by asking him how he could do reverence to the priest of a church in Lombardy, which he had entered in order to pray, when the priest kept a 'concubine' and had therefore 'polluted hands'. Francis replied with a symbolic gesture in the presence of the parishioners, kneeling down and kissing the priest's hands while explaining that,

---

[6]   R. D. Sorrell, *St Francis of Assisi and Nature* (Oxford, 1988), chs 5, 6, 7; trans. p. 101; '*per*' is rightly translated 'for, on account of' rather than 'by', so 'Be praised, my Lord, for Sister Moon ...'; Cathars, pp. 77–9, 137, 147–8.

[7]   E. Dupré-Theseider, 'Gli eretici nel mondo comunale italiano', *Mondo cittadino e movimenti ereticali* (Bologna, 1978), pp. 233–59 (orig. *BSSV* LXII (1963), pp. 3–23).

[8]   II Celano, *Analecta Franciscana* X (Ad Claras Aquas, n.d.), pp. 78–9; Habig, *Writings*, pp. 427–9.

whether the accusation was true or false, he could kiss them because of the sacraments they administered and the authority under which they did so. It may be that other preachers in Italy followed Francis's approach, stressing positively what the pillars of belief were and enjoining respect for the priesthood and hierarchy rather than attacking heresy explicitly, and that this explains the lack of anti-heretical sermons in extant collections in contrast to German-speaking lands where Berthold of Regensburg's sermons are a mine of information on heresy. A possible exception is to be found in the *Summa* against heretics once attributed to the Franciscan Capelli, which has passages directly apostrophizing Cathars and may represent portions of sermons once preached.[9]

Street theatre, demonstrations of ecclesiastical power, skilled pulpit rhetoric on the one side, governmental repression of religious demonstrations, attacks on convents and inquisitors on the other, all formed part of the conflict, part political, part religious, in which slowly and painfully the Church began to get the upper hand as the thirteenth century went on. A Dominican, Brother Robaldus, was the object of a trick designed to expose his powers of healing as a deceit, when a man claiming to be ill presented himself and asked for a cure. Suspecting what was afoot, Robaldus expressed the hope that if he was ill God would cure him and, if he was not, that He would give him a salutary penance, whereupon the man fell ill with fever; Robaldus visited him at home, where he was converted and healed.[10] In time, the story was transferred to the more famous preacher, thaumaturge and enemy of heresy, Peter of Verona. Exhuming and burning of bodies at the order of inquisitors, following canon law, was another potent demonstration – not only distressing to the relatives of the dead and menacing because of the possible attendant penalties of disinheritance, but also a vivid reminder to the population that the unrepentant heretic was damned and his corpse barred from consecrated ground. Anticlericals, fautors of heresy and Cathars themselves could reply to ecclesiastical pressure by publicizing the weaknesses of the clergy: so at Arezzo the anti-episcopal faction, reacting against an unpopular and avaricious warrior-bishop, catapulted a dead donkey equipped with mitre over his palace walls.[11] At Viterbo, a hostile regime for imperialist reasons expelled Rose, an eighteen-year-old Franciscan tertiary, from the city in winter simply for carrying an image and singing *Laudes* in the streets.[12]

The stakes were high. Fired up by the effects of persecution or the hope of breaking free from repression, attacks on convents and friaries or on inquisitors went on sporadically. At Rimini there was a conspiracy to kill a

---

[9]   L. Lemmens, *Testimonia minora saeculi XIII de S. Francisco Assisiensi* (Ad Claras Aquas, 1926), pp. 93–4; Habig, *Writings*, pp. 1605–6; for lack of sermons explicitly attacking heresy, M. D'Alatri, 'I Francescani e l'eresia', *Eretici e inquisitiori: studi e documenti* I (Rome, 1986), pp. 91–112.

[10]   *Vitae fratrum*, ed. B. M. Reichert, pp. 225–6.

[11]   Miccoli, 'La repressione ...', p. 652.

[12]   M. D'Alatri, ' "Ordo paenitentium" ed eresia in Italia', *Eretici* I, pp. 45–63 at pp. 59–61; G. Abate in *Miscellanea Francescana* LII (1952), pp. 151–2.

podestà who had delivered heretics up to Frederick II; at Brera in 1254 Pietro d'Arcagnano was assassinated on the piazza because he refused to cancel names from inquisitorial registers; in 1279 a mob attack on the convent at Parma killed an old, blind Dominican.[13] To be an inquisitor was to run a considerable risk.

On the other side, the leading preachers, holding large audiences hanging on every word, exercised great power – albeit temporarily – which could be used to devastating effect. Beneath the violent, confused externals of Italian politics lay a deep, if often inarticulate, yearning for peace aroused by the failure of existing institutions to settle inner feuds and city quarrels. The *popolo* had come into power but had often not been able to provide tranquil government: in the absence of satisfactory secular authority, men looked spasmodically, sometimes feverishly, for a divine source of power. This was the background for the success of John of Vicenza and the ten-month epoch of the Alleluia.[14] Crowds assembled in the expectation of miracles, themselves the guarantees of prophetic power. When a savage horse blessed by John became tame, he was acknowledged to have a supra-natural power which even dumb creatures would accept. With such authority, a preacher's word took on extraordinary weight – so, for example, a crowd stirred up by John burned to the ground the house of a usurer, Pasquale Landolfo.

In Verona, the impetus already won by preaching and peacemaking elsewhere carried him forward on a tide of high expectation and religious feeling, febrile but for the moment irresistible. He persuaded Lombard troops to abandon their trophy of war, the caroccio of Verona and return it to the city, an action which at once reflected glory on to John. A mass burning of heretics in the amphitheatre was sandwiched between an intervention in which he requested and received the office of '*dux et comes*', in effect absolute power, and his great preaching from the text 'My peace I give you, my peace I leave with you' from a specially erected tower some twenty-eight metres high in the meadow at Paquara in August 1233, attended by a crowd of overwhelming size, including the bishops of nine cities and leading men of the region. Reporting the burning, the chronicler describes the victims as 'Patarenes' (Cathars) and the 'Poor of Lyons' (Waldensians), who refused to take the oath to obey John's precepts; both sects rejected the oath out of a literal interpretation of the words in Matthew's gospel, 'Swear not at all.' As at the heart of John of Vicenza's peace process lay the swearing of oaths, formally recorded to bind the participants, this could well have smoked them out and, in the excitement of the peacemaking, condemned them; or they may just have been unwilling to put themselves effectively in the hands of a Dominican. On 21 July and the three following days, John presided over the burning of

---

[13] D'Alatri, 'I Francescani e l'eresia', pp. 91–112 at pp. 94–5, 102; Guiraud, *Inquisition* II, p. 575.
[14] Thompson, *Revival* (vivid and illuminating); *Storia di Vicenza* II: *Età medievale* ed. G. Cracco (Vicenza, 1991), pp. 97–9.

sixty victims, including men and women from the best families of the city such as would often expect to be able to escape such a holocaust: the effect would have been immense. From the burning, John went on to his greatest triumph in the meadow of Paquara, part political, part penitential. Many came barefoot: it was a great religious occasion, but also a political one as John induced concessions from opposing groups and secured a marriage between children of the rivals Azzo d'Este and Alberico da Romano.

All that happened, the adaptation of the city's statutes, the burnings, the denunciation of usurers, the making out of written peace agreements flowed from John's eloquence, his reputation, skilfully managed theatre and a revulsion from faction fighting and war. For a matter of months he could do as he wished: the restoration of moral order through the repression of usury and heresy was bound up with the restoration of peace, and in the blaze of his eloquence, the sense of guilt and the yearning for peace in his audience, all compromises, sectional interests and power-seeking were swept away.[15] But from the pinnacle of success the way downhill was rapid. He made a fatal error in Vicenza when he disappointed the expectation that he would dismiss the *podestà* and use his power to appoint a new one acceptable to the two opposing factions within the city. By continuing with the existing *podestà*, he was felt to have favoured the da Romano side; a pro-Padua faction reacted; as he felt his power slipping, John formed a military force and at once his authority disappeared, like snow in warm sunshine. A prophetic power had to be sustained by continued evidence of even-handed justice and succeeded only as it brought into the open the 'unspoken or unspeakable desires of its hearers'. John was made to seem only a faction leader after all and within days lost his charismatic leadership.

One of the lasting consequences of the Alleluia movement, even though heresy was not its main target, was the development of lay confraternities concerned with putting down heresy. In themselves, confraternities of various sorts were not new. Lay penitents, who adopted a rule of life and committed themselves to certain observances without renouncing marriage, were to be found in Italy in the later twelfth century and grew in popularity, encouraged by popes who protected them, further stimulated by friars whose evangelizing attracted laity who wished to deepen their spiritual life without entering the monastic state. Commonly included among the requirements of membership were the refusal to shed blood, to carry arms or swear oaths, and an insistence on the restitution of unjust gains, which correspond precisely with the evangelical tenets prominent in heretical movements of the twelfth century. Volpe long ago believed that the confraternities and the heresies attracted similar recruits: certainly extant statutes show a concern to guard against any infiltration of heretics.[16]

---

[15]   Thompson, *Revival*; see discussion of style of preaching, pp. 83–135; the prime aim of the Alleluia was not the repression of heresy.
[16]   G. Volpe, *Movimenti religiosi e sette ereticali nella società medievale Italiana (secoli XI–XIV)* (Florence, 1926), p. 169.

In practice, they acted as a conduit away from heresy even where their principal aims were charitable or devotional, for they offered a disciplined way of life, perhaps with a habit, and with regular meetings, the encouragement of participation in a common endeavour within Catholicism. The refusal to bear arms led to clashes with municipalities and the requirements of military service: this was not harmful to their cause, for it gave a welcome publicity and demonstrated to the sympathizers of Catharism that literal observance of gospel texts was not its monopoly. The confraternities were effective competition, for they offered a spiritual life within the lay state where Catharism could only provide its believer class with an auxiliary, attendant role of serving and adoring their perfect.

In the most advanced part of medieval Europe, confraternities were the fruit of a wider development, leading to a revaluation of the lay condition.[17] Flight from the world was becoming an internal matter, no longer seen simply as a renunciation of carnal life in an exterior sense. Monasticism was losing its monopoly: the confraternities offered a halfway house. Conjugal chastity, that is, periodic continence, gave a place in the ascetic life for married couples and increased the possibility of salvation in the lay state. Lay associations, backed by churchmen, were asserting their place, with particular fasts, prayers and obligations of attendance at mass, of confession and communion. In the resistance of heresy, they formed a bulwark, better instructed than run of the mill faithful, heavily committed to the worship of the Church, yet at the same time jealous of their institutional independence, for they chose the priests whom they wished to serve them and maintained the right to manage their own affairs.[18] Some had practical, charitable objectives: utility confirmed their appeal. The congregation and confraternity of S. Maria of Misericord at Bergamo in 1265, for example, were the main instruments for the organization of charity, especially the distribution of food. The confraternity had links to both Franciscans and Dominicans and included the repression of heresy among its aims.[19]

Orientation towards active measures against heresy added another dimension, pre-eminently the work of Dominican friars supported by the papacy with grants and indulgences and boosted by the emotions released in the Alleluia. Two such confraternities were founded at Milan, probably through the agency of Peter of Verona, also known as Peter Martyr, a Dominican like John of Vicenza, of great eloquence and ascetic life, with a similar power of holding large audiences in his hand:[20] at the height of his

---

[17] G. G. Meerssemann, *Ordo fraternitatis: confraternite e pietà dei laice nel Medioevo*, Italia Sacra XXIV–XXVI (Rome, 1977) (definitive exposition), review, A. Vauchez, in *RSCI* XXXII (1978), pp. 186–94; A. Vauchez, 'Pénitents', *Dictionnaire de spiritualité au moyen age* XII (Paris, 1984), coll. 1010–23; *Les laics au moyen age* (Paris, 1987); D'Alatri, ' "Ordo paenitentium" ', pp. 45–63.

[18] See esp. Vauchez, *RSCI* XXXII (1978), pp. 186–94.

[19] L. K. Little, *Libertà, carità, fraternità: confraternite laiche a Bergamo nell' età del comune* (Bergamo, 1988).

[20] A. Dondaine, 'Saint Pierre Martyr: études', *AFP* XXIII (1953), pp. 66–162, should be read in conjunction with criticism of G. G. Merlo, 'Pietro di Verona – San Pietro

powers he requested the communal authorities of Florence to enlarge the piazza by S. Maria Novella to accommodate the crowd. In Milan, he had to have a special carriage to shield him from the mass of people who wished to touch him; at Cesena, matrons of the city were so eager to hear him they hurried out without stopping to put on the normal, modest covering of their overmantles. He lacked John's moral flaws and never achieved his dizzying political eminence, but he constantly appears as a preacher, spiritual influence and hammer of heretics. He sprang from a part-Cathar family, had a heretical uncle and is the probable author of a treatise against the Cathars:[21] he plainly saw the confuting and repression of heresy as a prime vocation. One confraternity, the Society of the Virgin, so dedicated in honour of Mary in hostility to the Cathars, was designed to assemble the faithful who chose to join in defence of their faith: the other, the Society of the Faith, had the function of providing supporters for direct action against heretics. They supplemented the lay committee of twelve already in existence for the arrest of heretics there and were envisaged as providing voting power for orthodoxy. This was one major service of the confraternities; they organized the opposition to heretical evangelizing and its influence on municipal governments, pressing within cities for the acceptance of anti-heretical legislation and the imposition of penalties on heretics. As the executives of the communes, *podestàs* had the function of initiating action against heresy: confraternities of the latter type formed bodies capable of negotiating with them, putting pressure on the unwilling and supplying manpower to find and hold heretics for trial.[22]

The Militia of Jesus Christ at Parma, founded by another Dominican, Bartholomew of Vicenza at the time of the Alleluia, a military order for patricians and their wives, put the defence of the faith against 'every sect of heretical depravity' at the head of their list of duties. But there was also an appeal to social conscience – they were not only to look after churches and religious, but also widows, pupils and orphans and defend them from oppression. Action against heresy (and significantly the Cathars headed the list of named sects) combined with social action and with obligations of fasting, abstinence and prayer. Gregory IX seems to have hoped that this militia could be a model for confraternities of the same type elsewhere, but was disappointed: it did not last at Parma, Salimbene witnessing both its birth and death.

Martire …', *Culto di santi: istituzioni e classi in età preindustriale*, ed. S. Boesch Gajono and L. Sebastiani (L'Aquila, Rome, 1984), pp. 471–88. G. G. Meerssemann, 'Etudes sur les anciennes confréries dominicaines, II. Les Confréries de Saint-Pierre Martyr', *AFP* XXI (1951), pp. 51-196. Dondaine, *AFP* XXIII (1953), p. 72 doubts whether Peter founded confraternities in Milan; not generally supported. Peter did not act as inquisitor before 1251: Thompson, *Revival*, p. 38. n. 36 corrects H. C. Lea, *A History of the Inquisition of the Middle Ages* (New York, 1906 edn) II, p. 214.
[21]   T. Kaeppeli, 'Une somme contre les hérétiques de S. Pierre Martyr (?)', *AFP* XVII (1947), p. 295–335.
[22]   N. J. Housley, 'Politics and heresy in Italy: anti-heretical crusades, orders, confraternities, 1200–1500', *JEH* XXXIII (1982), pp. 193–208.

It may be that there was a certain ambiguity about crusading and ancillary action against heresy in Italy: politics and the problem of heresy were inextricably interwoven and there was sometimes an incongruity between the high phrases of a Gregory, speaking of martyrdom and crusading and drawing clear lines between heresies and orthodoxy, and the realities of family quarrels, Ghibellinism, the contests of cities over rights and territory and inner-city factions, which formed the context in which the heretics and their sympathizers lived. The clarion calls to action, effective when summoning Northern Frenchmen to root out heresy in the South, did not easily fit the Italian scene. There is a certain implausibility about calling the Paduans 'special athletes of Christ' because of their conflict with Ezzelino da Romano in 1231 and offering remission of three years' penance for support against him. Dark tyrant as he was, Ezzelino was opposed by Padua for temporal and territorial reasons rather than spiritual ones.[23]

Confraternities had come to stay and were reinforced when Raniero Fasani, a penitent in Perugia, touched off the movement of the Disciplinati in 1260, issuing in massive processions, passing southward to Rome, then northward through much of Central and Northern Italy, beating themselves with leather thongs, praying and chanting, recollecting the Passion.[24] Like the Alleluia, it was in part borne up by the will to peacemaking: its origin follows closely peace legislation by the *popolo* of Perugia in 1260. It remained a strongly orthodox movement in Italy, condemning heresy, usury and sodomy, by its very nature anti-Cathar, practising flagellation till the blood ran in order to share in the sufferings of Christ at the crucifixion, issuing in the foundation of new confraternities to sustain their aims amongst the faithful. The Laudesi, first known from a confraternity founded by a Dominican in 1267, chanted religious ballads in the vernacular celebrating the saints, the joys and sorrows of Mary and Christ's Passion, focusing popular devotion in a style far removed from that of the Cathars.[25]

Obscure individuals linked to no organization also played a role. The way for the Alleluia in Parma was prepared by a bizarre lay brother, Fra Cornetto, who played a horn and sang religious songs, including a troped version of the Hail Mary. The cult of Umiliana di Cerchio del Cherchi, a widow in Florence who, not finding a suitable confraternity, led a sternly ascetic life and worked for the poor, was promoted after her death in 1246 as an example of a lay woman who had achieved holiness without joining an order, a pattern for women who might otherwise have felt the perilous appeal of the life of a *perfecta*.[26] The Milanese poet Bonvesin de la Riva, who

[23]   G. G. Merlo, ' "Militia Christi" come impegno antiereticale (1179–1233)', *Militia Christi e Crociata, Miscellanea del Centro di Studi Mediaevali* XIII (Milan, 1992), pp. 335–86, on Ezzelino, pp. 73, 383.

[24]   G. Dickson, 'The flagellants of 1260 and the crusades', *JMH* XV (1989), pp. 227–67 (illuminating); G. G. Meerssemann, 'Disciplinati e penitenti nel duecento', *I movimenti dei disciplinati nel settimo centenario del suo inizio (Perugia – 1200), Convegno internazionale: Perugia 25–28 sett. 1200* (Perugia, 1962), pp. 43–72.

[25]   Vauchez, in *Laics*, pp. 391–8.

[26]   Thompson, *Revival* (Cornetto); A. Benvenuti Papa, '*In castro poenitentiae': santità e società femminile nell' Italia medievale* (Rome, 1990), pp. 59–98 (Umiliana).

died c.1313–15, was a lay member of the Humiliati, and in his poem cast as a debate between a fly and an ant shows awareness of current terms for a perfect and a believer; in his Debate between Satan and the Virgin he reveals knowledge of radical dualist doctrine on free will and arguments put in play by the author of the major Cathar treatise, the *Liber de duobus principibus*. It has been suggested that the Virgin is modelled on one of Bonvesin's fellow Humiliati and Satan's arguments, a fair representation of Cathar polemic, derive from his own personal contact with a Cathar.[27] This vernacular anti-Cathar work is unlikely to have stood alone: there may well be a lost literature, some produced earlier in the thirteenth century, fruit of the openness of Italian society where knowledge of Cathar beliefs and internal debates was widespread.

A lay movement had arisen which, in its independence and positive enthusiasm for Catholicism, attracted an elite in the cities and provided a counterpoise to Ghibellines, anticlericals and fautors of heresy.

The cities, the Ghibellines and the protectors

When the Cathar bishop of Cremona, presiding over what was evidently an *émigré* Languedocian Church, sent over to Montségur offering asylum to his co-religionists, he illustrated in the most vivid fashion the contrast which existed between Cathar Languedoc and Cathar Italy. Despite occasional inquisitions and burnings, the denunciations of popes and bishops and the growing competition of the confraternities, Italian Cathars were still in many cases able to move about, receive the visits of their perfect and practise their beliefs while, after Montségur, the Church in Languedoc was fast becoming the Church of the Desert, existing in subterfuge and secrecy. The reasons for this contrast lay pre-eminently in the cities, in their long tradition of anticlericalism, struggles with their bishops and tensions over the rights, liberties and endowments of the Church, and to a lesser extent in the *contados* where a certain number of aristocrats and confraternities provided patronage and refuge for leading Cathars moving away from periodic persecutions. Certain city governments so valued their autonomy that they were unwilling to accept anti-heresy legislation or allow inquisitors freedom to act: their leaders were not necessarily personally sympathetic to heretics, but they feared offering churchmen any additional powers, or were already embroiled with an ancient complex of ecclesiastical authorities over strictly temporal issues, perhaps enjoying usurped ecclesiastical revenues, unwilling to surrender them and fearing that the acceptance of an external authority on the issue of heresy would involve surrenders in other spheres as well. Dissatisfaction with torpid or concubinary clergy also played a role.[28]

Frederick II's court propagandists, his rhetors, poets and publicists, his distinguished Latin and appeal to ancient imperial traditions might weigh

[27]   F. Zambon, 'L'hérésie Cathare dans la société et la culture italienne du XIIIe siècle', *EO*, pp. 27–52.
[28]   Dupré-Theseider, 'Gli eretici ...' is a balanced guide.

Map 4 The diffusion of Catharism in Italy
Source: Sketch map of some principal Cathar localities kindly given by Professor
F. Zambon for his lecture in *EO* (delivered 1992)

less heavily than the friars, but they were not without influence which, whatever the official tenor of imperial legislation, tended to favour the toleration of the heretics. Frederick's plea for a poor, apostolic Church,
convenient as it was for his political aims, was not necessarily wholly insincere, and it struck a chord in some quarters, automatically favouring the
Waldensians and Cathars.[29] Ghibellinism was much more than a simple
support for emperors, involving as it did a multitude of local interests,

---

[29] See Schaller, in *DA* LI (1995), pp. 493–513.

families and factions, but it had an anticlerical undertow and it was the most important force in Italy for the protection of heretics, pre-eminently the Cathars.

Gregory IX had been concerned about Catharism in Florence in 1227: it is clear that it lived on and penetrated the ruling elite, who were revealed in the searching enquiry of Ruggero Calcagni, the Dominican inquisitor in 1244.[30] This was not simply casual tolerance, for the Nerli family described by Dante as one of the oldest and most honourable in Florence, produced a *perfecta*, who was visited by her four sisters; Lamaldina, wife of Rinaldo Pulci, of the banking and trading house of Pulci, kept open house for the perfect and allowed the administration of the *consolamentum* while her sister-in-law was a *perfecta*. The wife one of the rich clan of Caponsacchi, Adalina Tribaldi, lived outside the city at Ripoli, entertaining the perfect and allowing the *consolamentum* to be administered, calling in two perfect to her dying husband. The De Barone family were among the leading families of Florence; Baro de Barone was a member of the city council in 1245 and his brother, Pax, had been witness in 1232 to an agreement between the cities of Florence and Colle. No respecter of persons, Calcagni initiated proceedings against the brothers and gathered evidence. Catharism had penetrated deeply. The brothers were believers, their mother a *perfecta*, a woman believer lived in one of their houses and in another they received the perfect, allowing consoling to take place and instruction to be given. They gave refuge to a perfect freed by force from prison in the Marinetta Tower by believers, who was then joined by another perfect also hiding in their house, and made off to the countryside where they, along with other perfect and a bishop, were protected by a nobleman, who first kept them in his palace, then in a private house and finally with priests in a dwelling owned by the Catholic Church in Pontefonio. When the inquisitor condemned the Barone brothers to suffer penalties, including demolition of one house, loss of goods and a heavy fine, he was not allowed to prevail. Support was obtained from Frederick II who issued an imperial rescript protecting them; the messengers of the *podestà* appeared at the Dominican convent on 12 August 1245 to demand the withdrawal of the inquisitor's sentence and the captains of the anti-heretical confraternity of the Society of the Faith were ordered to desist from intervening.

The rescript itself could be taken as a provocation by the Church party in Florence, since Frederick had lately been deposed as part of Innocent's campaign against him. The *podestà* sprang from a Ghibelline family of Bergamo and his set of mind was opposed to the inquisition. On 13 August, Calcagni countered by assembling his supporters in the piazza before S. Maria Novella and citing the *podestà* as a fautor of heretics; Peter of Verona addressed members of the Society of Faith in the cathedral later in the

[30]   D. Corsi, 'Aspetti dell' inquisizione fiorentina nel '200', *Eretici e ribelli del XIIIe secolo*, ed. D. Maselli (Pistoia, 1974), pp. 65–91. R. Davidsohn, *Geschichte von Florenz* II (Berlin, 1909), pp. 290–309. For social composition of heresy in detail, G. Šemkov, 'Die Katharer von Florenz und Umgebung in der ersten Hälfte des 13. Jahrhunderts', *Heresis* VII (1986), pp. 61–75, tables, pp. 67, 72.

month on St Bartholomew's Day, but the *podestà* had worked to collect forces hostile to the Church party. The commune's bell sounded to summon the citizens into action and the inquisitor's supporters were worsted in a pitched battle in the piazza and in the cemetery. The Barone brothers won by force of arms. Despite his legislation against heresy, Frederick was aware that proceedings against Cathars and their protectors in Florence necessarily damaged his own political support; to back the inquisitor meant undermining a valuable asset in his campaign to sustain his power in Italy. Some citizens backed the *podestà* for secular rather than religious reasons, fearing for the commune's long-term autonomy. In consequence, the Cathar elite could live on undisturbed, and it is surely significant that as late as 1260 the leader of the Florentine forces in the victory at Montaperti, Farinata degli Uberti, was a Cathar.[31]

Catharism had spilled into the countryside as the case of the nobleman protecting the fleeing perfect reveals, and another episode in which peasants in Ronco allowed their house to be used for the consoling of a woman who later returned with her companion *perfecta* to live with them for some years. Evidence for support below the level of leading citizens is, however, very scanty: perhaps the inquisitor was led to the high-born and wealthy in the first instance, who then occupied all the time available to him, perhaps records are deficient. It seems difficult to believe that the rich did not diffuse their beliefs to dependents and servants. Two physicians were deeply involved and the two perfect who were sprung from the prison were arrested in the house of one of them.

What must be plain is that the calibre of Cathar patrons and adherents enabled them to influence the leaders of the Florentine government in a way that humbler followers could not, and that political calculation, the emperor's support and the fierce will to independence stifled the forces in the city hostile to heresy and led to the inquisition's defeat and, more significantly, that of Peter of Verona. In 1244 his preaching had deeply stirred the citizens, yet he and the Society of Faith could not in the end prevail; indeed, his very success in strengthening the consciously Catholic forces of the city roused reaction and no doubt contributed to the crisis of August 1245 when the Ghibellines bestirred themselves and counter-attacked. They won, Peter left the city, the inquisitor ceased to act and Guelf supporters suffered in the following years.[32] Even a great preacher, who could move his hearers to tears of repentance and change lives, did not necessarily prevail against deep-seated political commitments and the emotions of proud citizenship.

Ezzelino III da Romano's case was a very different one.[33] He was not a conventional Ghibelline but a coldly ambitious local lord, reared as a young

---

[31]   Comment, Housley 'Politics and heresy in Italy', p. 201; Guiraud, *Inquisition* II, pp. 489–94 blurs the inquisitor's defeat.

[32]   See also Thompson, *Revival.*

[33]   R. Manselli, 'Ezzelino da Romano nella politica italiana del secolo XIII', in *Studi Ezzeliniani*, ed. G. Fasoli et al. (Rome, 1963), pp. 35–70; F. Lomastro Tognato, *L'Eresia a Vicenza nel duecento* (Vicenza, 1988), esp. pp. 21–5, review G. G. Merlo, *Ricerche di storia sociale e religiosa* XXXIX (1991), pp. 201–9; Cracco, *Vicenza*, pp. 97–110.

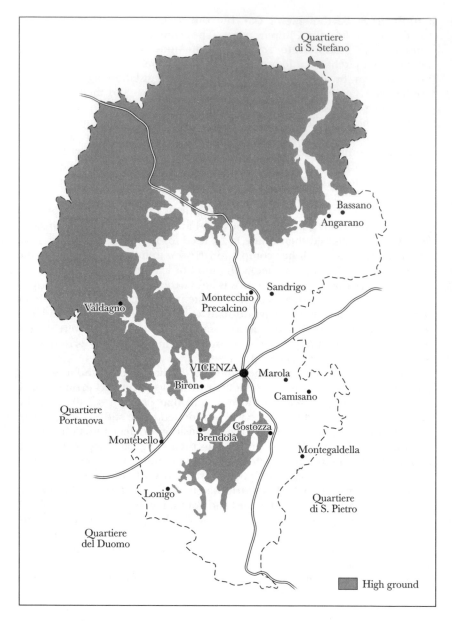

Map 5 Catharism in Vicenza and its *contado*
There is no geographic concentration: heretics are to be found in the hills at the foot of the mountains and in the plain, although there are clearly more recorded to the south and east. Bassano was the seat of the Da Romano. Within Vicenza a number of powerful families who supported Catharism had residences in the central district of the Colle. The map records provenance and habitation of Cathars.

Source: F. Lomastro Tognato, *L'Eresia a Vicenza nel duecento* (Vicenza, 1988), p. 68

man in the ruthless politics of the communes, who broke with the family's traditional hostility to the Empire to reach an understanding with Frederick in 1232, so advantageous that it lasted till Frederick's death: he held no imperial title but fought for Frederick who gave him his bastard daughter in marriage. Ezzelino and friends desired Verona and took it; a key position on the route between Germany and Italy, Frederick needed to neutralize its enmity and helped him to hold it. When Frederick took Vicenza, he handed it over to Ezzelino, who took Padua with the help of imperial troops. In 1241 Frederick entrusted the governing of the territory of Treviso to Ezzelino, who took the city by a coup. He thus came to rule a substantial territory by arms, personality and terror, plus the desire of some citizens to gain economic advantage by a strong and secure rule even at the expense of their freedoms. He foreshadowed the *signori* of a later age, yet was unlike them in his lack of interest in founding a dynasty.

While Ezzelino lived, his great territory was closed to proceedings against heretics. He pursued absolute power: the chronicler Rolandino of Padua said simply that 'he made laws and governed.' To such a man the independent authority of an inquisitor represented a perilous breach in his supremacy: he was indifferent to excommunication and papal exhortation or threat, though he recognized Church authority for the annulling of his marriage to Isotta Lancia; formally correct in his relationship with the Church in his territories, he even exerted a curious fascination over his churchmen, for which they were rebuked by Innocent IV.[34] He quietly appeared among the mass audience of John of Vicenza, recognizing that, for some months, John was a true political force, accepted the reconciliations John imposed, then resumed his political and military strategy as the enthusiasm for the Alleluia faded. In Vicenza, certain ecclesiastical communities such as the canons of the cathedral or the Humiliati enjoyed his protection and Bishop Manfred could rule his diocese – always provided that the issue of the repression of heresy was not raised. The situation of the Church only fell back decisively in the years following the death of Frederick II.

Ezzelino's toleration of heresy was no innovation: his father had followed the same policy and died excommunicate, but it mattered much more because of the size of the region which Ezzelino III, the major power-holder in north-eastern Italy from 1236 to 1259, commanded, where heretics and their supporters could move freely. The Cathar community in his far-flung lands had an unusual immunity; it was not, as elsewhere, forced to become a close-knit, fearful body, carefully protecting its perfect and avoiding pressure from inquisitors and spies. Pietro Gallo, a figure of stature and member of one of the leading families of Vicenza, rose to the status of bishop from being *filius major* to Nicola of Vicenza and for long added to the prestige of Catharism there; teaching was easily and broadly diffused, and, knowing of the freedom in Ezzelino's hands, Cathars flowed in from elsewhere. Viviano Boglo, later bishop, was recruited in this way. For a time Catharism could impose itself on the orthodox. Innocent appeared to believe that the monastery of S. Pietro had been infiltrated and the district of S. Pietro was still a focus for Catharism some two years after Ezzelino's death.

[34] Ibid., p. 106; Church life under Ezzelino, pp. 404–6.

Around Ezzelino's private views doubt hangs still. It has been argued that he had a Cathar family inheritance, that his father, who was reported as having become a monk at the end of his life, had in fact been consoled and was a perfect,[35] and that Ezzelino himself was more than a casual tolerator of heresy – 'one of the foxes that laid waste the vineyard of the Lord'. His sister Imiglia, who long outlived him, was the subject of a posthumous condemnation for heresy.[36] For all his formal acceptance of the traditional rights of the Church as he saw them, his culture was profoundly non-Christian. His passion for astrology, his interest in magic, his relations with Arabs are straws in the wind:[37] he was an unusually cruel politician even by the standards of the time and allusions to his atrocities formed part of the case mounted against him by the papacy. He was the object of profound hate, yet also of an ambiguous respect for an amoral but courageous and determined man who brought order as well as terror. His childlessness has excited interest. Married more than once, he yet had no heir, and though Rolandino believed he had fathered a bastard, he chose never to adopt an heir. It was said that he abstained from the love of woman (in contrast to the greedy sexuality of his brother and ally Alberico)[38] and the suggestion has been made that this sprang from Cathar convictions.

It is unlikely that a man of his temperament would submit wholly to any system. His own fortune was his lodestar; he was the apotheosis of the solitary *condottiere*, immersed in his own bloodstained career. And yet some line of principle may be discerned in his support of the ideal of *imperium*, of an imperial power above the conflicts of families and the individualism of the communes, bound up with a personal reaction against the obligations of the *domus*, the family and its widespread kin, in which he had been brought up. The pope, pressing home his attack in 1248, accused him of not honouring the 'order of nature', of rejecting the sacrament of matrimony with its purpose of procreation, and preferring 'foul unions'.[39]

Yet, despite the denunciations and excommunications, Innocent IV declared himself ready in 1254 to offer Ezzelino pardon and the tranquil government of his lands.[40] Ezzelino preferred the rich material prize open to him by taking up an alliance with Oberto Pallavicini, also a Ghibelline and *condottiere* in spirit, looking to enjoy with Ezzelino a joint hegemony in Northern Italy. Behind 'pardon' would have doubtless lain a reciprocal obligation to yield on the toleration of heretics; they, and the anticlerical forces who backed Ezzelino, could breathe again.

---

[35]   Lomastro Tognato, *L'Eresia*, p. 31; flourishing of Catharism in Vicenza, Cracco, *Vicenza*, p. 405.

[36]   Lomastro Tognato, *L'Eresia*, p. 22, n. 45.

[37]   Ibid., p. 24, n. 52; P. Marangon, *Alle origine dell'aristotelismo Padovano (sec. XII-XIII)* (Padua, 1977), pp. 43–9; Lomastro Tognato believes it to be no accident that Ezzelino was both a protector of Catharism and a patron of courtly love; see also M. L. Meneghetti, *Il publico dei Trovatori* (Modena, 1984). I owe offprints to Dr D. Rando.

[38]   Lomastro Tognato, *L'Eresia*, p. 50.

[39]   Cracco, *Vicenza*, p. 101, with ref.; ideal of *imperium*, p. 102.

[40]   Ibid., p. 108.

In the event, the alliance with Oberto heralded Ezzelino's decline. It alerted other forces, the papacy, Venice, the communes, to the dangers of an overweening da Romano–Pallavicino power. Innocent had seen this clearly: Alexander IV acted. He moved to provoke dissension against Ezzelino, appointed a first-rate reforming bishop to Vicenza, the Dominican Bartholomew of Breganza, and at the end of 1255 called a crusade against him under the fighting archbishop of Ravenna, Philip of Pistoia. It was a 'ruffianly' army[41] but it had papal resources behind it and backing from Venice.[42] For a time, the crusade army pressed Ezzelino and captured Padua, but it was finally defeated and the archbishop taken prisoner. Thus Ezzelino rode the storm but in his overall policy from 1254 had aimed too high. Advised by the subtle Buoso da Doara and angered by Ezzelino's unwillingness to hand over Brescia, Oberto broke with him and in 1259 formed a hostile alliance. Ezzelino's fortune failed after an attack on Milan; he was captured, mortally wounded and, though treated with respect and given medical care, died quietly, showing no concern over family succession to his rich inheritance. Heresy, excommunication and crusade played a part in his downfall but balance of power and local patriotisms were more significant.[43]

Oberto lived to see a widespread Ghibelline collapse and found himself compelled to yield to a new political constellation. Basing his dominion on Cremona and the middle Po, he was as tolerant of heresy and as anticlerical in his sympathies as Ezzelino, differing only in being more closely bound first to Frederick II and then to his German successors. The freedom of the Cathars of Cremona was made possible by Oberto's policies. He meant to keep control of any external force that had potential to upset his dominance, whether the inquisition or the Disciplinati, kept out by the grim spectacle of the gallows he erected on the bank of the Po to terrorize them. Even when for political reasons he had to come to terms with the papacy, it brought no immediate threat to the Cathars.[44]

Viterbo is a case of another kind, where a long continuity of complacency to heresy by Ghibelline families, never completely broken for all Innocent's efforts, and the imperial interest in a city which lay on a key route to Rome, prevented the heresy being totally uprooted. It was not an individual tyrant who prevented sustained, effective persecution, but powerful local families of which the Tignosi are the best known.

Denounced by Innocent III as 'a son of perdition', Giovanni Tignosi was nevertheless in the city in 1214 and two years later was involved in litigation there; in the 1240s, Tignosi were still active in the contest between Empire and papacy. Gregory IX was constrained to intervene when he got wind of

[41] C. W. Previté-Orton, *A History of Europe 1198–1378* (London, 1937), p. 84.
[42] N. J. Housley, *The Italian Crusades* (Oxford, 1982); comment, G. A. Loud, 'The missing martyrs', *SCH* xxx, pp. 141–52.
[43] Cracco, *Vicenza* on Ezzelino's fall preferred to other accounts; Guiraud, *Inquisition* ii, pp. 447–51, 534–8 gives quotations, but no analysis of Ezzelino's attitudes.
[44] Manselli, *L'Eresia*, p. 285, comment p. 282 (Catharism known in Cremona only because of letter); Violante, in *Hérésies et sociétés*, p. 183.

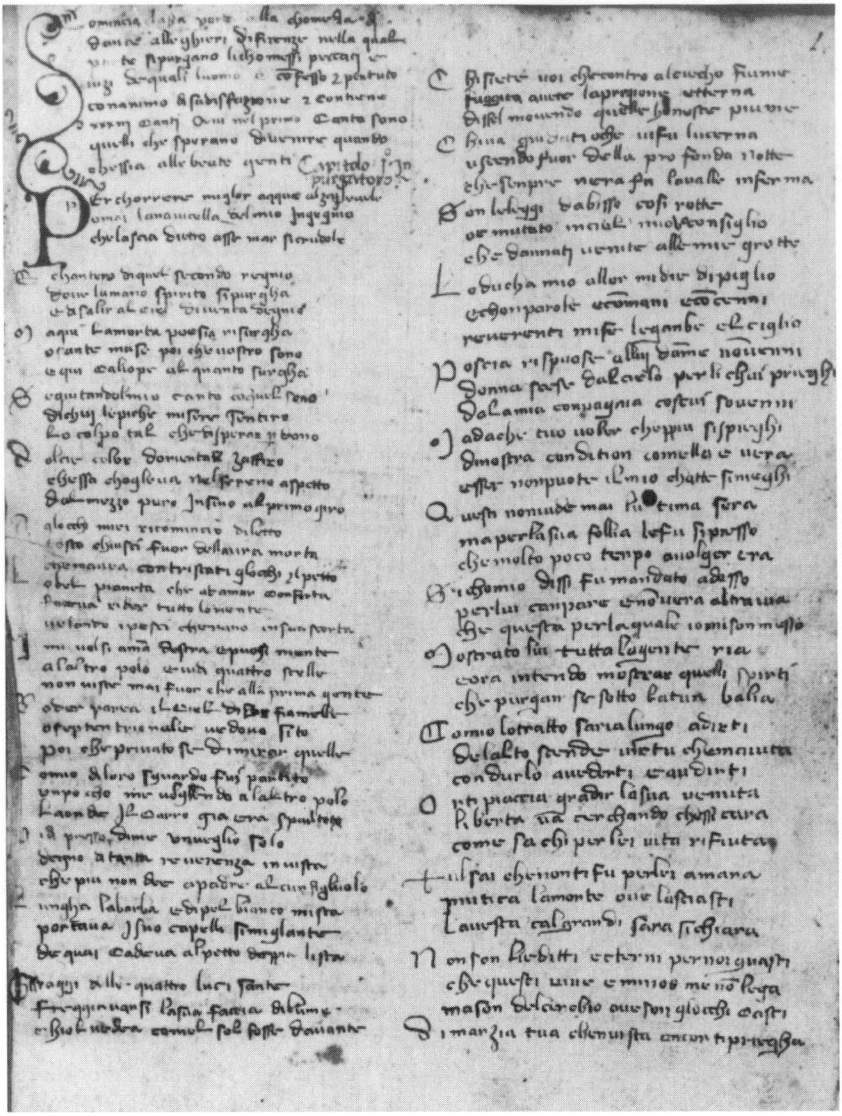

Figure 5   *Liber de duobus principibus*
Reproduced by permission of Bibliotèca Nazionale di Firenze

the supposed election of a 'pope' of the heretics in the city in 1231.[45] The expulsion of St Rose and family in 1250, even though her activities were religious, not political, demonstrates the influence which the protectors of heresy still possessed.

[45]   Manselli, *L'Eresia*, pp. 290–1; Violante, in *Hérésies et sociétés*, pp. 183–4.

As in Viterbo, the protection of Catharism in Orvieto lay among powerful families. The desire for autonomy and its territorial interests pulled the commune in one direction, the advantages to be gained from peaceful relations with the papacy and the pope's own interests in a city within the Papal States lying along a strategic route from Rome to Florence pulled in another. Tactical submissions to authority seem never to have ended in an uprooting of Catharism, whose presence is revealed in a scattering of episodes between 1223, when a married couple were sentenced for giving hospitality to two perfect, and the thorough inquisition conducted by Franciscans in 1268–9. The heretics seem to have lain low after the storm over the killing of Pietro Parenzo, but they had aggressive members and supporters who fired the Dominican convent and wounded the inquisitor Ruggero Calcagni in 1240, shortly after the rupture between Gregory IX and Frederick II. In 1249 eight heretics, including one who participated in the attack, were sentenced for various offences, including an attempt to constrain the inquisitor's notary to delete names from the register.[46]

Grumbling territorial conflicts with the papacy, the sensitive position of Orvieto and, probably, a delicate balance of power between factions easily upset by external events, account for the failure to put heresy down in the decades following the Parenzo affair. The heretical movement at that time 'comes across largely as a political faction'[47] – in other words, Ghibellinism and family interest were crucial. By 1268–9 Catharism had spread widely in Orvietan society; politically orientated protection had given it time to develop its religious attractions.

The inner life of the Italian Cathars

One famous manuscript from the Florentine archives, discovered by Dondaine, epitomizes the likeness and unlikenesses between the Catharism of Italy and Languedoc. The manuscript is a curiosity.[48] Using a thirteenth-century Lombard script, two scribes copied the major extant work of Italian Cathar scholarship, the *Liber de duobus principibus*, possibly directly from an autograph, certainly at no great distance from the original. Scribe B inserted a partial transcription of a Latin version – the only one extant – of the ritual for the administration of the *consolamentum*; another crude unprofessional hand added some individual texts. The manuscript passed into the hands of an Italian perfect, proud of his *consolamentum* and fearful of giving clues about his identity to pursuers in the inquisition. At the foot of the folio

[46]   Episodes, Henderson, *Piety*, pp. 41–5; Manselli, *L'Eresia*, p. 289, Violante, in *Hérésies et Sociétés*, p. 183.
[47]   Henderson, *Piety*, p. 43.
[48]   A. Dondaine, *Un traité néo-manichéen du XIIIe siècle: Le Liber de duobus principibus, suivi d'un fragment de rituel cathare* (Rome, 1939) (original discovery): C. Thouzellier, *Livre des deux principes. Sources Chrétiennes* CXCVIII (Paris, 1973) (edn with commentary, French trans.), for MS see pp. 15–32; cryptogram, pp. 29–32, Borst, *Katharer*, pp. 258–9, nn. 17–19; dating, *GRK* IV (1), p. 211; authorship and doctrinal analysis, pp. 211–79 (outdating all others); summary, pp. 272–9; *WEH*, pp. 511–91 (excerpted trans. with introduction).

where the *Liber* comes to an end he wrote three lines in partial cipher recording in Latin that he, Sagimbenus, had been consoled by the Lord Henry when he was about fifty-one and a half. In much the same way as baptisms and weddings were recorded on the flyleaves of family Bibles, Sagimbenus was using a precious manuscript that had come into his hands to record what must have been to him one of the greatest days of his life, his consoling. He used a simple cipher, a variation of that known to the curia, the imperial court and to classical antiquity: consonants remained in place, vowels represented by numbers in one system and by the preceding consonants in the alphabet in another, the systems alternating so as to throw possible decipherers off the scent. In the most probable interpretation, he was recording a consoling which took place on 2 November 1254 near the beginning of the season of Cathar fasting before Christmas at a place now unknown, 'in Salmignono'. A Cathar fortress lay at Sirmione on Lake Garda; some have seen in 'Salmignono' a discreet reference to Sirmione where in 1271, according to the confession of a perfect from Languedoc, refugee bishops of Northern France, Toulouse and Lombardy were still in residence able to administer the *consolamentum*.[49] As a safe refuge, Sirmione disappeared in consequence of a destructive expedition under the bishop of Verona and an inquisitor in 1277.

In 1254 the golden days of Italian Catharism were past, Innocent IV had reinforced the inquisition and, despite islands of toleration, adherents of heresy had to proceed more cautiously, as Sagimbenus's cryptogram witnesses. A marginal annotation elsewhere in the text praises a certain Alberic, referring to him as *mallexardus*. The clue is unmistakable. A *mallexardus* was a supporter of the imperial power, Ghibelline, and the allusion is to Alberic, brother of Ezzelino da Romano, and must have been inserted sometime between the brothers' reconciliation in 1257 and Alberic's death in 1260.[50] It is yet another reminder of the crucial role played by individual secular power in maintaining places of security from persecution.

For all its mysteries, what the manuscript so clearly shows is the common ground between Languedoc and Italy – the awe and reverence felt by believers and perfect alike for the *consolamentum*, the making of a perfect and the attaining of salvation. The Latin text conveys the same passionate conviction of the potency of the *consolamentum* as the sole rite of salvation as the Provençal text – albeit with the odd remark implying that Catholic baptism, or perhaps life within Catholicism, still had merit although falling short of the true Cathar baptism of the spirit: 'let no one conclude', the officiant says, addressing the candidate for consoling in the Latin ritual, 'that through this baptism which you receive in understanding you disdain the other baptism – either Christian observance or any good thing which you have done or said up to the present moment; on the other hand you must understand that it is fitting for you to receive this holy consecration of Christ as a supplement to that which was insufficient for your salvation.'[51]

49   *JDH*, p. 190–1.
50   Borst, *Katharer*, p. 254n.; Thouzellier, *Livre*, pp. 21, 28.
51   *WEH*, p. 481.

Through a long sermon, the presiding officer, customarily a member of the Cathar hierarchy, explained the significance of the spiritual baptism of the *consolamentum* with a plethora of biblical texts and allusions, confirming the power of the apostles to administer this baptism, which they had received from Christ. 'Baptism', he commented, 'means a laving or superbaptism. Now, one must understand that Christ did not come to wash the filth of the flesh, but to cleanse the filth of God's souls that have been soiled by contact with evil spirits'[52] – in other words, it was not water but spiritual baptism through the laying on of hands which was efficacious.

Unmistakably, in Cathar interpretation of Scripture, Christ came in order to reveal his spiritual baptism and hand it on to the apostles and so, down through lines of 'Good Christians' to the Cathar perfect of the thirteenth century. The president stated the unique claim of the perfect:

> No wise man believes that the Church of Jesus Christ performs this baptism by imposition of hands without manifest proof from Scripture nor imagines that the Church of God performs this consecration out of the presumption and human intuition of its members or by unknown and unseen inspiration of spirits. No, the disciples of Jesus Christ actually went forth and stood with the Lord Jesus Christ and they received from Him the authority to baptize and to forgive sins. So today do true Christians . . .[53]

There follows a justification of the Cathar imposition of hands as the true spiritual baptism, leading on through a disquisition on the meaning of Noah's ark, and more biblical proofs, to the decisive conclusion that only the Cathar *consolamentum* could save. 'True Christians, then', the prior concludes, 'taught by the primitive Church, actually perform this ministry of the imposition of hands without which, we believe, no one can be saved.'[54]

The theme of the supreme authority of the *consolamentum* is thus the same as in the Provençal rite, albeit more fully expounded and with more biblical allusions. Just as in the Provençal, the ministration of the prayer, i.e. the rite whereby a believer received authority to say the paternoster, immediately precedes the consoling itself – possibly held on a separate occasion but clearly a normal preliminary. The Provençal version of both rites is more curt and less reflective. The core of the ceremony in the use of the book, and the laying on of hands remained the same in all lands. Because it has more detail, the Latin version enables the modern reader to reconstruct vividly the sequence of gestures and prayers.

After the administration of the prayer, the candidate approached the prior accompanied by the *ancianus* of the community where he or she had trained and passed through the requisite fasts. The two then made three

---

[52]   Ibid., p. 475.
[53]   Ibid., pp. 476–7.
[54]   Ibid., p. 479.

obeisances to him and prayed for the 'good' of the candidate, that is, for reception into the ranks of the consoled. The prior and all the perfect present, both male and female, then said seven prayers to God asking that the point be heard. The *ancianus*, standing beside the prior, asked for forgiveness for all: 'May the Holy Father, just, true and merciful ... forgive you and have mercy on all your sins ...' [55] The prior replied, then with three obeisances all the perfect asked God's pardon for sins.

It was a characteristic sequence of acts and supplications on the most sacred of all occasions, seeking to brush away every fleck of sin from them all before the consoling. The prior then arranged a table in front of himself, the candidate took the book, a gospel or New Testament, from the prior who asked the candidate if he was willing to receive the 'spiritual baptism' and pardon of his sins 'through the supplication of Good Christians'.[56] He assented, the prior's sermon followed and an exhortation to the candidate to fidelity to the law of Christ, including a commitment 'never knowingly or of your own will' to 'eat cheese, milk, the flesh of birds, of creeping things, or of animals, prohibited by the Church of God' [57] – and an injunction to be ready to endure 'hunger, thirst, dissension, persecution and death'. Then the candidate gave his assent to receiving the *consolamentum*, repeating the words of the *ancianus*: 'I come to God, to you, to the Church and to your holy order to receive pardon and mercy for all my sins ...'.[58] The prior replied, the candidate rose and, leaning, put his hands on the table, while the prior held the book on the candidate's head and the perfect also put their right hands on his head or shoulders. Prayers, paternosters and supplication for the newly initiated followed, spoken by the prior, then a reading from the opening chapter of St John's gospel. The whole sequence of ritual and sermon was studded with scriptural texts, just as in the Provençal version; only two quotations about chastity and virginity, possibly from the Fathers, form an exception.[59] This could only enforce the impression that it was the Cathars who were in possession of the authentic, scripturally based tradition.

The candidate, now for the first time referred to as a Christian, kissed the book three times, made three obeisances and prayed for a rich reward for those who had administered it to him. The ceremony closed with the confession of the perfect, the *apparellamentum* – a reminder of the eternal watchfulness demanded of them to push away their sins and retain unflecked their status till death release them from the envelope of Satan. Supporters would have been present but they played no active part.

This final act, together with the emphasis throughout on repeatedly asking pardon for sins, conveys something of both the strength and weakness of Catharism. With their fasting, their meticulous care to avoid pollution and their monthly collective confessions, the perfect stood out in

[55]   Ibid., pp. 473–4.
[56]   Ibid., p. 474.
[57]   Ibid., p. 480.
[58]   Ibid., p. 482.
[59]   Ibid.

their passionate zeal against sin (as they interpreted it) in contrast to the broad mass of Catholic clergy and religious, imperfectly disciplined, often involved in internal, ecclesiastical conflicts or the troubles of the cities, embracing with the saintly very many imperfect human beings. In comparison, the perfect were an elite, aristocrats of fasting in an age which still valued asceticism, adherents of a rigidly disciplined way of life which attracted their believers and kept them in a kind of cocoon of veneration. With the passionate concern to avoid the clutches of Satan and his evil spirits, however, went a tense anxiety about faults and a watchfulness among the leading perfect so vividly portrayed in the narratives about Nicetas and Petracius[60] and the inner conflicts of the twelfth century, lest one of their number had committed a sin, forfeited the *consolamentum* and dragged down with him those he had consoled. The perfect walked a tightrope and their anxieties were a potential source of dissension.

On the other hand, the Ritual also conveys the strong sense of collegiality, as all the perfect present, male and female, join in prayers and, at the key moment of consoling, put their right hands on the head of the new 'Christian'. The prior of the Ritual was *primus inter pares* and there was a strong sense of community amongst them, linked together in their pursuit of salvation and a holy life. Pseudo-Capelli, writing probably around 1240 and concerned both to confute Catharism and to expose slanders about it, spoke of Cathar deacons running hospices 'in which brethren who come from other places receive the boon of hospitality, cheerfully providing for the latter's necessities with careful attention, for they are strongly linked to each other by a bond of affection.'[61] He may once have been a Cathar believer, who, having felt its attractions, was still able to convey them to his readers while warning of the dangers of yielding to them.

Language divides the rites of Languedoc and Italy, Provençal against Latin. The conservative choice for ritual, Latin had the advantage of being supra-national and probably still comprehensible to many in Italy 'as an archaic form of the vernacular'.[62] There is little doubt that the Bogomil rite of consoling emerged in a Latin version in Western Europe in the twelfth century, archetype of the extant Provençal and Latin versions. An affinity between these and the Radoslav liturgical MS from mid-fifteenth century Bosnia, itself demonstrably of much older origin, makes clear what the prototype of all Cathar ritual was: this naturally developed along regional lines with variations incorporated in usage by leading perfect, producing texts characteristic of Cathar communities in Languedoc, Italy and Germany. Translation into the vernacular was no doubt a necessity for Languedoc, given the low level of comprehension of Latin there, though

[60] Above, pp. 49–54.
[61] *WEH*, pp. 302–3.
[62] Hamilton, 'Wisdom from the East' in *BHL*, pp. 38–60 at p. 49; Radoslav MS, below, p. 300: M. R. Harris, 'Prolégomènes à l'histoire textuelle du Rituel Cathare occitan', *Heresis* VI (1986), pp. 5–14 decisively rejects Borst's hypothesis, *Katharer*, pp. 121, 279–83, of the priority of the Occitanian version. See *GRK* IV (1), pp. 62–7 for differences between Occitanian and Latin versions.

the translator still left certain well-known elements such as the Prologue to St John's gospel and the paternoster in the original Latin.[63]

In the Latin rite, the prior enjoins the candidate to promise to the best of his ability to be 'obedient to God and to the Church, at the will of God and his Church';[64] this is not found in the Provençal rite, where the emphasis is placed exclusively on fidelity to the commandments of Christ. Perhaps Italian Cathars were at this point more influenced by the practices of the Catholic Church, or were concerned to stem the disunities which afflicted Italy by maintaining firm lines of control from the hierarchy to individual perfect.

If, despite these details, Sagimbenus's manuscript of the Ritual shows the profound underlying likeness between the rites of Languedoc and Italy and the role of their perfect, the *Liber de duobus principibus*, by contrast, points up a major difference between them. No comparable piece of writing ever emerged from Languedoc or was likely to do so, so great was the distinction between the academic capacities of leading perfect in Italy and Languedoc. The Italian cities were forcing-grounds for lay skills in the twelfth and thirteenth centuries: it was easier for Catharism there to pick up men of talent and academic or legal training and, since it was only effectively persecuted a good deal later than in Languedoc, its protagonists were given a greater freedom of debate and speculation. Whatever academic developments within Catharism were possible in Languedoc were in any case cut short by the heavy hand of crusaders, inquisitors and the lay supporters of Catholicism.[65]

The *Liber de duobus principibus* is one fruit of this debate. It is not a unified work: it presents in a fragmentary fashion a version of Albanensian theology, that is, an exposition from the school of Catharism especially associated with Lake Garda, which believed in the existence of two eternal principles, one Good, one Evil. Whether there ever was a certain Albanus who gave his name to the school remains a mystery. One passage in a controversial treatise, the *Liber supra stella*, mentions an Albanus but it has been demonstrated that it is a scribal error for Albanensis and all attempts to link the school with Albanus or a place in Italy or the Balkans remain wholly speculative. In his constitution of 1238, Frederick II denounced a group of Cathars under this name and adherents used it of themselves: they were also variously known after their centre, Desenzano by Lake Garda or after one of their leaders, Belesmanza.[66]

The most rigorous of the Cathars in belief, the Albanensians were the smallest of the Italian schools and the most distant from medieval Catholicism. The anonymous author was busy with controversy. As we have it, the *Liber* consists of seven sections, which may originally have been

---

63   Hamilton, in *BHL*, p. 48.
64   *WEH*, p. 480.
65   L. Paolini, 'Italian Catharism and written culture', *BHL*, pp. 83–103 (reassesses cultural life of Cathars).
66   *GRK* IV (1), pp. 165–76 (Belesmanza and Albanensians discussed in relation to John de Lugio).

independent pieces of writing. One, the *Contra Garatenses*, is avowedly polemical, directed against the followers of Garattus, the unlucky leader elected probably in the 1180s at the council of Mosio as the universally acceptable candidate after the conflicts following the visit of Petracius from the East and then discredited by a sexual scandal.[67] But, in some sources, it is none the less Garattus who gave his name to the moderate dualists, who did not accept the existence of an eternal evil principle and adopted a position less dramatically opposed to that of the Catholics, holding that Satan in the last resort was controlled by God. This, a much larger grouping than the Albanensians, was also called after their centre at Concorezzo.

The set of short treatises which compose the *Liber* are marked by a vigorous polemic style – opponents are stigmatized as 'ignorant', 'un-learned' and 'cowards' and the author battles against Catholics as well as moderate dualists. He is aware of his minority position – in the first treatise in the MS, 'On free will', as he begins his refutation of belief in one prin-ciple he notes his expectation that he will thereby contradict 'well-nigh all religious persons'.[68] His stated aim was 'to explain our true faith by evidence from the Holy Scriptures'. It is Albanensian Catharism defended in the light of a substantial body of scriptural citations and what he describes as 'eminently suitable arguments', principally a set of basic axioms, common-places of scholasticism. There are learned allusions and a level of debate attained to which there is no parallel in Languedoc, but the axioms and allusions might well have come from *florilegia* and do not provide evidence *per se* of a direct reading of the Fathers or medieval theologians.[69]

None the less, the author knew his Scriptures well and quotes widely. Unlike many other Cathars, he is not dependent on myths: Scripture holds the central place. He is a theologian in whom rational truth is constantly confirmed by the witness of Scripture.[70] Above all, the *Liber* witnesses to the great range of opinions embraced within the schools of Catharism in Italy, and the intensity of debate between the leading masters and their followers.

Catharism lacked a structure of authority capable of dealing decisively with doctrinal controversies comparable to that which was evolving in Catholicism. Their bishops exercised jurisdiction and might, as individuals, have a personal charisma; in practice, however, in Italy, once Nicetas and Petracius had made their fatal visits from the East and dissensions had sprung up, ruining the pristine unity of the missionary age, the leadership was never able to heal differences. Dated at various points between 1230 and 1250, the *Liber*, the only extant treatise to come directly from an adherent of the Albanensian school, is proof that the controversies stimu-lated over a generation earlier had not died down but continued with vigour not only between rival schools, especially Albanensians and Con-corezzans, but also within them. Despites its miscellaneous and fragmentary

[67]   Above, p. 51.
[68]   Thouzellier, *Livre*, p. 161: attitude to opponents, *GRK* IV (1), pp. 214–15.
[69]   Axioms discussed, *GRK* IV (1), pp. 215–17; Thouzellier comments, *Livre*, pp. 60, 65.
[70]   Dondaine, *Traité*, p. 21.

character, there is a certain unity in the author's aims, for in attacking both the Concorezzans and the Catholics, denouncing the latter in words reminiscent of Catholic authorities as 'the unskilled', he is deploying arguments against those who, for all their differences, have a common opposition to the doctrine of two principles. Though firmly based in the Albanensian tradition, the author interpreted this doctrine in his own distinctive way: both major authorities on the *Liber* have underestimated his calibre and independence.

The Albanensians

Within the school of Albanensians, the writer of the *Liber* stood in a tradition of revisionism dating back to a major split between the Bishop Belesmanza of Verona and his *filius major* John de Lugio of Bergamo, largely a conflict of generations, reported in detail by Rainier Sacconi, once a perfect who had spent seventeen years with the Cathars before being converted by Peter of Verona, entering the Dominican order and becoming an inquisitor in Lombardy. Sacconi's *Summa* of mid-thirteenth century is the work of a cool-headed observer listing concisely Cathar beliefs out of his own knowledge, personal contacts and interrogations.[71]

A long-standing bishop of the radical dualists in line of succession from Johannes Bellus, the candidate elected by the adherents of Nicetas at Desenzano and sent East for consecration, Belesmanza kept the adherence, he said, of 'most of the older and a few of the younger persons of that sect', while John de Lugio drew to his party the 'younger men and a few of the older ones'. Sacconi was a methodical man and he liked to assess the numbers of perfect in the various Churches: John de Lugio's group he classified as 'somewhat larger'. It sounded as if John's school had the future in its grasp – or would have had if force, peaceful competition and the movement of opinion in Italy had not pushed the Albanensians out of existence in the decades following Sacconi's *Summa*. John de Lugio struck out against the myths and exotic ramifications of the school of Belesmanza; Sacconi refers to them as 'the old beliefs which all the Cathars and Albanenses used to hold in the period of approximately AD 1200 to 1230.'[72] In fact, we can assume that the main lines of Belesmanza's were an inheritance going in outline further back to the time of Nicetas.[73]

Old-style Albanensians laid great stress on the independence of two principles, Good and Evil, each with their own spheres; the *Brevis summula*, a late source on Italian Catharism, initiated by a Franciscan jotting heretical tenets into a MS Bible, has a vital clue on the Albanensian approach, taking

[71]   Šanjek, in *AFP* XLIV (1974), pp. 31–60; *WEH*, pp. 329–46; Rottenwöhrer uses dogmatic analysis to distinguish John de Lugio's writing, known through Sacconi, from the *Liber de duobus principibus*, *GRK* IV (1), pp. 165–279, largely rejects R. Nelli, *La philosophie du Catharisme: le dualisme radical au XIIIe siècle* (Paris, 1975) and supersedes all others including Borst, who underestimates the *Liber*, and Dondaine (Nelli biblio. *GRK* IV (3), p. 398).
[72]   *WEH*, p. 337.
[73]   *GRK* IV (1), pp. 33–4.

off from a text attributed to Solomon in the apocrypha, 'All things are divided, one against one.' [74] With extraordinary thoroughness, the Albanensians evolved a theology which postulated an almost unlimited duality of kingdoms, of worlds, of groups of men, of Old Testament patriarchs and prophets, of souls and bodies, clarifying thereby the manner in which the people of God seeking salvation through the Cathar *consolamentum* were to engage with the two great spheres whose endless struggle shadowed their lives. The Old Testament and the history of God's people which it enshrined was not neglected by them – it was, rather, reconstructed as taking place in two settings, an 'earthly' earth and a 'heavenly' earth, the former being an underworld or hell.

The doctrine of the opposing principles, the good God and Satan, both creators, both eternal, had a certain appeal: superficially at least, it appeared to offer a solution to the problem of the nature and origin of evil and sketched a powerful vision of fallen angels passing through bodies, unable to escape transmigration in the age of the Old Testament, but enabled by the coming of Christ to receive the *consolamentum*, to be awakened to the memory of the sin in heaven which led to their fall and to do penance in their bodies before returning to heaven and taking up again the crowns of righteousness which they had lost through Satan's seduction. [75] In this interpretation the number of imprisoned souls was ever diminishing as they received the *consolamentum* and, dying, escaped the chain of being.

With this central doctrine of the incompatibility of the two principles came curious oddities of belief, such as the warlike attacks of God or Satan in the other's sphere; the demons who were alternatively occupation troops in the sphere of God or his hostages; the notion of a crucifixion in God's world of Lucifer, son of Satan and prince of the earthly world; the origin of Christ, born of Lucifer's intercourse with a wife of God or a bad 'Holy Spirit'. [76] The very existence of such fantastic speculations, perhaps held by individual masters and their followers and perhaps, as in the case of Christ's origin, retained as a 'great secret', witnesses both to the lack of any effective central control of what was taught within Catharism and to the rich play of the imagination among some perfect unfettered by Scripture or the Fathers.

But the main lines of Albanensian belief were also in vivid contrast to contemporary Catholic doctrine. The Trinity was denied: Christ was either engendered or created by God and was consequently not eternal: from Mary he received no earthly body, but brought with him a heavenly one. In one account he entered and left her through her ear. He had but one, heavenly nature: his earthly body was a body in appearance only and neither crucifixion nor resurrection in fact took place. He is not the Saviour of

---

[74] Ibid., pp. 351–61; 'put together ... almost entirely from pre-existing documents', W. L. Wakefield, 'Notes on some antiheretical writings of the thirteenth century', *FS* v (1967), pp. 285–321 at p. 320 (demonstrates extent of mutual borrowing); this ref. *WEH*, p. 357, Eccles. 42: 25, see *GRK* IV (1), p. 68.

[75] *GRK* IV (1), p. 148.

[76] Ibid., p. 69.

mankind in the customary, Catholic sense, but rather a messenger of God, an angel whose mission it was to bring knowledge of the means of salvation, the *consolamentum*: Christ's suffering on the cross was a matter of appearance only and his death and resurrection had no significance.[77] The good God, holy and merciful, is God alone, his substance distinct from that of Christ and the Holy Spirit: he is not all-powerful, but was damaged by Satan who seduced some of his angels. The contrast to the doctrines of the medieval Church could hardly be greater.

In the treatise against the Cathars attributed to Peter of Verona, Albanensians were divided in explanation of God's failure to protect his angels from the assault of Satan, some arguing that God knew nothing of Satan's intervention, others that he knew of it but could not defend his sphere, or that he permitted Satan to take the angels with him. Such contradictions, coupled with the exotic speculations of certain masters, both in the Albanensian school and their rivals, were naturally seized on by the orthodox controversialists and inquisitors whose work flowered in Italy for a century, from Bonacursus down to Anselm of Alessandria and including the massive work of Moneta, a Dominican authority, the treatise attributed with high probability to Peter of Verona and the work of a nobleman, Salvo Burci of Piacenza.[78]

There was clearly much more debate and reasoned refutation in Italy than in Languedoc, sometimes abusive, with unfair imputations made about Cathar morality, but more often careful, conscientious analyses based on converts' personal knowledge, the fruit of inquisitors' interrogations or the scrutiny of Cathar works, now lost, such as the *Stella* against which Salvo Burci wrote his polemic, the *Liber supra stella* in 1235.[79] Believers and perfect were not necessarily moved by the hostile, logical analyses of the tenets launched by their opponents; at the heart of the Cathar experience lay a profound conviction of the incompatibility of flesh and spirit, the fundamental Gnostic view of the jewel in the mud, the spirit imprisoned.

From that conviction sprang the theology of Catharism. At its centre lay the question of the salvation of the people of God, and round that passionate concern, plus the conviction of the evil character of the flesh and all material creation, revolved the effort of explanation, seen in its most radical and dramatic form in Albanensian teaching. Scripture was mined to

---

[77]   Ibid., pp. 91–6; general exposition of Albanensian beliefs, with variants, reconstructed from controversialists, pp. 68–164.

[78]   Texts, edns, *GRK* I (1), pp. 47–73, I (2), pp. 71–237, extracts *WEH* (see esp. Moneta excerpts, pp. 307–29); orig., Moneta of Cremona, *Adversus Catharos et Valdenses* ... , ed. T. A. Ricchini (Rome, 1743, reproduced Gregg Press, Ridgewood, NJ, 1964); introduction with notes on Moneta's significance: P. S. Timko, *The Ecclesiology of Moneta of Cremona: Adversus Catharos et Valdenses* (STD thesis, Catholic University America, 1989); G. Schmitz-Valckenberg, *Grundlehren katharischer Sekten des 13. Jahrhunderts* (Munich, Paderborn, Vienna, 1971) (based on Moneta); for Peter of Verona, see Kaeppeli, in *AFP* XVII, pp. 295–335; for Burci, Ilarino da Milano, 'Il "Liber supra stella" ...', *Aevum* XIX (1945), pp. 309–41, *WEH*, pp. 265–6, 269–74.

[79]   Rottenwöhrer broadly supports controversialists' statements, summary, *GRK* IV (3), pp. 280–1. Duvernoy is deeply suspicious of controversialists and underestimates doctrinal division, a weak point in his survey (summary *JDR*, p. 346).

provide justification for dualism and texts which cut against dualist interpretations were glossed away. Philosophical axioms were taken into service
but their function was decorative rather than formative. Neither the interpretation of Scripture nor a metaphysics shaped Cathar theology even when
they occupied space in Cathar discussions and polemic – at the core of the
movement and its theology lay the conviction of the nature of mankind and
life on earth.

If oddities and logical contradictions emerged within this theology they
did not apparently unduly trouble Cathar adherents *en masse* because their
interest focused not so much on God, Satan or the personalities of the Old
and New Testaments as on the history of the salvation of God's people,
among whom they were to be reckoned. They were prepared to tolerate
some idiosyncracies identical to Cathar beliefs given the conviction of the
importance of salvation and the explanation and justification for the practice and theory of the status of the perfect and *consolamentum* in which they
had invested so much.[80]

Certainly there were perfect and believers of no strong critical sense with
vivid and creative imaginations, who delighted in the play of metaphor, the
use of myth, the sheer literary power of Cathar stories, who are likely to have
been immune to criticism made by controversialists, preachers or casual
aquaintances from the Catholic world. But others may not have been so
impregnable, for though a strong convention on the Catholic side damned
heretics as 'idiots', simple and illiterate, incapable of handling and understanding theology, another equally strong convention damned them as
subtle, deceiving, proud, misusing their skill in letters to lead the orthodox
flock astray, and the words of controversialists, Dominicans and papal letters
clearly imply that the Cathar masters were using academic skills and had to
be refuted at an academic level. All the evidence is that at certain times and
at certain levels a real debate was taking place. A higher standard of education raised the level of controversy. Paolini speaks of the 'reality of Italian
cities, where laymen wrote, studied, used books and knew Latin', creating
an ambience in which laity as well as priests were capable of debate and even
wrote polemic, as in the case of Salvo Burci or the author, whose Christian
name of George is alone known, of the *Debate between a Catholic and a
Patarine* – all of which implies that the Catholics expected to make converts
among Cathar supporters or, perhaps more importantly, deter possible
Cathar neophytes from being drawn into the movement. Standards on the
Cathar side certainly rose with time from the comparatively unsophisticated
oral instruction, the likely stock in trade of the early masters of Mark the
Gravedigger's day, through the stimulus given to debate over the pillars of
Cathar belief resulting from the irruption from overseas of first Nicetas,
then Petracius. Fragmentation of Churches, then of belief, followed by a
wrestling between leading perfect for doctrinal victory or for unity was a
forcing-ground for thought about beliefs and more effective instruction of
the perfect.[81]

---

[80] Summary on Cathar doctrine, *GRK* IV (1), pp. 279–383, *passim.*
[81] Paolini, 'Italian Catharism …', quotation, *BHL,* p. 84; A. Reltgen, 'Dissidences et
contradictions en Italie', *Mouvements dissidents, Heresis* XIII–XIV, pp. 89–113 (with

Cathars were aware of the scandal of their disunity, tried to reach deci-sions to overcome it and failed. Salvo Burci gives the most vivid description of these attempts from his vantage point at Piacenza, noting how divisions of belief led to loss of believers.[82] Speaking of the time before the emergence of the Dominicans in 1217–20, Stephen of Bourbon gives a similar account, which, despite its legendary overtones, carries conviction, and he too describes how dissension deterred.[83] His informant who, he said, had witnessed a failed pro-unity conference, felt himself much strengthened in orthodox belief by this spectacle of failure. The gulf maintained between the perfect and the mass of believers to some degree blocked realization of the tensions existing between different schools, for it was generally under-stood that there were inner secrets only to be imparted to those who prepared themselves to be given the *consolamentum*, gradually receiving the hidden truths, while those outside, as it were, had to be content with less demanding fare. Sacconi said that John de Lugio and his followers 'do not dare to reveal to their believers the errors described, lest their own believers desert them … and because of the schism existing among the Albanensian Cathars, of which they are the cause' [84] – in other words, the conflict between the adherents of John de Lugio and those of Belesmanza was a conflict among the perfect kept from the knowledge of the mass of the faithful.

Such measures can never have been wholly water tight; the major dissension between the Concorezzans and Albanensians was in any case widely familiar. If believers would have preferred the conflicts to be forgotten, controversialists on the other side were enthusiastic in making them known.

Eleven treatises, strung out in time between c.1176 and c.1273, stand for a larger volume of Catholic polemic of all kinds in Italy, no doubt supports and reference works for a body of contemporary preaching now lost. There is evidence to suggest that the full-blown treatises themselves evolved from lists of scriptural texts compiled for the use of preachers in the refuting of heresy: popular polemic played a vital role from the earliest days of the Catholic counter-attack and was greatly stimulated by the emergence of the Dominicans as an order specifically dedicated to the reasoned refutation of heresy. There was common ground between the treatises and mutual borrowing. Themes recur – on the distortion of Scripture, the discordance between Scripture and heretical teaching, logical failures within Catharism and their internal disagreements. It is reasonable to think that these attacks on the Cathar position at various levels stimulated some re-thinking of doctrine by their masters and that this combined with the need to defend positions against rival Cathars to produce a considerable fluctuation and

discussion of term 'Patarine', pp. 111–13), defence of controversialists esp. pp. 91–4; the *Debate*, WEH, pp. 289–96; text, Martène-Durand V, pp. 1705–11, Ilarino da Milano, in *Aevum* XIV (1940), pp. 85–140.

[82]   WEH, pp. 270–1; edn of full text in preparation, P. D. Diehl (*Christendom and its Discontents*, p. 47). Extracts, I. von Döllinger, *Beiträge zur Sektengeschichte* (Munich, 1890), II, pp. 52–74.

[83]   GRK IV (3), p. 289, rejecting *JDR*, p. 346, n. 199.

[84]   WEH, p. 343.

development of doctrine. Anne Reltgen has argued that Cathars began to face difficulties with their own faithful objecting to the more exotic and 'shocking' teaching which had prevailed in some quarters, that this in turn led certain masters to modify doctrinal positions in ways which brought them in practice closer to Catholicism.[85]

The profound hostility to Catholicism had not changed, but standards had risen and the work of preaching and popular polemic had begun to create a climate of opinion less readily receptive to aspects of Cathar theology. In consequence, though dualism was still ardently defended, modifications were made to come to terms with this changing atmosphere. The *Liber de duobus principibus* is witness to this process, and incidentally demonstrates by implication the authenticity of Rainier Sacconi's reporting of the movements of Cathar doctrine. The *Liber* stands at the end of a line of thinking. Rottenwöhrer's dogmatic analysis demonstrates beyond doubt that it was not written by John de Lugio at all, as some historians have suggested, but by an author who belonged to his school but differed from him in important ways; analysis of the text and comparison with Sacconi's summary of John de Lugio's beliefs makes clear where likenesses and unlikenesses lie.[86]

While retaining fundamental ideas of the Albanensian school, John made major modifications. Though a creation of the good God and not a person of the Trinity, his Christ took real flesh from Mary, was a sacrifice in the sense of the New Testament, truly suffered and was a saviour. His function, though not very clearly expressed, was not solely to bring mankind the *consolamentum*. John the Baptist pleased God; he was not a tool of Satan. The good God was more influenced by Satan; the customary accounts of the fall of Satan and the seduction of the angels are absent. He accepted fleshly men in the sphere of God, for though he accepted the transmigration of souls, he believed they would end with their own body in God's world. He does not have angels in the usual sense of pure spirits: what fell from heaven were not angels but souls, who will one day be restored to heaven. John accepted the Old Testament; his good God is also the God of the Old Testament, the source of the punishment of His people, the fallen souls, for which He made use of Satan. Most striking in John is the jettisoning of the highly coloured myths which had played so large a part in Cathar exposition and the acceptance of the whole Bible, interpreted literally rather than allegorically.[87]

Like John, the author of the *Liber* believed in the two eternal principles in accord with the central doctrine of the Albanensians, to which he claimed allegiance, though he too saw the good God influenced by the evil principle. Like John again, the centre of his interest lay in the history of

[85] Reltgen, 'Dissidences', pp. 100–2, 104; treatises and edns, pp. 92–3.
[86] Summary, *GRK* IV (1), pp. 272–9 (with correction of an earlier judgement I (2) 11; ibid., p. 217).
[87] Rottenwöhrer's analysis, using Sacconi, ranged under headings, *GRK* IV (1), pp. 176–207, summary, pp. 207–10, rejecting *JDR*, p. 117 following Nelli, arguing that the views of John de Lugio and the *Liber* author represented only minor deviations from Albanensian tradition. Rottenwöhrer insists there are major movements of thought.

God's people rather than systematic theology. He, too, believed that Christ took human flesh from Mary, accepting the whole Bible and abandoning myth. He stood, therefore, in the same tradition of revisionism but with distinctive features of his own, believing in God's pre-knowledge of evil, an evil which served his plan of salvation. The evil principle was a creator and lay behind the bad events of the Old Testament, but Satan is to be distinguished from the evil principle and must be seen as an effect of this cause. Angels exist, in contrast to John de Lugio's teaching. Ingenious inter-pretations of '*creare*' and '*facere*' lay behind some of his distinctive views.[88] There was only an earthly earth and Christ lived in it; there was no earth of God.

Rottenwöhrer's analysis reaches the conclusion that the author of the *Liber* was an independent thinker who followed through the implications of his ideas and contrived to reconcile an acceptance of the Old Testament with Albanensian thinking without finding the necessity of taking up the cumbersome Albanensian notion of 'mirror-repetition' with its seemingly endless dualities. A profound clash with orthodoxy remained but the author in the end stood in some respects closer to medieval Catholicism than the school of Belesmanza had done.

Of the influence of the *Liber de duobus principibus* we know little. It is not impossible that the most exhaustive and erudite controversialist of all, Moneta, made use of it,[89] but there is in general remarkably little evidence of the *Liber*'s being read: perhaps the epoch of debate was in any case drawing to a close, as more effective persecution took hold. Bernard Gui's classic maxim written at the end of the Cathar age, 'One should not engage in disputation with heretics', informed the work of inquisitors well before his period of office and led to a dwindling emphasis on persuasion and less opportunity for discussion. Perhaps at a deeper level both the *Liber* and the work of John de Lugio had only limited impact, not only because the protagonists in the debate among the perfect deliberately willed to keep the believers away from it, but because the believers and maybe some among the perfect had little taste for debate and scholastic-type analysis.

On the one hand, the movement of opinion within the Albanensian school can be seen as a sign of continuing vitality within Catharism, as some masters kept pace with the developing educational standards of Italy. As Rottenwöhrer observes, Albanensian theology was anything but unified, in one sense a sign of vitality. That tradition went on attracting men with lively and ingenious minds who adapted the tenets they inherited. Even in the late twelfth century Joachim of Fiore, who had direct experience of the Cathars in Southern Italy, had complained of their dialectical skills and what he saw as a 'perverted' understanding of Scripture; a similar complaint about their skill in argument was later made to Honorius III c.1222 by Bishop Rainerius of Toscanella.[90] Plainly, they managed texts well: it may

88   *GRK* IV (1), pp. 239, 242, 258, 263.
89   Ibid., pp. 278–9.
90   Refs from Joachim's *Expositio in Apocalypsim* and Rainerius in Paolini, 'Italian Catharism …', in *BHL*, pp. 90–1.

even be that the practice of collecting texts in summaries designed for preaching and disputation originated with them rather than the Catholics and was imitated in orthodox circles.[91]

Schools of Cathar instruction profited by the freedom of the Italian scene. Cesarius of Heisterbach knew of Cathar schools in Rome c.1209.[92] When Ivo of Narbonne fled from his native land, he found refuge in Italy in 1214 and wandered amongst Cathar communities, learning their secrets and hearing how they 'sent to Paris capable students from nearly all Lombard and from some Tuscan cities. There some studied logic, others theology, with the aim of strengthening their own error and overthrowing the Catholic faith.'[93] Ivo may have exaggerated the extent of Cathar infiltration and the sending of crypto-heretics to Paris, his memory perhaps heightened by the passage of time, for he seems to have written his report decades after the event, but his account still bears witness to the existence of a substructure of Cathar schools from which the most capable future masters would have received the necessary groundwork to compete in controversy. According to his own self-description '*olim heresiarcha*', Rainier Sacconi must have given instruction.[94] Peter of Verona himself may well have been a Cathar scholar in his early years, for he sprang from a Cathar family and was sent to Bologna to study 'for the defence of perfidy'.[95] The impression given is of places of instruction at all levels, capable of carrying the most promising pupils up to university level – a miniature counterpart, in fact, of the educational structure of the Dominican order.

This educational armament at the back of the Cathars increased the fears of churchmen, which may not in the last resort have been justified. The case is arguable that the tilt towards the rational and the jettisoning of the myths, for all the calibre displayed in the work of John de Lugio and the *Liber de duobus principibus*, was not a sign of strength but rather of weakness. Anne Reltgen, reflecting on the work of John de Lugio, points out that, while on the one hand he further radicalized the doctrines of the Albanensians, on the other his theory of dualism 'despite everything permits reconciliation with Christian sensibility'.[96] This was pre-eminently the case with his treatment of Christ, according to his teaching both human and divine. Certainly we have Sacconi's witness that John was carrying with him a majority of the younger perfect; whether he could have had a similar effect on the believer class, how far his views leaked to them, how far the believers preferred their myths, yet, living in an environment which had shifted appreciably towards orthodoxy, found themselves on the receiving end of a more effective Catholic counter-attack, we cannot tell. Our knowledge fades. Extant anti-

[91] Paolini's hypothesis, in *BHL*, p. 92 following R. Morghen, *Medioevo Cristiano* (Bologna, 1951, 2nd edn, 1968), p. 229.

[92] *Dialogus miraculorum*, ed. J. Strange (Cologne, Bonn, Brussels, 1851) I, p. 309. Paolini, 'Italian Catharism ...', pp. 96–7.

[93] Matthew Paris, *Chronica Majora RS* LVII 4, p. 271; *WEH*, p. 186.

[94] *AFP* XLIV (1974), p. 44.

[95] Paolini, 'Italian Catharism ...', p. 102.

[96] Reltgen, 'Dissidences ...', p. 104.

Cathar literature in Italy reaches a peak in roughly the decade 1240–50 and we know little of inner Cathar movement after the *Liber*.

Anne Reltgen's hypothesis receives further support from analysis of a parallel movement of thought, *mutatis mutandis*, taking place within the rival camp of the Concorezzans. The division between them and the Albanensians was profound, and was never healed. When Sacconi summarized the interrelations of the various Cathar Churches, he said that 'all the Churches of the Cathars recognize each other, although they may have differing and contrary opinions, except the Albanenses and the Concorezzenses, who censure each other.'[97] It is highly likely that the views of Concorezzo represent the earliest strand of Cathar opinion. They believed in one principle, not two – hence the profound division. The good God is in the last resort in charge of events and there is no evil principle all powerful in his own sphere – a view much more compatible with orthodoxy whether in Byzantium and the Balkans or the Latin West. The likelihood is that early Catharism remained moderate dualist, or, as Rottenwöhrer prefers, 'mono-principial', and only subsequently changed. It is inherently more likely that the movement of thought proceeded from this moderate dualism, in which Satan's role is that of a fallen angel, to the more radical belief in two co-equal principles than vice versa.[98] From this movement of thought, most probably sparked off by intervention from the East,[99] sprang the divisions of the Italian Churches.

The Concorezzans

Concorezzo itself, however, was far from monolithic.[100] A central pillar of Concorezzan belief lay in their acceptance of one God or principle, eternal and almighty, who allowed his creature Lucifer, an angel whose name was changed to Satan at his fall, to 'order' the visible world from material which God had created, the four elements of earth, air, fire and water. God used Satan as a servant; in due time, Christ, also a creature, was sent to rescue from this world those who would be saved. The Holy Spirit was also a creature; in this respect the Concorezzans, like the Albanensians, denied the Trinity.

Though once a prince of angels exceeding the others in his talents, and after his sin of pride in heaven, his seduction of other angels and his Fall, prince of this world, of darkness and the God of the Old Testament, their Satan was far removed in his power from the evil principle of the Albanensians, for he was in no true sense a creator of this world. He acted like a potter, making human bodies from mud, but he had to force angels into them, even seeking God's aid to do so. He made Eve so that she could

---

[97]   *WEH*, p. 345.
[98]   *GRK* IV (3), p. 284.
[99]   Above, pp. 56–7.
[100]   See subdivisions in Rottenwöhrer's exposition, *GRK* IV (1), pp. 310–426; summary, pp. 432–6. *Liber*, an authentic Cathar work, arguing from within the movement against Concorezzans, provides a double check on what the Concorezzans believed.

seduce Adam into the sin of sexual intercourse.[101] In a vivid phrase derived
from the *Debate*, attributed to the layman George, the tree of the knowledge
of good and evil was the vulva of the woman, her desire aroused through
intercourse with the tail of the serpent and then transmitted to Adam.[102] Sin
was the consequence of the freedom of the will, fundamental to the
Concorezzan interpretation of the history of angels and men and of the
origins of evil. The sex act was the original sin on earth – a doctrine absent
from the Albanensian system.[103] Through it, bodies were reproduced, and
angels, once imprisoned, continued to be imprisoned in new bodies. A
common Concorezzan view believed that one angel was forced into a body
by Satan, that of Adam from whom Eve was made as in the Genesis story.
Sacconi reported that the angel imprisoned in Adam had sinned
'slightly':[104] other versions spoke of a good angel who had not sinned in
heaven and another postulated two angels being used by Satan.

Demons were generally fallen angels who still possessed their natural gifts
and were correspondingly dangerous to mankind; others were stars, their
light deriving from an angel, their bodies formed by Satan. Metempsychosis
was an Albanensian doctrine; Concorezzans believed in the reproduction of
one soul from another via the act of sexual intercourse.[105] There remained a
fundamental Gnostic-type dichotomy between the body, the work of Satan
which would dissolve first into the four elements and then, at the Last
Judgement, into chaotic matter and a soul, an imprisoned angel. But where
Albanensians believed in two types of men, the one a carrier of a demon,
the other of an angel, Concorezzans understood that the souls of all
humanity were angels with freedom of will, capable of both good and evil.
Their bodies were the tools of the soul, ever liable to draw the soul down
into Satan's clutches but still controlled by it. As in Catholicism, on the
choice made between good and evil rested the eternal fate of mankind: a
part of mankind would be saved through the *consolamentum* administered by
the Cathars, but a greater number would be damned. Only the *consolamentum* held securely with the faithful observance of the way of life of the
perfect could save.[106]

Frontiers of belief between Cathar denominations, for all the open
conflict between Concorezzans and Albanensians, were surprisingly fluid in
practice, as the doctrines of Nazarius, long bishop of Concorezzo, demonstrate; he had been the *filius major* of the Garattus whose followers were
attacked by the author of the *Liber de duobus principibus*, then reigned as
bishop between c.1190 and 1240. Sacconi calls him '*antiquissimus*',[107] referring to his age rather than his office, and remembered, while still a Cathar
before c.1245, hearing him expound doctrine. It is all the more surprising

101   On Satan, *GRK* IV (1), pp. 33–7, creation, pp. 366–75.
102   *GRK* IV (1), p. 333.
103   Ibid., p. 337.
104   *WEH*, p. 334; *JDR*, p. 111 argues phrase provides background to parable of
prodigal son: see *GRK* IV (1), pp. 351, 356–60.
105   *AFP* XLIV, p. 58; background, *GRK* IV (1), pp. 395–8; doctrine, pp. 399–410.
106   Ibid., pp. 238–81.
107   *AFP* XLIV, p. 58.

to find that his Christology is touched by Albanensianism, and that on Mary he held part-Albanensian views on her as an angel and only an apparent mother of Jesus.

Nazarius was the recipient of the Eastern apocryphon from Bulgaria, the *Interrogation of John* or *Secret Supper*, in which, in a dialogue in heaven between John the Evangelist and Christ, are elicited the inner secrets of the origins of the world, the fall of angels, the making of man and the means of his salvation. A version fell into the hands of the inquisitors' staff at Carcassonne; on the MS an inquisitor or an office scribe wrote: 'This is the *Secret* of the heretics of Concorezzo, brought from Bulgaria to Nazarius their bishop. It is full of errors.'[108] Its sense of mystery, its powerful story-telling and carnal imagery makes it an effective addition to the armoury of the Concorezzans, carrying with it the special prestige of the East as the birthplace of the Cathars. The Devil bade two angels to enter bodies of clay, differentiated according to gender, and 'bade them to perform the works of the flesh ... but they did not know how to commit sin.' Then he planted a bed of reeds in paradise and made a serpent of his spittle, entered the serpent and had intercourse with Eve with the tail and both angels in consequence 'were affected by a lust for debauchery'. This is a strangely organic, sexual emphasis in a text presumably created or transmitted and read by celibates, Eastern monks or Western perfect. Consciously banished from the life of the elite, sexuality makes its return by the back door in apocryphal literature.[109]

The power of this Gnostic-style exposition would lead one to expect that the *Interrogation* would sweep the board as a standard canonical text, finally enshrining Concorezzan views. But it was not so: Nazarius picked and chose, influenced by the *Interrogation*, not overcome by it. His idiosyncratic mix of Catharisms did not prevent him holding sway as bishop for decades and illustrates again the individualism of leading masters. In essentials, he belonged to the past and was at heart a traditional weaver of fantasies, a believer, for example in the curious theory based on a misunderstanding of a technical expression in astronomy, that the sun and moon, which he believed had souls, fornicated once a month, giving issue to honey and dew.[110] Honey was not forbidden to Cathars but Nazarius abstained from it, mindful of its doubtful origin. Such fantasies were rejected by his *filius major*, Desiderius, and his party within the Concorezzan Church, who

---

[108]   *Le Livre Secret des Cathares: Interrogatio Johannis apocryphe d'origine bogomile*, ed. E. Bozóky (Paris, 1980), p. 26 (from Vienna MS; attribution confirmed, *TDH*, *AFP* XX p. 319); *WEH*, pp. 448–9, 456–65; Rottenwöhrer argues on basis of dogmatic analysis, *GRK* IV (1), pp. 313–27 (including elements only in Vienne text), that *Interrogatio* is not strictly Bogomil, but the product of an 'eastern Catharism', an intriguing hypothesis developed in *GRK* III: *Die Herkunft der Katharer nach Theologie und Geschichte* (Bad Honnef, 1990), pp. 17–44 (dogmatic contrasts between *Interrogatio* and Bogo-milism, pp. 41–2). At least a third party intervenes in possible transmission from Bogomilism to Catharism. On Bozóky edn, G. Firmin, *ETR* LVII (1982), pp. 113–17.
[109]   M. D. Lambert, 'The motives of the Cathars: some reflections', *SCH* XV, pp. 45–59 at pp. 52–3; *WEH*, pp. 460, 461.
[110]   *GRK* IV (1), p. 408; summary, pp. 409–10.

spurned Nazarius's approach as 'the old opinions' and the *Interrogation* which, Sacconi tells us, they regarded as 'bad'.

Desiderius's Christ was a real man with a human body taken from Mary (though not from Joseph), who ate, was crucified and rose again. Christ and his disciples performed real, corporeal miracles. His earthly body would be laid aside at the ascension, taken up again for the Last Judgement, then finally dissolved into primeval matter. He is of one essence with God, but as Son of God in a lesser position; the Holy Spirit is also of God's essence but subordinate to the Son. The souls of the righteous, with Mary, the apostles and saints, would remain in an earthly paradise till the Last Judgement.[111]

For all his idiosyncracies and subordinationism, there is an appreciable swing under Desiderius away from myth and Docetism towards a more solid, rational style of exposition, a greater acceptance of the corporeal in general and of the humanity of Christ in particular. He is no longer created by God and Desiderius gives him both a human and a divine nature. A gulf between even the Desiderian revision and the doctrines of the medieval Church remained but the Christology had changed profoundly. That this movement of thought occurred within the Concorezzan school, accompanied by a general acceptance of at least portions of the Old Testament, in a word, a shift towards medieval orthodoxy from within Catharism, running parallel to the revisionism within the rival Albanensians under John de Lugio and the author of the *Liber*, seems, as Reltgen argues, more than a coincidence.[112] It is rather a sign that leading lights within Catharism had begun to feel the effects of a change in sentiment, of controversial work directed against them and, it may well be, of their own wrestling with the foundation texts in Scripture for their beliefs.

Sacconi's Summa

The result of the struggle within the Concorezzan Church between bishop and *filius major* remains unknown. When Sacconi wrote his *Summa* in mid-century he gave greatest space to the battle within the Albanensian Church on which he was best informed, having in his possession John de Lugio's work 'in ten quires'.[113] But he was aware of a division amongst the Concorezzans, between the doctrines of Nazarius and others, whom he does not name but who must be Desiderius and supporters. Concorezzo in his day had much the largest membership among Cathar Churches – Sacconi rated it at one thousand five hundred or more perfect of both sexes 'scattered throughout most of Lombardy'[114] – and it would have been difficult for Desiderius to convince such a large and scattered membership and take over doctrinal leadership. Moneta tells us that supporters of Desiderius (perhaps in fact only a segment) did not accept his revisions completely but

---

[111] Ibid., pp. 411–22.
[112] Reltgen, 'Dissidences ...', p. 104.
[113] *WEH*, p. 343.
[114] Ibid., p. 337.

reverted to Docetism.[115] The implication is that Desiderius was less successful with the Concorezzans than John de Lugio was with the Albanensian perfect, for he had carried with him most of a younger generation.

Sacconi implies that the divisions still existed in his time, for after describing the beliefs of Nazarius he goes on in the present tense to talk of those who 'profess that Christ assumed a true human body'.[116] He was aware, too, that yet another Church with some variant beliefs existed side by side with the Concorezzans and Albanensians at Bagnolo,[117] not clearly identified, but possibly Bagnolo S. Vito near Mantua. They were close to Concorezzo in thought, for they accepted one principle and believed that Satan was a fallen angel, ultimately subject to the power of the one good God, but were subject to certain idiosyncracies such as the belief that God had sent three angels, Christ, Mary and John the Evangelist to the earthly world, had views of their own on the false body of Christ, which clothed and concealed His true, heavenly body, and held that God made new angels at intervals of time and put them in bodies, apparently to do penance on earth. It was an illogical view, for, being new creations, these angels had not sinned in heaven and therefore should have needed no penance.[118]

From the Albanensians they seem to have borrowed metempsychosis and the belief that demons were the souls of a portion of mankind, who were correspondingly doomed. It is likely that the Bagnolensians began in the allegiance of Concorezzo and evolved towards the Albanensians, assimilating some of their doctrines but, as Rottenwöhrer points out,[119] never coming to share the Albanensians' central preoccupation with the history of God's people. Movement in belief was still taking place as Sacconi wrote, for certain smaller Churches, those of the March of Treviso, Tuscany, the Valley of Spoleto, which he describes as having more in common with the Bagnolensians than the Albanensians, were none the less 'little by little ... being drawn to the Albanensians'.[120]

Sacconi was too honest to argue that all the divisions of belief among the Cathars had led to excommunications and open hostilities: 'all the Churches of the Cathars recognize each other', he said, 'although they may have differing and contrary opinions',[121] the only exception being the Albanensians and Concorezzans, who remained in enmity. Though they had their distinct hierarchies and organizations, the others shared an underlying set of beliefs and attitudes which Sacconi is careful to list, and common rites which he describes as four sacraments, 'the imposition of hands, blessing of bread, penance and consecration',[122] that is, *consola-*

---

[115]   *GRK* IV (1), pp. 411–12, noting conflict with Sacconi's testimony; see corrections on Desiderius of *JDR*, p. 119; Schmitz-Valckenberg, *Grundlehren*, p. 338.

[116]   *WEH*, p. 344.

[117]   *GRK* IV (1), pp. 427–60; superseding G. Rottenwöhrer, 'Foi et théologie des Cathares bagnolistes,' *Heresis* VII (1986), pp. 27–32.

[118]   *GRK* IV (1), pp. 448–9.

[119]   Ibid., pp. 442–50.

[120]   *WEH*, p. 345.

[121]   Ibid.

[122]   Ibid., p. 331.

mentum, the blessing of bread by the perfect at meals, the *apparellamentum* and the ceremonies used for the establishment of the hierarchy of bishop, *filius major* and *filius minor*. He still thought of Catharism as a substantial menace to orthodoxy, its doctrines and beliefs deserving precise exposition and refutation, but with long scornful passages based on a Dominican's grasp of moral theology and a thirteenth-century churchman's understanding of confession, penance and purgatory, denouncing the undifferentiated rigidities of Cathar attitudes to 'sins'.

He wrote with the passionate conviction of one who, having been a Cathar for seventeen years, had experienced its attractions, and with the emotions of a convert rejecting his former beliefs. His fierce attacks on Cathar lack of true contrition, avarice, lack of care for the poor and vainglorious boasting form the weakest, most biased portion of his *Summa*, where his feelings get the better of him.[123] It can hardly be expected that he should convey openly one crucial point – that it was precisely this utter, unswerving commitment of the most devoted perfect, this lack of flexibility, which had won converts in the past and in the right intellectual and emotional environment would still continue to do so. The very fierceness of the attack shows where he felt that a peril from Catharism still existed. They were for him the great enemy: he did not feel it necessary to give anything like the same space to the Waldensians.

Catharism in Sacconi's day had retained its structure, yet the *Summa* conveys a sense of impending doom. At its opening, Sacconi rejoices that though the sects of heretics were once numerous 'by the grace of Jesus Christ they have been almost completely destroyed',[124] leaving just the Cathars and Waldensians: in his crisp summary of the strength and distribution of contemporary Cathar Churches, he concludes with implicit triumph: 'O reader, you can safely say that in the whole world there are not as many as four thousand Cathars of both sexes ...'[125] Sacconi knew better than anyone that the success of Catharism rested on a continuing recruitment of perfect, and evidently the numbers were in decline. Italy was the last refuge of Cathars from elsewhere and the number of perfect in the refugee Churches was quite low. The Church of France (by which he meant Northern France) which had fled to Verona and Lombardy was about one hundred and fifty strong; all the Churches of Languedoc, the Toulousan, the Albigensian, that of Carcassonne with 'some who were formerly of the Church of Agen, which has been almost totally destroyed', amounted only to 'nearly two hundred'; it was a pathetic remnant of once substantial Churches, which Sacconi presumably knew to be still under heavy pressure in their homelands.

The two major Italian Churches, Albanensian and Concorezzan, numbered five hundred and fifteen hundred respectively; the former, Sacconi said, 'dwell in Verona and several cities of Lombardy', while the Concorezzans were scattered 'throughout almost all Lombardy'. Other

---

[123] Ibid., pp. 331–2.
[124] Ibid., pp. 330–1.
[125] Ibid., p. 337.

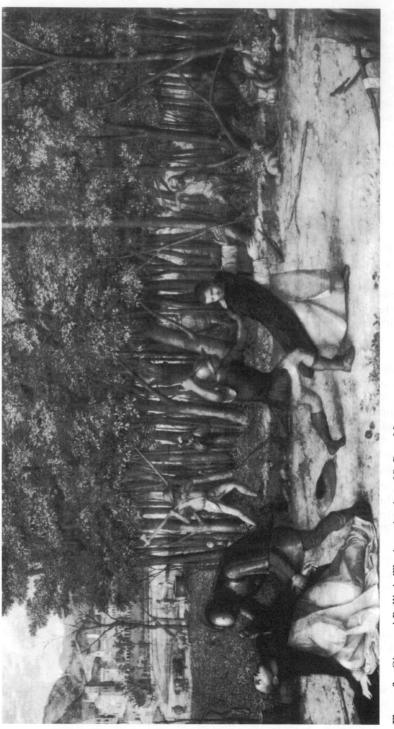

Figure 6 Giovanni Bellini, *The Assassination of St Peter Martyr*

churches were small and localized. Bagnolensians had a certain denominational character, since they existed in Milan where other Cathars were represented, Sacconi adding in parenthesis 'but in very small numbers';
otherwise he placed them in Mantua, Brescia and Bergamo and in
Romagna, to a total number of two hundred. Bagnolo, from which the
Church took its name, lay in the countryside outside Mantua: a move of the
seat of the bishop from Mantua may have been due to the search for greater
security or from the chance that the second Cathar bishop originated
there.[126] The Church of the March of Treviso 'persists' he said, at Vicenza
but not at Verona, to a total of one hundred, while those of Tuscany and the
Spoletan Valley he assessed at not quite a hundred.

He said nothing of Southern Italy and gave cursory attention to the
East, listing the six Churches, of Sclavonia, the Latins and Greeks of
Constantinople, 'Philadelphia in Romania', Bulgaria and Drugunthia,
noting that all the Western Churches had taken their origin from the last
two, and assessing the perfect of the East at 'something under five
hundred', the Church of the Latins contributing 'less than fifty' to the total.
In the crucible of Italy, the perfect of the indigenous Churches, in Sacconi's
estimation, formed more than half the total of perfect everywhere.

Though as a Dominican, inquisitor and convert, Sacconi had every inclination to believe in a victory for his church, he had more than *parti pris* to
buttress his conviction that Catharism was in decline. Divisions created by
personalities, local patriotism and clashes of belief in the late twelfth
century had lasted for over sixty years; Sacconi composed his *Summa* when
the faith had passed the peak of its popularity in Italy and visible inroads
were being made into the Cathar position.[127] In the following half-century
the way for the Cathars was to be downhill.

The consolidation of the inquisition

Twenty months elapsed between the death of Gregory IX and the election
of Innocent IV in 1243. Frederick II hoped for a cessation of conflict on his
terms, only to discover that Innocent, master-diplomat and canonist, was a
yet more determined opponent than his predecessor, who crossed his plans
by taking refuge in Lyons, summoning a Council to depose him and using
all the resources of the papacy to rouse Germany and encourage anti-impe-
rial forces in Italy. Frederick was a tired man, worn by the struggle when he
died of fever in 1250. The most secular-minded of all thirteenth-century
popes, Innocent threw every available weapon into the battle against the
Hohenstaufen: he made unlimited use of provisions to benefices to obtain
money and allies and pushed the theocratic claims of the papacy to the
utmost. His instinct was to make the friars instruments in his propaganda
war, tarnishing both mendicants and papacy thereby.

---

[126]   Violante, 'Hérésies urbaines ...', p. 180.
[127]   'moving into an irreversible crisis', Merlo, in *Ricerche di storia sociale e religiosa*
XXXIX (1991), p. 207.

In the wake of Frederick's death, Innocent returned from his exile at Lyons in the spring of 1251 and soon turned his attention to heresy. In June he named Peter of Verona for an inquisitorial mission to Cremona – a brilliant choice, for though Peter had long been concerned with heresy, he had never hitherto received inquisitorial office and was able to bring to his task a high reputation, energy and asceticism. In 1252 he was in office as one of the inquisitors for Lombardy, based in Milan. He had little time to show his qualities in action, since a conspiracy of Cathar leaders from Milan, Como, Lodi, Bergamo and Pavia hired assassins to murder him. Peter was struck down from behind by a heavy rustic implement, a *falcastrum*, the murderer then stabbing him in the side. His fatally injured companion nevertheless lived long enough to give evidence of Peter's dying words, commending his soul to God and reciting the beginning of the *credo*. Innocent at first feared his death would intimidate the Dominicans and wrote to the convent at Bologna to encourage them, but public opinion swung against heresy, there was an immense funeral in Milan and a cult soon developed. One of the plotters, Daniel of Guissano, repented and became a Dominican.[128]

In significant contrast to the killings at Avignonet, where attempts at official recognition of martyrdom were unsuccessful,[129] Innocent took the cause firmly in hand and canonized Peter at Perugia in March 1253. The Dominican chapter-general resolved that his feast should be publicized, his name included in litanies and that he should be depicted in churches, where the crude instrument of his death was transmuted romantically into a sword. The legend developed that he had written '*credo*' on the ground in his own blood. In accord with the poverty and humility of his order, unescorted and walking rather than riding along a dusty road, not long after saying mass at Easter, he was wholly vulnerable to his enemies and the image of his killing became a powerful aid in the future struggle against heretics. And yet, as inquisitor, he held authority over life and death, to acquit or condemn, to impose an array of penances, decree imprisonments, confiscation of goods or to relax a recalcitrant heretic to the secular arm. On the road, he was vulnerable and beyond rescue; in Milan, to deal with heretics at the end of a period of grace, he would have been a man of power. In some quarters, he was a controversial saint, his fame especially bound up with the Dominican order and its circle of adherents, not always accepted elsewhere.[130] But the immediate reaction to his death created a climate favourable to counter-attack and to the legislation with which Innocent reinforced repression.

Patrons of heresy were from the first a prime target. In June 1251, Innocent had considered launching a crusade against Ezzelino da Romano but was too occupied with the problems set by Conrad and the continuing

---

[128]   See Dondaine, in *AFP* XXIII, pp. 66–162; Merlo, 'Pietro di Verona ...', pp. 471–88.
[129]   Above, p. 166.
[130]   Merlo, 'Pietro di Verona ...', pp. 479–85.

Hohenstaufen power in Southern Italy.[131] None the less, in September *Tunc potissime* publicized the potential of a crusade against obstinate supporters. In the atmosphere of hostility created by Peter's murder, Innocent launched *Ad extirpanda* in May 1252, a 'terrible decree',[132] massing the penalties for heresy and fautorship, ordering the institution of a form of inquisitional police in the localities, well equipped with powers to pursue and arrest and to decide the division of the goods of the convicted, one-third going to themselves, one-third to the commune and one-third to bishops and inquisitors to facilitate inquiries and pursuits and no doubt to provide rewards to informers. Most significant of all, Innocent requires *podestàs* or rectors to use torture to elicit confessions 'just as thieves and plunderers of goods are compelled to accuse their accomplices and confess the crimes they have committed',[133] thereby removing a fundamental distinction between the practices of civil and canon law. Confession was the queen of proofs and, influenced by Roman law, city authorities were accustomed to secure it by torture. Notoriously, torture distorts evidence and, while there is no indication that the application of the instruments to Italian suspects in the thirteenth century led to unjust condemnations, their use by inquisitors in later centuries brought a poisoned harvest of misinformation.

Confidently, in October 1252 Innocent made use of the vacancy in the Empire after Frederick's death to reissue Frederick's edicts on heresy in *Cum adversus haereticam*. In a real sense, Innocent was Frederick's heir, coolly making his own the imperial legislation, once willingly issued in the interests of imposing orthodoxy in the Empire and damming the cities' efforts at emancipation, but neglected after the renewal of conflict in 1239 because of Frederick's political fears. With one hand, Innocent battled on against the remnants of Staufen power, while with the other he took over imperial edicts, made them his own and enforced them with a personnel under his control, the friars, who knew intimately the life of the cities and were better placed than anyone to make anti-heresy measures stick. His success flowed from the deposition of Frederick in 1245 at the Council of Lyons, based on the concept derived from the heresy legislation of the 'contempt of the keys'.[134]

Patrons continued to be an object of Innocent's concern. In April 1253 he set in motion a crusade in south Tuscany, and in 1254 issued a series of Bulls requiring the preaching of the cross against heretics in Lombardy. He also brought in the Franciscans as inquisitors on a much larger scale, perhaps because he thought their popularity would make them acceptable,[135] and divided up Italy into eight provinces for inquisition,

[131] Housley, *Crusades*, p. 200.
[132] M. D'Alatri, 'L'inquisizione francescana nell' Italia centrale nel secolo xiii', *Collectanea Francescana* XXII (1952), pp. 225–50 at p. 230.
[133] W. L. Wakefield, 'Inquisition', *Dictionary of the Middle Ages* VI (New York, 1985), pp. 483–9; E. Peters, *Torture*, (Oxford, 1985); Miccoli, 'La repressione ...', p. 725.
[134] Walther, 'Ziel ...', pp. 126–9.
[135] R. Manselli, 'Aspetti e significato dell' intoleranza popolare nei secoli xi–xiii', *Medioevo ereticale*, ed. O. Capitani (Bologna, 1977), pp. 67–88 at p. 80.

leaving Lombardy and the Regno to the Dominicans, the remaining six to the Franciscans. Innocent understood very well the importance of symbols, and in his last year of life took up the bones of heretic bishops from a former Cathar refuge at the castle of Gattedo and burnt them, fulfilling the prophecy of Peter of Verona, now known as Peter Martyr, who had passed by the fortress in 1251 and foretold its ruin.[136]

His successors, Alexander IV, Urban IV, Clement IV, continued to reinforce and apply Innocent's legislation. Alexander allowed inquisitors to absolve each other for 'irregularities', in practice removing any residual restrictions on the use of the instruments of torture, which now to all intents and purposes lay at the disposal of any inquisitor. The formidable structure of law and organization confronting heresy passed into the manuals of inquisitors and into the canon law code of Boniface VIII, the Sext.

His successors also had to continue to battle against the Hohenstaufen heirs Manfred and Conradin, with the concomitant side-effects of financial problems, secularization and the waging of war, till the victories of a successful papal champion, Charles of Anjou, put paid to resistance in 1266 and 1268. It was a key point in the decline of Catharism, for forces in cities were often finely balanced and a small shift in the high politics of the peninsula had significant and widespread effects. Italian bankers played a major part in financing Charles's armies and this created interest-blocks in the cities in his favour.[137] He filled the Regno with his own men and whatever heresy existed there is likely to have been blotted out; in the rest of Italy he intended to secure his gains by close alliances in key positions, leading to the installation of Guelf governments unsympathetic to heresy. In a halting sequence through the last decades of the century, the way was opened for the entry of inquisitors and serious action against Cathar communities.

[136]   Dondaine, in *AFP* XXIII, pp. 66–162.
[137]   R. Manselli, 'La fin du Catharisme en Italie', *CF* XX, pp. 101–18 (posthumous publication, no footnotes, intuitive account) at pp. 104–5.

9

The Suffocating of Catharism in Languedoc

The fall of Montségur in 1244, Raymond VI's shift in policy towards active pursuit of heresy, and the falling away of former protectors created a climate favourable to hostile action. Two inquisitors, Bernard de Caux and Jean de Saint Pierre, set new standards in a massive investigation of Cathar-bearing localities far exceeding the type of restricted questioning of individual suspects, hitherto the norm. It was the most comprehensive enquiry into a region ever undertaken.

A partial record of this enquiry has survived in MS 609 of the Bibliothèque Municipale of Toulouse, a fair copy made in 1260 of two registers concerning the work of the inquisitors in the Lauragais and the region of Lavaur in 1245–6. The enquiry itself spread well beyond these bounds and filled ten volumes of registers in all. The bulk of these has perished; what remains includes the depositions of some 5,605 witnesses who were transported from their native villages to answer standardized questions. The inquisitors wanted facts, dates, meetings, consolings, together with a sprinkling of information on belief: this was in effect a comprehensive police-type survey, investigating every male over fourteen and every female over twelve, a census conducted at one spot, the vast cloister of Saint-Sernin, Toulouse, by inquisitors, their scribes and notaries in the presence of local clergy and other clerical witnesses; an interrogation on an unprecedented scale by clergy into laity based on mass transportation of witnesses, locality by locality, to face routinized questioning, the basis for checking and cross-referencing, the process clearly illustrated in the manuscript itself. Fortunately, the record which survives is concerned with the heartland of Languedocian Catharism, including Dominic's selected target of Fanjeaux, Laurac and the site of Nicetas's Council of S. Félix de Caraman.[1]

It was the third enquiry into this region; it was being investigated by William Arnold and Stephen of St Thibéry when they were killed at Avignonet; it was the subject of a subsequent inquisition led by the keen-minded Catalan Dominican Ferrier, a refiner of inquisition techniques. Witnesses moving up and down the roads, the coming and going of clergy,

---

[1] Dossat, *Les Crises*; concise outline of inquisitional procedure, *WHC*, pp. 168–94; MS described, Abels and Harrison, in *MS* XLI, pp. 220–5, esp. nos. p. 220.

Map 6   Inquisition versus Catharism: the enquiries of 1245–6
Source: adapted from Y. Dossat, *Les Crises de l'inquisition toulousaine au XIIIe siècle (1223–1273)* (Bordeaux, 1959), pp. 228–9

the taking of oaths, the answering of questions one by one was in itself a demonstration of the power of the church and the energy of the inquisitors: a house was bought near Saint-Sernin to serve as a prison.[2]

___

[2]   Y. Dossat, 'Une figure d'inquisiteur, Bernard de Caux', *CF* VI, pp. 253–72 at p. 259.

Groups were brought in, sometimes twenty to thirty persons at a time, even as many as seventy-five; occasionally prisoners were brought out to confirm old confessions or make new ones; suspects who had kept silent, betrayed by neighbours, were brought back again to retract an earlier denial. Many gave formal replies to all the questions, others were taken beyond the routine and either wanted or felt compelled to continue into fuller evidence, introduced by the phrase, 'Afterward he said'.

Time was never spared. Nine and a half months of interrogations were recorded; taking of testimony in Le Mas-Saintes-Puelles occupied thirty-eight days.[3] A total, all-embracing picture was being sought; so, for example, at Fanjeaux the inquisitors took the trouble of re-examining, despite the fact that all but eight of the ninety-eight deponents had confessed earlier to Arnald or Ferrier, in the hope of breaking down deceitful denials: an investigation at Pamiers designed to deal with the heretics of the county of Foix between September 1246 and May 1247 issued in seven life sentences.[4]

The enquiry had two effects. It changed attitudes to inquisitors: sympathizers with heresy were thereafter led to think of the inquisition more as 'an entrenched institution than a single, unrepeated ordeal'.[5] Thousands dutifully accepted the inquisitors' summons, went to Toulouse and testified. Secondly, it smoked out more false statements than ever by simple cross-checking, revealed in marginal comments such as 'Before other inquisitors he admitted that he adored heretics and ate with them twelve times.'[6] Dossat has argued that one could count 'a hundred false statements discovered by the inquisitors'.[7] Secrecy pacts had been made and deceived earlier inquisitors: these now broke down. Mercy was shown to those who surrendered and confessed voluntarily; stiff penalties were applied to those who persisted in deception.

There was a pattern of punishment and flight. Using the admittedly imperfect evidence, Dossat calculated that about one in four of those who came to the inquisitors' serious attention escaped by flight. 'Out of every hundred persons who receive some punishment, perhaps one was burned and ten to fifteen were imprisoned':[8] the others were condemned to wear yellow crosses or to go on pilgrimage. A thorough inquisition placed the Cathars and their supporters in a harsh dilemma: confronted with the oath-taking and compulsory deposition were they to confess fully – and face the wrath, sometimes murderous, of their former associates – or prevaricate, suppress evidence and try to get away with a partial confession, or flee to the *maquis*, to another area less harassed, into the mountains or to Italy? A further option lay in confessing fully and offering services to inquisitors for the future as double agent, trapping old acquaintances, using knowledge to

---

[3] Wakefield, in *CHR* LXIX (1983), p. 221.

[4] Dossat, in *CF* VI, p. 257; W. L. Wakefield, 'Friar Ferrier, inquisitor', *Heresis* VII (1986), pp. 33–41. Survey, J. Duvernoy, 'De Guillaume Pelhisson à Bernard Gui: les inquisiteurs méridionaux et leurs temps', *Persécution, Collection Heresis* VI, pp. 217–39.

[5] Abels and Harrison, in *MS* XLI, p. 223.

[6] WLW commenting on MS 609.

[7] Dossat, *Crises*, p. 243.

[8] *WHC*, pp. 184–5, following calculations of Dossat, *Crises*, pp. 266–8.

penetrate Cathar circles, even giving the *melioramentum* or attending a consoling in order to allay suspicions. Such services were given in return for mitigation of sentence, for money, land or property or out of religious zeal. An enthusiasm that once flowed in Cathar channels could be redirected into Catholicism. Inquisitors seem never to have felt scruples about the use of double agents: they were engaged in a battle against the forces of evil, and if double agents were forced to participate in acts condemned by canon law, they were doing so in a higher cause and could be absolved.

Pressure and terror caused old securities to break down. Though knowing they were heretics, Peter of Gouzens, for example, had harboured his mother and cousin for five years[9] before driving them out of his house. Peter Gaubert was a perfect who converted: the alarm thus created is revealed by the attempt by a Cathar supporter to raise funds to bribe him to keep silent. On the very day knowledge of this reached the inquisitor, 'Peter Gaubert, convert' was listed as one of the official witnesses to abjurations. He had gone over to the enemy; a later document mentions a property assigned to him.[10] Personal security was a major factor, especially when the convert had made many enemies through major betrayals. One example is that of Arnaud Pradier, a native of Cambiac who had been a perfect c.1215 and who ended up living in the safety of the Château Narbonnais in Toulouse with his wife, the former *perfecta* Stéphanie de Châteauverdun, whom he had once consoled. We know from accounts which list expenditure for her clothing and feeding of their son that they were living at the inquisition's expense. It was an investment made not only to protect and reward a major source of information but also to put in place a pair now committed to Catholicism who had had intimate and prolonged experience of Catharism, most fitted to influence prisoners at the Château, bringing them to the full confession which inquisitors desired above all things, both as policemen and priests.[11]

Flight drew off from the ordinary community some of the most committed, who, if they did not take to the woods and hills near their former homes, moved on to other regions. The mountain lands of the Sabartès in the Haute Ariège and parts of Catalonia had long had a Cathar presence. There is evidence of heresy in the Spanish Pyrenees early in the thirteenth century; the future count of Foix, Roger-Bernard II, son and nephew of *perfectae*, entered into a marriage contract with the heiress of Castelbon; Cathar strength was sufficient to justify the appointment of Pierre de Corona as deacon for Catalonia. The heresy's influence spread over both sides of the mountain range. Lordat had a Cathar burial ground as early as 1209. Castelbon, a well-established centre, underwent a major

[9] *BF*, p. 264.
[10] Griffe, *Inquisition*, p. 112.
[11] A. Cazenave, 'La chasse aux Cathares', *L'Histoire* LVI (1983), pp. 22–31; 'La résistance Cathare de la defaite à l'exil', *Histoire et clandestinité du Moyen Age à la Première Guerre Mondiale, Colloque de Paris (Mai 1977), Revue du Vivarais*, ed. M. Tilloy, G. Audisio and J. Chiffoleau (Albi, n.d.), pp. 357–52 (psychology of defeat incisively sketched). Effects of increase in inquisitorial efficiency, Hanssler, *Katharismus*, pp. 196–220.

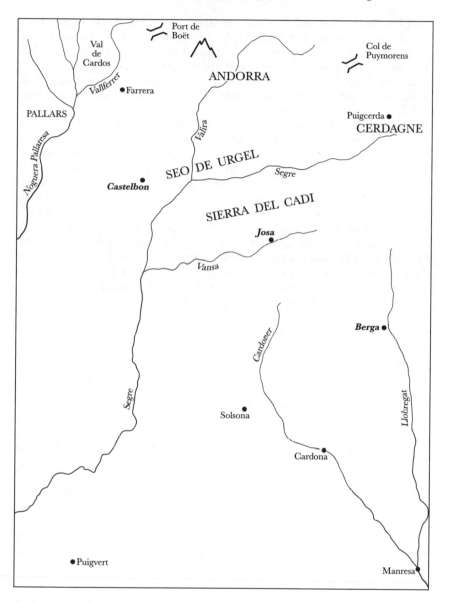

Map 7   The Cathar circle of Castelbon–Josa–Berga
Source: A. Cazenave, 'Les Cathares en Catalogne et Sabarthès après les registres d'Inquisition: la hiérarchie Cathare en Sabarthès après Montségur', *BPH Année 1969* (Paris, 1972), p. 395

investigation, with condemnations and exhumations in 1239; a second campaign led to the poisoning of an inquisitor and an armed attack on the castle. Damaged at Castelbon, Catharism lived on elsewhere; the spillage of heresy from the mountain lands of Foix to the Spanish side of the Pyrenees long continued. Arnaud de Bretos of Brega, consoled by Bertrand Marty, for example, moved easily between his native land and the Haute Ariège. The sympathy of certain nobles remained an important factor. While Montségur remained in Cathar hands, there was coming and going between it and the Sabartès; inquisitors became aware of these connections and their attention moved on to the Haute Ariège. But for a short time these mountain lands were a valuable refuge.[12]

Stéphanie de Châteauverdun herself sprang from a family of local lords who produced Cathars over five generations; in the Sabartès she moved from the role of sympathizer to that of postulant, was consoled by Arnaud Pradier at Rabat, lived at various sites, then attempted for a month to live in her own house before, fearing discovery, she went to join other women perfect in cabins in the Pays d'Alion. Her confession makes clear that some sort of Cathar hierarchy was then in existence in the mountains including Arnaud Pradier, once deacon of Laurac who had taken refuge in the Haute Ariège, another deacon specifically appointed for the Sabartès and Arnaud Roger, probably designated by Bertrand Marty, who died at Montségur, as his successor in the see of Toulouse. For a time the centre of gravity shifted farther south towards the Pyrenees; then, as pressure on former safe lands grew, some fugitives passed on to Lombardy. A nucleus none the less remained and their existence prepared the way for the last revival of Catharism under Pierre Autier in the early fourteenth century.[13]

Although the actions of the Dominican inquisitors were checked for some years following 1248–9, because of a dispute with Innocent IV, bishops and their officials resumed their traditional role of pursuit. In the diocese of Carcassonne, Bishop Guillaume Arnaud, a native of the city, set about reconstituting the registers which had been stolen at Caunes where inquisitors' assistants were murdered in 1247,[14] and initiated a massive enquiry, using an inquisitional procedure involving extensive oath-taking and precautionary fines, sometimes of high value, and the use of guarantors designed both to ensure the appearance of defendants and fulfilment of penalties.[15] He may well also have intended to give greater emphasis than was commonly the case to the defendant as penitent. There were many voluntary submissions; some took the opportunity to clear the slate so that they would never again be troubled. The bishop was inclined to mitigate penalties in cases of good behaviour, allowing release from prison and the remitting of the wearing of yellow crosses, with mixed results. Some were

---

[12]   Cazenave, 'Les Cathares en Catalogne ...', pp. 387–436; for Catharism in Spain, L. Vones, 'Krone und Inquisition: Das aragonesische Königtum und die Anfänge der kirchlichen Ketzerverfolgung in den Ländern der Krone Aragon', *Anfänge*, ed. P. Segl, pp. 195–233, with refs.
[13]   Cazenave, 'La chasse ...'; I accept her reconstruction; Pradier, *JDH*, p. 301, Stephanie, BF, p. 271.
[14]   W. L. Wakefield, 'Friar Ferrier, inquisition at Caunes, and escapes from prison at Carcassonne', *CHR* LVIII (1972), pp. 220–37; Ferrier's efficiency, *JDH*, pp. 297–8.
[15]   J. Paul, 'La procédure inquisitionale à Carcassonne au milieu du XIIIe siècle', *CF* XXIX, pp. 361–96.

never again brought before a court, others such as Guillaume Sicre of Cavanac reverted to heresy immediately. Granted an early release from prison, he played a pivotal role in restoring the perfect Bernard Acier, who had taken refuge in the Razès, to an active life in the Carcassès and was participant in the successful search in a wood for Cathar money buried in bottles by the vanished Cathar bishop of Carcassonne, Pierre Polhan. Guillaume's freedom diminished as pressures on heretical circles grew; in mid-Lent 1258, Bernard Acier and a fellow perfect recommended that he should follow them to Lombardy – indeed, Guillaume may have set about finding Polhan's treasure in order to make the journey. In event, he chose instead to make a pilgrimage to Rocamadour, only to find on return that Bernard Acier had abjured and confessed; he fled from Cavanac but was captured in 1259.[16] Acier's defection and the secession in 1259 of the deacon Bernard Gausbert were grievous blows.

Pressure, delation, fatigue whittled away the number of effectives; in the Carcassès investigations continued after the death of Bishop Arnaud in 1255. Dominicans returned generally to duties, their powers more extensive than ever after a settlement was reached with Alexander IV. A special register was opened to contain depositions of converted perfect, followed inevitably by long lists of believers and sympathizers whom they had betrayed.[17] There was no substantial break in anti-heresy action.

The Cathar diocese of Albi had been seriously damaged by one of the most notable defections of all, that of the *filius* Sicard de Lunel between 1242 and 1244, who denounced a series of noble families as fautors and listed sympathizers in considerable numbers, subsequently serving as informer and witness for decades; in 1274 he was in the Château Narbonnais attending to a prisoner in irons who had attempted suicide by beating his head against a wall;[18] there were other renegades.

Increased pressure and the rising number of defections affected the way of life of survivors. The houses of perfect visited regularly by deacons had vanished; their inmates now sought refuge wherever they could find it and security came to have priority over missionizing. The way of life of women perfect was especially vulnerable, as they retreated into the woods and hills; it was not easy to disguise the purposes of women wandering singly or in groups. They, more than men, were in the hands of sympathizers and, as in the case of Arnaude de Lamothe, were subject to endless movement from refuge to refuge. At some stage after the fall of Montségur the numbers of women who receive the *consolamentum* dwindles, perhaps because the men who consoled made a policy decision not to encourage women's vocations, perhaps women no longer came forward in such numbers as postulants.[19] Praticalities, the effects of the retreat to cabins in forests from their houses rather than ideology, are likely to have been the major factor. But no less

[16] Griffe, *Inquisition*, pp. 110–13.

[17] Archives de la Haute Garonne MS 124: see *CF* III, pp. 259–61, *JDH*, p. 301.

[18] *JDH*, pp. 301–3; J. Duvernoy, 'La vie des prédicateurs Cathares en Languedoc et dans l'Albigeois vers le milieu du XIIIième', *Revue du Tarn* CXXI–III (1986), pp. 26–54, 257–77, 455–505.

[19] Abels and Harrison, in *MS* XLI, pp. 236–40.

than men, women were eager as ever to receive the death-bed consoling, and their support role as believers, discreet messengers, hostesses and sources of family influence was undiminished. They arrange and attend consolings, and many a perfect, answering inquisitors' questions, recalled with nostalgia bread, fruit and fish received from the hands of a woman sympathizer and the overnight hospitality of her household.

The males became less accessible to their faithful; it was too dangerous to stay long in one place and, as they took to movement, the whereabouts of a perfect to console the dying could only be ascertained via a grapevine of sympathizers. Some perfect joined with wandering bands of armed *faidits*, dispossessed men unwilling to submit to authority or face imprisonment, thereby obtaining the protection which they, forbidden to shed blood, could not provide for themselves. Such bands were given hospitality by a young knight in the Albigeois, Amblard Vassal of La Roque Arifat and his wife, who gave the *melioramentum* to the perfect among them; sick and in expectation of death he was consoled, then captured and brought before an inquisitor. Released on the strength of a massive financial caution and the promise that he would betray his Cathar contacts, he preferred to join the *faidits*, eventually finding his way to Lombardy. His family was ruined; his wife had to beg her bread. He was recaptured in 1274.[20]

As the call of Lombardy became more insistent, so Languedoc slipped farther back towards the role of mission station. Pierre de Bauville, merchant of Avignonet, advised to leave by Raymond d'Alfaro after the killing of the inquisitors, spent long years in Northern Italy, at Cuneo, Piacenza, Cremona and Pavia, carrying on his business, maintaining his faith and seeing in his time a series of refugee perfect and members of the hierarchy. Many years after leaving, he returned to Avignonet, was captured and forced to reveal the detail of his contacts.[21] Many who fled never returned. Bishops, deacons and perfect remained in Italy, a microcosm of the Languedocian Cathar Church of the past in a milieu where they were unlikely to make converts, while hopes they may yet have entertained of new prospects in their native land never materialized. Towards 1300, the hierarchy of the Churches of Languedoc disappears from the records of Northern Italy; all that is left, it seems, is a 'major deacon' and several perfect in Sicily.[22]

The use of blessed bread as a quasi-relic is a late development in response to persecution; morsels carefully transported and hoarded were a welcome reminder of the perfect who could no longer visit believers as of yore. Navarre of Belleval near Caraman sent to inform her niece of blessed bread concealed in a trunk, which she believed at the moment of death would have as much value as the presence of a perfect.[23] But such treasuring up of

---

[20]   *BF*, pp. 279–80, 282–4; vivid account of women under persecution, ch. 20 to end; J. Duvernoy, 'Cathares et faidits en Albigeois vers 1265–1275', *Heresis* III (1984), pp. 5–34; G. Passerat, 'Un dignitaire de l'église Cathare de l'Albigeois: Guilhem de Caussade', *Journée d'etudes à Caussade* (Montauban, 1986), pp. 121–6.

[21]   *JDH*, pp. 304–6; journey, Hanssler, *Katharismus*, pp. 202–4.

[22]   *JDH* p. 308; see below, pp. 235–6.

[23]   *BF*, pp. 280–1.

bread in believers' houses represented all unconsciously an assimilation of Cathar worship to the pyxes and monstrances of Catholic devotion.

The words of the vernacular *Vindication of the Church of God,* a Provençal source with affinities to the Cathar rituals, about the persecutions to be suffered by the true Church, would have echoed in the minds of those suffering under persecution who read or listened to it. The text focuses on the ethical superiority of the Cathar Church to the Roman, conveying its meaning in incantatory chapter headings: 'This Church of God has received such power from our Lord Jesus Christ that sins are pardoned by its prayer ...'; 'This Church refrains from adultery ...'; 'This Church refrains from theft ...', and so on through a list of moral failings renounced, including in customary Cathar style the swearing of oaths. At the heart of the *Vindication* lies its confident statement: 'This Church keeps and observes all the commandments of the law of life ...', conveying the sense of the completeness of Cathar observance in contrast to the Roman Church's stained record.[24]

The text gives no clear indication of either the date or provenance within a radical or moderate dualist denomination, but the force and length of the chapters on persecution make a late date plausible. The 'Alpine-Provençal' vocabulary leads Duvernoy to suggest an origin among emigrants from Languedoc seeking refuge in Piedmont, who, having lost their homes, knew the meaning of persecution.[25] The text comforts its readers by quoting Christ's words to his disciples on the persecutions they must expect to suffer, 'words which contradict the wicked Roman Church'.[26]

In the same MS, possibly from the same stable,[27] also in the vernacular, is a gloss on the paternoster with biblical citations, reference to the *Vision of Isaiah* and the salvation of God's people as a characteristic *leitmotif,* which has intriguing quasi-mystical reflections on a hierarchy of seven substances, with no parallel elsewhere in Cathar literature. Both the *Vindication* and the Gloss can readily be related to the ritual of the *consolamentum,* to the delivery of the prayer, that is the paternoster, and to the type of sermon addressed to a candidate before the laying on of hands. If it, too, is of late date, then it is evidence of a Catharism near its end which none the less has sustained its literary power and creativity.

Side by side with the development of the slow but patient machine of inquisition, an economic revival played its part in reconciling part of the population to the change of regime and the suppression of heresy. Crusade

[24]   T. Venckeleer, 'Un recueil Cathare: le manuscrit A.6.10 de la collection vaudoise de Dublin, I: une Apologie, II: un glose sur le Pater', *RBPH* xxxvIII (1960), pp. 815–34, xxxIx (1961), pp. 758–93; trans. *WEH,* pp. 592–606, quotations, ibid., pp. 597, 599, 600, 602; A. Brenon, 'Syncrétisme hérétique dans les refuges alpins? Un livre Cathare parmi les recueils vaudois de la fin du Moyen-Age: le MS 269 de Dublin', *Heresis* vII (1986), pp. 5–23 modifies Venckeleer; *Vindication* as catechism, A. Brenon, 'La Parole Cathare: une catéchèse de l'évangile', *Catéchisme et Confessions de Foi: Actes du VIIIe Colloque Jean Boisset* (Montpellier, 1995), pp. 99–121.
[25]   Analysis, *GRK* IV (3), pp. 139–51, dating, p. 139, dualism, p. 148; Piedmontese hypothesis, *JDR,* p. 19, n. 37.
[26]   *WEH,* p. 603.
[27]   *GRK* IV (3), pp. 105–38; *WEH,* pp. 607–30.

and conquest were psychological blows which brought misery to many, but they were surmounted. Although the placing in power of royal administrators created tensions and was accompanied by abuses, Louis IX's unmistakable zeal for justice and his institution of *enquêteurs-reformateurs* did something to mitigate the worst excesses, while his skill in drawing potential rebels into his crusade and his personifying of chivalrous ideals, linking valour with traditional orthodoxy, helped to reconcile the Southern nobility. Philip III's amnesty pointed in the same direction. The conquest once secure, monarchy acted with moderation.

Acquiescence in the conquest and repudiation of heresy brought rewards as in the case of Olivier de Termes. The destruction and disruption caused by warfare was insufficient to halt the tide of demographic expansion and growing prosperity, which not only lessened old grievances about the exactions of the Church but was the background to a new phase of church building. Set against this economic background, Northern conquest was more than a source of oppression and loss; it offered new posts and new opportunities, making the surrender of the old faith an easier task.[28]

The decline of Catharism was assured so long as the working alliance between bishops, inquisitors and monarchy held, as generally over the century it did. Certain exceptional cases where the alliance failed or royal officers did not act in full cooperation with inquisitors, reveal in sudden, surprising glimpses the continued attachment to the old faith, suppressed but far from eliminated. Orthodoxy had made strides, had gained lay supporters and had been buoyed up by friars and reforming clergy; yet a general conversion of the heart had still not taken place. The long years of near-toleration had enabled Catharism to put down roots: the most determined statistical analyst of the Collection Doat has argued that even for the 1270s and 1280s there is evidence of considerable surviving support for Catharism at the level both of perfect and believer.[29]

Good fortune, the unwillingness of witnesses to betray, discreet withdrawals to Italy and perhaps, skilled management of money were enough to keep in the field one perfect, Guillaume Prunel, who appears at various times between c.1258 and 1283 in the southern Albigeois, the Cabardès and Toulouse. When he spent a month in Toulouse, he was recognized as a heretic but no one betrayed him. A residual sentiment in favour of deathbed consoling as the key to salvation was a standby for such wandering perfect: Prunel, though illiterate, had success with nobles and even relatives of clergy.[30]

Guillaume Pagès, perfect of La Tourette, also came back from Lombardy to undertake duties in the Cabardès, Minervois and Carcassonne in a career stretching from 1266 to 1283, with his companion consoling a remarkable number of people of standing – knights and their womenfolk, notaries, royal officers, even clergy. He was treated with complacency by those in

---

[28]   P. Wolff, 'Role de l'essor économique dans le ralliement social et religieux', *CF* xx, pp. 243–55; Griffe, *Inquisition*, pp. 121–6 (St Louis).
[29]   Hanssler, *Katharismus*, pp. 66–74, 222–3. Much depends on multipliers; the case deserves investigation.
[30]   Ibid., pp. 115–28; *JDH*, p. 310.

power: Jean Pennavayre, who held Cabaret as castellan for the crown, went through the motions of arresting Pagès in 1277, releasing him on being given the bribe he wanted, a pig and six rams. The old religion had power to penetrate circles which should have been most impervious to its attractions: Robert of Sens, of a Northern French family, whose first marriage brought him fiefs in the Cabardès, who had allied himself with the de Voisins, descendants of a companion of Simon de Montfort, though he held high office under the crown as *prévôt* of Carcassonne, castellan of Cabaret, even, finally, *procureur des encours heretiques* for the seneschals of Carcassonne, was a secret adherent and protector of Cathars who visited Pagès. With his second wife, sister and a niece, he was condemned by the inquisition and imprisoned in 1285. His influence accounts in good measure for Pagès's long freedom.[31]

He was not the only royal officer to be so convicted. Pierre Bougi, of meridional origin, who in 1330 became royal viguier of the Cabardès, held land in the region and bought territory confiscated from heretics, lived quietly through the disturbances over heresy in the Midi at the end of the century, then was convicted in 1330 of having visited and heard heretics a half-century earlier. Géraud Galhard, a jurist, also of Southern origin, held crown office as judge in Albi, the Minervois and Limoux, and also advised the consuls of Carcassonne in their conflict with inquisitors to compromise, thus to the populace becoming a symbol of defeatism and collaboration, and was killed by an angry crowd. This did not save him from a posthumous condemnation by inquisitors for having played a part in a plot to steal inquisition registers at Carcassonne and having been present at the consoling of Castel Fabre, a citizen of Carcassonne, father of a consul well known for his sympathy for the Franciscans, who certainly received Catholic rites at his death but was alleged by the inquisition to have indulged in the practice of assuring salvation by obtaining the services of a perfect as well as a priest. Vehement defence of Fabre by the Franciscans could not deflect the inquisition; later, his widow was also posthumously condemned.[32]

The alliance between the royal power and the inquisitors, fundamental for the success of the assault on Catharism, was affected by the inclinations of individual royal officers as well as by major shifts in attitude and policy either by inquisitors or the crown. At Narbonne in 1262, anger against the inquisitors had so diminished that Ferrier was asked by the citizens to plead their cause in a secular dispute with Béziers and actually led a delegation to the seneschal Guilhem de Pia on their behalf. In the Albigeois, a long-running conflict between the bishop and the royal administration included among the points of dispute the pursuit of heretics and the confiscation of their goods; pressure against them from both bishop and inquisition diminished, while royal officers insisted on the necessity of condemnations and confiscations; the bishop was inclined to blunt the edge of confiscations and prevent the families of the condemned being ruined, leaving the royal

[31]   Ibid., pp. 310–11 (Pagès); A. Friedlander, 'Les agents du roi face aux crises de l'hérésie en Languedoc', *CF* xx, pp. 199–220.
[32]   *JDH*, pp. 318, 333; Griffe, *Inquisition*, pp. 160–1 leaves open culpability.

officers as the prime objects of popular discontent. In 1253 it came to open violence as sergeants of the king were attacked by citizens and the viguier in revenge pillaged bastides of the bishop.

In the last two decades of the century the situation changed: inquisitors pressed home their pursuits, while royal officers hesitated and no longer gave automatic, full-hearted support to their activities. The volume of Southern complaints to the bishop against inquisitors grew to such a degree as to influence the crown; under Philip the Fair a number of decisions hostile to the inquisition were made. Inquisitors counter-attacked by accusing royal officers of complicity with heresy. The figures are startling: for the period 1226 to 1275 only two accusations against them are recorded, against thirty between 1275 and 1306. The accusations, sometimes against the office-holders themselves, sometimes against their relatives, range from protection of heretics, dining with them and lending them money to the giving of the *melioramentum*, attendance at consoling, affirmation of belief and actual reception of the *consolamentum*.[33] Whether they came originally from Northern families or were of Southern origin, as was true of the majority, all were vulnerable to accusations. Sometimes there seems no doubt these were justified. In the Albigeois the viguier, sousviguier and judge backed popular resistance to inquisitors at the end of the century and officers of the royal bastide of Réalmont were fautors; in the Cabardès, Pagès's work had ensured that many officers were involved in heresy.

A complicity with heresy on the part of leading citizens in Carcassonne is revealed by the plot to seize and burn the inquisition archives in order to check unwelcome enquiries by the inquisitor Jean de Garland. In 1285, meetings were held involving three of the consuls, the diocesan official and certain other notables; it fell through because the plotters' agent could not find the requisite key and Bernard de Lagarrigue, a former perfect and inquisition spy, took fright at the prospect of being condemned for relapse if the plot went wrong. Jean de Garland believed in the reality of the plot and the involvement of Sans Morlane, archdeacon, one of the administrators of the diocese during the long episcopal vacancy. It was a startling accusation. Though supporting the inquisitors in their proceedings against the plotters, the pope made no decision about Sans Morlane; whatever connection he may have had with heretics he seems to have given up. He became a benefactor of both Carmelites and Augustinians and died in his bed in 1311 untroubled by inquisitors. Subsequent investigation showed that his brother Arnaud, *curé* of Pennautier, had plotted against the inquisitors, given the *melioramentum* and was himself consoled during an illness; his body was exhumed and burned in 1325. Another plotter, the professor of law, master Guillaume Garric, was subsequently convicted. This independent investigation confirmed decisions made by de Garland.[34]

Carcassonne was a 'nodal point'[35] for the history of late Catharism: there

[33] Friedlander, 'Les agents …', pp. 208–11.
[34] Griffe, *Inquisition*, pp. 136–70, thoughtful analysis; plot at Carcassonne, pp. 152–8.
[35] J. L. Biget, 'L'extinction du Catharisme urbain: les points chauds de la repression', *CF* xx, pp. 305–40 at p. 310 (summary related to royal policy).

were close links between the city and the surrounding countryside, where Pagès and others had been active. When de Garland followed the threads which led from the country into Carcassonne, he roused a storm of protest. Some citizens moved to Albi or Castres, where the heresy had never been completely uprooted; appeals were made to the pope and king. Authority stood firm; the evidence is sufficient to show that the accusations were not generally based on prejudice and that despite irregularities the old religion still had a residual hold, even among its high officials and leading citizens.

The same must be said of Albi, where the dominant figure in the pursuit of heresy was Bishop Bernard de Castanet, 1276–1308, a jurist originally from Montpellier, friend of the Dominicans, an authoritarian ultramontane of similar tradition to his contemporary Boniface VIII, determined to dominate the spiritual life of his diocese and a builder who enlarged the episcopal palace and set in hand a remarkable cathedral. He was determined to uproot heresy: his statutes include a stipulation that refusal of the last rites should incur suspicion of heresy.[36] It was at the death-bed that the Cathars retained their power. In face of the anti-inquisitional disturbances in Carcassonne, the bishop and inquisitor cooperated in an investigation and four defendants were taken for interrogation to the episcopal palace at Albi: probably confessions of the Carcassonne plotters alerted Bernard to the extent of surviving heresy in the town and diocese of Albi. He then saw that those in his diocese suspected of working with the pro-Cathar party in Carcassonne were also put on trial: nine were convicted, imprisoned and dispossessed. Information about other suspects came to light, much not being immediately put to use.[37]

Strife over heresy was complicated by the tensions between the papacy and Philip the Fair, which caused the monarchy in the 1290s to move from restraining the actions of inquisitors, especially as the conflict between Philip and Boniface heated up, to the abandonment of such checks, as the papacy made peace. Disturbances were renewed. The Bourg of Carcassonne, excommunicated because of resistance to inquisitors, finally surrendered on terms in 1299; at Albi, a conflict between citizens and bishop over his temporal powers in the city ran side by side with the struggle over heresy and stimulated the bishop's actions. Following waves of arrests, trials of suspects from Albi and elsewhere took place in 1299–1300, brought to a conclusion with remarkable speed, sometimes following the use of torture, and issuing in stiff sentences, often *murus strictus*,[38] confinement on bread and water or preventive detention without trial. Of the thirty-five defendants, twenty-five came from Albi itself and seven more were arrested in 1301–2, the bishop and the inquisitor Nicholas of Abbeville presiding.

---

[36]   Comment, J. L. Biget, *CF* XXIX, 'La législation synodale: le cas d'Albi aux XIIIe et XIVe siècles', *CF* XXIX, pp. 181–213 at p. 202.

[37]   J. L. Biget, 'Un procès d'inquisition à Albi', CF vi, pp. 273–341 (classic analysis, political background); G. W. Davis, *The Inquisition at Albi, 1299–1300* (New York, 1948, repr. 1974) (for events – superseded on motives); orig. text, pp. 103–266, analysis, pp. 11–91.

[38]   Biget, 'Un procès …'; p. 283.

The arrests, trials and sentencing recorded in a series of curt but damning confessions, fruit of brief, formal sessions sometimes cramming as many as four to six statements into a single hearing, formed a sudden, brutal sequence of events – no leisurely and thorough investigation as earlier, but a campaign designed to eliminate the guilty in short time.[39] The timing and selection of defendants was above all due to the bishop's will to strike at the urban oligarchy which, from the years 1265 to 1270 onwards, broke its quondam alliance with the bishop and set out to seize a greater autonomy at the episcopal expense by making use of royal officers and appeals to the crown. Bernard de Castanet was disposed to see no division between his temporal and spiritual rights: an attack on one was deleterious to the other.

The arrests for heresy in 1299 are intimately linked with the long drawn-out battle over episcopal temporal jurisdiction which opened with the arrest by the bishop's bayle of thirteen citizens in April 1297: a judicial conflict dragged on as the urban oligarchy backed the citizens and used every device to prolong proceedings. Heresy was one issue where the bishop, working with the inquisitor, held the whip hand; inquisitorial proceedings were swift, if successful extremely damaging to defendants, in practice not usually subject to appeal and supported by the crown, following the Capetian tradition of hostility to heresy. So bishop and inquisitor seized their chance. In the archives remained many names against whom evidence had been laid in the Carcassonne investigation; political considerations more than anything else dictated the selection, since demonstrably the great majority were of the urban oligarchy and had been active in the government of the town and a majority of those imprisoned were involved in the conflict of 1297–9 over the temporal jurisdiction of the bishop. There was an evident concern to convict men of the king. Generally these were men of some wealth; opponents complained that the bishop was driven by a desire for gain, but analysis of episcopal resources and outgoings and the net gains he might expect from confiscations do not bear this out.[40]

These were guilty men; whatever the motive for arrest, the outcome was not unfair. The convicted formed part of a relatively homogeneous social grouping, including merchants, royal officers, men of law, linked in a good number of cases by matrimonial alliance, who had long been involved in Catharism. Though brief, the confessions are of good calibre, lacking the suspicious uniformity and repetition characteristic of forced and false evidence; there is corroborative detail. The town provided the majority of convictions but defendants also came from Cordes, Lescure, Réalmont – in other words, though there is a predominance of Bernard's opponents from within Albi itself, the investigation still had the character of a general enquiry.[41]

With relatives and friends, the hostile among the oligarchy fought back, gained an eloquent defender in Bernard Délicieux, lector at the Franciscan convents of Carcassonne and Albi, and appealed to Philip the Fair, who

[39]   Davis, *Inquisition*, p. 36.
[40]   Biget, 'Un procès …', pp. 304–10.
[41]   Ibid., pp. 291–2.

intervened.[42] In the end it was all in vain; as the quarrel of king and pope ended in the death of Boniface VIII, Philip ceased to see the popular movement against bishop and inquisitors as a useful source of support. Carcassonne and Limoux turned to treason and were punished with mass hangings. Délicieux was imprisoned. Clement V removed Bernard Castanet to Le Puy and had abuses corrected but did not release the incarcerated. In fundamentals, bishop and inquisitors were vindicated and the inflamed proceedings of the end of the century dealt a heavy blow against urban Catharism.

What was significant was that the old religion had made such inroads in ruling classes. Clearly, the hunting down had been patchy; in certain districts the perfect had been driven into emigration and a twilight existence. But at the same time a few surviving missionaries had been able to operate with relative impunity, and a minority of royal officials, lawyers and merchants continued to give the *melioramentum*, to assist at consoling and listen to their perfect. More disturbing still, some churchmen were ambivalent. Catharism had struck deep roots because of the decades of toleration before the Albigensian Crusade; an ancient feeling that the Good Men were heirs of the apostles and held the key to salvation lingered on in old Cathar families and among men of wealth and status. Perhaps no more than 10 per cent of the urban population were adherents but their power, the complicity of royal officials and meridonial toleration allowed them to lead a discreet double life, attending mass and conforming to Catholicism while maintaining secret contacts with the persecuted faith.

Between 1244 and the end of the century, Catharism in Languedoc suffered grievous blows but was not wholly eradicated. A final revival early in the fourteenth century centred on the highlands of the county of Foix was a disturbing reminder to the defenders of orthodoxy that their old enemy, though battered, still had evangelistic power.

---

[42] B. Hauréau, *Bernard Délicieux et l'Inquisition albigeoise, 1300–1320* (Paris, 1877) (orig. in *Revue des Deux Mondes*, reissue Portet-sur-Garonne, 1992, with introduction, trans. J. Duvernoy).

10

The Last Missionary

Origins

Pierre Autier was the last major force in the history of Catharism in Languedoc, author of the revival in parts of the county of Foix which lasted effectively from 1299 to 1310, although authority was deeply concerned with rounding up remnants well beyond this date. It so happens that these Cathars attracted the attention of a leading inquisitor, Geoffrey d'Ablis,[1] then Bernard Gui, a still more notable figure,[2] and finally the supremely competent investigator, Jacques Fournier,[3] subsequently Pope Benedict XII – these men left records of interrogations of such detail that together they exceed in value all other sources of Cathar life and beliefs whether in Languedoc or Italy.

Recent research has shown that, though it had special features, Autier's revival cannot in any way continue to be classed as decadent or aberrant: it deserves to be analysed as part of mainstream Catharism surviving under harsh circumstances. It is therefore appropriate to devote substantial space

---

[1]   d'Ablis's inquisition: *L'Inquisiteur Geoffrey d'Ablis et les Cathares du comté de Foix (1308–1309)*, ed. A. Pales-Gobilliard (Paris, 1984) (*GA*), (text, Fr. trans.; analysis, pp. 1–77), review, J. H. Mundy, *Speculum* LXI (1986), pp. 883–4.

[2]   P. van Limborch, *Historia inquisitionis cui subiungitur Liber Sententiarum inquisitionis Tholosanae ab anno Christi MCCCVII ad annum MCCCXXIII* (Amsterdam, 1692) (*L*); corrections, J. Duvernoy, *Heresis* XII (1989), pp. 5–12 (from British Museum MS: M. A. E. Nickson, 'Locke and the inquisition of Toulouse,' *British Museum Quarterly* XXXVI (1972)). *Practica inquisitionis haereticae pravitatis*, ed. C. Douais (Paris, 1886); extracts, *WEH*, pp. 373–445 from G. Mollat, *Manuel de l'inquisiteur*, 2 vols (Paris, 1926, 1927); *CF* XVI (Gui as inquisitor and author).

[3]   *Le Registre d'Inquisition de Jacques Fournier (1318–1325)* (Latin original) ed. J. Duvernoy, I–III (Toulouse, 1965) (*JF*); review, A. Dondaine, *RHR* CLXXVIII (1970), pp. 49–56, correction list, J. Duvernoy (Toulouse, 1972); *Le Registre d'Inquisition de Jacques Fournier (Evêque de Pamiers, 1318–1325)*, trans., annotated, J. Duvernoy I, pp. 1–396, II, pp. 397–749, III, pp. 751–1346 (Paris, La Haye, 1978) (*JFD*) (complete, but note trans. vols do not correspond to edn vols); preface, E. Le Roy Ladurie, 'La domus à Montaillou et en Haute-Ariège', pp. i–xxx, introduction, J. Duvernoy, pp. 1–25 (Fournier, pp. 1–4); J. Duvernoy, 'A la recherche de la personnalité de

Figure 7   Sculpture of Jacques Fournier, bishop of Pamiers
Photograph: Roger-Viollet, Paris

Jacques Fournier', *Actes du Colloque du 7ᵉ centenaire du diocèse de Pamiers*, Septembre 1995 (Société historique de Pamiers et de la Basse-Ariège, Saverdun, 1997), and 'Benoit XII et le pays de Foix', *CF* XXVI, pp. 19–37, J. Paul, 'Jacques Fournier inquisiteur', *CF* XXVI, pp. 39–67; A. Fössel, 'Denunziation im Verfahren gegen Ketzer im 13. und beginnenden 14. Jahrhundert', in *Denunziation*, ed. G. Jerouschek, I. M. Marssolek and H. Röckelein (Tübingen, 1997), pp. 48–63 (uses esp. *JF*).

to this movement and its implications despite its short existence and the fact that it played out its life overwhelmingly in the highly specialized environment of a remote and mountainous part of Southern France. Autier's mission field in fact extended beyond his own homeland down through the Lauragais to Toulouse and beyond into Lower Quercy: he and his colleagues were beginning to take steps to revive the faith in its ancient heartlands. Embers still glowed, were missionaries sufficiently appealing and audacious.[4]

On a November day in 1322 one of the more sensitive and observant Cathar supporters, the widow Sibille Peyre, gave evidence before Jacques Fournier, bishop of Pamiers. She had the misfortune to appear before one of the greatest of all inquisitors, a Cistercian, a master of theology of the University of Paris. Born at Saverdun in the Ariège, son of a revenue collector to the count of Foix, he was both a Southerner who knew the dialect and customs of his native land and a bishop of the highest calibre, who had a taste for acquiring knowledge in minute detail. He was concerned to draw from Sibille Peyre details which had not been brought out by the Carcassonne inquisitor to whom she had earlier confessed, then fled and hidden. At the end of his first interrogation, the defendant said ruefully that if she had been so interrogated at Carcassonne, she would have revealed everything she knew.[5]

The story which Sibille had to tell throws light on the reasons for the revival of Cathar fortunes in the county of Foix at the very end of the thirteenth and beginning of the fourteenth centuries and also on the limitations of its leadership. The protagonist in the revival, Pierre Autier, never appeared before Bishop Fournier – a disappointment for the historian, since it would have brought together a supreme, albeit idiosyncratic, inquisitor and one of the greatest of all Cathar evangelists.[6] Autier was burnt in 1310 and Fournier never met him. But he and all concerned with the final elimination of Catharism in the South would have been well aware of his personality and his achievements as he appears over and over again in the recollections of his erstwhile flock. In many hours of interrogations, often led by him in person, Fournier grappled with the effects of Autier's revival between 1318 and 1326, when he was translated to

---

[4]   Events, *JDH*, pp. 315–33, *JFD* I, pp. 4–21, Duvernoy, 'Le Catharisme ...'; (*CF* xx, pp. 27–56, penetrating analysis), *BF* chs 22–5, conclusion, pp. 373, geography, p. 307, map, p. 309, background, E. Le Roy Ladurie, *Montaillou village occitan de 1294 à 1324* (Paris, 1975) (*LRLM*), trans. (abridged), B. Bray, *Montaillou* (London, 1978) (analysis of Cathar-dominated village using anthropology, literary quality; based on *JF*), essential critique, L. E. Boyle, 'Montaillou revisited: *mentalité* and methodology', in *Pathways to Medieval Peasants: Papers in Medieval Studies*, et. J. A. Raftis, II (Pontifical Institute of Medieval Studies, Toronto, 1981), pp. 119–40; M. Benad, *Domus und Religion in Montaillou* (Tübingen, 1990), review, J. Duvernoy, *Medievistik* III (1990), pp. 417–18, doctrine, *GRK* IV (2), pp. 156–374. I have been unable to use H. C. Stoodt, *Katharismus im Untergrund* (Tübingen, 1997).

[5]   *JF* II, p. 424, *JFD*, p. 583.

[6]   J. Duvernoy, 'Pierre Autier', *CEC* xxI (1970), pp. 9–49, accepting Autier's descent from Cathar adherents; doubts, *GA*, p. 45.

Mirepoix: he caused the burning of the last of Autier's perfect in 1321,[7] though persecutions continued as late as 1329.

Sibille Peyre had come into contact with Catharism when she and her husband Raimond, then living at Arques, were mourning the death of a daughter. They were comforted by a widow, Gaillarde Escaunier, who promised she would introduce them to the brothers Autier. She related what can fairly be called the Autier *legenda*, the edifying story of their conversion passed from mouth to mouth in the process of evangelization.[8]

The Autiers, she said, were clerks – i.e. literate men – and knew the law, had wives and children and were well off. One day Pierre was reading a book and, handing it to Guillaume, said, 'Well, brother?' Guillaume replied that it seemed to him that they had lost their souls, to which Pierre answered: 'Let us leave, brother, and go and seek the salvation of our souls.' The story has an echo of the *tolle, lege* of St Augustine's conversion.[9] They gave up all they had, the widow said, and went to Lombardy, where they were consoled, then returned to their native land to save souls. They would save the Peyres' souls and so instruct them that they would cease to feel the weight of their grief for their daughter.

Sibille's husband went to Ax, met the brothers and brought back a vivid memory of their exhortation, denouncing the abuses of the Church, rejecting the power of priests and asserting that of the perfect: only they could save and the souls of those they received went at once to paradise, leaving the body so fast that they could pierce a brick wall. Sibille was more cautious but promised to receive them when they came in secrecy to their house and not betray them. Pierre came with his son Jacques, who, the proud father said, was more eloquent than himself and spoke with the mouth of an angel.[10] On this visit Jacques read from a book, unspecified, and his father expounded the doctrines of the Fall, of transmigration of souls and final salvation through the hands of the perfect; then, on another night, preached again, vividly attacking the practice of baptism, the mass and transubstantiation, and carnal marriage. If, he said in derision, Christ's body was present, then even if it was as big as Mount Bugarach, it would still not be enough to be consumed by so many priests. Cathar followers would all in the end be saved, even those who recanted or denounced the perfect, though they would have to suffer much first. He ended with a vision of the Cathar paradise, where each soul would have the same happiness as another; they would all be one and each soul would love any other just as much as those of father, mother or children. Here lay the nub of the comfort for the bereaved – a future in which all individual affections and earthly sorrows were caught up in a universal love.

---

[7] *JDH*, p. 331.
[8] *JF* II, p. 404, *JFD*, pp. 566–7.
[9] J. M. Vidal, 'Les derniers ministres de l'albigéisme en Languedoc: leurs doctrines', *RQH* LXXIX (1906), pp. 57–107 at p. 64; confession of Sibille Peyre, *JF* II, pp. 403–29, *JFD*, pp. 566–88.
[10] *JF* II, p. 406; Autier's view, not Sibille's as mis-stated, *JFD*, p. 569.

Sibille had been impressed. Difficulties none the less emerged later when the widow Gaillarde fell ill, was consoled and put in *endura*,[11] but after a fast of eight days was persuaded by Sibille to start eating again. Then Sibille's daughter Jacqueline, still less than a year old, fell seriously ill; her father wanted her to be consoled and secured the services of the perfect Prades Tavernier, one of the weakest members of Pierre's team. Pierre had ruled strictly that under-age children were not to be consoled, but Tavernier nevertheless consoled the little girl with full ceremony, 'making many inclinations and elevations and placing a book on her head',[12] instructing Sibille not to give her anything to eat or drink that had been born of the flesh (which included milk); if she lived, she would be subject to the dietary restrictions normal to the perfect. Sibille rebelled and after Prades and Raimond had gone, gave her child the breast. Another Cathar believer, Pierre Maury, told her she was a bad mother and that women were demons: her action precipitated a sharp quarrel and split the family.

She noticed, too, a darker side to the brothers. Pierre and Guillaume amassed money, she said, and she disliked the justification for killing informers given from Scripture, using the words of Jesus on hewing down a tree that does not bring forth good fruit. Her daughter died. In her heart she had abandoned Catharism when she suckled the child, but she continued to receive the perfect since, as she said, she 'greatly feared and loved her husband'[13] and saw that he had a great affection for them.

Defendants commonly minimized their participation in Catharism and put blame on the absent and the dead – in this case, Sibille's husband. And yet her evidence, the build-up of facts and events, her recall of Pierre's phraseology, even to a dialect phrase,[14] and the bishop's acceptance of her story will make the reader believe that Sibille is giving us a fair picture of her own development as a failed adherent and of the strengths and weaknesses of Autier's revival.

Pierre Autier was in his fifties when in 1295–6 he felt the call to be consoled and devote himself to the life of a Cathar missionary. The widow Gaillarde was quite right to draw attention to the earthly position which Pierre and his brother gave up. Pierre was a notary with high connections, of the *noblesse de robe*. He had an extensive family, three sons and four daughters by his first wife Aladaycis and two bastard children by his mistress Moneta, sister of another Ax notary. Although at his departure for Italy he was deeply in debt and left his guarantor in Ax to pay up for him, he was a capable businessman and planned a missionary campaign with an adequate treasure chest behind it. Years later, when he had built up resources, he repaid him with an apology and had sufficient to finance his wanderings,

[11]   Below, p. 241; *JF* II, p. 414, *JFD*, p. 575; compare *JF* III, p. 143, *JFD*, p. 939.
[12]   *JF* II, p. 414, *JFD*, p. 575; another report, *JF* II, p. 17, *JFD*, p. 562 speaks of pressure on Tavernier to console after he had initially refused and wrongly says the daughter recovered.
[13]   *JF* II, p. 424, *JFD*, p. 582; see case of Mengarde Buscail refusing consoling of baby son because she would have to refuse her breast, *JF* I, p. 504, *JFD*, p. 538.
[14]   *JF* II, p. 406, *JFD*, p. 568; I cannot share Brenon's low view of Sibille's evidence, *Heresis* XI (1988), p. 64 (see n. 179 below).

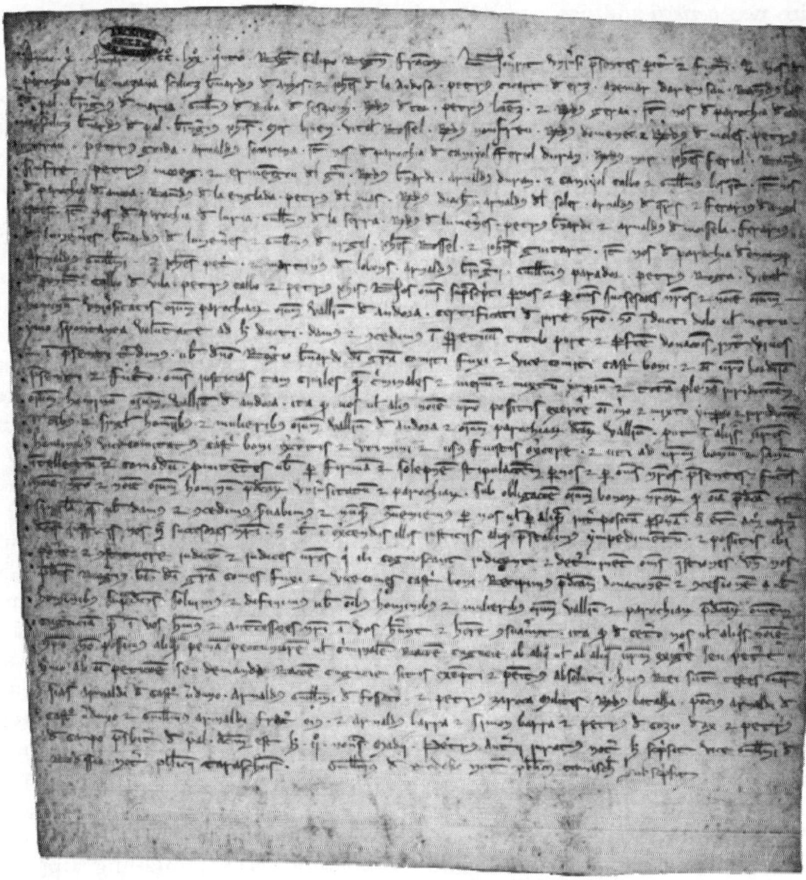

Figure 8   The writing of a heretic: Pierre Autier
Reproduced courtesy of J. Duvernoy

buy books and parents, keep a deposit at money changers in Toulouse, give
payments to poorer followers and obtain a batch of Parma knives intended
as a blind to cover his missionizing.[15]

The traditional route to Italy ran by the Var and the Alpes Maritimes, Nice
and the Col de Tende, thence into the plain and to Cuneo in Piedmont, a
commercial point where heretics could be lost in a busy entrepôt and where
Pierre and Guillaume received the *consolamentum* and came into contact
with Bernard Audouy de Montégut-Lauragais, the *ancien* of the Church.
Much further to the south, Raymond Isarn Major, deacon, lived in Sicily

---

[15]   *JF* I, pp. 295–6, *JFD*, p. 373; *JF* II, pp. 202–4, 216, *JFD*, pp. 595–6, 605; Duvernoy,
CEC XXI, pp. 16–17; knives as presents, *GA*, pp. 226, 384.

with two *perfecti* and two *perfectae,* a tiny remnant of the old Church's hierarchy, whom the Autiers may well never have visited.[16]

Already informed, the brothers would have needed little instruction but required training in the dietary and ethical requirements of their new status; they needed to gain an automatic adherence to the schedules of fasting and abstinence, to the routine of the paternosters and to be weaned first from eating meat, then all animal fat.[17] Audouy had contacts with the underground Church's supporters, Pierre Raymond de Saint-Papoul, remembered as a handsome man, first coming to Lombardy in 1219 and Prades Travernier, a weaver of the village of Prades in the Pays d'Alion, a high plateau north-east of Ax-les-Thermes, who, as he grew in enthusiasm for the perfect, practised his weaving less and less, then one day sold his tools, formed a party with the widow Stéphanie de Châteauverdun and her daughter Catalane and went to Barcelona to seek *perfecti,* Catalane supporting them by work in the silk industry: finding no one, Prades went on to Italy.[18] Another enthusiast was Amiel d'Auterive, who took the name Amiel de Perles. Bon Guillaume, the elder of Pierre's illegitimate children, acted as courier, spying out the land in Languedoc.

With this tiny missionary group, Guillaume, Pierre Raymond, Prades and Amiel, Pierre Autier launched his offensive, returning late in 1299 to his native land, abandoning the relatively passive role enjoyed by Bernard Audouy on the Lombard slopes of the Alps and by Raymond Isarn in Sicily for the terrors of a life as active perfect in a land where orthodoxy was backed by force. He never returned to the greater security of Italy; instead he carried on a guerilla existence, guided by an iron sense for secrecy, passing from one safe house to another, sleeping often by day and moving far and fast by night, unservingly endeavouring to bring to life a new church from the embers of the old.

The ramifications of Autiers formed an essential background to the success of the enterprise. His brother Guillaume was his unfailing support. Their brother Raimond, who, ostensibly at least, had been told nothing of their life in Italy, described to the inquisitors his joy at meeting Pierre and Guillaume again at his house in Ax, probably in 1300.[19] Bon Guillaume came by night in the season of Lent to ask if Raimond would receive them: yes, he said, he would, 'he could not abandon them because they were his brothers.'[20] Towards midnight came their knock at the door; Raimond received them with joy, embraced them and gave them a bed. They stayed about eight days and Raimond's house became one of the secure resting points for the missionaries. Arnaud Teisseyre had married Pierre's daughter Guillelme – although not very happily – and was deeply implicated before the brothers went away to be consoled; he was accused of having counselled

[16]   Duvernoy, *CF* XX, pp. 38–9; *GA,* p. 118.
[17]   Duvernoy, *CEC* XXI, p. 20; *GA,* pp. 154–6.
[18]   *JF* II, p. 417, *JFD,* p. 577; Pierre Raymond's appearance, *L,* p. 185.
[19]   *GA,* pp. 116–34.
[20]   Ibid., pp. 116–17.

them to go to Lombardy and had bought them a razor at the Pamiers fair to avoid the risk of going to a barber.[21]

At Tarascon, Guillaume de Rodes, a nephew of the Autiers, described how he gradually came to do more and more; first, asked by Raimond if he would put them up for the night or give them something to eat, he refused to do more than give them some food; later, as Raimond led Pierre and Guillaume through the countryside near Tarascon by night, the dawn came up and Raimond concealed them in a shed in a meadow Guillaume owned, then went to tell him what he had done. Guillaume went out to feed them, brought them into his house for the night and concealed them in his grain store; later still they stayed for three weeks. Guillaume claimed that he had heard little of the heretics' preaching and had not adored them, explaining that he had concealed and protected them because they were of his family and he did not think they had sinned or done evil.[22]

Pierre's children did humble tasks; Arnaud and Jean brought fish to Raimond's house.[23] Bon Guillaume was a nervous agent, not kept *au fait* with all his father's plans; he stayed only a little time with the brothers at Cunco, enjoying plentiful supplies of food and drink, then was sent back. In Ax he moved from house to house for fear of the authorities and made his contact with Arnaud Teisseyre in the utmost secrecy, throwing a stone at the window, tapping, whispering so that no one should overhear.[24]

Pierre's legitimate son Jacques was made of sterner stuff. He followed his father's teaching with devotion and, by accepting the *consolamentum* in full health, helped to make up the yawning gap in the number of active missionary perfect. With Pons of Ax, he was ordained in 1301[25] and thereafter shared the hunted, fugitive life of his father and uncle. Wives backed husbands. So Blanche gave full support to her husband Guillaume de Rodes and Gaillarde, Guillaume Autier's wife, reinforced the resolve of Sibille, wife of Pierre Pauc of Ax, to be consoled.[26]

Thus the extensive Autier family gave a convenient and safe nucleus for the missionary drive. How deep family feeling ran can be learnt from the curious episode of Raimond de Rodes, Pierre's nephew, who stood quite outside the family tradition and was a Dominican friar at Pamiers. Despite their secrecy, the return of the brothers was soon bruited abroad. A beguin of Pamiers, Guillaume Dejean, offered his services to the friars as double agent, promising to ingratiate himself with the perfect and hand them over to the inquisition. Hearing of this, Raimond sent urgently to his brother Guillaume asking him to come at once, took him aside and told him about the beguin and the alarming fact that he had said Guillaume had received and fed heretics. Guillaume lied and

---

21 *JF* II, pp. 194–220, *JFD*, pp. 589–609.
22 *GA*, pp. 134–62.
23 Ibid., p. 94.
24 JF II, p. 209.
25 Below p. 244. Jacques apparently did not go to Italy; Philippe d'Alayrac did, *JDH*, p. 325, *BF*, p. 332.
26 *GA*, pp. 134–62, 212–40; *JF* I, p. 294, *JFD*, pp. 371–2.

reassuringly said it was quite untrue but within a fortnight two believers had killed the beguin by night in the mountains above Larnat and thrown his body into a ravine.[27]

Family feeling reinforced and sustained religious belief: from casual fautorship to the commitment of a believer, step by step, a child or brother could be drawn along; preaching and instruction could be concealed in casual house gatherings; the ties of blood made betrayal less easy.

The beguin episode showed none the less how simply the movement might be infiltrated. So the cloak of secrecy remained as thick as possible. One of the most zealous of all supporters, Sibille den Baille, kept a secret chamber for the Autiers; the brothers de Area at Quié had a grain chest below which was a concealed place where the missionaries could be completely hidden.[28] Literary convention depicted heretics as habitually lurking in cellars and underground places; it was an attribute of unorthodoxy to be concealed and to love darkness. In the case of the Autier mission, the use of darkness and the living and preaching in out of the way places, in sub-solars and the like, was a matter of survival: when Pons Arnaud conducted Philippe de Larnat to Quié to meet the Autiers, he took the neophyte to the village in the dead of night when all were asleep.[29]

Daylight movement was concealed under commercial activity. The Parma knives made the Autiers seem to the uninitiated like travelling pedlars.[30] Raimond de Saint-Papoul pretended he was a travelling merchant when he went to Ax to seek out the Autiers.[31] The secrecy was justified. Guillaume Autier was nearly surprised by the sergeants of the count of Foix in the house of Alamande, widow of Arnaud de Vicdessos Tarascon. They had come for a quite different purpose, to claim the possessions of a merchant captive in the castle of Foix; the widow only narrowly averted disaster by alerting Guillaume Bayard, an officer of the count but a friend of heretics, who ordered the sergeants to enter by one door while Guillaume slipped out of another.[32]

Although the prosecution of heresy in this remote region had not been as rigorous as in some other parts of Languedoc, there was awareness of the massive penalties for heresy and fautorship. Men and women needed to be persuaded before they would take the risk of associating with heretics. Arnaud Piquier feared that involvement would cost him his goods; it needed his wife's persuasion before he was ready to accept the perfect. But then they came to stay over and over again, some twenty times in all.[33] Sometimes respect and affection for the perfect was muffled by prudence. So Esclarmonde den Garrabet would not see the Autiers because she had

[27]   *GA*, pp. 150–4, comment, p. 58; see *JF* II, p. 423, *JFD*, pp. 581–2.

[28]   *GA*, pp. 140, 158–60.

[29]   Ibid., p. 114; movement and whistles at night, p. 386.

[30]   *JDH*, p. 323; Raymond Issaurat as a boy seeing heretics with knives at his father's house, thought they were coiners, *GA*, p. 260.

[31]   *GA*, pp. 124–6.

[32]   Ibid., pp. 154–6.

[33]   Ibid., pp. 164, 168.

already been penanced for heresy and feared the penalty for relapse; none
the less she showed her true feelings by sending them presents – wine,
bread called *tonholt* and raisins called *bromests* in a painted bowl.[34]

Bertrand de Taix of the fallen nobility of Limoux lived as a *rentier* in
Pamiers and was wont to lament the passing of the time in which the Good
Men were to be found in the land: he was one of a few surviving members of
noble house who kept an attachment to heresy. His second wife was hostile,
so he was inclined to conceal his true position; none the less, he repeatedly
sent wine to the perfect and planned a visit to the baths at Ax as a cover for
an attempt to contact the Autiers.[35]

The consolamentum *and the* endura

The perfect saw a prime duty in the consoling of the dying: it was an overriding necessity, an integral part of their duties, which they fulfilled again
and again in the teeth of rain, storm, cold and threat of betrayal. No longer
was consoling a public event; it had become a secret matter, concealed in a
household with only one or two supporters at hand.

Guillaume Autier's wife persuaded a dying woman, Sibille, wife of Pierre
Pauc of Ax, that she could arrange for Guillaume to come in so quietly to
console her that her hostile husband would not notice. So it was. From his
concealment in a nearby house, Guillaume was brought into the kitchen at
night where Sibille lay in bed while her husband slept on in another room;
unluckily, Sibille's illness had gone too far, she was in delirium and could
not make the responses, so died unconsoled.[36] A similar secrecy prevailed at
Savart, near Tarascon, where the daughter of the dying Mengarde Alibert
fetched Guillaume from Raymond Marty's dovecote at Junac to console her
in bed by the light of the kitchen fire with the candle blown out for security.
Here, too, the candidate could not make the responses, yet Guillaume
consoled her.[37] The reason for this distinction is not made clear.

At Tarascon itself, carefully placed in the house in order to console the
dying mother of Pierre de Gaillac, Guillaume dared not enter her room
because of the press of visitors. Raimond Autier's wife Esclarmonde found a
solution by persuading Pierre to ask the crowd to leave about the time of
vespers because of the effect of the heat on the dying woman. Guillaume
slipped in disguised in Esclarmonde's clothes and administered the *consolamentum*.[38] Raimond Garsen, ill near the altar in the church of the hospital of
Saint-Suzanne at L'Hospitalet, was consoled by Guillaume Autier and
Prades Tavernier. His daughter, Guillelme Garsen of Ax, a simple and easily
led believer, related how the party of heretics came in one night before
dawn and asked Raimond if he believed he was going to die. When he said
that he was sure this was so, they asked him if he wished to be received by

34   Ibid., p. 234.
35   Ibid., p. 47; *JF* III, p. 322–4, *JFD*, pp. 1178–80.
36   *JF* I, p. 294, *JFD*, pp. 371–2; *consolamentum, GA*, pp. 67–71.
37   *JF* II, pp. 305–7, *JFD*, pp. 675–7; Griffe, *Inquisition*, pp. 202–3.
38   *GA*, pp. 350–2.

them and if he could assure them that he would keep the will of God and of them. On his assenting, they held a book over his head and spoke words which she could not understand. To Guillelme and the other bystanders they gave their orders – nothing should be given to the dying man except water and that only if he was very thirsty, and if he drank he should say the paternoster every time.[39] On his diet of water, Raimond could be expected to slip from life and be secure that he could hold his *consolamentum* to the end without fear of breaching the obligations of a perfect, even by oversight or accident. Cathars had no doctrine of intention and an accidental fall lost the *consolamentum* as completely as a deliberate breach.

This proceeding of fasting to death in order to hold the *consolamentum* was the *endura*, foreshadowed elsewhere, but more widespread by far in the mission field of the Autier revival than at any other time or place in Cathar history.[40]

Long a committed believer, Gentille d'Ascou came in her last illness to the baths at Ax more for the sake of being consoled than for the thermal waters. Guillaume Autier, tapping gently at Raimond Vaysièrre's door at the time of the first sleep of the night, induced him to act as guide to the baths. Together they went into a field at the back of the hospital where Gentille was staying while a friend assisted her, so frail she could neither move nor stand without help, to go out to them; sitting in the field, she received the *consolamentum*. It seems she did not eat after that and died five or six days later.[41] Another woman from Coustaussa, in far better health, left her husband, fled to the Sabartès where she put herself into *endura* at the home of Sibille den Baille; it took her twelve weeks to die.[42]

When Sibille Peyre had completed her evidence before Fournier, she was astute enough to ask the bishop to allow her, if she subsequently remembered more, to confess more without danger, i.e. without incurring the penalties for concealing information. She did remember more and, among stray details in a later interrogation, recalled a conversation with Pierre Autier in which he described consoling Huguette, wife of Philippe de Larnat junior, in her last illness.[43] She put herself in *endura*; then 'for love of heretics', as the register puts it, was moved into a *sotulum* at the lowest point of the house where the perfect, including both Pierre and Guillaume

[39]   Ibid., pp. 190–2, 196.
[40]   Duvernoy, *JDR*, pp. 164–70, seeing *JF* II, p. 426 as essential clue to *endura*'s evolution (*JDR*, pp. 164–5). Rottenwöhrer, *GRK* II (2), pp. 586–604, thorough but preceding publication of *GA*, misses this. Pales-Gobilliard, *GA*, p. 72, follows C. Thouzellier, *Rituel Cathare* (Paris, 1977), p. 169 in hypothesis of importation by Autier from Lombardy. But evidence is slender (see Pavia case 1275). I prefer Duvernoy's evolution in Languedoc, but believe he underplays *endura*, underestimates Autier's role and wrongly links *endura* to decadence.
[41]   *GA*, pp. 206–8.
[42]   Ibid., p. 226. This sounds like a healthy believer's will to die: otherwise death would not have been so long delayed. It also suggests Autier approved since (a) deposition attributes recounting of story to Autier, (b) Sibille was close to him (*GA*, p. 204).
[43]   *JF* II, p. 426, *JFD*, p. 584.

Autier, could safely watch over her till her end, being prepared to reconsole if it became necessary, i.e. if by chance she breached the obligation of the perfect. They were there 'to see and hear her till she died'. Pierre remembered an exchange between Huguette and her mother-in-law Sibille when she, with many others, stood by her in the *sotulum* as she lay dying. Huguette asked if she would soon be 'finished' and Sibille replied that she would live (*adhuc vivetis*) and together they would look after her children. Pierre heard this exchange and smiled. Sibille was saying, he believed, that if she lived, Huguette would be one of the perfect and fulfil in her life the obligations of that state, the requirements of fasting and prayer which would make it so much harder for her without help to fulfil also her obligations to her family. Pierre still held the scene in fond recollection and was surely smiling at the time because of the evidence of devoted self-sacrifice by both his supporters. Huguette looked to her end and as a devout Cathar wished it to come quickly so that she might soon be in paradise: if she did, in spite of all, live, she would not be one of the more half-hearted supporters who promptly gave up the obligations of the perfect, but would go on with the fasts and abstinences. Like many a bedside watcher, Sibille seems to have hoped that Huguette might yet live and was confident that she would honour her obligations if she did: for herself, she was reassuring her daughter-in-law that in that case she would be there for the children.

It is unlikely that Sibille Peyre or even the bishop understood the clue given by this episode to the nature and origins of the *endura*.[44] It sprang from a profound insecurity about dying people successfully maintaining the rigid requirements of the state of the perfect. Receiving the *consolamentum* at death had become more usual, and in the early fourteenth century a small band of perfect was heavily occupied moving to and fro administering it to a small and scattered flock. They had to move in secrecy for fear of betrayal. Inevitably, they often arrived too early or too late. In disunited or uninstructed households they could not be sure that some well-meaning relative would not comfort the consoled with chicken broth,[45] a well-known panacea in the region, thereby destroying his or her status. In delirium or in consumptive cases when the mouth could fill with blood, or through weakness, the patient might be unable to recite the regulation paternoster after sustenance.[46] Reconsoling was difficult. The *endura* was the practical answer.

[44]   Duvernoy (above, n. 40) is first historian to have understood.

[45]   *JDR*, p. 168; J. Duvernoy, 'La nourriture en Languedoc à l'époque cathare', *Congrès d'études régionales de la fédération des sociétés académiques et savantes de Languedoc, Pyrénées, Gascogne, 1968* (Carcassonne, 1970), pp. 235–41.

[46]   *JDR*, pp. 168–9. Sacconi's description of Italian practice is relevant: 'since many of them when ill have sometimes asked those who nursed them not to put any food or drink into their mouths if the invalids could not at least say the Lord's prayer, it is quite evident that many of them thus commit suicide' (*WEH*, p. 334). Is this not a parallel to developments in Langedoc? See also Fanjeaux case, Thouzellier, *Rituel*, p. 169, *JDR*, p. 166, n. 93, correcting R. Manselli, 'Un'abjura del XII secolo e l'eresia catara', *BISIAM* LXVII (1955), pp. 212–34 on alleged twelfth-century case.

Drinking cold water could be held to be so minor a consumption as not absolutely to require the Pater and it met the natural thirst of the dying. It needed to be cold, since heating water in a *foganha* of the Sabartès might well involve the use of pots in which meat had been cooked. Cold or fresh water is the normal prescription; sometimes sugared water is mentioned.[47] Prades Tavernier, generally insecure in his understanding, was known to prescribe bread and water, but that was an eccentricity.[48]

Pierre, Guillaume and Jacques Autier, Prades Tavernier, Philippe d'Alayrac are all recorded to have ordered or recommended the *endura*.[49] In Provençal the word meant and continued to mean fasting or hungering; in the hands of the perfect, believers and more fringe supporters of the Autier revival, it came to have the precise and technical meaning of fasting to death after receiving the *consolamentum*.[50] Its appearance so late in Cathar history was a consequence of the pressures of persecution coupled with the steely pastoral determination of Pierre Autier and his colleagues to rescue as many imprisoned spirits as possible from the realm of Satan, and to do so with security for their salvation. In one case Autier consoled a sick woman, ordered her not to be given anything to eat or drink and left her in charge of her daughter, assisted by a servant. As the record runs, they kept to Autier's order, refusing the mother all nourishment by day and night although she asked for it, 'lest she lose the good which she had received and lest she do anything against the *ordinatio* of the said heretic'.[51] It was not until the third day that they yielded and the sick woman recovered.

In the past, supervision of the last hours of the dying was simplified by transporting the candidate for consoling and care to the house of the perfect. The procedure resembled nothing so much as oblation *ad terminum*, the Catholic practice of committing oneself to a religious house when dying, taking the habit and being transported there to be cared for by monks or nuns and to benefit from their prayers. Guilhem de Malhorgas did both, being consoled when he thought he was dying, recovering, thinking better of it, eating meat and finally having himself taken to die at the Cistercian monastery of Boulbonne.[52] Catharism ran parallel to Catholicism with the important distinction that for the Cathar final salvation depended on the full observance of the food prohibitions and prayer requirements in a way that for the Catholics it did not. Alternatively, when the perfect could move more freely, they could call at a dying candidate's house and ensure that all was well. Pierre Autier's stay in the house

---

[47]   *GRK* II (2), pp. 592, 597; water as concession for those who cannot abstain, *JF* III, p. 247, *JFD*, p. 1019.

[48]   *JF* I, pp. 494–5, controversy, pp. 498, 501, *JFD*, pp. 530, 532, 535; uncertainty, *JF* II, p. 15, *JFD*, p. 561.

[49]   *JF* II, p. 426, *JFD*, p. 584, *GA*, pp. 302, 306 (Pierre); *JF* III, p. 265, *JFD*, pp. 1139–40, *GA*, p. 190 (Guillaume); Tavernier, above, p. 234; *GA*, p. 304 (d'Alayrac), *L*, p. 126 (Pierre Sans).

[50]   *GRK* II (2), p. 587.

[51]   *L*, p. 143.

[52]   Above, p. 135; *JDR*, p. 167.

observing and hearing Huguette harked back to those earlier days. The treatment of Huguette was in fact a throwback; such close supervision was no longer normally possible and the *endura* evolved to meet the need.

In conversation with Pierre Maury, Jacques Autier remembered a case where a candidate in *endura* could not succeed in dying for thirteen days and nights, though he had been a believer in good standing. Jacques interpreted the discomfort of waiting so long as a penance for his conduct in another tunic, i.e. incarnation. Conversely, he remembered another believer who had done ill dying swiftly; that, he concluded, must have been because he had merited a swift death through good conduct in a previous time. One of the most intelligent of the team, Jacques was beginning to form a theology of the *endura*.[53] His words to Pierre Maury have interesting implications. It does not seem as if Jacques was considering that death in such cases could be 'accelerated', to use the inquisitor's phrase. That certainly occurred sometimes, as in the case of Guillelme Marty of Prouade who had already been for many days in *endura* and yet lived and feared detection and capture; she sought help to make away with herself more speedily to cheat the inquisitor's agents. She tried the effects of bleeding, cold and poison, and procured a shoemaker's cutting instrument to kill herself. In a macabre episode, she and her helper conferred on the exact position of the heart so that she could be sure of death if the inquisition arrived.[54]

Medical science was not so developed as to make it easy to decide whether a young candidate was likely to die. Guillaume Autier consoled Bernard Marty, a shepherd at Junac, at the insistence of his more zealous brother Arnaud: years later in evidence Bernard remembered how Autier and Raimond de Saint-Papoul, each holding an arm, took him, racked by fever, and put him in position to kneel before Guillaume, make a response and have a book applied first to his head and then his shoulders. Guillaume said some words he did not understand, then briskly tucked the book under his arm and gave orders that he should eat neither bread nor meat nor drink wine, but have fresh water only. Thus, Guillaume said, he would go to paradise. Arnaud was pleased. Bernard drank only water. But the fever left him and on the third day he said he was very hungry. Reproachfully, Arnaud acceded to his request and brought him bread, wine and meat. Bernard ate and forfeited his *consolamentum*.[55]

It was sometimes agreed that if a candidate put him or herself in *endura* and then deliberately abandoned it, there could be no other valid consoling in that incarnation.[56] The normal *endura* saw a sick candidate, often near coma in any case, gently to the end; Pierre Maury, however, alluded to the darker possibility, a speedier end brought about by deliberate bleeding.[57]

---

[53] *JF* III, p. 31, *JFD*, p. 930; Jacques Autier's reflections, not Bélibaste's, as *JDR*, pp. 169–70, and so emanating from an alert perfect instead of one 'most poorly initiated', partaking of a 'popular point of view', ibid., p. 169.

[54] *L*, pp. 33, 70–1, 76, 94.

[55] *JF* III, pp. 265–6, *JFD*, pp. 1139–40; compare *JF* II, pp. 13–16, *JFD*, pp. 559–61.

[56] *JF* III, p. 143, *JFD*, p. 939; compare *JF* II, p. 484, *JFD*, pp. 881–2.

[57] *GRK* II (2), p. 595; *JF* III, pp. 247–8, *JFD*, p. 1020; see *L*, p. 33.

Jacques Fournier understood that the *endura* was suicide and incitement to murder.[58] The Cathars would not have seen it in this way. Sporadic and uncertain as its incidence before 1300 may be, the *endura* – making the escape from Satan – was always a possible deduction from their world view. How far more aggressive means of ending life to maintain the validity of the *consolamentum* were used and how far the *endura* was self-applied by the healthy remains uncertain: what is clear is that the *endura* for those thought to be already dying was becoming an established custom in the Autier revival.[59] It was no marginal or decadent phenomenon.

The perfect

A small category were consoled with the intention of keeping the requisite rule of life in order to serve as the active leadership: it was the equivalent of ordination. Pierre Autier was neither bishop, *filius* nor even deacon, but finer points of procedure and hierarchy were abandoned. When his son Jacques was consoled in the house of Arnaud Issaurat of Larnat together with Pons, son of the determined Sibille den Baille of Ax, there was no general congregation. Jacques and Pons knelt with their hands in prayer and asked to be received, made promises and listened to 'many words about the apostles and the gospels' and then were embraced and kissed on the mouth by the Autiers, welcoming them to their ranks.[60] At another ordination held at the same house two men were received, clad in blue mantles and green tunics, who took the names of Peter and Paul, this time in a wider gathering including the Issaurat family, mother, father, two sons and two daughters, and five leading missionaries, the three Autiers, Prades Tavernier and Pierre-Raimond de Saint-Papoul:[61] Peter and Paul had a special significance for the Cathar mission: we hear of a book of Peter and Paul amongst their collection of edifying literature.[62] The Autiers sent Philippe d'Alayrac from Coustaussa down to Sicily to be consoled; he returned to action in a party including Aude Bourrel of Limoux who had been consoled in Italy.[63] Pierre Autier consoled no healthy adult woman.

Newly fledged perfect continued the life of abstinence of the novitiate; they ate separately from believers and did their own cooking, no doubt of necessity if they were to avoid all contact with animal fat and meat, however accidental. Eggs, cheese and meat were totally excluded as products of

---

[58]   *JF* III, p. 247, *JFD*, p. 1020; compare Sibille Peyre, *JF* II, p. 414, *JFD*, p. 575.
[59]   See Pierre Clergue's praise for those who practised it ('saints of God'), *JF* I, pp. 230–1, *JFD*, pp. 271–2; compare Guillaume Belot ('martyrs of God'), *JF* I, p. 473, *JFD*, p. 471.
[60]   *GA*, p. 314.
[61]   Ibid., pp. 98–100; A. Delpech, 'La famille Issaurat de Larnat', *Heresis* XVI (1991), pp. 1–19 (evocative photos, J. L. Gasc).
[62]   *GA*, pp. 57, 60.
[63]   *JDH*, p. 325; Bourrel, *BF*, pp. 332–5. Aude Bourrel lived in the little Cathar centre at Toulouse: functions are not clear.

coition. When he stayed with Alamande de Vicdessos, Jacques Autier bought wine, bread and fruit from her but reserved all preparation to himself, using oil for cooking.[64] The perfect had their own *pot au terre* and their own dishes which no one else touched, except a few of the most committed women supporters who were allowed to cook for them.

The diet was not wholly austere. The perfect were skilled in the preparation of fish, especially with spices. Pierre de Gaillac of Tarascon remembered with pleasure the piece of trout he had bought very well cooked by the Autiers.[65] Pierre de Luzenac remembered the salmon and trout he had eaten at Toulouse with Pierre Autier, Pierre Sans and supporters.[66] Raimond Autier, travelling to sell sheep, took the opportunity at his brothers' request to buy two ounces of pepper and saffron for them.[67] Supporters liked to bring them presents of food and wine, including little delicacies such as figs in honey; on the other hand, if a supporter was too poor to cater easily for them, they arranged for food to be bought out of their own money. They might take a glass of wine with a supporter – but not seated side by side.[68] Their rule was that they ate apart from the rank and file – if it had to be at the same time, then there would be the length of the table between them. At the ritual blessing and distribution of bread, a perfect with his knife would cut slices for each and hand them over with a set form of words. The physical separation, the special dishes and the segregated cooking threw into high relief the profound gulf between those who had been consoled and the rest.

Hardest to bear for the active perfect must have been the great fasts three times a year, the dates of which emerge from Bernard Gui's *Practica inquisitionis*, from 13 November to 24 December, from Quinquagesima Sunday to Easter, from Pentecost to the feast of the apostles Peter and Paul, that is, 29 June.[69] These austerities won them support: repeatedly the great fasts and abstinences are cited as proof of the missionaries' devotion.

The mission

The *melioramentum*, the adoring of the good men, was an essential sign of commitment, the inquisitors' standard subject of enquiry as they tried to sift the truly committed from the casual and occasional hearer of sermons of pro-Cathar conversations. Witnesses knew this and were concerned to argue that their greeting to the perfect was that of any polite acquaintance.

Pierre and his team were determined to secure the *melioramentum* as early as they could. Technique varied. Pierre de Luzenac, student, a man of high potential and subsequently a notary, was a fine catch, but one who had to be played in carefully through a series of meetings, with loans and gifts of

[64] *GA*, p. 244.
[65] Ibid., p. 334.
[66] Ibid., p. 372.
[67] Ibid., pp. 118–20.
[68] *GA*, p. 73.
[69] Mollat, *Manuel*, p. 8; *GRK* II (2), pp. 569–85, *JDR*, pp. 212–13 (blessed bread).

money, the present of a silk bonnet and an enticing glimpse of a book of the gospels and epistles in Bologna letters with illuminations. Autier broached the giving of the *melioramentum*. It was refused. Again the request was made. Pierre excused himself on the grounds of his fear of publicity. It was finally secured in the dead of night when he, Pierre and Jacques had to take shelter from a shower in a deserted mill.[70]

Pierre Maury, an impressionable shepherd of Montaillou, a village on the high plateau of the Sabartès near the Aragonese frontier, was the object of a virtuoso performance by Pierre Autier, who, on meeting him, greeted him with joy, took him by the hand, sat next to him in the room where he was eating, told him that he would put him in the way of salvation where he would become a good believer, engaged him in dialogue and asserted the moral superiority of the perfect over the Catholic clergy. When Maury objected that he had recently heard a good sermon from a Franciscan, Pierre swept this aside and secured his adherence that very evening: closing the door to ensure they would be alone, Pierre got him to practise genuflecting to him, thus obtaining the *melioramentum*.[71]

First contacts with Cathars were commonly remembered in vivid detail despite a lapse of time, partly because of the calibre of medieval memory, partly because of their significance. An ethical appeal was commonly the first step. Talking to Raimond after their arrival from Lombardy, Pierre and Guillaume emphasized that they followed the way of the apostles and did not swear, lie, eat meat, cheese or eggs.[72] Arnaud Piquier, who claimed to have been drawn in through his wife's influence, heard Pierre and Jacques claim they were the Church of God, who followed a good life and had a good faith, better than that of Catholicism.[73] Walking with Pierre Autier's sister one Sunday morning, Guillelme Garsen was asked if she wanted to know the way by which she could be saved. There followed a disquisition on the faith and ethical calibre of the perfect, opening the way to salvation and, a less common twist, to prosperity and riches in this life. Sometimes a sympathizer alluded first to the persecution of the perfect, explaining that they were nor heretics at all but unjustly persecuted by representatives of an evil Church.[74]

Anton du Château de Rabat was led into Catharism by his friend Philippe de Larnat who asked him if he was a good man: when he said he was, he went on to explain what this meant in Cathar terms, the title 'Good Men' being for them for a claim and a programme. When he finally met Pierre and Guillaume in a storeroom, he heard them read from the *Vision of Isaiah*,[75] the ethical claim to superiority thus rapidly followed up by intro-duction to the special revelation of one of Catharism's apocryphal books. Pierre de Luzenac, on first meeting with Pierre before he left for Lombardy,

---

[70]   *GA*, pp. 370–4, 378–82, 384–90.
[71]   *JF* III, pp. 122–5, *JFD*, pp. 924–6.
[72]   *GA*, p. 118.
[73]   Ibid., p. 164.
[74]   Ibid., p. 180.
[75]   Ibid., p. 325; see also p. 110.

was asked whether he knew what was good and evil and whether he knew how souls were saved. When he replied 'in doing good works and obeying God', Autier rejected the answer, claiming that no one could be saved except those commonly called heretics.[76]

Ethics, exposure to persecution and exclusiveness of salvation were bound up together. Always we have an impression of the confidence of the perfect and their unswerving hostility to the Catholic Church. They were steeled by hard, regular fasting. Their total diet was not unvaried or lacking in delicacies but these were interludes in the rigorous routine of the three days of bread and water per week. Fasting demands determination: the novitiate must have weeded out the less committed. The routine, the fasts, the separate cleansing and cooking, the saying of the paternosters, the celibacy, coupled with the secrecy and wandering of these last occitanian perfect created hard men, whose aura gave an extra edge to their words. Even the lesser members of the team carried the aura of the perfect. Bernard Clergue, the bayle of the village of Montaillou was married in the church by the *curé* but the day was fixed because the perfect Guillaume Autier thought it the most propitious.[77] The perfect Philippe d'Alayrac, consulted by Pierre Maury about the personal problem of his sister maltreated by her carpenter husband, firmly ordered him to get her away from him and absolved Pierre on the spot 'on behalf of God' for any sin he might incur in so doing.[78] The Good Man, conscious of his rectitude and the power of the *consolamentum*, had taken over the authority – and more – of the Catholic priesthood.

Pierre Autier was the powerful personality whose impact runs through all the reminiscences: his jocular greeting to his nephew who came late and missed a solemn consoling,[79] his urbane opening words to Sibille Peyre,[80] his patiently graduated approach to Pierre de Luzenac, his insistence that there must not be even an accidental touching of the skin of a perfect woman,[81] his clear understanding of the essential restriction of consoling to the adult,[82] his successful encouragement of the *endura*, his determination to continue a hard life of hiding and nocturnal movement across several departments of modern France despite being in his fifties or sixties and having suffered an illness, and the utter conviction which led him to tell a nephew who pleaded with him to give up his ministry, that he would not abandon it even if all his friends were burnt before his eyes, show his stature. A supporter remembered how in April 1310, in his last moments before he was burnt, he defied his judges and told the crowd that if he were free to preach he would convert them all.[83]

---

[76]   Ibid., pp. 368–70.
[77]   Griffe, *Inquisition*, p. 230.
[78]   *JF* III, pp. 151–2, *JFD*, p. 945.
[79]   *GA*, p. 100.
[80]   *JF* II, pp. 405–6, *JFD*, p. 568.
[81]   *GA*, p. 286.
[82]   *JF* III, p. 144, *JFD*, p. 940.
[83]   *L*, p. 220. Autier had humour (*BF*, p. 586) but also chilling rigour. Of leadership

Rationalism was a second major weapon.[84] In his second sermon to the Peyre family, Pierre Autier used the ancient *mot* about Christ's body needing to be as big as a mountain to feed the priests.[85] Defendants most commonly denied transubstantiation and said that the host was only dough.[86] Guillelme Garsen remembered the host being compared to the '*oublies*', unconsecrated bread presented by children on the occasion of their New Year resolutions.[87] Jacques Autier, instructing Pierre Maury as they journeyed together, asked him in a *reductio ad absurdum* how the host could be the body of God when men handled it and it passed through the processes of digestion and so ended up in the latrine.[88] Géraud de Rodes remembered Cathar preaching in which it was pointed out that if a consecrated host was left where there were mice, they would eat it and so would be eating the body of Christ. Popular scepticism had an intellectual parallel among students of the natural sciences at Toulouse, almost all of whom doubted transubstantiation, in the witness of one defendant.[89] Jacques Autier said there was nothing worthwhile in the mass but the gospel and the paternoster; chants and the rest were a deceit of the priest.[90] The mass came under especially heavy fire because of its central role in Catholic devotional life. Catharism had no substitute for it, although the blessing of bread had a liturgical significance. The object of the Cathar leadership was to de-mystify it and destroy its hold.

Other sacraments underwent similar attack. Confession was ridiculed on the grounds that priests betrayed the secrets of the confessional.[91] Infant baptism was dismissed on grounds in which scepticism, hostile anecdote and dualism all played a part: it was the water of the mire of corruption in contrast to the water of the spirit, the word of God;[92] it was valueless because infants could not make decisions, in contrast to the decision of the Cathar adult to be consoled.[93] Either Pierre or Jacques – Arnaud Piquier could not remember which – related how a child died of cold through the baptismal water.[94] Marriage was inevitably condemned on dualist grounds: sexual

---

there is no question: see his use of *endura*. It is he who praises it (*GA*, p. 226), presides over end of Huguette de Larnat (*JF* II, p. 426, *JFD*, p. 584), consoles Guillaume Sabatier of Limoux who dies in *endura* (*GA*, p. 306), is in charge when consoled woman put in *endura* (*L*, p. 143), is closely followed by Pierre Sans, who imposed *endura* (*L*, p. 126). Arguments for diminishing his responsibility (*JDH*, p. 326) or arguing for misunderstanding of his aim (*JDR*, p. 169) have no adequate base.

[84]   M. D. Lambert, 'Catharisme et le bon sens populaire', *Persécution, Collection Heresis* VI, pp. 193–214.

[85]   *JF* II, pp. 410–11, *JFD*, p. 572; alleged Saracen derision, *JF* III, p. 60, *JFD*, p. 1075.

[86]   *GA*, pp. 118, 228, 250, 263, 312, 364.

[87]   Ibid., p. 188.

[88]   *JF* III, p. 133, *JFD*, p. 932; compare *JF* III, p. 233, *JFD*, pp. 1008–9.

[89]   *GA*, p. 104 (mice), p. 358 (natural sciences).

[90]   *JF* III, p. 133, *JFD*, p. 932.

[91]   *JF* III, p. 229.

[92]   *GA*, p. 336.

[93]   Ibid., p. 312.

[94]   Ibid., p. 172.

intercourse was a sin *per se* and worse when performed in marriage than otherwise because it was done more frequently without shame; true marriage was between soul and spirit in paradise or between the soul and God.[95] Catholic images were idols.[96]

The object of the leadership was to break down the structure of custom and ritual which retained Catholicism's place in daily life, and to replace it by a set of Cathar observances. The perfect and their hearers were all familiar with the Catholic pattern of life, crossing oneself at mealtimes, on getting up or going to bed or on entry to a church, genuflecting at the elevation of the host, having infants baptized. Outward observance of some of these rites might be necessary as a blind in Catharism's underground existence, but the leaders wished to destroy their emotional hold. So when Pierre de Luzenac crossed himself at a meal with Pierre Autier, he was criticized for doing so.[97] Autier also derided the practice of crossing oneself with invocation to the Trinity on entering a church and made his hearers laugh when he said it was suitable for brushing flies away in summer; if they made the sign, they could say, 'Here is the forehead and here is the beard and here is one ear and here is the other.'[98]

In this process of destruction, the leaders made use of scepticism rather than their own underlying doctrines. Cathar Docetism was incompatible with the doctrine of the mass, and bread and wine were in any case part of the evil creation of Satan, but in practice the mass was denigrated on grounds of a generalized rationalism. The *canard* about Christ's body and the mountain, though not exclusively Cathar, appears early in its history.[99] Béatrice de Planissoles, who certainly used the phrase about the host, claimed that she first heard it used by a stonemason watching people going to church for the elevation of the host at Celles in the Ariège when she was a young girl. There was a general scepticism too among the peasants on the utility of prayers for the harvest, which Cathars found a useful springboard into their own teaching that soil and crop alike were part of the evil creation and not subject to the good God.[100]

If the initial stage of conversion called for sceptical attitudes towards Catholicism, it was not expected that these would be carried over to Catharism itself. Pierre Maury was warned by Pierre Autier against asking questions of other perfect, aware of the lower standards of some of his team. If they answered questions incorrectly, he said, they could be subjected to a penitential fast of three days.[101] But Maury was an inveterate questioner; when Jacques Autier was instructing him as they journeyed and came to the

[95] *JF* II, p. 411, *JFD*, p. 572.
[96] *GA*, pp. 250, 338; *JF* II, p. 410, *JFD*, p. 572; contrast of Churches, *GA*, p. 166.
[97] Ibid., p. 372.
[98] *JF* II, p. 422, *JFD*, p. 581; compare Bernard Clergue, *JF* II, p. 284, *JFD*, p. 501.
[99] G. Macy, 'Berengar's legacy as heresiarch', *Auctoritas und Ratio: Studien zu Berengar von Tours*, ed. P. Ganz, R. B. C. Huygens and F. Niewöhner (Wiesbaden, 1990), pp. 47–67; *PL* CXCV, col. 92.
[100] *JF* I, p. 218, *JFD*, p. 263 (Béatrice); *GA*, pp. 60–1 (harvest).
[101] *JF* III, p. 126, *JFD*, p. 927.

passage where the Father puts his foot over the hole through which the angels were falling out of heaven and addresses those below, Pierre could not resist asking how the Father's voice could be heard below when he had stopped up the hole: Jacques replied that the Father is heard as well by his little children in the world as by those who are beside him when he speaks.[102] Pierre Maury was, however, the exception: most hearers sat mutely by.

Sceptical sayings emerge more frequently in sources late in Cathar history, not only and probably not mainly, because they were part of the commonplaces of society in the mountain lands of the Sabartès, the centre-point of Autier's movement, but because the inquisitors from the late thirteenth century onwards began to investigate much more closely the beliefs, as opposed to the actions, of their suspects.[103] The new interest in beliefs, coupled with Fournier's own curiosity, throws into relief the existence of a current of spontaneous disbelief side by side with Cathar allegiance. Sometimes, it may be, aware that they would be sentenced to imprisonment anyway, defendants took the opportunity to display insolence towards the Church.[104] Rationalism acted as an escalator carrying recruits away from Catholicism: it was a forerunner to the exposition of dualism.

Doctrines

The Autiers and their followers drew their beliefs in the first instance from the traditions of Albigensian radical dualism.[105] Pierre was sufficiently equipped to expound the Cathar interpretation of the *nihil* in the first verses of St John's gospel to his brother-in-law before he left for Lombardy,[106] but no doubt the most profound instruction came from the Albigensian exiles in Italy. He and his team were individualists and Pierre did not impose a uniformity of belief on the perfect in the mission field, not even on his own son Jacques, and alongside a core of Albigensian radical dualism, the perfect reveal in their teaching twists of doctrine peculiar to themselves.[107]

Pierre was a radical dualist who accepted the existence of two principles, good and evil. To Sibille Peyre and her husband[108] he expounded the story of the Fall, brought about by Satan, who, after standing at the gate of heaven for a thousand years, finally gained entrance through a trick and seduced the angels who had been created by God, and consisted of soul, heavenly body and spirit.[109] He lured them out of heaven with promises of possessions, gold, silver and wives, till they fell like rain upon the earth over

---

[102]   *JF* III, p. 131, *JFD*, p. 930.
[103]   Duvernoy, *CF* XX, pp. 43–7; inquisitors, Hanssler, *Katharismus*, pp. 138–48.
[104]   Perhaps related to the quarrel of the men of the Sabartès with Fournier over levying of *carnalagia* (*CF* XX, pp. 46–7).
[105]   *GRK* IV (2), pp. 15, 156–8, 185–6, 197, 211–12, 226, 247–8, 365–9, 406–12.
[106]   *JF* II, pp. 213–14, *JFD*, p. 603.
[107]   I am indebted to Professor Rottenwöhrer: see *GRK* IV (2), pp. 159–369, *passim*.
[108]   *JF* II, pp. 406–8, *JFD*, pp. 569–70; *GRK* IV (2), pp. 161–2.
[109]   Ibid., p. 165.

nine days and nights, to be shut up in bodies ('tunics') by Satan. Pierre distinguished two types of angel according to the degree of their guilt, drawing a line between those who took the lead in accepting Satan's seductions and those who passively followed.[110] Noticing the desertion of heaven, God put his foot on the hole through which so many had left, threatened those who remained with the consequences of leaving and told those who had gone that they could go 'for the moment and for now' ('*per ia*');[111] by which Pierre understood that all the fallen angels would one day be able to return to heaven. Fallen to earth, they sorrowfully replied to Satan's demand that they should sing the songs of the Lord with words of psalm 136, 'How can we sing the Lord's song in an alien land?' Satan pushed the angels into the bodies he had created so that they could forget what they had lost. Then he could not make the bodies move and had to call on the Father to do it for him.

Angels were brought to salvation by transmigration through as many as seven or nine bodies[112] till they came to be in that of a Cathar, who, accepting the *consolamentum* and keeping it valid, finally returned to heaven. Pierre equated the higher clergy of the Catholic Church with the guilty leaders of the angels who in punishment for their higher level of guilt would have to suffer more in transmigration but in the end would be saved. A bodily resurrection was naturally excluded since bodies were the work of Satan. The Old Testament history of God's people, wandering and suffering but despite their waywardness assured of God's protection, was transmuted into a history of the Cathar perfect, persecuted by Satan on earth but assured in the end of their places in heaven.

Christ was a pure spirit, not in reality or even appearance born of Mary, who was not a woman at all: she was simply the will to do good.[113] Christ therefore had no human attributes, for he did not eat, drink, suffer hunger, thirst or cold, neither did he die,[114] He went back to God and obtained from him the right to bestow on his apostles the power of binding and loosing: in effect, his task was to transmit to his apostles and so to the true Church of the Cathars the *consolamentum*, the rite which liberated from sin. Like other radical dualists, Pierre believed that the present world was hell and would become so in the full sense when all the fallen angels had returned to heaven.

Pierre evidently continued in the Albigensian radical-dualist tradition, but not slavishly; one meets variations, as in the episode where Satan has to call on God to give his bodies the power of motion, a doctrine which recalls the tradition of Concorezzo or even Bagnolo. He remained an individualist, most of all in his startling doctrine of Mary's non-existence. In his mind the

[110] Pierre follows an Albigensian radical-dualist view here, in contrast to Bagnolo, passed on to Guillaume and Jacques, who build individual variants (Rottenwöhrer, *GRK* IV (2), pp. 159–369, *passim*).
[111] *JF* II, p. 407, *JFD*, p. 569.
[112] *GRK* IV (2), p. 168.
[113] Ibid., pp. 166–7, comment, pp. 163, 186.
[114] Ibid., pp. 162–4.

dichotomy between body and spirit was intense: hence his rigid Docetism and his punctilio over the most innocent and fortuitous physical contact with a woman. Woman represented sexuality: to be saved, a woman's soul would become that of a man.

Though influenced by Pierre and his vocabulary – his phrase referring to the *consolamentum*, 'passing through the hands of the Cathars', was widely used[115] – the other perfect followed their own paths. Guillaume was more conventional.[116] He implicitly rejected Pierre's views on Mary, whom he interpreted as a real woman, though only spiritually the mother of Christ, about whom he thought as Pierre did. On metempsychosis he followed him too, only adding toads to the list of creatures in which reincarnation could take place. On the destiny of those who betrayed, persecuted or brought about the imprisonment of Cathars, he was harder than Pierre: they were condemned to lose their hope of salvation for ever.

In many things Jacques followed his father, but, though rejecting the Catholic doctrine of the Trinity, nevertheless thought that God was for a time divided into Father, Son and (probably) Holy Spirit.[117] It may be that, as one of the more scholarly Cathar teachers, he wanted to do justice to the New Testament texts which refer to Christ as God. He developed a doctrine of two Scriptures, one good, that of the Cathars and their God, the other of Satan and his followers, thus removing the last vestige of value from the enemy, the Catholic Church.[118] Like his father, he would not allow that women as such could enter heaven; on the return of a woman's soul to heaven it would be changed. It was with a vision of a woman that Satan had seduced the angels, so a woman would never be allowed into heaven.

Jacques was concerned about the conduct of some believers: he was too honest not to accept Pierre Maury's judgement that they committed evil acts in the expectation that whatever they did, all their sins would be remitted by reception of the *consolamentum*. He assured Pierre that the perfect did not encourage such a reaction: believers who sinned in this way might be brought to court and condemned, thereby putting themselves beyond the reach of the perfect and the possibility of being consoled.[119]

Guillaume Bélibaste has a special role as the last survivor, who, after his escape from prison at Carcassonne in 1309 and subsequent wanderings, led a group of Languedocian exiles in Catalonia.[120] Pierre Maury who was his friend and shared his exile, lamented the loss of the calibre of Pierre and Jacques Autier's preaching and example; Bélibaste kept a mistress and attempted to pass her off as his wife, in an odd echo of the white marriages of corrupt Catholic clergy,[121] though the followers were led to believe that

115   Ibid., p. 186.
116   Ibid., pp. 187–97.
117   Ibid., pp. 227–9; compare pp. 244–6.
118   Ibid., pp. 227, 247.
119   *JF* III, pp. 131–2, *JFD*, p. 931.
120   *JF* II, pp. 20–81, *JFD*, pp. 751–801; *GRK* IV (2), pp. 249–369.
121   *JF* II, p. 28, *JFD*, p. 757 (Maury's lament), *JF* III, pp. 188–92, *JFD*, pp. 973–6 (passing off mistress; see Duvernoy, *Heresis* XVIII, p. 50).

Raimonde was not in reality his wife, but only a servant whose presence in the house would deceive informers. At home in Morella, it was said that they slept in separate beds and if, when travelling, they had to sleep together, it was always in their clothes so that naked flesh never touched. But when Bélibaste, Raimonde and her sister Blanche were living together at Prades, Blanche one day unexpectedly entered their room and found them in a compromising position.[122] She lost faith in Bélibaste and he, to recover his status, had recourse to reconsoling. In personal morality, Bélibaste's leadership was a degeneration, yet his teaching was not unworthy of his predecessors.

Bélibaste's Satan was the greatest of demons and not a fallen angel; not God, but one who called himself God and was a reverse image of the good God, with his creation, his son Lucifer and seven kingdoms, just like God's, represented by seven kinds of demons scattered in earth, water and air, carrying out Satan's will, unable finally to prevent the ascent of saved spirits escorted towards heaven by angels, but capable of hindering the progress of spirits from body to body, as air demons scalded those moving from a dead body to a live one, so forcing them to move with indiscriminate speed[123] – so fast, he said, that it might pass from one body in Valencia to another in the county of Foix in heavy rain and be touched by but three drops of water. The bodies of animals formed part of the chain of transmigration, though since they could not speak, no soul or angel imprisoned there could reach salvation.[124] It was a penitential process for fallen angels, lasting till they reached the body of a man or woman who had 'the understanding of God' and could be saved.

Satan ruled the visible earthly world and was responsible for bad weather and hail. Unable to seduce Christ from his purpose of bringing the means of salvation to the imprisoned spirits, he made use of the Jews – described as belonging body and soul to Satan and destined for damnation – to bring about Christ's death.[125] Yet even demons, fallen Cathars and Catholics might be saved: all rested on the mercy of God. In a unique twist of Cathar doctrine, the Father was described by Bélibaste as having a spiritual body – probably a personal reflection on the words of Genesis: 'Let us make man in our own image, after our likeness' – a more positive view of the first man and a doctrinal position nearer to the Catholics than that of the majority of Cathars.[126] Although Bélibaste was second to none in the fierceness of his denunciation of Catholics and their representatives – he spoke for example of the four devils who ruled the world, the pope, the king of France, the bishop of Pamiers and the inquisitor of Carcassonne[127] – in some respects

---

[122] *JF* II, p. 31, *JFD*, pp. 759–60, *JF* III, p. 198, *JFD*, pp. 980–1.
[123] *GRK* IV (2), pp. 252–68, 288–96, air demons, p. 295 Valencia, *JF* II, p. 35, *JFD*, p. 762.
[124] *JF* II, pp. 34–5, *JFD*, pp. 762–3; *GRK* IV (2), p. 316.
[125] *GRK* IV (2) pp. 259, 267–8, 306–7, 343.
[126] Ibid., pp. 254–5, 327–8, 366; salvation, pp. 293, 340–3; Gen. 1: 26.
[127] *GRK* IV (2), pp. 260, 335–6.

he stood closer to Catholicism than one might expect. He accepted purgatory: he believed that the Cathars who had been saved would pray for their colleagues still imprisoned in bodies on earth, addressing their prayers to God and to Mary. He also used the concept of 'persons': there was one God, divided into three persons from the time of the mission of Christ to the end of the earthly world, where there would be a reversion to one person – not orthodox Trinitarian teaching, but nearer to Catholicism than the more common view that Christ was, and remained, an angel.[128]

Elsewhere in Bélibaste's teaching there was unequivocal heresy. His Christ was Docetist, one who neither ate nor drank nor was crucified: he had no human body and only appeared to die. He took an apparent body from Mary, herself sometimes interpreted as the Cathar Church and sometimes as an actual figure, albeit without a true human body. Bélibaste adhered to the Autier tradition of the Father failing to notice the fall of the angels from heaven and then belatedly putting his foot over the hole: in his exposition of the manner of Christ's coming to earth, he borrowed from earlier Languedocian tradition and depicted him as one of the angels who remained faithful to the Father. In anthropomorphic terms, Bélibaste describes the Father 'almost alone' surveying the empty seats in heaven, wondering how he might recall them from their forgetfulness and bring them back, then hitting on the idea of rewarding with the position of Son any angel who would leave heaven to go down to earth bearing a message of salvation to recall those imprisoned. Many were ready to volunteer but swooned after reading a little of the book, wherein for forty years the Father had written down all the afflictions, sicknesses, insults, hatreds and the like which can strike humanity: then one called John rose up to accept the task, but even he after reading four or five pages fainted and lay for three days and nights before being splashed with water, reviving and weeping. But he kept his promise and came to earth as Christ, seeming to be born of Mary.[129]

In the evening by the fire, after walking among the vines and drinking with his flock, Bélibaste seems for a moment to have forgotten his Docetism and interpreted the sufferings of Christ as if they were as real as those which he and his flock had endured. It was one of the last recorded, mythical, multicoloured sermons with which the perfect to the end retained their authority over their followers.[130]

In his audience was Arnaud Sicre, son of Sibille den Baille and brother of a perfect; in reality a spy, commissioned to capture Bélibaste. Not long afterwards, he contrived to lure Bélibaste into the town of Tirvia in the diocese of Urgel which, though over the Pyrenees, belonged to the count of Foix. There the agents of the count took him and transported him away for trial. In the search for his victim in Aragon, Sicre had picked up casual work in an atelier in San Mateo, Tarragona, where a colleague told him he had noticed a countrywoman of Sicre's, a carrier advertising her services in the street.

[128]   *JF* II, p. 38, *JFD*, p. 766 (purgatory), *GRK* IV (2), pp. 253–4, 256, 321, 350 (God, prayers).
[129]   *GRK* IV (2), pp. 270–85; *JF* II, pp. 45–6, *JFD*, pp. 770–1.
[130]   *JF* III, pp. 44–5, *JFD*, p. 770.

When Sicre got into conversation with her, she soon revealed that she 'spoke the language of Montaillou' and that she was of the faith. 'Have you the understanding of Good [*entendement de Be*]?' she asked. He pretended he was a Cathar and was eagerly welcomed by the little group of exiles.[131] Their resources were insufficient to support Bélibaste, who had to work to support himself, his mistress and her daughter at Morella, some distance from the nucleus at San Mateo. All lived in fear of betrayal; they devoted anxious time to debating whether and how they could be rid of the nagging, hostile daughter of a believer at Beceite who threatened to turn informer.[132] The exiles seem not to have won new recruits in their localities: yet they had lost nothing of their reverence for the role of the perfect, laid great weight on securing the *consolamentum* at death and consequently did not wish to live too far away from one of them. Bélibaste encouraged them with the report of a vision seen by a perfect, one of the most beautiful of all Cathar descriptions of heaven. Mounted on the shoulders of an angel, he was carried up to the seventh heaven, where he saw a sky of great clarity, many angels, fine orchards and singing birds, where there was joy without sadness, no hunger, thirst, cold or heat but a great mildness of temperature.[133]

Bélibaste had moved to meet the needs of a diminished Church. Unlike all other Cathars, he taught that the giving of the *melioramentum* was sufficient to ensure salvation; it was a demonstration that they who made the ritual gesture had the requisite, saving faith, even when it had not been possible for them to be consoled. In such cases, the *consolamentum* would be administered by an angel after death.[134]

He had an unformed but original mind, genially willing to draw material for his individual structure of belief from a wide range of sources, to invent and think for himself. Biblical texts were used with some abandon: there were folklore elements, like the explanation of the Adam's apple in men or the description of a man's spirit, a lizard-like object, coming and going from the mouth of a sleeping believer. Catholic legends were used in his sermons and he was most likely the author of a strange vernacular prayer revealed by Jean Maury to the inquisitor at Aragon, part prayer proper, part sermon, part fragment of a cathechism.[135] Homespun, lacking the eloquence of Pierre or Jacques Autier, Bélibaste was still to be reckoned with and, without the sly intervention of Arnaud Sicre, would have continued successfully to preside over his little flock in exile.

---

[131] Sicre's deposition, *JF* II, pp. 20–81, *JFD*, pp. 751–801; language of Montaillou, *JF* II, p. 22, *JFD*, p. 752; narrative, Vidal, *RQH* LXXIX, pp. 100–5.

[132] *JF* II, pp. 55–7, *JFD*, pp. 777–8.

[133] *JF* II, p. 51, *JFD*, p. 775.

[134] *GRK* IV (2), pp. 323–4.

[135] Adam's apple, *JF* II, p. 492, *JFD*, p. 888, comment, Duvernoy, ibid., p. 912n.; probable attribution, *GRK* IV (2), pp. 285–6; lizard, *JF* III, pp. 152–3, *JFD*, pp. 945–6; legends, *GRK* IV (2), p. 303; vernacular prayer, *JF* II, pp. 461–2, *JFD*, p. 860, *GRK* IV (2), pp. 250–1, *JDR*, pp. 188–9.

The destruction of the movement

The heyday of the Autier revival lay in the earliest years of the fourteenth century, as shown by the frequency of contacts between perfect and believers (figure 9) derived from the confessions of seventeen defendants who came before the tribunal of Geoffrey d'Ablis, chief inquisitor at Carcassonne 1308–9.[136] It gives a rough guide to the prospering and decline of the mission, rising after the return of the brothers from Italy late in1299, then dipping as the agents of the inquisitors begin to establish their hold, and the perfect under pressure find it harder to meet their followers. A Dominican from Chartres, a 'soul without feebleness', d'Ablis was appointed in 1303 and came capably to grips with the Autier movement. The register of 1308–9 is only one chance survival from a large number of such records, fruit of the labour of d'Ablis and other inquisitors. It is enough to enable us to surmise that d'Ablis more than anyone else brought the revival to an end. The register gives a glimpse of his technique, hearing and re-hearing, personally or through his lieutenants, giving the accused time for reflection or a guarantee against the penalties of perjury in case of lying the first time round, so as to ensure that suppressions and distortions were eliminated. d'Ablis and his men lacked the time and the exceptional talent of Bishop Fournier, yet they had method and organization – the heart of police work – and pushed the heresy back, leaving Fournier to winkle out remnants later.

Betrayal was the starting-point for decline.[137] A believer imprisoned in Carcassonne, who ran into debt paying the gaoler for his food, was angry at fellow believers who refused to help him meet his debts. In prison he stayed silent: in revenge on his release, he gave information which led to the sentencing of many and he set a trap for Jacques Autier, who knew nothing of his defection. He called him to console a woman on her sickbed in Limoux. Autier responded and was there arrested in September 1305, together with Prades Tavernier. d'Ablis decided to give special attention to the village of Verdun in the Ariège valley and summoned the inhabitants to Carcassonne for questioning. Pierre Autier and Amiel de Perles only narrowly contrived to keep one jump ahead of their pursuers.

The arrest of a perfect was always a blow because of the fear inspired in all followers that the perfect, bound never to lie if the *consolamentum* was to be kept valid, would tell all.[138] In reaction, a majority at Arques went off to seek absolution for heresy from the pope. Then Jacques and Prades somehow escaped, the scene lightened and Pierre Autier consoled another helper, Pierre Sans. Nevertheless, he felt it imprudent to return to the Sabartès till early 1307.

The arrival at Toulouse of Bernard Gui in 1307, an inquisitor of the highest calibre, strengthened the forces of repression. He held his first

---

[136]   *GA*, table 11.
[137]   Best narrative in *JDH*, pp. 328–33; betrayal, *JF* II, pp. 57–8, *JFD*, p. 779.
[138]   Duvernoy's hypothesis, *CF* xx, p. 50, *JDR*, pp. 223–4; support in *JF* III, p. 145, *JFD*, p. 941.

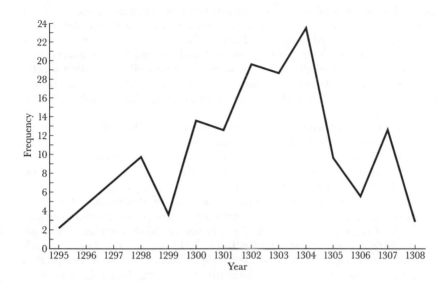

Figure 9   Heretical activity in the register of Geoffrey d'Ablis, showing incidence of meetings with the perfect from confessions in the register
Source: A. Pales-Gobilliard (ed.), *L'Inquisiteur Geoffrey d'Ablis et les Cathares du comté de Foix (1308–1309)* (Paris, 1984), pp. 76–7

sermo generalis in March 1308. Gaston I, count of Foix, for political reasons had to make his peace with the papacy in 1308 and promise to defend the Church and orthodoxy.[139] This gave d'Ablis more freedom of manoeuvre. In the spring or early summer of 1309, henchmen of the inquisition searched homes in Montaillou, Guillaume Autier and Prades Tavernier escaping in the nick of time disguised as woodcutters.[140] In August, Gui issued a proclamation for the capture of Pierre Autier, Pierre Sans and Sans Mercadier. In the same month, Montaillou underwent the same treatment as Verdun had, when all the inhabitants over fourteen years of age were arrested in a sweep led by the gaoler of Carcassonne and Arnaud Sicre, notary, estranged husband of Sibille den Baille and father of the spy. Interrogations and imprisonments followed.

The perfect were taken one by one. Pierre, Jacques and Guillaume Autier, Amiel and Prades Tavernier were captured at various dates during 1309 and

[139]   *JDH*, p. 329.
[140]   Revised dating, Benad, *Domus*, pp. 154–64, tables of events, pp. 324–44; Duvernoy, *Mediaevistik* III, pp. 416–19 accepts revised date for search of Montaillou, but not all points. See Benad for bibliography (excellent), economic background, chronology; care is needed on Pierre Clergue and 'ideology'.

burnt. Pierre survived a year in captivity, probably because of the need felt by inquisitors to carry out long interrogations, and was burnt, defiant, in April 1310 in the presence of d'Ablis, Gui and a great concourse of notables.[141] The leadership was decimated and the years of expansion over. Very few perfect were left; Sans Mercadier killed himself in despair after the capture of Pierre Autier; Philippe d'Alayrac and Bélibaste broke prison after capture in 1309, but d'Alayrac was retaken and burnt; only Bélibaste survived in exile.

d'Ablis's investigations missed some cases. At Montaillou, the *curé* himself, Pierre Clergue, deeply stained by Catharism, escaped detection. Wholly unaware, d'Ablis even occupied the *curé*'s room when he came to investigate in person, his French-born notary working with him. Pierre knew too much about his parishioners for them to dare to betray him.

Other rank and file not caught in the nets of d'Ablis and Gui were rounded up under Fournier. In accord with the cooperative procedure laid down by Clement V to check the abuses of inquisitors in *Multorum querela*, Bishop Fournier, who took office in 1318, worked hand in hand with the inquisitor of Carcassonne, Jean de Beaune, and was assigned a Dominican Jean de Pomiès as assistant, but it was Fournier who gave the lead and stamped his personality on his remarkable inquisitions, painstakingly recorded in volumes taken with him when he left Pamiers. Eventually conflict arose with the tribunal at Carcassonne, which was not settled till 1329 after Fournier had left. But by then Catharism was effectively killed off.

Fournier's methods were shaped by his experience interrogating the Waldensian deacon Raimond de Sainte Foy;[142] his Cathar quarry only fully emerged into his view after he began to interrogate Béatrice de Planissoles, widow of the former lord of Montaillou, guilty of certain superstitious practices, but much more informed about Catharism. From her he learned the truth about Pierre Clergue and brought him and a series of others before his court. He made no use of torture: remands to prison to refresh memory were effective enough, coupled with skilled use of information derived from other defendants.[143] He preferred to interrogate with a reserve of concealed knowledge. Arnaud Sicre was backed by Fournier with finance and absolution from penalties normally incurred by contacts with heretics to bring down Bélibaste. Sicre wanted to regain the inheritance of his mother, confiscated when she was burnt. Lured out of his security, Bélibaste was burnt at Villerouge-Terménès on territory of the archbishop of Narbonne.

---

[141] I retain Duvernoy's dating, *JDH*, p. 330; compare Benad, *Domus*, p. 21, *GRK* IV (2), p. 157, n. 3.

[142] *JF* I, pp. 40–122, *JFD*, pp. 55, 122.

[143] Béatrice, *JF* I, pp. 214–15 (witnesses), pp. 216–50 (deposition); on torture, I prefer Benad, *Domus*, pp. 9–14 to Duvernoy, *JFD*, p. 289, n. 59 and do not believe she was made ill by torture. Paul stresses Fournier's severity and failure to understand gulf between him and defendants (*CF* XXVI, pp. 42, 52–3, 63–5); Duvernoy is more sympathetic.

Pierre Autier and his colleagues had given a remarkable amount of work to inquisitors. Vidal's classic survey lists a hundred and twenty-five localities where adherents were found, some ninety-five of which subsequently came under the scrutiny of the inquisition.[144] Six hundred and fifty defendants were dealt with by the tribunals of d'Ablis at Carcassonne, Gui at Toulouse and Fournier at Pamiers over the period 1308–9, when the last sentences were carried out on Cathars in Languedoc. Another three to four hundred believers or sympathizers were mentioned in depositions, making a total of at least a thousand persons who were influenced by the heresy.

Records are, notoriously, defective. Much of d'Ablis's work has not come down to us; a second volume of Fournier's register in which Verdun played a major part has disappeared; Gui's work is represented by the book of sentences of his tribunal at Toulouse without the record of the preceding interrogations. Vidal's figures from these records must therefore represent an underestimate.

The Sabartès, the mountainous region south and west of Foix and including Ax, the Autier home town, was the heartland. Out of his hundred and twenty-five localities, Vidal listed forty-eight in the modern French *département* of Ariège, the greatest number of which lay in the Sabartès together with the Pays d'Alion immediately to the west. Three modern cantons, Ax, Les Cabannes, Tarascon supply thirty-three of Vidal's localities, lying mainly along the high valley of the river Ariège between the towns of Ax and Tarascon. It was poor, remote country, a place of refuge abutting the Pyrenees, with a long tradition of Catharism. The existence of sympathizers here, who had lain low under orthodox pressure and were revitalized by the Autier group, helps to explain the success of the revival in the early fourteenth century.

Pamiers was a new diocese created in 1295 by Boniface VIII to improve oversight of the faithful and protect them against the inroads of heresy; but the bishops who held office before Fournier were too distracted to direct the diocese on the lines Boniface desired. The counts of Foix had a family tradition powerfully sympathetic to the Cathars. The Countess Philippa had been a perfect and had presided over a house of perfect women from 1204; her daughter Esclarmonde was consoled in 1206. The comital house was hard pressed by the inquisition, but a tradition of support survived. Roger Bernard III had made use of the services of Pierre Autier as notary and Pierre claimed to Sibille Peyre that he consoled him in the castle of Tarascon during his last illness in 1302, with the complicity of his officer Guillaume Bayard, a genial fixer who boasted of his sexual prowess, not a practising Cathar but a man who praised the perfect and made merry with his friends over a priest who said in a sermon that Christ ate and drank but was careful not to swallow.[145] A long and bitter dispute over the imposition

---

[144] *RQH* LXXIX, pp. 84–92.

[145] *JF* II, p. 427, *JFD*, p. 585 (consoling); *JF* III, p. 61, *JFD*, p. 1076, *JDH*, p. 327 (Roger Bernard and perfect); Duvernoy, *CF* XX, p. 35 (comital officers); J. Duvernoy, 'Le droit de cugutia et le paréage d'Andorre', *Heresis* XVIII (1992), pp. 45–53; 'La noblesse du comté de Foix au début du XIVe siècle', *Actes du Congrès* (as above, n. 45) XVI (Auch, 1961), pp. 1–44. I owe offprints to Dr Duvernoy.

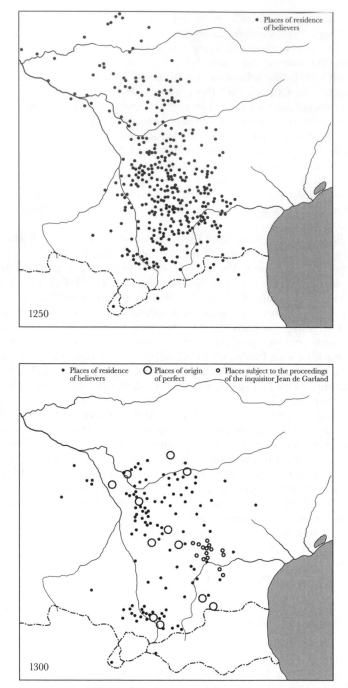

Map 8   The decline of Catharism in Languedoc
Source: adapted from J. Duvernoy, 'Le Catharisme en Languedoc au début du
XIVe siècle', *CF* xx, pp. 29, 30

of *carnalagia* in the diocese of Pamiers, seen as a means of extending tithing to animal husbandry, embroiled the bishop and clergy with the laity, nobility and peasantry alike.[146] They were all circumstances from which the perfect could profit. The Autiers made earnest efforts to capture for their cause men of education and substance, and were not entirely unsuccessful, but the majority of converts sprang from families of small resources, shepherds, peasants, artisans.[147]

Although the Sabartès provided the largest body of believers and sympathizers, the Autier mission reached out to the west into the Razès. Movement between winter and summer pastures linked the pays d'Alion with Arques, Coustaussa and Cubières, and the routes followed by the flocks were also followed by the perfect. Limoux was a strong point, at least until the inquisitional action of 1305.[148] At Toulouse, where Pierre Autier deposited money reserves and his son-in-law rented a house, there was a group of artisan supporters in its new suburbs and Jacques Autier defiantly preached on one occasion in a church and on another in a suburban garden there.[149] The revival reached as far as Bas-Quercy and into the Albigeois. To the south of Toulouse the records register localities in the Lauragais, familiar from the prosperous days of the heresy, where old attachments were brought into new life. Other traditional names recur: Castelsarrasin, Verfeil, Vielmur, the region of Lavaur, Lanta and Caraman. Pierre Autier undertook long journeys to keep in touch with supporters and make fresh contacts, exercising a certain prudent economy of information about supporters and localities, so that his guides and sympathizers were never *au fait* with the full extent of the mission field.

The perfect, similarly, were drawn from a wide range of localities. The largest number came from the Sabartès and the Pays d'Alion: the three Autiers, Tavernier, Amiel d'Auterive, Pons the son of Sibille den Baille, Arnaud Marty and presumably the two known as Peter and Paul. Two others, Philippe d'Alayrac and Raimond Fabre, the only two of the group to escape the fire by recanting, came from the village of Coustaussa between Ax and Carcassonne and close to Arques in the Haut-Razès south of Limoux; Aude Bourrel, the last active woman perfect, came from Limoux, was consoled in Italy and went to live in Toulouse. Bélibaste also came from the Razès: he had once killed a shepherd and so had to flee from his native village of Cubières on the border of the Fenouillèdes. This most dubious member of the whole group was probably consoled by d'Alayrac.

Others came from the northern end of the mission field. Pierre Sans, originally a believer active in assisting Pierre Autier and his instrument in attempts to win over Pierre de Luzenac when he was studying in Toulouse, came from Lagarde, near Verfeil; an indomitable missionary, he was preparing for the consoling of Pierre Fils, a young man from Tarabel in the

---

[146] Griffe, *Inquisition*, pp. 197–8.
[147] Compare Vidal, *RQH* LXXIX, pp. 89–92 and Duvernoy, *CF* XX, pp. 34–8.
[148] Geography, Duvernoy, *CF* XX, pp. 28–34; map, *BF*, p. 309.
[149] *CF* XX, p. 33.

Lantarès, when he disappears from history. Sans Mercadier, a weaver consoled by Pierre Autier in 1309, had his origin in Born in Haut-Garonne. Pierre-Raimond de Saint-Papoul, a perfect of earlier vintage who had fled to Lombardy in 1291, came from the village whence he derived his name near Castelnaudary between Toulouse and Carcassonne. Pons de Na Richa, companion to Pons den Baille, was from Avignonet. Bernard Audouy, the *ancien* of the remnants of the Cathar Church of Languedoc who possibly became a *filius*, the dignitary to whom Amiel de Perles was sent, came from Montégut in the Lauragais. He was resident in Italy, but there is evidence that he came to visit sometimes in Languedoc, for he is described as administering the *apparellamentum* to the dying Guillelme Marty of Prouade. There was thus a nucleus of perfect outside the Sabartès, some, of old and new vintage, linked to the former Cathar land of the Lauragais. Their numbers were growing when the inquisitors cut the movement down.[150]

Montaillou

Apart perhaps from Verdun where records have not survived, the village of Montaillou represents a summit of late Cathar achievement: here Catharism came nearer than anywhere else, omitting the special case of Montségur before the siege, to taking over an entire settlement.[151] The weaknesses of authority and Catholicism in the mountain lands were magnified to a remarkable degree in Montaillou because of the chance, firstly, that in the early fourteenth century there was no lord in residence to check the spread of heresy:[152] Bérenger de Roquefort died about 1299 leaving a susceptible widow, known to history under her maiden name, Béatrice de Planissoles, who moved from the castle at the edge of the village to a house below. Secondly, Pierre Clergue the village priest, who took office before 1300, was a Cathar believer who favoured the perfect and, while accepting their teaching, outwardly conformed to Catholic practice, conscientiously saying mass, hearing confessions, marrying, burying, saying the office and being careful not to rouse suspicion by neglecting his duty to attend synods. He was the favourite son of one of the most prosperous families in the village, who had been educated as a priest and returned there. In Montaillou there was little to stand in the way of this passionate and vengeful village Napoleon: there was no other priest, and friars did not come up to these heights. Catharism was endemic and the scattering of pro-Catholic families forming a weak counterweight, which Le Roy Ladurie believed he had detected, has been demonstrated by Matthias Benad to be virtually non-existent.[153] Certainly there were individuals hostile to Catharism and innocents who did not understand the true role of the Clergues, but not

---

[150]   Lists and discussion, Vidal, *RQH* LXXIX, pp. 73–83, Duvernoy, *CF* XX, pp. 31–4, *JDH*, pp. 322–7, Griffe, *Inquisition*, pp. 180–1, 286; Pierre Fils, *BF*, p. 344; Fabre, *JFD* II, p. 694, n. 3.
[151]   Discussed by Le Roy Ladurie in *LRLM, passim*.
[152]   *LRLM*, p. 513 and n.; Benad, *Domus*, p. 43, n. 124.
[153]   Benad, *Domus*, pp. 29, 35, 230–2 correcting *LRLM*, pp. 402–13.

cohesive Catholic families capable of providing conscious resistance to the pervasive ethos.

Both Pierre's parents were Cathar sympathizers: his mother Mengarde was probably the most important influence. She fed and concealed perfect on their visits and employed a bastard daughter of Prades Tavernier[154] as her servant, quietly favouring Cathars while maintaining outward Catholic observance. Like another strong-minded matron, Na Roqua,[155] Mengarde echoed at village level the role of the matriarchs in Languedoc society who had favoured Catharism in its springtime. Benets, Belots and Clergues were all leading families who leaned to the Cathars and exerted influence in their favour. Family members consoled at the deathbed were none the less buried by Pierre Clergue in consecrated ground.

Pierre's hold was reinforced when his brother Bernard became bayle, standing for the authority of the count of Foix; together they were representatives of both ecclesiastical and secular authority in Montaillou and could cooperate to prevent unwelcome external intervention. Bernard was as sympathetic to the Cathars as Pierre and handed on corn to the perfect. Pierre acted cautiously: when an innocent who had chanced on evidence of Cathar activity questioned him, he blandly denied its presence. He manipulated the role of parish priest as contact point for the inquisition, taking a bribe to allow a condemned Cathar sympathizer to abandon his crosses. Pierre's lechery was well known; he used threats to force his attentions on women at the baths in Ax: his pro-Cathar stance was much more discreet. His manipulations created rage in some quarters, the Maurs family going some way towards setting up an assassination before abandoning their plan.[156]

Pierre and his clan continued to prosper. Guillaume Autier, the principal contact between the Cathar leadership and the village, benefiting from a family connection with the Benets through his wife, boasted of the freedom which the perfect enjoyed in Montaillou and regretted that there were not more village clergy of the stamp of Pierre Clergue. This freedom rested in part on blackmail and force. Arnaud Lizier, who was hostile, was found dead at the gate of the castle; Mengarde Maurs had part of her tongue cut out and it was generally assumed that this was done at Pierre's instigation.[157] Pierre had ridden out d'Ablis's investigation and no doubt he believed he would continue to dominate. But for Fournier that might well have been the case.

The bishop was careful to examine cases of scepticism to ascertain whether they were the fruit of Cathar teaching: thus in 1318 he questioned Aude Fauré of Le Merviel about her disbelief in transubstantiation, found

[154]   Ibid., pp. 90–2, 127; *JF* I, pp. 229, 243, *JFD*, pp. 271, 280.

[155]   Benad, *Domus*, pp. 91, 92; Griffe, *Inquisition*, p. 230.

[156]   *JF* I, pp. 316–17, *JFD*, p. 312, *JF* II, p. 276, *JFD*, p. 495 (corn); *JF* I, p. 324, *JFD*, p. 319 (denial); *LRLM*, p. 224 (lechery at Ax); *LRLM*, p. 102 (crosses); Benad, *Domus*, pp. 177–80, 185–6, Griffe, *Inquisition*, pp. 246–8 (assassination).

[157]   Ibid., pp. 234–5 (Guillaume); *JF* II, p. 427, *JFD*, p. 585 (Lizier); Benad, *Domus*, p. 154, n. 100, *JFD*, p. 488, n. 4 (legal interpretation) (Maurs); *JF* III, p. 76, *JFD*, p. 1090 (part of tongue).

that she was a devout woman who had had nothing to do with Cathars and that her disbelief, personal and involuntary, sprang from one traumatic experience working on a highly sensitive personality; he imposed a medicinal penance.[158] In 1320 he took up a denunciation of Béatrice de Planissoles, widowed for a second time, for sceptical remarks about the mass uttered some ten years previously, and queried her about these, about contacts with the Autiers and a sorceress, Gaillarde Cuq. He already knew that Béatrice's father had been accused of heresy.[159] He began quietly, asking her for simple statements without the customary oath, which if false or incomplete would not attract penalties for perjury; then, finding the answers inadequate, set another hearing with the oath, whereupon she panicked and fled, only to be picked up with items in her possession that amply confirmed suspicion of sorcery, including the umbilical cords of her two grandsons, designed to bring her success in court, and underwear stained with blood from her daughter's first menstruation, destined to be squeezed out to make a philtre for her son-in-law to drink to bind him in love to her daughter for ever. Sorcery was left behind as Béatrice abandoned evasion and spoke freely of her Cathar past, above all of her eighteen month long affair with Pierre Clergue, from Lent 1300 to August 1301, in which he revealed his heresies to her. Fournier already had evidence against Pierre, but nothing as devastating.[160] Thereafter the Cathars of Montaillou were doomed.

Seduction had begun in church, where Béatrice knelt before Pierre to make her Lenten confession and he kissed her, saying there was no woman in the world he loved so much. Stunned, she left, but he pressed his suit, a masterful personality with a young widow whom he knew to have a sexual relationship with his bastard cousin.[161] He knew was he was doing. A herbal contraceptive insured against pregnancy,[162] while Cathar arguments in the mouth of a man with a priest's education overpowered Béatrice's Catholic beliefs. She told him she would rather sleep with four men than with a priest, since she had heard that a woman who had intercourse with a priest could not see the face of God: he replied with Cathar orthodoxy that the sin of carnal relations was the same whether committed with any man, even a husband. She said that marriage had been instituted by God between Adam and Eve as the first sacrament: he asked why, if God had created Adam and Eve and instituted marriage, he had not prevented them from sinning. She took this to mean that God had not created Adam and Eve and had not instituted marriage. Eventually she gave in. He went regularly to

---

[158]   *JF* I, pp. 82–105, *JFD*, pp. 31–48.

[159]   *JF* I, pp. 214–17, *JFD*, pp. 260–2, *JF* I, p. 246, *JFD*, p. 282; see *GA*, p. 96.

[160]   Deposition, above, n. 143; *LRLM*, pp. 229–41, 247–50, 253, 275, 309, 469, 484–5, 488, 512. Boyle, 'Montaillou revisited ...', pp. 125–6, 128–30, corrects *LRLM* on Barthélemy Amilhac. See also Griffe, *Inquisition*, pp. 236–8, 282–3, Benad, *Domus*, pp. 338–41 (chronology); change of testimony, *JF* I, p. 245, *JFD*, p. 281. Duvernoy, *Mediaevistik* III, p. 417 sees Béatrice's testimony as crucial. I agree.

[161]   *JF* I, pp. 238, 244, *JFD*, pp. 277, 281.

[162]   *JF* I, pp. 243–4, *JFD*, pp. 280–1.

her house and she to his, often making love on Saturday night before mass on Sunday.

For a time she accepted Catharism, even ardently. Pierre denigrated the Catholic clergy for their greed, told Béatrice that they heard confessions and imposed penances for the sake of revenues, and referred to Catholics who were not Cathar sympathizers as 'dogs and wolves'.[163] Only the perfect could save; the believers who came to them to be consoled did not need to confess their sin, the laying on of hands was sufficient. The perfect who were caught and burnt would not feel great pain, for God helped them not to suffer; they alone formed the true Church.

Much of the exposition of Catharism which unfolded during their love-making revolved round the sensitive issues of marriage and the sexes and the practice of confession. At the back of Pierre's mind lay the fear that Béatrice, who despite her aberrations had had a religious upbringing and sporadically practised her religion, would repent, go to confession else-where and so betray him. When she reproached him with saying mass on a Sunday after their love-making on the night before without going to confession, he stressed that the only worthwhile confession was that made to God, who knew the sin before it was committed and who alone could absolve, and that she should confess her sin of fornication to God. No man could absolve, he emphasized, and went on to deny even papal powers of absolution. St Peter had not been pope while he was alive; his bones were washed and put in the chair where the popes sat; they conferred no powers of absolution. On marriage, Pierre combined commonplace Cathar sentiments about sexual activity with flights of fancy about incest: in the beginning, sisters and brothers had intercourse legitimately; rules against it had been made by the Church only because of jealousy between brothers who competed for possession of their pretty sisters.[164] He spoke of the prosperity of the Clergues and the damage done to their *domus* by the necessity of paying out dowries for his two sisters; how much better, he said, if brothers married sisters and dowries were not lost to other houses – a reflection which revealed not only the common preoccupation with the economic vitality of the family and household, but also probable acts of incest by this obsessively carnal man.[165]

Pierre was a caricature of a Cathar believer. His respect for the perfect, his knowledge of their teaching, his high valuation of the *consolamentum* were genuine enough, but he was too great an egoist to put himself to any incon-venience to defend a Cathar. When in 1308 he boasted to Béatrice about using the inquisition to keep the men of Montaillou under his feet and she

---

[163] *JF* I, p. 231, *JFD*, p. 272.

[164] *JF* I, p. 225, *JFD*, p. 267; Peter's bones, *JF* I, p. 227, *JFD*, p. 269; parallel legend, confession, P. Guillermi Respaut of Avignonet, July 1245 hearing Arnaldus de Mirepoix, MS 609 fol. 130r (WLW).

[165] On Clergue's seductions as expressions of power in Montaillou, R. I. Moore in *Headstart History* I (1991), pp. 170–1; true and an implicit correction of Le Roy Ladurie's tendency to fairyland eroticism. But still I cannot underestimate Clergue's sheer sexual energy – note lechery in Ax, not so directly linked to power in Montaillou. I suspect youthful incest.

reproached him, he only said that he wished the Cathars well but would be revenged on the churls of Montaillou who hated him, in any way he could, and after that would settle his position with God.[166] This was for him a key point: he could allow himself anything he wished and then at the end be saved by the *consolamentum*. Relaxed in his passion, Pierre had given vent to his true Cathar beliefs to a woman who was not a committed believer, whom he could not intimidate; he remained uneasily aware of his vulnerability. He tried to keep his hold on Béatrice; when she moved to Prades and he was doing duty in the church there, he made up a bed for them in the building and made love to her, possibly as a means of desensitizing her to the emotional attractions of the Church as well as being an act of personal braggadocio. He continued his efforts even after she had decided to remarry and make her home below the mountains, first in Crampagna, then Dalou; twice he sent Bernard Belot to remind her of her Cathar past and warn her of the danger to her soul of being in territory where the perfect were not readily to be found; once he came himself and they made love in the cellar while her servant kept watch at the entrance; they met again for the last time in 1308, when he sat at her bedside in Varilhes where she lay seriously ill, afterwards sending her a gift of an engraved flagon with sugar.

Away from the Pays d'Alion, Béatrice's views changed: at Crampagna she heard the sermons of Dominicans and Franciscans and came into contact with devout Catholics. Her sister Gentille at Limoux influenced her and while staying with her, she made confession of her sins to a Franciscan friar, only omitting her contacts with heresy, as former Cathar sympathizers were wont to do out of fear of the consequences.

Brought back from her flight in 1320, Béatrice spoke unreservedly, pouring out information about every Cathar contact of her life, not because she was a woman accustomed to obedience and submission,[167] but because she had long abandoned Catharism, had failed to escape and saw a full deposition as the only way out. She talked on in a sequence of hearings through August, till on the 25th Fournier felt obliged to hold a special session because she had fallen ill, it was feared she might die and he wished to proof her confession, to make sure there had been no omissions or misattributions so that he could safely absolve her on the threshold of death.[168] She corrected a misattribution, answered questions on sorcery and was absolved. She recovered and ultimately served fifteen months in prison, followed by the wearing of crosses.

The Clergues promptly showed their calibre by seeking to undermine witnesses against them by threats and bribes, Pierre, now in prison, employing Bernard as tool for the purpose. As bayle, he was entrusted with the administration of land confiscated from heretics and he used his

---

[166]   *JF* I, p. 239, *JFD*, p. 277.
[167]   Benad, *Domus*, pp. 212–15. Fournier was just as capable in breaking men's resistance: see *JF* III, pp. 75–88, *JFD*, pp. 1089–1100.
[168]   *JF* I, pp. 245–50, *JFD*, pp. 281–5.

position to suggest to one witness that he could put a meadow into his hands provided he bent himself to the Clergues' interest and gave false evidence. Even in prison, Pierre offered a bribe to his companion in the cell, who happened to be Béatrice's lover Barthélemy Amilhac, to persuade her to withdraw her evidence against him. The brothers did not succeed. No deposition from Pierre survives: Bernard boasted that neither he nor Pierre gave anything away. But both were ruined. Pierre died in prison in 1321, extravagantly mourned by his emotionally dependent brother,[169] and Bernard was condemned to *murus strictus*, prison in fetters with bread and water, and soon died. Fournier was free to complete the destruction of a minor fortress of Catharism.

Montaillou shows the importance of a third force, pagan, folkloric, existing alongside Catharism and Catholicism and intertwining with both. Béatrice's actions in her desperate flight from Fournier's court reveal unmistakably what she valued, for in these straits she still encumbered herself with a strange collection of objects – the umbilical cords, the blood-stained underwear – admitted to be designed for magic, and other odd items which she convinced the bishop, perhaps a little easily, were not intended for magic and sortilege. And yet Béatrice was an instructed Catholic who after childbirth offered a coloured purification candle at St Marie de Carnasses, the pilgrim church of Montaillou, and was attending Lent confession when Pierre Clergue began his seduction.[170] Magic and Catholicism co-existed in her mind. At his father's death, Pierre Clergue cleared the house after the villagers had paid their respects to the body lying in state in the *foganha*, leaving two women ritually to cut off locks of hair and finger- and toe-nails lest good fortune should leave the Clergue *domus* when Pons's body was taken away for burial.[171] Pierre Clergue with his brutal opportunism combined folk-magic, Catholicism and Catharism.

Le Roy Ladurie's work has taught the historian to appreciate the vital role of house and family, *domus* or *hospitium* in the Latin, *ostal* in the vernacular, for the understanding of the lives of the peasants and shepherds of Montaillou.[172] Where the parish church and the pilgrim church of the Virgin formed the focus for Catholicism, the *ostal* was the focus for Catharism, as the perfect moved from one house to another instructing, consoling, receiving the *melioramentum*, talking of their faith and entertaining their audiences with their powerful narrations of the fall of angels, of Satan's mud bodies and the lake of fire awaiting an evil creation. The

[169]   Griffe, *Inquisition*, pp. 274–81; bribery attempt, Benad, *Domus*, p. 79. I cannot agree with Benad, pp. 210–12, who attributes human feelings to Pierre Clergue.

[170]   *JF* I, pp. 247–9, *JFD*, pp. 283–4 (magic); *JF* I, p. 223, *JFD*, p. 266 (candle); see Boyle, 'Montaillou revisited ...', p. 124 correcting *LRLM*, p. 237.

[171]   *JF* I, pp. 313–14, *JFD*, pp. 309–10, *JF* I, p. 328, *JFD*, p. 322; Benad, *Domus*, p. 150.

[172]   *LRLM*, pp. 51–87, 446–522 (magic); G. Sergi, G. Filoramo, G. G. Merlo and A. Petrucii, 'Note su storia totale fra ricerca e divulgazione', *Quaderni Storici* XL (1979), pp. 205–27; G. de Llobert, 'Variété des croyances populaires au Comté de Foix au début du XIVe siècle d'après les enquêtes de Jacques Fournier', *CF* XI, pp. 109–26; J. Paul, 'La religion populaire au moyen age (à propos d'ouvrages recents)', *RHEF* LXIII (1977), pp. 79–86.

ostal was the target of Catholic authority, armed with canon law provision for its destruction in cases of grave pollution by heresy. Burnings, imprisonments, house demolition, confiscation of land, could literally destroy an *ostal* as villagers well knew. Gauzia Clergue, great niece of Mengarde, discussing with Pierre Azéma her past complicity with heresy – of which, she claimed, she had repented – wondered aloud if she should go back to Fournier and confess more than she had already to the bishop 'who had received and heard her generously'. He told her she would thereby 'extinguish the fire in her house' and leave her sons to beg. He added he had planned to marry a daughter to one of her sons, which, he said, would raise the status of her *domus*, but would be inconceivable if heresy struck her house. In the event, Fournier caught up with Gauzia anyway and she went to prison, condemned because she had had her sick daughter consoled, a young married woman, victim of a long illness, when her godfather, Guillaume Benet, promised a better doctor than those who treated her in vain, namely a doctor of the soul, Prades Tavernier: Gauzia worried about the consequences but, wishing to do her best for her daughter, let in Prades. The sick woman willingly consented to be consoled, stretched out her arms in welcome, thereafter ate and drank no more and died.[173]

Gauzia and Béatrice illustrate how Cathar sympathizers could be made and lost. Gauzia like Béatrice returned to Catholicism, went to confession but omitted all reference to heresy, which she planned to confess only at death. Catharism was not a monolithic force in which converts, once made, were necessarily retained. The class of sympathizers waxed and waned for a variety of reasons in which friars' sermons, family tradition, the force of individual personalities, the salvation of a dying child, love, hatred, fear of inquisition and judgement all played a part. Defendants before a court naturally wished to ingratiate themselves and somehow mitigate the penalties they feared; it was in their interest to profess repentance and throw themselves on the mercy of the court. None the less, it is presumptuous to assume that all defendants who say they regret their Catharism are doing so out of self-interest. Conversion took place both ways.

Some remained genuinely uncertain. Pierre Maury, who lost his share in the family *ostal* because of his heresy, never wholly made up his mind. He remained part Catholic, part Cathar to the end. Others may perhaps have viewed the *consolamentum* as a bolt-on feature, a desirable extra for the dying, not necessarily involving any whole-scale future commitment to the Cathars for those admitting the perfect for the ceremony. In Montaillou, folklore practices, Catharism and Catholicism were all marked by the characteristic features of a propitiation religion: it might be wise to insure all ways.

The significance of the Autier revival

The Autier revival was a heroic but doomed guerilla action. It stood no realistic chance of success. The constellation of political power in Southern

---

[173]   Gauzia's confession, *JF* III, pp. 356–68, *JFD*, pp. 1119–29; quotations, *JF* III, p. 366, *JFD*, p. 1127.

France had long moved decisively against the Cathars. Autier and his followers were faced with anti-heretical procedures operated by men of high calibre, d'Ablis, Gui, Fournier. Gui's classic treatise on the procedures to be adopted for the detection and punishment of heretics, with its crisp questions and its detailed notes of the appropriate formulae to be adopted in all possible circumstances was shaped by his experience in office at Toulouse.[174] It shows his quality, a quality immediately deployed against the Autier group.

It is probable that at no time could the revival call on the services of more than sixteen perfect. Autier had to be content with what he had and quality was variable. Prades Tavernier opened the way to conflict with Sibille Peyre by consoling her year-old child; he was uncertain of himself and less esteemed by the rank and file who realized he was a simple man, lacking knowledge of Latin. There were tensions over money and resentment by Prades of the greatly superior wealth of the senior Autiers.[175] It may not be a coincidence that the betrayal of Jacques Autier was sparked off by a conflict over money between supporters, a sign, perhaps, that a weakness in the leadership was echoed amongst the membership. Sibille Peyre remembered her husband taking action to funnel contributions to Prades rather than the Autiers as he was disillusioned over their way of living and said he regretted having become a perfect 'so quickly'[176] before he knew more about their lives.

The revival was marked by conservatism. Autier and his followers worked along the lines of Albigensian radical dualism and traditional rituals were sustained. Belief and practice retained their ancient force: ordinary members were as fascinated by the perfect and respectful of their renunciations as ever they had been. But in the circumstances of persecution, a full novitiate for the perfect was no longer possible. Emphasis shifted from consoling in health to administering the *consolamentum* to the dying, and the use of the *endura*, well on its way to becoming an established custom as the movement was cut short, was the fruit of this development. And yet, in essentials, Autierian Catharism remained the old Catharism of Languedoc.

Autier respected earlier hierarchical arrangements, sent Amiel de Perles over the Alps to the *ancien* Bernard Audouy after he had committed a grave sin, and would not supervise the *apparellamentum* because he did not hold the rank of deacon.[177] Till Bélibaste, celibacy was maintained; indeed, restrictions on contact between men and women were heightened by Autier, a natural rigorist. Bélibaste breached celibacy, and in his manoeuvres over his mistress betrayed the friendship of the faithful Pierre Maury. Moral

---

[174]   A. Pales-Gobilliard, 'Bernard Gui, inquisiteur et auteur de la Practica', *CF* VI, pp. 253–64; J. Paul, 'La mentalité de l'inquisiteur chez Bernard Gui', *CF* VI, pp. 279–316.
[175]   Duvernoy, *CF* XX, p. 31 (nos); *JF* II, pp. 416–17, *JFD*, pp. 576–7 (Tavernier, Autier wealth).
[176]   *JF* II, p. 417.
[177]   *CF* XX, p. 38; *GF*, pp. 333–4.

decadence appears for the first time, and yet in his expositions, idiosyncratic, even creative as they were, Bélibaste was far from decadent.

Rottenwöhrer has shown that Catharism was marked from first to last by individual strands of belief, emanating from the perfect reflecting on their traditions and exercising a sovereign power of interpretation. There is, he has demonstrated, no classic Catharism from which Autier and his group deviated and no late decadence within the Autier revival. Duvernoy's full edition of Fournier's register has made a comprehensive analysis of doctrine possible for the first time and overthrown the interpretation of J. M. Vidal,[178] who relied on the extracts copied from the register by Ignaz von Döllinger, which were unconsciously slanted, giving too much weight to the revelations of one minor figure, Jean Maury, folkloric and debased, untypical of the leadership.[179] In Autier's time Catharism was still a living force: it had not decayed, as an older generation of historians once believed.

Autier's success had grave implications. It made apparent that the old faith in the right hands, working on ancient families and drawing in converts who were dissatisfied within orthodoxy, still had potency. That the heresy could make such progress in Montaillou, a remote village unaffected by reform under a priest who was in effect a Cathar double agent, is not surprising: what must command attention are the inroads the last perfect were able to make, not merely in the mountain lands at the southern extremity of France, where standards of Church life might be expected to be lower and there was a count sympathetic to them, but also in a swathe of localities outside the mountains stretching northwards as far as Toulouse and beyond. Even at this late stage, Catharism in the Midi was evidently not succumbing to inner weaknesses or Catholic competition.

Whether reforming Catholicism alone would have quenched the revival of Catharism must remain uncertain, though there were signs of some orthodox vitality. Aude Fauré's deep distress over her disbelief and her conversations with an older friend whom she called Auntie, who comforted her with a story of a eucharistic miracle from James de Voragine and taught her the beautiful occitanian prayer she customarily said at the elevation of the host, are evidence of a sincere orthodox piety.[180] The reactions of Pierre Maury and Béatrice de Planissoles show that friars could preach moving sermons. The case at Unac where the *curé* was brought before Fournier's court for preaching heresy is instructive. Expounding the *credo* at a low mass attended by fifty persons, probably early on Sunday morning, the *curé* fell into error on the fate of the body at the Last Judgement; this passed unremarked, but when he repeated his error at high mass, he was checked by his

[178] Vidal, 'Les derniers ministres …', *RQH* LXXIX (1906), pp. 57–107; 'Doctrines et morale des derniers ministres albigeois', *RQH* LXXXVI (1909), pp. 5–48.
[179] *Beiträge,* Duvernoy's corrections, *CF* XX, pp. 40–3; *JDH,* p. 326; summary and judgement on Vidal tradition, *GRK* IV (2), pp. 409–12; A. Brenon, 'Le Catharisme des montagnes: à la recherche d'un Catharisme populaire', *Heresis* XI (1988), pp. 53–74 (but metempsychosis appears earlier, see also Rottenwöhrer's comments, *GRK* IV (2), p. 409).
[180] *JF* II, pp. 82–105, *JFD,* 31–48.

assistant priest and a nobleman. At another high mass attended by a great multitude, he was detected spreading error on the soul. The inference is that, although one of the heresy-bearing localities in the Sabartès listed by Vidal, Unac had a well-attended church with a sensitivity to heresy, served by two priests. The judgement by Le Roy Ladurie that the *curé*'s congregation was 'lukewarm' is untenable. Annie Cazenave is nearer the truth when she refers to the Unac episode as evidence that a change of mentality was taking place.[181] How far that change would have affected the chances of Catharism regrowing we can never know. The perfect were not given the chance to evangelize for long. They and the movement they inspired were bludgeoned into oblivion.

[181] *JF* III, pp. 7–13, *JFD*, pp. 1033–8; *LRLM*, p. 485, criticized, Boyle, 'Mountaillou revisited ...', pp. 137–9; reflections, Cazenave, 'Les Cathares en Catalogne ...', p. 418.

11

The Decline of Italian Catharism

Politics and repression

The ripple of change which followed Charles's victories of Benevento and Tagliacozzo acted as a catalyst for movements of opinion hostile to Catharism which had been stirring before the 1260s; self-preservation also had a part to play, for there were dangers in resisting the development of Guelf alliances outside a city which were likely to be backed by exiles. Ghibellines fell out of favour and the Cathars lost their natural protectors.

Ghibellinism had in fact led the Italian Cathars into a blind alley. They were dependent on pro-imperialist factions and families for their security but could never establish an independent power base. Ghibellines used them as propagandists and allies in battles over clerical rights and lands, but were under no lasting obligation to them. Ghibellines battled for themselves or their cities, not for Catharism *per se* and, although in some instances complicity with heresy blossomed into more active support, in the main no strong bonds were forged. The heretics remained minorities and when the political fashion changed, they went down to defeat. Having no new initiatives, Catharism came to seem somewhat old-fashioned in the age of the great scholastics. It kept a passionate support among adepts and believers but was not finding it easy to win new recruits. What remained within the cities and could create sudden, fierce reactions against persecution, was a feeling of tolerance, a desire to escape confrontation and a suspicion of inquisitors – not wholly unjustified. The later thirteenth century was the age of victory for the Italian inquisitors, but also the age of their growing corruption.

Founded for religious purposes, confraternities now came to be used as political counterweights to the Ghibellines. In some cases, defence of the liberty of the Church had been one of the confraternity objectives and there was a logic about this, since temporal resources were necessary adjuncts to attempts to put down heresy; without them, the hands of churchmen were tied. At Parma, a Society of St Hilary, formed in 1263 and backed by Urban IV, was dedicated to the defence of the faith and the liberty of the Church and played a part in resisting the attempted take-over of Oberto Pallavicini. According to Parma's chronicler Salimbene, its successor the *Societas*

Cruxatorum, inscribed in letters of gold Charles of Anjou's name first in its register as its 'captain ... prince, duke, count, king and mighty victor'.[1] Although Salimbene got some details wrong, the attachment to Charles was a reality, for the *Societas* played a part in securing Parma for the Guelf interest and was asked by Charles to assist him against the surviving Ghibellines in Lombardy. Here there was an unequivocal political commitment which went well beyond that envisaged in the Society of Faith of St Peter Martyr at Milan.[2]

Oberto Pallavicini's empire began to crumble in the face of Angevin success; legates sent by Clement IV in 1266 attempted to negotiate a deal with him in the new political climate, but foundered on the issue of surrender of heretics to inquisitors. To secure cover for himself, Oberto's adviser Boso was prepared to be more obliging and used the issue to push Oberto aside, aided by pressure from pope and legates, eliminating Pallavicini power and with it another bastion of heresy; within two cities formerly controlled by Oberto, Piacenza and Cremona, the confraternity, the Consortium of Faith and Peace, took extensive authority. At Piacenza heretics were burned and Cathar refugees from the South of France sent back in chains; at Cremona the Consortium pledged itself not only to arrest heretics and fautors but also to keep Cremona faithful to the Roman Church and prevent disturbance to the peace of the city. In effect, they were guarantors of the Guelf settlement which had replaced Pallavicini power and had started putting down heresy.[3] In Bologna, the Militia of the Blessed Virgin Mary, founded in 1261 by a Bolognese noble together with others from Bologna, Parma, Reggio and Modena, took on a similar dual role of defending the faith and the liberty of the Church; the pope sent two of its knights to Florence to secure the city in the papal interest in the aftermath of Charles of Anjou's victory at Benevento.[4] Although such actions were a valuable aid in securing settlements acceptable to the papacy and so providing a platform for the prosecution of heresy, they inevitably exposed some confraternities to the charge of factionalism and tended to damage their spiritual calibre. In the decades which followed Charles's victories, the Cathars were driven away from their old security and progressively reduced to a twilight existence; but successful Church actions were not necessarily accompanied by any positive Catholic revival.

The repression of heresy at Vicenza carried on initially by Bartholomew of Breganza, one of the most noteworthy of all mendicant bishops, illustrates the point. There was a clear victory over heresy, but no major revival of Church life. The death of Ezzelino opened the way to the bishop's entry into his episcopal city, carrying with him precious relics, the gift of St Louis, a fragment of the Cross and a thorn from the Crown. These gave occasion to miracles and brought prestige to Vicenza: civic pride could again find a

[1] *Cronica,* ed. O. Holder-Egger, *MGH SS* XXXII, pp. 371–5; Housley, 'Politics ...', p. 202.
[2] Comment, Housley, 'Politics ...', p. 203.
[3] For this phase, Housley's exposition, ibid., pp. 201–6, *passim.*
[4] Guiraud, *Inquisition* II, pp. 550–1.

religious focus. Echoing St Dominic's tactics at Fanjeaux of seeking out a prime site of the enemy for counter-attack, a Dominican convent with church was erected in the inner-city district called Colle (the hill) which had been a focus for heresy and the place of residence of leading families of fautors. Bishop Bartholomew confronted the Cathars and confuted teaching which went back to Pietro Gallo, long bishop of Vicenza. The 'archipresul' of the whole March of Treviso was converted, Viviano Boglo bishop of Vicenza was either converted there and then or imprisoned, escaped and was subsequently burned by the Paduans; two deacons and eight other heretics were burned in Vicenza.[5]

It was the end of the age of prosperity for Catharism in the March; it descended like other Cathar Churches into clandestine existence. Statutes issued in 1264 contained a passage exalting procreation and the function of the city organizing civil life and making possible the perpetuation of the species as part of the cosmic order willed by God – a manifest hit at Catharism.[6] Inquisitors succeeded Bartholomew in the duty of repression and wrestled with adherents like Marco Gallo, a relative of Pietro and supporter of Ezzelino, who were married, had progeny and attended mass while maintaining an attachment to the Cathars. Marco deceived one inquisitor about his beliefs in 1269; Philip of Mantua, inquisitor in 1287, put the case before a commission, who adjudged that Marco's oath of innocence in 1269 had been a deception and rejected his heirs' submissions on his behalf. There were also problems about distinguishing between heresy proper and a yielding to the power of Ezzelino, which led Benedict XI in 1304 to order inquisitors not to molest fautors of Ezzelino's regime and their heirs. A scattering of cases emerged over the decades following Bishop Bartholomew's victory, including that of a rich man, Bartholomew di Sandrigo, convicted in 1292 of mocking the elevation of the host.[7] But it was only a scattering: the bishop had inflicted a major defeat on the Cathars. His disappointment was that his achievement was primarily negative and that, for all his zeal and talents, the legacy of Ezzelino's last years and the cramping effect of Padua's political dominance over Vicenza inhibited a true revivifying of the diocese.

In Verona it was not the bishop who played the key role. Ezzelino's death left the city, weakened by his dominance, ripe fruit to fall into the hands of the Della Scala; their political hue was Ghibelline, but in time it became convenient for them to work for an understanding with the papacy and this led inexorably in due course to action against heretics.

The pursuit of heresy in Orvieto is a case where one thorough enquiry leading to mass departures, destruction and confiscation appears to have smashed Catharism.[8] The inquisition of 1268–9 followed hard on the heels

---

[5]   Lomastro Tognato, *L'Eresia*, pp. 23–49; Bartholomew battled, not with the living Pietro Gallo, but with his theories, Cracco, *Vicenza*, p. 406, n. 276. On Gallo's fate, *WEH*, p. 187, Borst, *Katharer*, p. 238, Lomastro Tognato, *L'Eresia*, p. 35.

[6]   Lomastro Tognato, *L'Eresia*, p. 32.

[7]   Ibid., pp. 45–6.

[8]   Henderson, *Piety*, the most thorough analysis of Catharism in Orvieto, combining financial and other evidence with the *Liber inquisitionis 1268–9*; analysis of personnel indispensable, pp. 57–150.

of Charles of Anjou's purging of Ghibellines in Florence and may well be associated with a faction victory for the Monaldeschi, early backers of Charles and the principal Guelf family of the city whose rise had been facilitated by gains from confiscations in the aftermath of the Parenzo killing.[9] It has the hallmarks of a thorough enquiry, mounted by two Franciscans, one of whom came from Orvieto, involving eighty-eight persons, of whom sixty-one were still living, and gives the impression that it chopped away the local roots of Catharism: certainly there is no evidence of further investigations. No perfect was caught, evidently because Orvieto lay on the circuit of wandering missionary perfect who had their base elsewhere, principally in local centres such as Viterbo, Spoleto, Narni or Florence, or such smaller places as Regno, Gradoli, 'Casalveri'.[10]

There was evidence that Catharism was on the wane, yet it was far from dead. Franciscans had had a settlement in Orvieto well before the foundation of the church of St Francis in 1240; the Dominicans' church and convent was founded in 1233–4; Pope Urban IV had resided from 1262–4; a miracle at close-by Bolsena had led to the institution of the feast of Corpus Christi in 1264; a confraternity with St Peter Martyr as patron was in existence in 1258. In other words, there was a substantial and active Catholic presence, yet in the years preceding the inquisition, Cathars evidently led a normal life, serving on councils, acting as witnesses to private and public deeds, some holding high office as rector, then captain of the *popolo*, consul or town chamberlain. Amideo Lupicini, whose body was exhumed by order of the inquisitors, was rector of the commune in 1266 and took part in negotiations with Clement IV to make peace between Orvieto and Siena: it is difficult to believe that his heretical sympathies were unknown to contemporaries.[11]

Clearly, part of the city's elite was involved in heresy; some were of Ghibelline allegiance, others not. Traditional Ghibelline families such as Tosti, Ricci, Miscinelli and Lupicini had a complicity, but the leading Ghibelline family, the Filippeschi, enemies of the Monaldeschi, was not convicted and there were no sentences passed on the della Terza, della Greca and della Tasca families. The highest ranking of all those convicted, Domino Rainerio, a nobleman of great wealth, so far from having any known Ghibelline links, was related to the Monaldeschi. Politics had not been crucial and the inquisition cannot be crudely stigmatized as an act of force by a Guelf commune against the Ghibellines.[12]

All levels of society had been touched. Borst's generalizations about the fall in social class as Catharism neared its end should not, on the Orvietan evidence at any rate, be applied too early in the century. Wealth was well represented. There were certainly three, perhaps eight, money-lenders and the three operated on a substantial scale.[13] Some wealthy heretics suffered

[9] D. Waley, *Medieval Orvieto* (Cambridge, 1952), p. xxv.
[10] Henderson, *Piety*, p. 156.
[11] Ibid., p. 70.
[12] Ibid., p. 74.
[13] Ibid., pp. 96–102.

demolition of houses: Bivenio Blasii had several houses and a fortified tower armed to resist the inquisitor.[14] Symeon Lanarolo was a big woollen manufacturer, deeply implicated; he taught an adherent how to adore a perfect, allowed the *consolamentum* to be administered in his house and once rescued the body of an executed perfect and gave it burial. He had been a believer for ten years, his mother had been consoled, whether in the expectation of death or so that she could carry out a perfect's duties is not clear. His house was destroyed after his conviction.[15] Jacobus Arnuldi, whose body was exhumed, had received both men and women perfect in his palace, to both of whom he had given the *reverentia*, the Orvietan term for the *melioramentum.*[16]

Heresy also penetrated lower into Orvietan society: a cohesive group was uncovered by the inquisitors – a skinner and his wife, son and daughter-in-law and family friend 'whose father had also had heretical leanings'.[17] A young trumpeter, clearly of no financial weight, received a light fine: he lived down his conviction and subsequently rose in civic employment.[18] Influence could cross barriers of class and wealth, as when the sick servant of Domina Verdenovella persuaded his mistress to fetch two 'patarenes'[19] to console her. How widely diffused heresy was in terms of rich and poor is amply demonstrated from the census conducted for tax purposes in 1292, which shows that the value of property owned by people linked to those convicted in 1268–9 ranged from sixteen thousand to fourteen lire. Involvement ranged from the nobleman Rainerio to a household servant and from a merchant's consul to a cobbler.[20]

In Orvieto, as well as carrying out their customary duties, including presiding at meals and blessing bread, the perfect in certain instances gave *munuscula* to their hearers, little gifts reminiscent of the pins and small household items which Waldensian preachers distributed.[21] Some forty to fifty *perfecti* were active over the years compared with only four or five *perfectae.*[22] A number of upper-class widows took the risk of sheltering them and allowing meetings to be held in their houses: perhaps the underground movement gave them a sense of purpose after the death of their husbands and offered comfort in grief which orthodoxy had not provided. A Cathar bishop Iannes Robba was repeatedly received by an Orvietan widow.[23] Analysis of families of suspects shows how, once heresy had entered, it was sustained through a variety of relationships; some parents allowed their children to earn pocket money guiding perfect who did not know the locality; sympathizers were prepared to take the risk of putting perfect up

14   Ibid., p. 107.
15   Ibid., pp. 79–80.
16   Ibid., p. 65.
17   Ibid., pp. 83–4.
18   Ibid., p. 189.
19   Ibid., pp. 91–2.
20   Ibid., p. 117.
21   Ibid., pp. 47, 111.
22   Ibid., p. 153.
23   Ibid., pp. 68–9, 153.

overnight or, more dangerous still, allowing a consoling to take place there; others, more wary, confined themselves to giving alms in money or kind or listening to them in other venues. This was the case for Rainerio, who did not receive the perfect at his home but went to see them, on one occasion asking for medical as well as spiritual counsel. Filippo Busse confessed under pressure that he had allowed four named men to stay 'by day and night' in his house on their visits for approximately twenty years.[24]

By contrast, connections of Neri, a believer wanted for questioning, were intensely nervous for their own safety although they lived in the *contado*; when his brother Masseo refused to allow an overnight stay, Neri broke in to force the issue. For years, the *contado* was safer for the movement than the city and larger assemblies were held there for safety reasons.[25]

Few of those convicted revealed much depth of doctrinal understanding. A majority appreciated the perfect, reverenced them, believed that they were good and holy and accepted their teaching that the Roman Church could not save and that the keys of salvation were in their hands.[26] Stradigotto of Siena, possibly a furrier, who was able to recite a detailed creed[27] and knew the theological implications of Catharism, was an exception. He was a committed member whose wife was consoled and who had twice abjured before being brought before inquisitors in 1268-9. A widow Bonadimane had been among the devotees of a local saint Ambrogio and in 1240 had vowed to bring a wax image to his shrine if a child, her nephew or grandson, was healed of mortal illness. The child recovered and she gave evidence in the canonization proceedings, yet was discovered in 1268 to have been a Cathar believer who had listened to preaching, taken part in rituals and received a *perfecta* into her home. Although by 1268 she was dead, her memory was damned, her will revoked and her property confiscated.[28] Still more striking was the case of Domenico di Pietro Rosse, a Franciscan tertiary who combined his duties in a Catholic confraternity controlled by friars with an active life as a Cathar believer. A blot by his entry in the record may reflect the emotions roused in the Franciscan inquisitors. But the penalties show they believed that he had come to understand the evils of Catharism and would not relapse, for they included the wearing of yellow crosses, going on pilgrimage, clothing the poor, confessing three times a year to a Franciscan and other procedures such as abstaining from cooked food in Lent, fasting every Friday and saying fifty paternosters and fifty Aves every day, which could never have been effectively supervised.[29] He may not have been the only tertiary so affected. He was not a double agent like Armanno Pungilupo or Pierre Clergue, but had evidently found pleasure in participating in both religions. Despite the instruction, agitation

---

[24] Ibid., pp. 49–50, 152 (pocket money), pp. 61–4 (Rainerio), p. 84 (Busse); family links, pp. 126–9.
[25] Ibid., pp. 163–4.
[26] Ibid., p. 52.
[27] Ibid., p. 50; see also pp. 37–8, 155–6, 161, 167–70.
[28] Ibid., p. 167.
[29] Ibid., pp. 92–4; D'Alatri, ' "Ordo paenitentium" ...', pp. 45–7.

and menaces about Catharism from the Catholic side, he and Bonadimane had evidently seen no danger to the soul in their pro-Cathar activities.

This gives a clue to what was occurring in Orvieto. The citizens by and large had been unwilling to sponsor any drastic action against the Cathar community, while the Cathars themselves, who were not apparently fighting battles either for their own preservation or in aggression against existing Catholic institutions, were unwilling to renounce the visits of the perfect and their rituals and preachings, which they valued. A horror of heresy seems not to have taken hold and the new vitality of Catholicism had not sufficed to push Catharism out of existence; inquisitorial action was needed for that.

The inquisition was carefully conducted. The sentences were finely grad-uated according to degrees of guilt in a way which argues for a close knowl-edge of the convicted. Cristoforo Tosti and his son, who had both fled, were sentenced early on in the proceedings; destruction of their properties 'without hope of rebuilding'[30] was intended as exemplary punishment, to strike heavily at the nexus of families, among whom the Tostis were promi-nent, who protected and favoured Catharism. Destruction, fining and confiscation to the benefit of Church and commune, which unusually received two-thirds rather than the customary one-third, was speedily and efficiently imposed. There were no executions and no heroic refusals to recant. Many had fled before the sentencing. Of the eighty-eight sentences pronounced, nineteen concerned the dead. The indications are that this inquisition was intended to root out Orvietan Catharism, and that it succeeded. When in 1295 a movement against the Church in Orvieto again arose, it took the form of a riot on Maundy Thursday in which men ran amok, jostling the churchgoers and taking holy water and altar bread from the churches to conduct depraved rituals.[31] Catharism proper was no longer in the forefront; heresy as a vehicle of dissent had been replaced by blasphemy and atheism.

Florence was a different case. Heresy was tenacious and, although Charles of Anjou, appointed peacemaker in Tuscany by the pope, carried out a massive purge of Ghibellines in 1267, installed Guelf bankers and nobles in power and rewarded the Guelf faction with Ghibelline lands, there was no speedy uprooting of heresy. As part of Innocent IV's reorganization, Franciscan inquisitors had replaced the Dominicans in 1254 and, unlike them, avoided being tainted by involvement with factions: nevertheless, there remained in the city an intense suspicion of external interference and Cathars had adapted to a more clandestine existence.

The case of Saraceno Paganelli, a believer who appeared before one of the most formidable of all Italian inquisitors, the Franciscan Salomone da Lucca in 1282, is instructive both for the continuing importance of politics for the prosecution of heresy and for its durability.[32] Paganelli had been

---

[30]   Henderson, *Piety*, p. 106.
[31]   Ibid., p. 190.
[32]   R. Manselli, 'Per la storia dell'eresia nella Firenze del tempo di Dante. Il processo contra Saraceno Paganelli', *BISIAM* XII (1950), pp. 123–38.

drawn to Catharism thirty years before this hearing by a rich believer from Orvieto, Pietro Bonamsegne,[33] had then been instructed by perfect in Florence and implicated in heresy ever since without being betrayed. He was a committed Ghibelline and, together with his son and nephew, suffered exile as a result of the Guelf reaction. In Pisa, still a Ghibelline city, he found both a personal refuge and an opportunity to continue to practise his faith; the presence of two resident perfect suggest the undisturbed existence of a nucleus of heretical supporters. Evidently the political allegiance of a city still counted: if Ghibelline, it was likely to offer comparative freedom, but it did not necessarily follow that, if Guelf, there would be a truly effective and sustained persecution, though the outlook was certainly harsher. He returned after the settlement made by Cardinal Latino in 1280, only to fall into the hands of Salomone.

At least nine perfect emerge from the evidence linked to Paganelli's case, which suggests a Cathar community of some weight well into the epoch of decline. His testimony shows Catharism in full vitality with perfect preaching, receiving the *reverentia*, consoling at the death bed while he himself provided an escort for the perfect from his house, worked on a recruit, reading in a 'book of the patarenes' and moved in a Cathar circle, largely Florentine but including a man from Lucca, a married pair described as Provençal[34] and a wide range of occupations. Catharism was not dead. On the other hand, the frequency of the entry '*ad fidem conversi*' (converted to the Catholic faith) bears witness to the pressure which a rigorous inquisitor could bring to bear on a supporter once he had a lead to follow.[35]

Languedocian refugees found themselves a living in Italy, but not a home; some, despite the dangers, returned. They had lost the communities in which Catharism had been accepted; their children tended to turn away from the old faith. Nevertheless, remnants of the old hierarchy remained in Italy. A chance glimpse of a safe refugee community in a delectable and isolated spot at Sirmione, once praised by Catullus, stretching out into Lake Garda, shows a group of Languedocian Cathars under their bishop Bernard Oliba, still carrying his title of bishop of Toulouse, with colleagues consoling, instructing, receiving the *reverentia*; a witness testified before the inquisition that on a visit he had seen Oliba and his brother and others from Languedoc living together in a hospice where he ate with them, received blessed bread and was taught their version of the paternoster with the reference to supersubstantial bread, the beginning of St John's gospel and the rite of the *servitium*.[36]

But this was simply a remnant and the visit dated from 1273, not long before an expedition destroyed all Cathar security at Sirmione. The

---

[33]   See Henderson, *Piety*, pp. 104, 214.
[34]   '*provincialis*' (*BISIAM* LXII, p. 136).
[35]   Manselli, *L'Eresia*, p. 318.
[36]   *JDH*, pp. 190–1, 308, using Doat 25; C. M. Cipolla, 'Nuove notizie sugli eretici Veronesi, 1273–1310', *Rendiconti della R. Accademia dei Lincei Classe di scienze morali* V (Rome, 1896), pp. 336–53 at p. 342.

Catharism imported from Languedoc dwindled down, pushed from one formerly secure site to another, able to carry out one final service by providing a springboard for Autier's revival at the end of the century, but otherwise sharing the fate of Italian Catharism.

The inquisitors working in Italy in the second half of the thirteenth century, their victory epoch, were working within an established framework which combined the pastoral and the punitive; the formal sermon, the exhortation warning of the perils of heresy and urging repentance was accompanied by the offer of much milder treatment for those who freely confessed their own complicity and gave information about others within the period of grace. Marginal adherents could be convinced of peril to their souls and so confess; calculating spirits could seize the opportunity to secure light penances, particularly if they believed in the determination of the inquisitor and the likelihood that he would penetrate the reticence of witnesses and extract damning evidence. The more the inquisitor was feared, as Salomone da Lucca was, the more likely was it that there would be voluntary confessions and leads to follow: and such confessions were likely to increase in number as hope of political protection dwindled and more perfect and adherents were rounded up. Where perfect voluntarily throw up the sponge and recant, there is the clearest of signs of failing morale.

Much still depended on personalities. How shaky the defence of orthodoxy might be, even as late as 1273, is shown by a case in Arezzo where the inquisitor had required a repentant Cathar to promise that when he came to die he would ask for a guardian to fend off perfect seeking to console him; at the point of death, Ridolfo did just that, inviting the bishop to make an appointment.[37]

Given the idiosyncratic nature of the cities and the jealousy of their independence, each had its own history of heresy, persecution and decline. Cathars in one city reached out to another and news passed from one group to another, so losses in morale and news of captures and confessions passed round. On the other side, suspicion of inquisitors, dislike of their exercising authority, reluctance of *podestàs* to round up suspects, their distaste for the business of exhumations and the disturbance caused within families and dependants by disinheritance worked against a smooth running of the machinery of persecution. As the century wore on, exhumations feature more largely: it was a sign of the success of inquisitions as the numbers of living suspects sank. But it was a potent source of opposition to their work. There were notorious frictions between the friars and the secular clergy and the mendicants' operation of inquisitions easily roused seculars and envenomed proceedings. Slipping into clandestinity, Cathars learnt how to hide themselves, find safe houses and disguise their activities. All these aspects can be detected in the strange case of Pungilupo of Ferrara.[38]

---

[37]   Guiraud, *Inquisition* II, pp. 523–4.

[38]   G. Zanella, *Itinerari ereticali: Patari e Catari tra Rimini e Verona* (Rome, 1986) review, A. Patschovsky, *DA* XLIII (1987) p. 289; M. D'Alatri, 'L'Eresia nella cronica di Salimbene', *Eretici* I, pp. 65–74 at pp. 70–3. I have not accepted Zanella's attempt, *Itinerari*, p. 44, to revise traditional chronology.

Armanno Pungilupo

For some twenty odd years, Armanno Pungilupo of Ferrara led a double life, as a committed Cathar, first believer, then perfect, while simultaneously making himself conspicuous as a devout Catholic. From 1244 he had a regular confessor; in 1247 he went on a local pilgrimage and confessed his sins on St Lucian's day, 13 December; in 1268, the last year of his life, he confessed more than twelve times to the bishop's chaplain in Lent and made his last confession on St Lucian's day before expiring three days later. A priest came to his house with communion for his sick wife.[39] His death was mourned in Ferrara and beyond; he was buried in the cathedral and a series of miracles were reported by visitors to his tomb. Yet it emerged that he had for years past enjoyed an active role in the Cathar church, as a believer visiting other believers, providing food and alms for poor Cathars and suspects in prison, bringing bread blessed by the perfect to sick Church members, discussing doctrine and being on friendly terms with a Cathar bishop.[40] He travelled to visit Cathars: a young man remembered being taken with him, observing how he gave the *melioramentum* to a perfect and then being instructed how to give it himself. He did it, he said, but did not know what he was doing.[41] In 1266 on a visit to Verona Armanno was consoled in the presence of several witnesses; his wife was also consoled on another occasion. He passes through the statements of subsequent witnesses as a kindly figure, a prison visitor and a safe man for Cathars to trust; two Cathars going to be burnt left him their shoes. He went repeatedly to Cathar preaching and his conversation was larded with denunciations of the 'rapacious wolves', the mendicants and inquisitors. The distinguished perfect who consoled him in Verona were uneasy about his willingness to go to Catholic confession and obtained his promise to give it up.

He kept quiet about his status. A sympathizer was present when, at the request of two perfect women, he and his companion administered the *consolamentum* to their maid Maria, who exclaimed with surprise at the ceremony that she had always thought he was only a believer.[42] Something of his views leaked out in Ferrara; the official of the inquisitor one day challenged him on casual meeting, having heard that he had spoken heresy about the eucharist. Armanno fobbed him off. An officer of a Catholic fraternity learnt that he knew houses of 'patarenes' and the secret signs whereby they could be recognized; Armanno declined to reveal them.[43] He had a past. In 1254 he had appeared before inquisitors accused of heresy, including a denial of transubstantiation which he passed off as a joke, confessed after torture, took an oath to follow the mandates of the Roman Church and even accepted that he would pay a substantial fine if he

---

[39] Zanella, *Itinerari*, pp. 88–9.

[40] Ibid., p. 52.

[41] Ibid., p. 63.

[42] Ibid., pp. 57–8; consoling, pp. 52, 57; shoes, p. 63, wolves, pp. 54, 65 (see also p. 25).

[43] Ibid., p. 62.

offended in future. In fact he continued his Cathar activities side by side with assiduous attendance at confession.[44]

The cathedral clergy believed in his sanctity, alleging the miracles and the evidence from his confessors, but inquisitors knew that he was a Cathar; and the dossier built up from a whole series of witnesses, revealing that Cathar believers had gone to his tomb to pay their respects and that the miraculous healing of a mute had been faked by a Cathar, exposing the authorities to derision. After a long, bruising contest, Armanno's bones were dug up in the night in 1301, burnt and thrown into the river.[45]

The conflict helps to explain why the struggle against Catharism in Italy lasted so long. An unwillingness to disturb neighbours and acquaintances, suspicion of inquisitorial power was enough to keep Cathars like Armanno in being provided they mounted no obvious challenge. Gabriele Zanella has challenged the common view that Armanno was a Cathar passing himself off as a Catholic, and argued that he was a man of wide sympathies, genuinely unwilling to choose between the Churches, given to charitable practices and opposed to the hostile judgement of Catholics on the Cathars. In fact, there was a streak of exhibitionism: it is significant that at one stage he asked to confess to the bishop, not just to his chaplain. One witness said he went to church rarely;[46] challenged on his orthodox practices, he told another frankly that he engaged in these to put authority off the scent. He enjoyed his double role and had something of a confidence trickster about him.

Two fragments of evidence suggest that he had had early contacts with the Waldensians: perhaps he was a dissident, with roving interests. That he settled in Catharism and that his heart lay with them seems plain enough from the evidence on his rationalism on the mass, denouncing the belief of the priests that, as he put it, 'God could be contained in a pyx',[47] engaging in hostile demonstrations about the eucharist at Easter and his repeatedly expressed belief that salvation could not be obtained from the Roman Church, but exclusively from the perfect.[48] The evidence that he regularly gave the *melioramentum* to the perfect is unequivocal. He was a much better and more interesting man than the other well-known crypto-Cathar, Pierre Clergue of Montaillou, who used his role for spiteful and lecherous ends, but Cathar he certainly was.

The end of Italian Catharism

A sharp twist to the downward spiral of the Cathar was given by the expedition to Sirmione in 1276, which put paid for ever to the tranquillity of the peninsula whither the leadership of the Church of Bagnolo had migrated for security from Mantua and which harboured not only the

[44]   Ibid., pp. 55, 67.
[45]   Ibid., p. 29; mute, p. 70.
[46]   Ibid., p. 50; confession to bishop, p. 21.
[47]   Ibid., p. 56; see also p. 55.
[48]   Ibid., pp. 50, 55.

refugee bishop of Toulouse, but a bishop of Northern France and one described as 'of Lombardy'. It was set in train by Timidio Spongati of Verona who had tried in vain to extradite a Cathar from Lasize near Sirmione in 1273 and so sent a spy, Constance of Bergamo, to explore the situation in Sirmione. She went so far as to have herself consoled in order to reach the secrets of the community, where she learned the truth about Armanno Pungilupo.[49]

The expedition had a devastating effect. Sirmione could not stand against the della Scala and delivered up its Cathars. About one hundred and seventy were captured straight away, others escaped only to be rounded up later; in February 1278 some two hundred were burned in a holocaust in the arena at Verona. The victims have been described as perfect, who notoriously were least willing to save their lives by recantation. Because of this loss of enthusiasts and the damage to morale, it was a blow parallel to the disaster at Montségur.[50]

The decline of Catharism is clearly illustrated in the last substantial record which has reached us of an inquisition against a Cathar community, held in Bologna.[51] The city had been Guelf since 1274. It had long been a seat of inquisitors and its university one of the greatest of all training centres for canonists, though it had never been a Cathar centre *per se*, but rather a mission ground for wandering perfect, yet there had been a Cathar presence over decades.[52] The evidence of Guido da Vicenza's pertinacious inquisition which began at the end of the century shows that by then Catharism had begun to wane of its own accord. The acts of the inquisition of Bologna 1291–1310 uncovered believers, generally of a low cultural grade, one hundred and three males and thirty-seven females, a very small proportion of a population of forty to fifty thousand.[53] Bologna was a large *studium*, but Catharism seems not to have touched it, for there are hardly any students in the register. Questioning often enough elicited information about long careers in Catharism but did not give evidence of new recruits.[54] A majority were, technically, relapsed,[55] for they had had a previous conviction and their Catharism was an inheritance from the past, not a recent conversion.

Tenacious questioning, probably with torture, produced a rich harvest of names: so Onebene di Volte Mantovava, one of the numerous Cathar

[49] Cipolla, 'Nuove notizie ...', p. 338.
[50] *JDH*, pp. 190–1; Guiraud, *Inquisition* II, pp. 572–3; Borst, *Katharer*, p. 136.
[51] L. Paolini, *L'Eresia a Bologna fra XIII e XIV secolo*. I: *L'Eresia catara alla fine del duecento* (Rome, 1975) (definitive); E. Dupré-Theseider, 'L'Eresia a Bologna nei tempi di Dante', *Studi storica in onore di G. Volpe* (Florence, 1958), I, pp. 363–444; *Mondo*, pp. 261–315 (pioneer work, valuable general reflections); L. Paolini, 'Domus e zona degli eretici. L'esempio di Bologna nel XIII secolo', *RSCI* LXXXV (1981), pp. 371–87 (pinpoints geographical distribution; note scepticism on Modena mills, p. 377).
[52] Paolini discusses reasons for a Cathar presence, *L'Eresia*, pp. 167–72.
[53] Ibid., pp. 85, 160–1; Cathar portion 1291–1300.
[54] Ibid., p. 84.
[55] Dupré-Theseider, 'L'Eresia ...', in *Mondo*, p. 276 (citations hereafter from this version).

strangers who settled in Bologna, named sixty-nine persons, perfect, believers and fautors, the fruit of contacts inside and outside Bologna over decades.[56] Catharism within Bologna rested on the support of groups of families, who provided support and audience for the itinerant perfect. If sufficient of these families and the commercial and industrial contacts they maintained were winkled out and their contacts destroyed, the basis of the heresy was gone.

The core of the movement lay in the *popolo*, families neither proletariat nor aristocratic but well-to-do, with shops and houses, participants on a minor scale in commercial and industrial life, producers and retailers, tanners, grocers, purse-makers, furriers, leather-sellers and textile producers, with some *negotiatores*, including usurers.[57] Bompietro,[58] a man who had inherited his faith from his parents at Ferrara, a fixer with a long Cathar connection, who gave hospitality to the perfect, found food and money and arranged meetings with believers and had been convicted of heresy in 1276 but neglected to fulfil the penance of wearing crosses and going on pilgrimage to Rome, and was consequently burned as a relapsed heretic under pathetic circumstances, was characteristic in his miscellaneous enterprises, supplying wine to the Carmelites of San Martino, making purses and putting resources into other investments.

These families consisted of practical, down-to-earth people whose occupations and outlook gave an ethical cast to their Catharism. What they valued most was the way of life of the perfect who, they believed, rightly described themselves as 'good men'. For them, Catharism was an outlet for a religious sentiment not satisfied by what they saw as a secularized Church. In their workshops, hostile talk about its corrupt customs and low standards of the clergy had led on easily to a devaluing of the sacraments and praise of committed Cathars for their contrastingly evangelical lifestyle. Family business and shops with regular customers were comparatively safe settings for subversive talk about churchmen, the so-called 'heresy of opinion', lacking a dogmatic base but a humus for true doctrinal heresy, Donatism often being the springboard to Catharism proper. Corrosive reasonings, hostile anecdote, a fragmentary rationalism acted to sensitize non-Cathars to the defects of Rome; the attraction lay not so much in the doctrines and myths of Catharism but in its out and out opposition to Rome.[59]

Something like a cult of saints had grown up among the Cathars, with stories of the virtues and miracles of the perfect. Onebene spoke of heretics who had been burnt at Mantua, how they performed miracles and lights had been seen over their bodies.[60] Not in essence different from popular

---

[56]   Ibid., p. 285 (Ognibene); see Paolini, *L'Eresia.*
[57]   Paolini, *L'Eresia*, p. 163; exposition on diffusion and social aspects generally, pp. 157–74, for socioeconomic and political factors, see also Dupré-Theseider, in *Mondo*, pp. 276–81, 309–11, Paolini, *L'Eresia*, pp. 87–8.
[58]   Dupré-Theseider, in *Mondo*, pp. 282–5.
[59]   Paolini, *L'Eresia*, p. 170 (the 'sensitizing' of neophytes). Dupré-Theseider, in *Mondo*, p. 275 (examples of *boni homines*, p. 275, n. 41).
[60]   Paolini, *L'Eresia*, p. 89, n. 32; Dupré-Theseider, in *Mondo*, p. 287; M. D'Alatri, 'Culto dei santi ed eretici in Italia nei secoli XII e XIII', *Eretici* I, pp. 23–43.

Catholicism, these stories showed the Cathars bending to the assumptions of the age. As the educational standards of supporters in Bologna were not high, there tended to be uncritical acceptance of the myths and a lack of dissension about doctrines of rival Cathar churches.[61] There was no hierarchy resident in Bologna to give firm shape to their belief; in consequence, the interrogations leave the impression of a confusion and superficiality of understanding of underlying beliefs. Even the best informed of all those convicted, Bonigrino da Verona, a man of substance who held office in Bologna as *ancianus populi* and was one of the *castaldiones* of the *arte della lana gentile,* fully capable of standing up to inquisitors and who, after abandoning attempts at evasion, expounded his faith, showed signs of eclecticism in his views. Though he had spent time at Lake Garda, the seat of the Albanensians and held their views on the soul and the crucial issue of the origins of the visible world, he was a moderate dualist, accepting the doctrine of the one principle.

A surprisingly high number of the convicted had been born outside Bologna, importing their heresy into the city as the chances of economic life caused them to move.[62] Often a defendant would speak of contacts in a more distant past. The threads were wearing thin: Bompietro recalled his mother's complaint that she no longer found good men who would maintain the faith and his sons did not follow him into heresy. Recruitment was lagging and there was a consequent loss of vitality.[63] Cathar defeats elsewhere may have had something to do with this: the mass burnings at Verona are likely to have reduced the numbers of perfect coming to Bologna: perhaps there were still consolings of believers who wished to exercise an apostolate but on grounds of security chose to do so outside Bologna and its *contado* where they would be less easily recognized. More fundamentally, it seems that in Bologna, as amongst the last remnants in Italy of the broken Churches of Languedoc, becoming a perfect had lost its attraction and that this more than anything else was taking the heart out of the Church. What remained as Guido and his fellows set to work was a core of families maintaining faithfully their inheritance of belief, served by a small number of idealists.

A significant number of defendants, perfect and believers, twenty-one in all, came from the district of the Capella of San Martino dell' Aposa, perhaps because it was an area of workshops involved in purse-making: certainly the workshops of Bompietro and Giuliano were located there. Cathars in the district of San Martino and a neighbouring parish provided support for the perfect and did something to offset the fragmentary character of Bolognese Catharism.[64] They aroused local feeling: people from this district were prominent in the tumult which blew up over the burning

---

[61]   Paolini, *L'Eresia,* pp. 96–100; for superficiality of knowledge among other Cathars, ibid., p. 85; L. Paolini, 'Bonigrino da Verona e sua moglie Rosafiore', in *Medievo Ereticale,* ed. O. Capitani (Bologna, 1977), pp. 213–27.
[62]   Paolini, *L'Eresia,* p. 173; Dupré-Theseider, in *Mondo,* p. 275; Paolini wonders (p. 141) whether Bologna at this period appeared more secure than Florence.
[63]   Paolini, *L'Eresia,* p. 114.
[64]   Paolini, 'Domus ...', pp. 308–1.

of Bompietro in May 1299. But it is significant that his fate aroused indignation, not so much because of any feeling for the heresy *per se*, but because of compassion for an honest man clearly muddled in his thinking, who had repented of his heresy and cried out to be given communion before his burning, only to be refused by the inquisitor.[65]

After the expulsion of the Lambertazzi and the end of Ghibelline leadership in Bologna in 1274, heretics had lacked support in the political classes. Only Bonigro had held political office; the bulk of the Cathars were relatively insignificant, influenced perhaps by the wish of the self-made and self-employed, restive at the Catholic Church's monopoly, to reach out for a religion of their own. The State was not eager to prosecute. *Podestàs* carried out their formal duties without zeal and did their best to avoid confiscations, which created odium.[66]

There was informal opposition to inquisitors. Giacomo Benintendi, rector of the church of S. Tommaso del Mercato, accepted the confession of Rosafiore, wife of Bonigrino da Verona, that she had not been guilty of heresy after a previous condemnation to wear crosses and did not think that the inquisitors were acting justly when they burned her and accordingly gave her remains an ecclesiastical burial: they forced him to dig up the body at his own expense and pay money as a caution.[67] There were scandals over money which lay at the back of accusations which labelled Dominicans 'rapacious wolves'.[68] The long heretical careers of certain Bolognese imply that neighbours and acquaintances had not been eager to betray Cathars and a degree of tolerance, or inertia, on the part of authority is implicit in the sequence of punishments recorded over years against certain names.

All the hindrances which worked against inquisitors and their evident unpopularity were none the less in the last resort ineffective in blunting or warding off persecutions and their effects, provided the leadership was determined. A formidable body of legislation, experience and custom had built up, material which reached its apogee in the great *Manual* compiled in 1320–5 for the use of the Dominican inquisitors of Lower Lombardy.[69] The Dominicans were wise enough to ride out the storm over the burnings of 1299, receiving self-inculpations but imposing no penances on those involved. Careful interrogations pulled facts out of defendants. A second interrogation with torture forced Giuliano to abandon his pretence that he had had nothing to do with Catharism after his conviction in 1279. Prison broke the resistance of Bompietro Bonigno, a stronger personality, who finally threw aside evasions and went to his death defiant.

Given the absence of significant political support in the commune or any widespread sympathy for the doctrines of the Cathars, as opposed to the

---

[65]   Paolini, *L'Eresia*, p. 72; tumult, pp. 63–79; Dupré-Theseider, in *Mondo*, pp. 287–92.

[66]   Dupré-Theseider, in *Mondo*, p. 307; Paolini, *L'Eresia*, p. 16.

[67]   Giacomo's motives, Paolini, *L'Eresia*, p. 41; case of Rosafiore, Paolini, 'Bonigrino da Verona ...', as n. 61 above.

[68]   Dupré-Theseider, in *Mondo*, pp. 273, n. 36, 289–92.

[69]   *Il de officio inquisitionis* ..., ed. L. Paolini (Bologna, 1976).

individual personalities suffering under persecution, Catharism in Bologna stood little chance. It was already in decline: inquisitors dealt fatal blows. Early in the fourteenth century they turned their attention to Dolcino and the Apostolics, based in the *contado*.[70]

A malign chance leaves the historian of Italian Catharism with detailed records of only two major inquisitions from the epoch of decline, at Orvieto and Bologna, both mission areas: a balance would have been provided by records of the mute, heroic two hundred who went to their deaths at Verona in 1278, for they are likely to have been, not sketchily instructed believers, but the hard core of perfect who had committed their lives to the Cathar case. From their lips we could have better judged how the movement had fared under the pressure of the Catholic counter-attack. The comparative poverty of inquisition evidence in Italy compared to Languedoc will always dog the historian. Nevertheless, despite this caveat, it does seem plain that the Bolognese inquisition marks a caesura. Decline is likely to show itself earlier and most plainly in the missionary areas rather than the head-quarters, and in Bologna the survivors were a remnant, using secrecy to preserve a marginal community, a small specialist grouping unlikely to make major fresh conquests. Force alone cannot explain decline. It certainly accelerated a downward trend, above all because of its effects on the numbers and confidence of the perfect, but it always interacted with changes in the Italian climate of opinion, often deep-rooted, working over a long period of time against the Cathar interest.

In Languedoc force mattered more. The Albigensian Crusade and its aftermath removed or ruined a ruling class and brought about a massive transfer of power, which in turn opened the way to sustained, effective persecution. The situation was never so clear cut in Northern and Central Italy. Bishoprics were frailer, less-effective entities, patterns of living more fluid, the populace more mobile and more susceptible to sudden unpredictable emotional movements such as the Alleluia or Flagellant processions of 1260. The Alleluia movement gave impetus to orthodoxy; the Joachimism which lay behind the 1260 processions provided a set of myths of great potency about the Last Times, which foretold a great struggle with evil followed by a state of bliss on earth, a foretaste of paradise; more positive in tone, these were an appealing substitute for the darker Cathar myths of the Fall and the works of Satan.[71]

The friars meant much more in both areas. They formed part of a pastoral revolution, raised standards of preaching and were, implicitly or explicitly, much concerned with heresy. The survival of fragments of evidence such as a marriage sermon of the Franciscan Servasanto da Faenza, long resident at Santa Croce in Florence, bears witness to what must have been a sustained volume of exhortation working against the Cathars.[72]

---

[70] Dupré-Theseider argues for continuity from old Catharism to new Dolcinianism, in *Mondo*, pp. 312–13; Paolini rejects this on geographical discontinuity.

[71] Lambert, *Medieval Heresy*, 2nd edn, pp. 145–6; Manselli, *L'Eresia*, p. 331; contrast between Languedoc and Italy, R. Manselli, 'La fin du Catharisme en Italie', *CF* XX, pp. 101–18.

[72] A. D'Avray, 'Some Franciscan ideas about the body', *AFH* LXXXIV (1991), pp. 343–63; I owe offprint to the author.

Servasanto, who could have expected a highly educated lay congregation including representatives of the business community at Santa Croce, was unusual in making use of scholastic techniques not normally used by preachers in order to reject Cathar teaching about marriage. So, for example, he says: 'Therefore if nature makes members which are apt and suitable for generation, and it is not making them as superfluous things, or to no purpose, therefore generation is intended by nature. But that which is nature is not a sin, if it is done in the manner for which it is intended. Therefore the act of generative [power] is not in itself a sin.'[73] Aristotle runs through Servasanto's thinking and conveniently, since the Aristotelian concept that the soul is in the form of the body, forms a good base for rejecting the Cathar denigration of the body as the work of Satan, decidedly more so than the Neoplatonic stress on the dichotomy between body and spirit more prevalent in the previous centuries. In another sermon defending the doctrine of the resurrection of the body, he explicitly cites Aristotle and regards the Aristotelian doctrine of the relation between body and soul as an agreed basis for his exposition. While few mendicant preachers could count on so sophisticated an audience, most speaking in favour of marriage in simpler ways, remembering matrimony as the first sacrament, instituted in the Garden of Eden, and recalling Christ's first miracle at the marriage feast in Cana, Servasanto's intellectual flight bears witness to a more general intellectual change which had taken place in the thirteenth century, as a generation of orthodox thinkers assimilated Aristotle. He was one major influence affecting trained clergy and also percolating through society in a movement away from the deep pessimism about the body characteristic of the early Middle Ages on to a more balanced, humane and positive view of the visible world and man's place in it. Over and above explicit denunciations of heresy and planned, logical demolitions of Cathar belief, which did not necessarily reach the Cathars themselves, this shift was important because it was so widespread, excited a largely unconscious sway over minds and was wholly alien to Catharism.

So also was the new piety, especially associated with St Francis of Assisi and his friars, stressing the humanity of Christ, dwelling on his passion and associated with veneration of Mary, which tended to shape the outlook and practices of the confraternities. Auricular confession, imposed by Innocent III in *Omnis utriusque sexus*, gave birth to a literature instructing clergy in their duties, developed moral theology and, at its best, drew priest and penitent together in a relationship based on counselling and sympathetic insight into the needs of the laity: here again, as in the confraternities, much more attention was being paid to the duties and needs of laypeople of all ranks. In face of a more flexible penitential system of this kind, which explored motive, occasion of sin, temptation, Cathar rigidities could easily seem out of date. The believers had no part to play; it was not envisaged that the perfect would fall – yet fall they did sometimes and had to be reconsoled in ceremonies which, though possibly kept private, damaged morale.

[73]   Ibid., p. 334.

For Cathar supporters there was stark contrast: between the believer still in the realm and power of Satan and with very limited duties and the perfect among the elect with their massive, sustained renunciations. Stark simplicity, an absence of fine distinctions, the high demands for the few, suited some and would continue to do so, but for others alternative paths to salvation had opened up.

The friars, not alone but certainly a spearhead force in this pastoral revolution, did not maintain their pristine zeal. The money scandals which came to dog inquisitors, Dominican and Franciscan, in the late thirteenth century, and required intervention and reproof from the papacy, were symptoms of a wider malaise as well as fruits of a system of jurisdiction which left near unfettered power in the hands of so few. Abuses and lacunae remained and ignorant, concubinary clergy; the pastoral revolution affected pre-eminently the upper levels of society. There remained too often what D'Alatri stigmatized as the formalism of much medieval Church life, irrelevant to the concerns of many, and a prime factor in the choice of the Cathar alternative.

Part of the impulse behind Cathar recruitment was reformist; the perfect believed they represented a stream of pure Christianity preserved from the days of Christ; they emphasized the New Testament, cut away all prayers save the paternoster, used a gospel book or the New Testament in their most solemn ceremony, cited Paul and the gospels in support of their teaching.[74] The search for authenticity, for a pastoral care, represented by the often heroic energy of the perfect in consoling the dying, and for a more living, personal faith were the factors which had kept up recruitment. A similar search for a personal religion aided the expansion of the confraternities as well as Cathar adherence; the like-minded entered both. The pathetic reflections of Spera, former maid to the Marquesa of Este awaiting execution about 1269, imply that it was a matter of chance that she had been consoled by Armanno Pungilupo rather than entering a Catholic confraternity.[75]

Catharism presented itself as a New Testament religion and recruits did not understand clearly the distinction between it and Catholicism. Instruction, exhortation and the penalties imposed by inquisitors began to change the situation; the perfect were inhibited in missionary work; dissatisfaction with the Church certainly did not disappear, but found other outlets; the perfect lost their hold. In Langedoc, so far as records go, Catharism came sharply to an end in the early fourteenth century, struck down by persecution; in Italy it dwindled down to its end. The last bishop to be recorded was arrested in Figline in 1321, while in Florence the last known Cathar was detected in 1342 and in the Alps syncretistic communities lingered on later still.[76]

---

[74] M. D. Lambert, 'Catharism as a reform movement', *Häresie und vorzeitige Reformation im Spätmittelalter*, ed. F. Šmahel (Munich, 1998), pp. 23–39.
[75] M. D'Alatri, ' "Eresie" perseguite dell' inquisizione in Italia nel corso del duecento', in *Eretici* I, pp. 9–22 at p. 14; general reflections, Volpe, *Movimenti*, p. 170.
[76] J. N. Stephens, 'Heresy in medieval and Renaissance Florence', *Past and Present*

Survival in the mountains

Italy long remained the land for fleeing Languedocian Cathars passing through the high valleys of Piedmont to the promised land of toleration. Cuneo in south-west Piedmont was a prominent staging post, for years unaffected by repression; but other routes, less well known, were also used and carried heretical travellers in both directions. Above all, the Valleys were a place of refuge for Waldensians who benefited from the inaccessibility of these sites and the determination of mountain people to maintain their independence.[77] It became a perilous region for inquisitors. Two were murdered, in 1365 and 1374 respectively, while one parish priest was killed in 1332 in Angrogna because he was believed to have been responsible for an inquisitor's intervention. Secular authority was reluctant to support the pursuit of heretics for fear of disturbing their workforce.[78]

Though well aware of the problem, the Dominicans of the province of Upper Lombardy nevertheless failed to coordinate a strategy with their fellow inquisitors on the French side of the Alps, where Waldensians had also found hiding places, and in the fourteenth century never mounted a major expedition using armed force comparable to that led by the Franciscan Borelli of Gap in 1375 against Waldensians in the Dauphiné, so the communities of the Valleys survived, damaged but not destroyed.[79]

An inquisition of Alberto di Castellario in Giaveno in 1335 uncovered Waldensian doctrines: at the core of the movement lay the conviction that Waldensians led an authentic apostolic life and that contemporary churchmen did not. Witnesses might refer to Waldensians and their masters as 'good men' as Cathars referred to the perfect, but the context makes plain that the allusion is purely Waldensian.[80] The enquiry of Tommaso di Casasco in the Val di Lanzo in 1373 caught whiffs of Catharism.[81] The inquisitor was plainly suspicious; he asked one suspect if he knew a Cathar prayer;[82] from a housewife he elicited the admission that she had been taught by an uncle the Cathar belief that to kill animals was a great sin and the standard Cathar greeting to a perfect, '*Benedicite, parcite nobis*'.[83] Though claiming to know nothing of the *consolamentum*, Fina da Lanceo admitted to having given *reverentia* to Pietro Garigli and other masters. On the mass she admitted to a rationalism characteristic of both Waldensians and Cathars.[84]

LIV (1972), pp. 25–60 at p. 30, n. 35, citing G. Biscaro, 'Inquisitori ed eretici', *SM*, ns II (1929), p. 363.
[77]   G. G. Merlo, *Eretici e inquisitori nella società piemontese del trecento* (Turin, 1977) (*ME*), analysis of trial records, fertile in hypotheses on geography and roots of heresies; for geography and social class, see esp. pp. 75–120.
[78]   *ME*, p. 132.
[79]   Ibid., p. 138; on inquisitors' methods generally, pp. 135–48; context, E. Cameron, *The Reform of the Heretics: the Waldenses of the Alps, 1480–1580* (Oxford, 1984).
[80]   Text of this inquisition, *ME*, pp. 161–255; beliefs, pp. 199–206, also p. 49, n. 81.
[81]   Text, *ME*, pp. 257–83.
[82]   Ibid., p. 275.
[83]   Ibid., p. 263.
[84]   Ibid., pp. 263–4.

With the confession of a tailor, Giacomo Borello of Viù, the inquisitor came closer to leaders of the heretical communities, with whom he had travelled to Rome in 1366.[85] He gave wary answers, shifting responsibility when he could. The masters Pietro Garigli and Martin de Presbitero had taught him that authority had left the pope and clergy because they did not keep the commandments of God, and he believed them; asked if he believed in purgatory, he replied that he had heard that it did not exist, but always believed in it himself; then changed his response and admitted he did reject it. He answered evasively when asked whether he had ever adored a heretic: he had not, he said, but he had embraced on his knees Pietro Garigli when he came back from a journey. Waldensian masters were being assimilated to Cathar perfect; a Waldensian substratum long settled in the Valleys was being invaded by Catharism.

An inquisition led by Antonio di Settimo di Savigliano in 1387–9[86] drove deeper into the heretical communities and laid by the heels two of the most important masters, Antonio di Galosna, once a Franciscan tertiary, and Giacomo Bech, one of the most remarkable of all medieval heretics. Mobility and eclecticism of belief were leading features of the strange, secret communities of the mountains, where the sun finally set on Italian Catharism. The Valleys became receptacles for a sediment of heretical belief nourished by heretical teachers working in intense secrecy, leading meetings by night, imposing oaths against betrayal, using a secret sign of recognition, pressing little fingers together.

Waldensians had long been forced to sacrifice open preaching and retreat into nicodemism, sustaining the existence of hidden groups of the faithful through the journeyings of a small elite of masters. The conditions of secrecy made it harder to sustain purity of doctrine and eccentric, folk-lore beliefs surfaced in interrogations as in the case of Giovanni Freyria of the Valle Germanasca, who, rejecting the Holy Spirit, adored the sun and moon while reciting the paternoster and the Ave.[87] Both Waldensians and Cathars came to see persecution as a special mark of the true Church;[88] both rejected oaths and the doctrine of purgatory; both were kept in being by a dedicated elite, celibate and in practice often itinerant,[89] revered by followers; both had come to share an out and out hostility to the Church, condemned as an *ecclesia malignantium*. Once, Waldensians had been the enemies of the Cathars, against whom they wished to preach; under persecution, old barriers tended to fall and the likenesses in communities with little depth of theology pushed them together.[90] None the less, it was a passing phenomenon: the Alpine Waldensians who emerged from obscurity

[85]   Ibid., pp. 276–7.
[86]   Text and comment, G. Amati, 'Processus contra Valdenses in Lombardia Superiori, anno 1387', *ASI* 3rd ser. I (1865), pp. 3–52, II (1865), pp. 3–61.
[87]   *ME*, pp. 31, 41; reasons for folkloric contamination, p. 60.
[88]   Ibid., p. 24.
[89]   Ibid., p. 104.
[90]   Ibid., pp. 25–6.

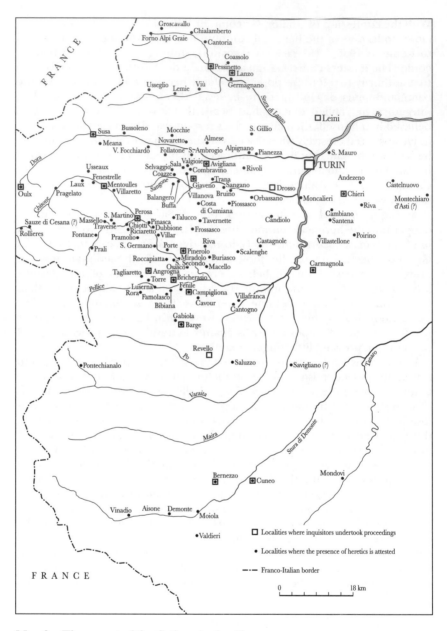

Map 9 The sunset of the Cathars in the Alps

A series of inquisitions in western Piedmont in the fourteenth century, plotted here, revealed the presence of Waldesians, eccentric individual heretics and syncretistic Cathar–Waldensian groups. Catharism came to its end in these remote valleys. Chieri, where the Cathar element was strongest and links were established with Bosnia, lies south-east of Turin.

Source: G. G. Merlo, *Eretici e inquisitori nella società piemontese del trecento* (Turin, 1977), p. 77

in the sixteenth century to link hands with the Reform were unmarked by any Cathar influence.[91]

Galosna had taken the habit of a tertiary from the Franciscan master of the third order in Chieri some fourteen years before his interrogation, but admitted to having had his first contact with heresy eleven years before that in the house of Laurentius de Lormea, a master who presided at nocturnal meetings at Andezeno. Young Galosna had kept the door but joined the others in a sacramental meal, consumed 'with great joy',[92] in which, to judge by other evidence, the Waldensian eucharist combined with confused memories of the Cathar ceremony of the blessing of bread. In the presence of this master, Galosna said, he had renounced belief in the incarnation of Christ on the grounds that God could not humiliate himself so greatly as to take on human flesh, and repudiated the sacraments of the Church. After two or three visits, he was hit on the head with a sword, causing blood to flow, presumably to induce this abjuration.[93] He was not deterred and recalled going to the meetings of a group numbering some thirty-seven souls about twenty-five times a year for three years. The master preached dualist doctrines, God was creator of heaven, not earth; a great dragon was creator of the earth and lord of the world and more powerful than God on earth.[94]

On his inquisition in 1373, Tommaso di Casasco found out nothing of Galosna's involvement and simply hit him with a stick, threatened him and gave him a light penance for minor infractions of discipline. Much later, caught redhanded at a meeting, Galosna decided to save himself and in a series of interrogations under Antonio di Settimo poured out details of decades of meetings in the Valleys, preachings and ceremonies, with a host of names of participants. In a simple annual ceremony, Martin de Presbitero had appointed him with others to hear confessions.[95] He kept a *pied-à-terre* in Andezeno, but wandered at various times through the Valleys preaching, confessing, presiding over ritual meals for the little communities where the blessing of bread had a great importance, being described as a sacrament above all others. Asked whether he had administered the *consolamentum*, he gave a curious answer, citing two cases in Andezeno of dying women each given with great solemnity a *bucellus panis* – in one case drink as well – and thereafter subjected to an apparent euthanasia by suffocation; his fellow master, Bech, gave a similar answer, with embellishments.[96] the name *consolamentum* survived, but these were not the classic Cathar consolings with the laying on of hands. Galosna testified that doctrine about the dragon as creator had been diffused through a number of villages; his own profession of faith in the beliefs of Martin de Presbitero included

[91]   Lambert, *Medieval Heresy*, 2nd edn, p. 166.
[92]   *ASI* 3rd ser. II, p. 12.
[93]   Ibid., p. 14.
[94]   Ibid., p. 15; compare pp. 6, 17, 21, 23, 25, 26, 30.
[95]   Ibid., p. 6.
[96]   Discussion with refs, *ME*, pp. 66–8; *ASI* 3rd ser. II, pp. 15–16.

reference to the dragon 'who fights with God and his angels and is ... more powerful than God'.[97]

Galosna's confession included sexual aberrations. At the opening of his career at Andezeno, he described as the greatest of the women in the sect a certain Bilia la Castagna, dead by the time of his interrogation, who made a magic philtre which, once drunk, ensured that the victim would never leave the 'synagogue' and who, by repute, kept a great toad under her bed and used its excrement together with pubic hair to make a powder for the philtre.[98] Meetings at Andezeno and a series of other sites, he said, ended with the ritual injunction '*qui habet teneat*' (hold what you have), the extinguishing of lights and an orgy. Desperate to escape the likely consequences of decades of heretical activity, Galosna, subjected to torture, said what inquisitors wanted him to say. There was a decadence not only among the Waldensians and Cathars but also among inquisitors, and stories of orgies, philtres and toads had become a commonplace slander applied to Waldensians, a bitter harvest of *Vox in Rama* and the habital use of torture. Galosna was tortured, probably as a matter of routine. His confession records the conventional phrase that he confessed freely: this means only that his formal confession was made outside the torture chamber and presumably after a pause. Torture distorts; all but the heroic are liable to say yes to any proposition.[99] This discredits the toads and orgies but it is much less likely that the doctrine of the dragon and the creation of the world by an evil power sprang from the inquisitor's imagination, for this is surely a debased version of Cathar doctrine.

Bech's confession corroborates that of Galosna on the existence of a dualist doctrine of creation, though less crude, featuring not a dragon but Lucifer fallen from heaven yet destined to return 'to his glory', and gives circumstantial detail on links to dualist heretics in Sclavonia. With his back to the wall, Bech, like Galosna, confessed freely; his attempted plea that he had only lightly and ignorantly been involved with Martin de Presbitero in the Val di Lanzo collapsed and a month after a simple abjuration 'without torture and outside the place of torture', in the hollow conventional phrase, he rejected his confession and poured out information.[100] A wandering connoisseur of heresy over decades, marked above all by the Franciscan spirit, he had in his time been a member of two groups of Apostolics, a heresy sprung from Franciscanism, had been in contact with Waldensians in the Dauphiné whose teaching he accepted and had journeyed in Tuscany and Umbria, to Rome and to Avignon. He received money from a well-wisher to cross the Adriatic in search of instruction from surviving dualists but, he claimed, had been driven back

[97]   *ASI* 3rd ser. II, p. 9.
[98]   Ibid., pp. 12–13.
[99]   Galosna and torture, ibid., p. 33; intervention of secular power and further torture, pp. 33–5. Orgy stories, *ME*, pp. 71–4. G. Gonnet, 'Casi di sincretismo ereticale in Piemonte nei secoli XIV e XV', *BSSV* CVIII (1960), pp. 3–36; Gonnet accepts promiscuity. Given tradition of slander, onus of proof must lie with accusers: Gonnet does not prove his case.
[100]   Career and wanderings, *ME*, pp. 93–4; confession, *ASI* 3rd ser. II, pp. 50–61.

by a storm.[101] He attracted reverence; the heretical group at Castagnole Piemonte made a great feast for Bech 'for love of him'.[102] Questioned about consoling, he gave a similar answer to Galosna's, adding a description of the strict requirements associated with the rite and describing the choice placed before the dying, of becoming a 'martyr' and undergoing an apparent euthanasia through suffocation or becoming a 'confessor' and undergoing a three-day total fast, including abstaining from drinking; the member who survived this ordeal would be one of the perfect and was expected to deprive himself of all his goods in favour of the master who had consoled him.[103]

Heresy in Chieri where Bech settled was profound, rejecting the incarnation, the resurrection of the body, the Last Judgement and the Church and its sacraments. Catharism had struck deeper roots here than anywhere else.[104] Masters were treated like perfect and given the *melioramentum* with the habitual Cathar greeting, a conventional one being substituted only in public.[105] They were moderate dualists who, in Bech's account, believed in the transmigration of souls, rejected the Old Testament as the work of the devil and were known by an Italian name for Cathars, '*Gazari*': Cathar tenets here outweighed Waldensian ones.

Bech's abortive journey of 1378 to learn wisdom from Slav masters may inspire suspicion, but he also mentions others who had earlier gone overseas in search of a full understanding of dualists teaching 'from masters ... staying in a place called Boxena'.[106] Boxena is Bosnia, the wild interior which lay behind Dubrovnik and the ports of the Dalmatian coast, in the fourteenth century the seat of the ancient dualist Church of Sclavonia and the one locality left in Europe where a remnant of dualists could live out their lives untroubled by persecution. The story of journeys to find wisdom rings true; it continues the twelfth-century Cathar preoccupation with masters in Byzantium and the Balkans and helps to explain why there was a more coherent and less crude dualism in Chieri than anywhere else.

Inquisition blackguarding probably blurs the picture of Bech's beliefs just as it did Galosna's: his confession also carries the orgy slander and includes a reference to antinomian views of Free Spirit type, which must be suspect.[107] None the less flaws in his evidence do not obscure the central outline of the story of the last known Italian Cathars. Catharism had run down; even in Chieri, its most substantial base, it was syncretistic and its last known practitioner was an unstable heresy-taster, drawn into Cathar beliefs at the end of a varied career in dissidence. In this obscure community, a part of Catharism remained – a good deal of doctrine, the practice of

---

[101]   Ibid., p. 53 (referring to Serbia); *ME*, p. 47.
[102]   *ASI* 3rd ser. II, p. 37.
[103]   Bech's confession, ibid., p. 56 et seq.; see *ME*, pp. 67–8.
[104]   *ME*, p. 30; Bech's own views (as expounded in sources), tabulated, pp. 34–5; see also pp. 20–2.
[105]   *ME*, p. 47.
[106]   Ibid., p. 43.
[107]   Ibid., p. 73.

reverencing the leadership, the name but not the original practice of consoling, a use of blessed bread, which probably had mixed Cathar/ Waldensian roots, and a reverence for a surviving dualist Church over the water. The old hierarchy had already disappeared; Antonio di Settimo's inquisition dealt a heavy blow.

In 1412 a highly charged ceremony in Chieri drew a final line.[108] Fifteen dead heretics, including some of those named by Bech as journeying to Bosnia for instruction and members of the aristocratic families of Balbi and Cavour, were condemned by the Dominican inquisitor for Upper Lombardy, their bones exhumed and burnt together with their images in the piazza of Chieri in the presence of Louis of Savoy. The inquisitor's citation referred to the beliefs of the dead as 'that pestiferous and horrid faith ... of the heretics of Bosnia'.[109] Evidently the inquisitor had found no living suspects to pursue; only in Bosnia was the heresy still to be found.[110]

[108]   M. Esposito, 'Un "auto da fé" à Chieri en 1412', *RHE* XLII (1947), pp. 422–32.
[109]   Ibid., p. 423.
[110]   M. Loos, 'Les derniers Cathares de l'Occident et leurs relations avec l'église Patarine de Bosnie,' *Historijski Zbornik* XXIX–XXX (1977), pp. 113–26.

12

Inertia and Survival: the Bosnian Church

Bosnia was the promised land of heresy, the ultimate outpost of the dualists,[1] as Giacomo Bech witnessed in his statement before the inquisition in 1388, when he spoke of his attempted journey across the Adriatic ten years previously.[2] Here, held in honour by the Bosnian rulers, a body of perfect with their own idiosyncratic hierarchy, lived out their lives, far removed from the ascetic missionaries who founded Western Catharism or their tormented heirs who at the end of Cathar history succumbed to the ravages of time, change of fashion, or the prisons and fires of the inquisitors.

A long historiographical tradition has gone further and placarded this Church as the only example in the history of the Middle Ages where the link between ruler, nobles and Church was such that one may fairly speak of an heretical State Church.

[1]   J. V. A. Fine Jr, *The Bosnian Church: a New Interpretation* (Boulder, 1975) (*FBC*) is the fullest account (analysis of sources, massive Serbo-Croat, international bibliography, with use of anthropology, assuming Church to be schismatic, not heretical); see F. Šanjek, *Les Chrétiens Bosniaques et le mouvement Cathare, XIIe–XVe siècles* (Brussels, Paris, Louvain 1976) for Latin sources (Croat-orientated discussion, convinced of heresy of Church; excellent analysis of Radoslav MS, pp. 185–94); introduction M. Loos, *Dualist Heresy in the Middle Ages* (Prague, 1974), chs 13, 15, 19 (Serbo-Croat research, assuming heresy); balanced survey, S. M. Ćirković, in 'Die bosnische Kirche', Accademia Nazionale dei Lincei, *Problemi attuali di Scienza e di cultura* (Rome, 1964), pp. 547–75; review of Ćirković's political history of Bosnia (in Serbian), J. V. A. Fine Jr, *Speculum* XLI (1966), pp. 526–9; J. Šidak, 'Das Problem des Bogomilismus in Bosnien', *Atti del X Congresso Internazionale* (Comitato Internazionale di Scienze Storiche) (Rome, 1957), pp. 365–9 (surveys research; announces personal conversion to theory of heresy of Church); S. M. Džaja, *Die 'Bosnische Kirche' und das Islamisierungsproblem Bosniens und der Herzegovina in den Forschungen nach dem zweiten Weltkrieg* (Munich, 1978) (full historiography: hypothesis of heresy of Church); S. Ćirković, 'The Bosnian Patarenes and Western heresies' (unpublished paper; I am indebted to Prof. Ćirković for access); O. D. Mandić, *Bogomilska crkva bosanskih krstjana* (Chicago, 1962; reissued 1979) uncritical, best not used except for sources reproduced pp. 435–51.
[2]   Amati, *ASI* 3rd ser., II (i) (1865), p. 53; see above, pp. 294–5.

Bosnia was a frontier land between the spheres of the Greek and Latin Churches. To the north, the kingdom of Hungary was an outpost of the Latins; farther south, Serbia represented the Orthodox tradition; along the coast Trogir, Split and Dubrovnik were Catholic, as was the strip of territory behind them. Dubrovnik, originally founded by Roman refugees fleeing from Slav tribes, an entrepôt between the Italian and Slav worlds, was between 1205 and 1358 under Venetian suzerainty. The interior of Bosnia, with its forests and mountains, was an ecclesiastical no man's land in which neither of the great Churches had effective jurisdiction.[3] Arguably, the monks whom Innocent's legate met at Bilino Polje were of Basilian, i.e. Orthodox background, but, if they were, they had wholly lost touch with the Church of their origin.[4] Innocent intended to draw Bosnia into his jurisdiction while sweeping aside heresy and eliminating a refuge for heretics. His assumption and that of his legate was that the heretics from whom the monks of Bilino Polje and the ban and nobles were to be protected were Cathars, and, as they were in flight from the Catholic archbishop of Split and one source of their heresy lay in goldsmiths of Apulian origin working on the coast at Zadar,[5] the assumption was reasonable. In the past, so ran the story which reached the inquisitor Anselm of Alessandria much later, heresy had been spread in the Dalmatian coastlands by merchants who went to Constantinople to trade and there assimilated heresy and carried it home. Constantinople, he said, had a heretic bishop of the Greeks and another of the Latins; bearers of heresy probably learned their doctrine from the Latins, then carried back to their homeland dualist teaching and dessiminated it in a Catholic environment, eventually sparking off the hostile reaction firstly of the archbishop of Split, then of Innocent III.[6]

In the West Catharism operated in a Catholic environment and drew strength from the movements of reform and dissent which flowered there in the twelfth century. The heresy of Bosnia had similar roots and can fairly be called Catharism, albeit of a peculiar and idiosyncratic kind. Anselm's narrative spoke of the merchants as originating 'from Sclavonia, that is from the land called Bossona',[7] lumping two broad geographical terms together. Far-flung trade was only associated with the Catholic coastlands; trade with the interior from the ports of Dalmatia was undeveloped and dealt primarily in raw materials and slaves; thus the merchants who came back from the Byzantine capital and missionized could only be operating in the first instance on the Catholic coast. Bosnia, it seems, did not itself produce heresy, but was a refuge point, certainly from the Dalmatian coastlands, possibly also from Serbia, where stiff persecution c.1172 during the reign of

---

[3]   Background, *FBC*; Loos, *Dualist Heresy*.

[4]   Above, pp. 107–8; reference to men and women living together may suggest origin in Basilian double monasteries lingering on, see M. Miletić, *I 'Krstjani' di Bosnia alla luce dei loro monumenti di pietra* (Rome, 1957); also E. Werner, in *Byzantinoslavica* XXI (1960), pp. 119–24.

[5]   *FBC*, p. 118; Šanjek, *Chrétiens*, pp. 39–40 (with quotations from source); Loos, *Dualist Heresy*, pp.163, 211.

[6]   *AFP* XX (1950), p. 308.

[7]   Ibid.

Stephen Nemanja condemned heretics to suffer the burning of their books and exile. It is usual in modern times to label this heresy Bogomil, but the designation is uncertain: the contemporary description refers to Arians.[8]

Once arrived in the interior, heresy was virtually impossible to eradicate for reasons both geographical and political. Heresy accusations were widely used to aid political ambitions, as, at the turn of the thirteenth century, by Vukan of Dioclea against Ban Kulin: there was exaggeration and confusion. Such accusations perennially stimulated the popes to appeal for action against Bosnian heresy but they could find no effective champion to impose a Catholic orthodoxy by force, and the bans, probably ignorant, certainly tolerant, in the long run eluded their pressure. The only realistic champion of orthodoxy was Hungary, but its own political and ecclesiastical weaknesses, coupled with the absence of communications and the rugged terrain of Bosnia, so resistant to an invader, spoiled its chances.

The interior had only been loosely attached to Catholicism by Innocent, and his successors were unable to maintain any effective allegiance. Honorius III had no success at all; Gregory IX, the father of the inquisition, had more, summoning the king of Hungary to lead a crusade into Bosnia. At first all went well: Coloman duke of Croatia, brother of the king, led the crusade: the ban Ninoslav, much like Raymond VI, renounced heresy and declared himself ready to repress it. The pope restrained Coloman and protected the ban, only to be disappointed. He then unleashed another Hungarian crusade, which, probably in 1236–7, brought much Bosnian territory under Hungarian control.[9]

Plans for better pastoral oversight within Bosnia following Bilino Polje had evidently come to nothing: it was reported in 1232 that the Latin bishop in Bosnia had obtained his place through simony, was uneducated, did not know the proper form in which to baptize and lived in the same village as heretics. He was deposed and replaced by a German Dominican, Johannes Wildeshausen, provincial of the Dominicans of Hungary, in turn succeeded by another alien, the Dominican Ponsa. Persecution, reform and mission went together: the first ultimately destroyed the hopes invested in the last. As Hungarian forces moved forward to defeat Bosnian resistance, Dominicans set about destruction of heresy and instruction in orthodoxy. Two Dominican convents were set up and there were burnings of heretics, handed over, so the Dominican chronicler informs us, to agents of Coloman. Ruined churches were repaired and there were plans for a cathedral to be built near Vrhbosna, the modern Sarajevo.[10]

---

[8] Ćirković, unpublished paper.

[9] *FBC*, pp. 134–45.

[10] Hypothesis of take-over by dualists following failed crusade, J. Šidak, 'Ecclesia Sclavoniae i misija dominikanaca u Bosni', *Zbornik Filozofskog fakulteta universitata u Zagrebu* III (1955), p. 11–40, German summary, p. 40, relying on *Commentariolum de provinciae Hungariae originibus*, Gerard of Fracheto, *Vitae Fratrum* ed. B. M. Reichert, *MOPH* I (Lovanii, 1896), pp. 305–8 (likely not to be a biased, distant source; the author wrote at Bodrog, near Sombor, close to the cockpit of events), adopted by Ćirković, *'Die bosnische Kirche'*, pp. 551–3; another interpretation, *FBC*, pp. 145–53, with account of events; comment on link to nobles, Džaja,, *Islamisierungsproblem*, p. 42.

Crusade, however, had only an ambiguous success. Ninoslav retained a certain independence and even in 1240 was free to enter into treaty negotiations with Dubrovnik. Mongol invasion in 1241 then weakened Hungary and, though in 1246–7 Innocent IV busied himself attempting to mount another crusade, he listened eventually to Ninoslav's protestations of orthodoxy and called off the Hungarians. Crusade spluttered out and with it all hopes of a Catholic take-over of Bosnia and a full repression of heresy. The cathedral was never built; the Dominican convents were burnt down. A list of convents dating from 1303 has no entry at all for Bosnia.[11] By mid-thirteenth century the Latin bishop had had to go into exile and continued to live for many years outside his see, on estates at Djakovo in Slavonia.

When in the fourteenth and fifteenth centuries sources for the condition of the Bosnian lands again become fuller, it is apparent that a Bosnian Church, the *crkva Bosanska*, is in existence, secure, endowed, respected by rulers and aristocracy, and yet marked, however formally, by unmistakable heretical traits – a quasi-Cathar Church which remained for many decades unpersecuted. Well aware of the anomaly of a heretical Church lying unscathed on the frontiers of their jurisdiction, popes continued in vain to denounce it and to call for action. Uniquely, the Bosnian dualists escaped the inquisitors.

The heretical tradition in Bosnia was an old one. The Radoslav collection, a manuscript copied by the *krstjan* Radoslav for his fellow *krstjan* Goïsak in the reign of King Stephen Thomas (1443–6) includes a short ritual consisting of the Lord's Prayer, phrases of adoration, the grace, an absolution and a translation of the first seventeen verses of St John's gospel, which is almost identical with the Western Cathar ritual, part Latin, part Provençal, published by Clédat in 1887.[12] Radoslav, like Clédat, has the form of the Lord's Prayer usual among Cathars, with the phrase 'Give us this day our supersubstantial (*našusni*) bread'; there are small differences – Radoslav omits the opening formulae preceding the Lord's Prayer in Clédat, which alone includes the lesser doxology, the *Gloria Patri*, ancient, but at this time much more common in orthodox oriental rites than in Western ones. Radoslav alone includes a pair of verses from St Paul's epistle to Titus, where he speaks of renouncing ungodliness and worldly lusts to live soberly in the present world – texts which would be taken by dualists to be an injunction to lead the life of the perfect. These Radoslav reproduces in glagolitic letters, in a form long fallen out of use and datable to the turn of the twelfth and thirteenth centuries. It suggests that though the Radoslav manuscript as it stands dates from the last years of the Bosnian Church, the original he was copying was probably over two centuries older, datable to the epoch of Bilino Polje.

The two extant Western Cathar rituals, the Clédat MS and the Florentine Latin version published by Dondaine, include much more material and

---

[11]   *FBC*, p. 144.
[12]   Best account of Radoslav in Šanjek, *Chrétiens*, pp. 85–91. I have not accepted Fine's explanation of this ritual, *FBC*, p.83.

culminate in the rite of the *consolamentum*. That is not included in Radoslav. What we have is in all probability a short ritual in regular, everyday use among the *krstjani*, the absolution being pronounced by the prelate, i.e. the senior *krstjan* or other churchman of rank, corresponding to the general absolution after the *confiteor* in a Western mass, for minor faults and breaches of regulations of insufficient severity to lead to the forfeiture of the *consolamentum*.[13] It was in fact the most common form of prayer in use.

Dualists took over an old, backward, monk-dominated indigenous Church in Bosnia; when exactly, it is difficult to say. Innocent's legate treated the representatives of the Church in 1203 as orthodox in doctrine, but ill regulated and in danger of infiltration by heretics ('patarenes'). Possibly he was wrong, and infiltration had already gone further than he assumed. Another Bosnian text written for the nobleman Batalo in 1393, extant only in a fragment consisting of the last four verses of St John's gospel, lists two columns of names, one being a list of the *djeds*, the leading churchmen of the old Bosnian Church, the equivalent of archbishop in the fourteenth century, and the other, by inference, a list of earlier leaders. It may be significant that the latter list includes the names of three of the 'priors' concerned in the agreement of Bilino Polje.[14]

The likeliest moment of transmutation, however, lies in mid-thirteenth century, in the aftermath of the failed Hungarian attempt at occupation, when Dominicans had apparently been chased out and Catholicism damaged by its association with an occupying power. In any case, the old Church had limited resources to defend itself. When the Church emerges again, fitfully, into the light of day in the fourteenth century, it is condemned by both Latin and Orthodox sources, and, feeble as they often are, its own sources reveal that its churchmen were heretics, holding their dualism in a kind of thin solution, without missionary or debating power, a half-understood heritage from the past.[15]

---

[13] See comment by Dondaine, in *Un Traité*, p. 45.

[14] Rival comments, *FBC*, pp. 215–18; Loos, *Dualist Heresy*, p. 165.

[15] I defend here my standpoint in a classic controversy, dating back to F. Rački, 'Bogomili i patareni', *Rad Jugoslavenske akademije znanosti i umjetnosti* VII (1869), pp. 84–179, VIII (1869), pp. 121–87, X (1870), pp. 160–263 (impressionistic account, L. Leger, 'L'hérésie des Bogomiles en Bosnie et en Bulgarie au moyen age', *Revue Historique* VIII (1870), pp. 479–517). Key points in favour of heretical character of Church are (1) Orthodox denunciations, not subject to possible Hungarian-influenced bias in Latin sources: A. Solovjev, 'Svedočanstva pravoslavnih izvora o Bogomilstvu na Balkanu', *Godišnjak istoriskog društva Bosnie i Hercegovine* V (1953), pp. 1–103 (French summary, pp. 100–3); (2) evidence of Dominican chronicle, locally written (above, n. 10); (3) the Franciscan *Dubia*, esp. qn. 21 (below, p.305), emanating from knowledgeable observers in Bosnia; (4) observations for practical purposes about Bosnian churchmen as diplomats by authorities in Dubrovnik – see M. Dinić, *Iz Dubrovačkog arhiva* III (Belgrade, 1967), pp. 181–236 (Serbian edn with transcripts in original languages, kindly given to me by Prof. S. Ćirković); (5) the Radoslav ritual (above, p. 193); (6) the Srećković glosses (below, p. 309). Fine, *FBC*, *passim* draws a subtle distinction between dualists in Bosnia and the Bosnian Church, which he believes schismatic, not heretical. His descriptions often illuminate, but I am not convinced by his arguments. See also Lambert, *Heresis* XXIII (1994), pp. 29–50, noting problems in Gost Radin's will for supporters of 'heretical' view.

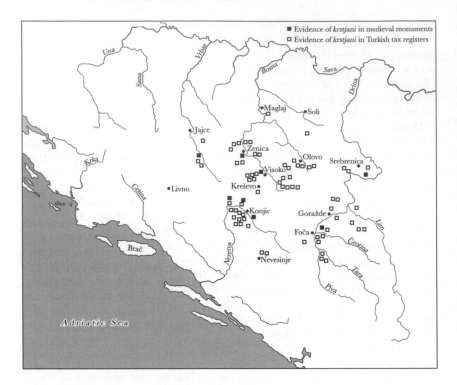

Map 10   The Bosnian Church
Source: S. Cirkovíc, *Istoŕija srednjovekovne bosanske države* (Belgrade, 1964), p. 284

Though popes continued to protest about the presence of heresy and to seek champions, they continued to fail. John XXII, pre-eminently an inquisition pope, wrote repeatedly, speaking in 1325 of 'many heretics' coming to the Bosnian state; Benedict XII, with his unrivalled experience of Catharism as Bishop Fournier, came closest of all to launching a crusade when he tried to mobilize Croatian nobles against ban Stephen Kotromanić.[16] Yet he failed also. Hungary, the natural Catholic champion had lost strength; Kotromanić, ban 1318–53, established friendly relations with her and strengthened his own position, conquering land, especially from the Serbs, and establishing a decentralized state, leaving a considerable autonomy to his nobles. He presided in tolerant fashion over three faiths, Catholicism, Orthodoxy and the Bosnian Church, each having their own spheres of influence.[17] His nephew Tvrtko I, who succeeded him, ruled till 1391 and,

[16]   *FBC*, pp. 177, 179.
[17]   Ibid., pp. 167–73.

after initial vicissitudes, achieved an understanding with Hungary and widened his territories; he took advantage of the distractions of Louis I of Hungary and the weakness of Serbia to have himself crowned at Mile in 1377 as king of Raška and Bosnia.[18]

It was the golden age of the Bosnia state.[19] Stephen Kotromanić was Orthodox at his accession but sympathetic to Catholicism:[20] he had a Catholic wife and received the Franciscan minister-general Geraldus Odonis with favour when he visited Bosnia in 1339. The visit was an immediate prelude to the establishment of a Franciscan vicariate sponsored by Benedict XII and formally set up in the ban's lands in 1340.[21] Though there continued to be talk of the repression of heresy by force, the balance had shifted to peaceful mission, facilitated by the fact that the enterprise was in the hands of Franciscans, untainted by association with the Dominicans and the age of attempted conquest. Kotromanić converted to Catholicism; Tvrtko was from birth a Catholic. Neither had any intention of acting like rulers in Western Europe and putting heresy down.

The Bosnian Church remained unpersecuted but it now had a peaceful rival in the vicariate – not at first a powerful one, for in 1372 the whole vicariate had a maximum staff of sixty brothers; missionary enterprise soon widened the field of activity beyond Kotromanić's state and the pastoral duties of the brothers included, beside missionary work among the Bosnians, the care of incoming Catholics, especially Dalmatians or Saxons established at mining settlements as the interior was opened up to economic development. The vicariate was put under severe strain as the Great Schism and inner conflicts linked to the rise of the Franciscan Observants led to the withdrawal of numbers of Italian friars; on the other hand, long term, this strengthened the vicariate as it led to greater emphasis on the employment and training of indigenous Bosnian recruits.[22]

Kotromanić's support and his friendly relationship with the first vicar, Peregrin of Saxony, put the vicariate on a firm footing. Convents in his reign, and subsequently, were skilfully placed to take advantage of political

---

[18] J. Džambo, *Die Franziskaner im mittelalterlichen Bosnien FF* XXXV (Werl, Westfalen, 1991), pp. 151–2, correcting Ćirković hypothesis on crowning at Serbian Mileševo; see also p. 27; reviews, B. Vadakkekara, *Collectanea Franciscana* LXII (1992), pp. 436–7 (in English), L. Lehmann, *Laurentianum* XXXV (1994), pp. 201–5, P. Vrankić, *Jahrbücher für Geschichte Osteuropas* XLI (1993), pp. 610–12.

[19] Best account of politics, *FBC*, pp. 167–210.

[20] Fine's hypothesis, *FBC*, p. 167; Džambo, *Franziskaner*, p. 80 asumes he had been brought up a Catholic.

[21] Džambo, *Franziskaner*, awarded Südosteuropagesellschaft prize, supersedes all others on vicariate (note esp. Franciscan historiography, pp. 17–25, origins and constitution, pp. 77–114, archaeology, *passim*). Emergence of Franciscans in Bosnia curiously linked with instituting of Franciscan inquisitors by Nicholas IV, a Franciscan, once provincial of Sclavonia, in 1291 (pp. 72–6); did they in fact operate as inquisitors – under Serbian protection? See review, C. Lohmer, *DA* XLVIII (1992), pp. 331–2; *FBC*, pp. 153–4. I am grateful for photocopies and help to Dr Džambo.

[22] Džambo, *Franziskaner*, p. 98; background, pp. 149–60.

Figure 10   Stone memorial of *Gost* Milutin

Photograph: Zemaljski Muzej, Sarajevo

and economic developments. He had a Gothic church built for the friars at
Mile, where he and Tvrtko I were buried; two other stone churches were
built, one near the castle at Bobovac, a strategic centre for the dynasty and
burial-place of the great, and the other at Sutjeska, also near a ruler's residence. At Olovo a convent catered for a mining community; similarly, at

Srbrenica the friars served miners and a colony of skilled workers and busi-
nessmen from Dubrovnik. The working centre for the vicariate lay at first,
most probably, in the Franciscan custody of Bosnia, well in the interior in an
area of strength of the old Bosnian Church.[23]

The problems which the Franciscans faced in a vast, undeveloped mission
field emerge from the *Dubia*, a list of twenty-three questions answered by
Gregory XI in 1373, asking, for example, what the correct attitude should
be to heathen-style, conditional marriages of Bosnians, who put away wives
as they wished; or whether, given the shortage of priests, the friars should
accept the services of certain rustics and schismatics not canonically
ordained but simply instituted priest by the custom of the land. They asked
whether friars should say mass in the presence of those who had aided
heretics, and whether laymen should dispute about matters of faith in the
presence of heretics. Though the heresy is not specified, question twenty-
one leaves little doubt. The friars ask how they should treat converts who
continued to adore heretics and participate in heretical rites while
observing their Catholicism secretly. It is unlikely that this 'adoring' can be
anything other than a form of the *melioramentum*. The question implies, too,
that the supporters of heresy were so influential that converts feared to
offend them.[24] Four years later Gregory had to deal with a complaint that
when the Franciscans celebrated mass in the presence of Tvrtko I, 'heretics
and Patarenes' sometimes appeared and were allowed to participate; when
the friars in consequence withdrew, Tvrtko turned to secular priests to say
mass for him.[25] Tvrtko was showing his power: he wished to have the
Catholic mass but he was resolute in tolerating the 'heretics', that is, the
Bosnian churchmen.

The power of the greater nobles within Bosnia was always a force to be
reckoned with, and as at least a section of that nobility continued to be
members and supporters of the heretical Bosnian Church, rulers felt bound
to treat it with respect. Probably in the aftermath of the defeat of the
Hungarians in mid-thirteenth century, the nobility in general, in so far as
they had any religious allegiance, were supporters of the Bosnian Church:
that changed as both the Orthodox and the Catholics gained a place in the
state; none the less, the adherence of certain families and a traditional,
regional strength maintained the Church's power. In one case between
1305 and 1307 a king of Serbia took as witnesses to a charter to a monastery,

[23]   Ibid., p. 81; map, p. 79; Mile (modern Arnautovići, near Visoko), pp. 81–5,
Bobovac, pp. 85–8, Sutjeska, pp. 88–9, Olovo, pp. 89, 91, 157, Srbrenica, pp. 90–3; on
Tvrtko I's grave, M. Wenzel, 'Bosnian history and Austro-Hungarian policy: the
Zemaljski Muzej, Sarajevo, and the Bogomil Romance', *Museum Management and
Curatorship* XII (1993), pp. 127–42.
[24]   Discussed, with other Latin sources, D. Kniewald, 'Hierarchie und Kultus bosnischen Christen', in *L'Oriente cristiano* (see n. 1 above), pp. 579–605; J. Šidak's
comment, *Istorijski Časopis* V (1955), p. 231 (German summary of Serbian article);
FBC, pp. 192–6 suggests friars may have confused a harmless local custom of reverence for priests with *melioramentum*. Many were Italians; would they have been
confused about this Cathar custom, even at this date?
[25]   *FBC*, pp. 196–7.

together with Orthodox bishops, a Catholic bishop and the *djed* of the Bosnian Church.[26] Between 1322 and 1325, Stephen Kotromanić issued a charter to a Bosnian nobleman at a *hiža*, a monastery of the Bosnian Church, using the *djed*, a *gost*, three elders and 'all the Bosnian Church' as his witnesses. As we know from the sources, there were three ranks in the Bosnian hierarchy – *djed*, *gost*, *starac* ('elder'), with the *strojnik* being a member of the *djed*'s council, and below them the *krstjani*, the ordained clergy corresponding to the perfect of Western Catharism. Another charter by Kotromanić from the same decade stipulates that nothing shall be done to the detriment of the beneficiary or his heirs without consulting the Bosnian Church.[27]

A *gost* was a man of substance, with a role comparable to that of many Western higher clergy who gained wealth and authority through secular service. The stone memorial, or *stećak*, of *Gost* Milutin, dated by Mark Vego to 1318, in its primitive carving and the ragged fashion in which the inscription to his memory begins behind his head, runs on to the side and then finally on to the back of the pillar, demonstrates the backward nature of this society. The wording emphasizes worldly power. It runs: 'In thy name, most holy Trinity, the gravestone of lord gost Milutin born Crničan. He perished as God willed it. He lived honoured by the lord of Bosnia, he received gifts from the great lord and nobles and from the Greek lord and was known to all.' His contact with the 'Greek lord' and the gifts he received may well have been an outcome of diplomatic service. He is buried at Humsko on the river Drina near Foča, eastern Bosnia, not far from his family's lands. His short tunic and the girdle of twisted cord correspond to the dress of the secular nobility; his clerical status is revealed by the book which he holds in his left hand and by the staff shaped in the form of a Tau cross on which he leans. Excavation has shown that his body was wrapped in a brocade robe adorned with lions and stars woven with threads of pure gold.[28] He represents a small literate elite within the aristocracy whom it would be natural to call into secular service.

The monasteries were headed by *gosti*, as is shown by the reference in Kotromanić's charter to the *hiža* of Gost Radoslav, and they had a secular as well as religious significance. Some were used as hostels and staging-posts: Vlach horsemen escorting caravans to the interior and Italian merchants made use of them. In one case, the subject of a dispute with a Dubrovnik

---

[26]   Ibid., pp. 155–7, arguing that presence of *djed* with a Serbian king implies the Bosnian Church was not heretical.

[27]   Ibid., pp. 173–5 (discussion of both charters; on *strojnik*, pp. 249, 318).

[28]   M. Vego, *Zbornik srednjovjekovnih natpisa Bosne i Hercegovine* III (Sarajevo, 1964), pp. 52–3. Mme N. Miletić of the Sarajevo museum, to whose kindness I owe photographs, doubts whether a precise date of 1318 can be proved; *FBC*, pp. 263–4 postulates a fifteenth-century date; see also Miletić, *I. 'Krstjani' di Bosnia*, pp. 122–78 (assuming orthodoxy of Bosnian Church). I have corrected the Vego version of inscription (see Lambert, *Medieval Heresy*, 1st edn, p. 145) in the light of *FBC*, p. 263. Ćirković argues that the Church acted as a balancing factor between ruler and aristocracy, ' "Verna služba" i "vjera gospodska" ', *Zbornik Filozofskog fakulteta u Beogradu* VI (1962), pp. 101–12 (in Serbian, German summary pp. 111–12).

merchant, a *hiža* was used as a border-post: in another, when a great man in fear of King Ostoja in the early fifteenth century took refuge in one, as a sanctuary. The terms used for them – *domus, casa, hiža* – imply they were quite small establishments.[29]

After Tvrtko I's death, the last phase of Bosnian history was marked, firstly, by a time of troubles in which Bosnia was drawn into the long Hungarian civil war between Sigismund and Ladislav of Naples, and secondly, by the steady growth of Turkish power dating from the battle near Doboj in 1415. Ostoja, king of Bosnia 1398–1404, 1409–18, was probably the one ruler who was himself a member of the Church.[30] He used a Bosnian churchman in 1403 in negotiations with Dubrovnik; the republic responded, giving him gifts, rewarding Ostoja's *djed* in the hope that he would influence the king, even giving the treaty into his safe-keeping while awaiting the king's assent.[31] The role of the Church remained significant under Tvrtko II when he finally succeeded Ostoja's son in 1420, but the major contribution of the Bosnian hierarchy lay in service over the years between 1419 and 1466 to a small number of noble houses, who used them repeatedly in negotiations with Dubrovnik.[32] They participated in forty missions; the largest number of all was sent by the great nobleman Stephen Vukčić Kosača, an adherent of the Church, who held a swathe of territory in what is now Herzegovina and who used pre-eminently a churchman called Radin, *krstjan* when first in noble service, then under Stephen, *starac*, finally *gost*, ultimately acting in effect as his foreign secretary.[33]

The utility of the Church to noble houses is entirely characteristic: it was an aristocrat-dominated Church, which struck roots in the Bosnian secular elite in the later thirteenth century and continued above all to serve the interest of nobles. Benko Kotruljić, a Dubrovnik merchant who had travelled in Bosnia and wrote a treatise in 1458 on trade and the model merchant, commented that 'the Bosnians, who follow Manichee customs, especially respect rich people and very hospitably receive them in their houses [i.e. *hižas*] while turning away the poor.'[34] His judgement confirms the impression left by diplomatic records, where we hear so heavily of secular service and the acquiring of wealth, and suggests that it is not merely a natural bias in this type of record that influences our picture of the Church hierarchy as conventional career men, little orientated to mission or the pastoral care of the people.

The *kristjani* retained from their religious inheritance certain customs, the refusing of the oath, for example. The authorities in Dubrovnik were well aware of this and repeatedly in negotiations with the Bosnians, ruler and nobles take an oath while representatives of the Bosnian Church are allowed simply to make a promise 'according to their custom'.[35] The

[29] *FBC*, pp. 256–60, 273, 276–7.
[30] Fine's hypothesis, *FBC*, p. 222; political events, pp. 219–38.
[31] Ibid., p. 226–7; original sources, Dinić, *Iz Dubrovačkog arhiva*.
[32] Penetrating analysis, *FBC*, pp. 238–44, 264–7; see list pp. 290–3.
[33] Ibid., pp. 239, 244, 249, 253–4, 256, 264–5, 267, 272–3, 307, 311, 314, 317–21.
[34] Ibid., pp. 329–30; Ćirković, in *'Die bosnische Kirche'*, p. 567.
[35] M. Dinić, 'Jedan prilog za istoriju patarena u Bosni', *Zbornik Filozofskog fakulteta u Beogradu* I (1948), pp. 33–44 (in Serbian, French summary, p. 44) at pp. 34–5.

position was comparable to that of the Cathar perfect who refused the oath, following a literal interpretation of Matthew 5, 'swear not at all', while leaving their followers who had not received the *consolamentum* free to swear as required. The republic treated them well, under the conventions of diplomacy, and even on one occasion asked to negotiate with a Bosnian churchman rather than anyone else.[36] To Radin, the last of the great *gosti*, they gave large sums of money over his long career in return for representing Dubrovnik's interest with Stephen Vukčić, and at the end, when his master had died and the Turks threatened, gave him and his followers asylum in the city. So, curiously, did Venice, with whom Radin arranged a species of insurance at the end of his life, asking that he and fifty or sixty 'of his sect and law' might settle on Venetian territory; a majority of senators voted to accept the request, though it was controversial enough for a minority to vote against or abstain.[37] In both cases, for Venice and Dubrovnik, the guiding principles were the same: they respected the wealth and skills of Radin and were aware that goodwill from Bosnian churchmen had helped to keep caravan routes open and trade flowing. The authorities in Dubrovnik were well aware of the character of the Church. They used the usual Italian term, 'patarene' applied to the Cathars and wrote back bluntly in response to a request for Bosnians to attend the Council of Basle, saying 'The Patarenes are called the religious [i.e. monks] of the said kingdom of Bosnia by the Bosnians, although they can truly be said to be without faith, order or rule', going on to explain the ranks in their hierarchy, much as in the charter of Stephen Kotromanić but with a minor error on the role of the *strojnik*, and concluding by saying, in effect, that they were heretics.[38]

That heresy, it must be said, lay remarkably inert. The churchmen used the sign of the cross, or accepted its use, and the invocation of the Trinity in documents. The gospels they employed were orthodox. The Batalo version was being used by an Orthodox monastery in the eighteenth century[39] and all the attempts made, especially by A. V. Solovjev, to argue for heretical nuances in words and phrases within Bosnian gospel texts have failed to carry conviction.[40] Like Bogomils and Western Cathars, the Bosnian

---

[36] *FBC*, p. 256.

[37] Ibid., p. 370. Decision in 1466; not acted on. Radin had been given a house in the city of Dubrovnik by the republic in 1455, *FBC*, p. 320.

[38] *FBC* trans., p. 248 corrected, Džaja, in *Münchener Zeitschrift für Balkankunde* I (1978), pp. 250–1. Fine argues that the 'Ragusans spoke of the Patarins not as they regarded them, but as they thought the clerics at Basel would' (*FBC*, p. 249). I am not convinced. See Dinić, *Iz Dubrovačkog arhiva* III, 221, no. 1; context, F. Šanjek, 'Le christianisme dans les Balkans au temps de Jean de Raguse (1390/95–1443)', *L'Eglise et le peuple chrétien dans le pays de l'Europe du Centre-Est et du Nord (XIV–XV siècles), Collection de l'Ecole Française de Rome* CXXVIII (Rome, 1990), pp. 289–300.

[39] *FBC*, p. 215.

[40] For Solovjev's approach, 'La doctrine de l'église de Bosnie', *ARBB* 5th ser., XXIV (1948), pp. 481–533; Bosnian gospel versions and textual variants, A. Vaillant, in *Revue des études slaves* XXVIII (1951), pp. 273–3, reviewing work of D. Kniewald; comment, Ćirković, *'Die bosnische Kirche'*, pp. 558–9.

churchmen used orthodox versions and bent them to their purposes by an aggressive exegesis of their own, making use of allegorical interpretations to void awkward texts. A vital clue is given by the marginal glosses contained in the Srećković manuscript of a Bosnian gospel, which reveal unquestionably heretical conceptions – on John the Baptist, for example, described pejoratively as the water-carrier, on the unjust steward and the prodigal son, with references to the two sons of God and to the angels imprisoned in bodies of men.[41]

When in 1466, Radin made his will in Dubrovnik, he made a definite distinction between those of his *zakon*, or law, and the Catholics of the city, and enjoins his nephew, another *gost* Radin of Seonica, solemnly 'for the sake of the faith that he believes and the fast that he keeps' to observe his instructions.[42] *Gosti* regarded themselves as monks; yet in Radin's case this must have been very much a formality, for he passed much of his time in secular service and amassed a fortune through simultaneously serving both Dubrovnik and Stephen Vukčić, which made him one of the richest men in Bosnia and Herzegovina, disposing of some 5,640 ducats. He lays out sums of money in 1466 for the deserving to receive charity from his bequests and for them to pray for his soul; three hundred ducats are to be given to his friend Prince Tadioko Marojević of Dubrovnik and the prince's nephew, Maroje Naoković to distribute to needy Catholics individually in amounts from three to eight dinars, in order that candles should be burnt for his soul 'in God's churches' on certain feast days; in a similar manner, in amounts from three to eight *perpere*, another three hundred ducats are to be given to needy members of his own Church, described as 'baptized people who are

---

[41] M. Speranskij, 'Ein bosnisches Evangelium in der handschriftensammlung von Srećković', *Archiv für slavische Philologie* XXIV (1902), pp. 172–83; comment, extracts (in French trans.) Šanjek, *Chrétiens*, pp. 175–81; see also Džaja, *Islamisierungsproblem*, p. 19. On this I accept Solovjev's interpretation (*ARBB* 5th ser., XXIV (1948), p. 500), Šidak's doubt on Bosnian origin of glosses (Džaja, p. 114) I believe over-cautious. See also S. Ćirković, 'Die Glossen des bosnischen Evangeliums aus der Handschriftensammlung Srećkovićs und die Lehre der bosnischen Kirche', in *Bogomilism in the Balkans in the Light of the Latest Research* (Skopje, 1982), pp. 207–22. On glagolitic MSS with denunciations of Bosnian dualist errors, Džaja, *Islamisierungsproblem*, pp. 21, 115–17. Doctrines attributed to Bosnian Church in Latin sources remain a problem for supporters of the 'heretical' view: see Šanjek, *Chrétiens* for texts. Ćirković, *'Die bosnische Kirche'*, p. 554, n. 17 provides an explanation for one difficulty; *FBC*, pp. 335–7, 355–61 discusses Torquemada renunciation (where I incline to see gratuitous, reach-me-down attributions of doctrine, as Fine).

[42] I follow Yvonne Burns's trans., kindly incorporated by her in Lambert, *Medieval Heresy*, 1st edn, pp. 374–80, with notes. She corrects C. Truhelka, 'Das Testament des Gost Radin: ein Beitrag zur Patarenerfrage', *Wissenschaftliche Mitteilungen aus Bosnien und der Herzegovina* XIII (1916), pp. 52–90 and A. V. Solovjev, 'Le Testament du Gost Radin', *Mandićev Zbornik* (Rome, 1965), pp. 141–56, reviewed J. Šidak, *Slovo* (Zagreb) XVII (1967), pp. 195–9. I owe photocopies to the kindness of the director, Historiski arhiv, Dubrovnik and Mrs Burns. Comparison of Burns with Solovjev, Lambert, *Heresis* XXIII (1994), pp. 29–50 at pp. 46–50; comment, Loos, *Dualist Heresy*, pp. 314–15, Džaja, *Münchener Zeitschrift für Balkankunde* I (1978), p. 250. Problems remain to be solved.

of the true apostolic faith, to the Christian peasants (both men and women), so that they, bending their knees to the ground, shall say a holy prayer for my soul ...'.[43]

The distinction between members of his Church and the Catholics is carefully maintained, yet the relationship between himself and Prince Tadioko is plainly an easy one, he diplomatically leaves an equal bequest to the needy of his host's city as to the needy of his own Church, and he refers to the churches of Dubrovnik as 'God's churches'. However, the duty to be performed for him by the legatees is different – candles in churches on one side, kneeling and praying on another. When he described his legatees, Radin did so in a repetitious, incantatory fashion which runs parallel for both Churches. The needy members of his Church were the 'blind or weak or crippled or poor, the unsightly leprous people ... the blind ... the crippled ... the hungry and thirsty ...'.[44] The likely pattern is the words of Jesus from the parable of the supper, when the host's servant is commanded to go into the streets and lanes of the city and bring in 'the poor and the maimed and the halt and the blind'.[45] He was acting like any wealthy Western Church dignitary at his end, thinking of distribution to the poor and of prayers for his soul. He clearly envisaged that members of his church would be baptized, a fact which sits awkwardly with the rejection of John the Baptist and water baptism in the Srećković gloss. Radin included the feasts of Orthodox saints Nedelja and Petka, whose cult was Serbian in origin, amongst the 'Great Days' on which he expects his needy legatees to light candles or pray for him – suggesting an Orthodox root to the old Bosnian Church.[46] It was, in a word, a syncretistic Church, with a top-hamper of doctrine and ritual inherited from dualist infiltration, but in practice not very different from the great churches with which it competed and it was not difficult in the special circumstances of the Balkans of the time for either Venice or Dubrovnik to make a place for Radin and his retinue.

The Church faded out after Radin. It was not a State Church, as has often been claimed, for, though at various times the Bosnian bans, kings and

---

[43]   Mrs Burns's trans. Prof. Šanjek in conversation asks whether it is *the* holy prayer, i.e. Lord's Prayer. Mrs Burns (Lambert, *Medieval Heresy*, 1st edn, p. 377, n. 14) on word trans. 'Christian', comments '*krstjanin* in the form found in Bosnia corresponding to *kršćanin* in Croatia and *hrišćanin* in Serbia in modern times. Although writers on the Bosnian Church have taken this word to imply a member of a heretical Church, there is much linguistic evidence that this word is merely an early form of *kršćanin* in which the palatalization of *st* has not yet taken place. Yet this term does have a specialized meaning, i.e. a member of the Bosnian hierarchy.' A puzzle remains.

[44]   On this see Lambert, *Medieval Heresy*, 1st edn, pp. 146–8, MS repro., p. 147, commentary by Yvonne Burns, pp. 378–9; also Lambert, *Heresis* XXIII, p. 41. Truhelka, part of a group of scholars of the Austro-Hungarian epoch who keenly defended the heretical character of the Church (Wenzel, 'Bosnian history ...', p. 134), read '*mrski*' (meat-eating) instead of '*mrsni*' (unsightly); false analysis of categories of Church membership followed.

[45]   Luke 14: 21.

[46]   There were others: the Bosnian Church was subject to composite influences.

nobles leaned on the Church or made use of the secular services of its churchmen, they also employed in diplomacy and the witnessing or guaranteeing of charters Orthodox or Catholic churchmen and laymen.[47] Radin's pre-eminence was due more to his native skill than to his status. Even Ostoja, a supporter of the Church, in 1418 twice used a Franciscan as diplomat.[48] Rulers had to reckon with the Church as a support or guarantor because it had a certain independent strength, based ultimately on endowments and aristocratic support in certain areas.

The independent strength of the Church and its freedom of action gives it a unique place in the conspectus of dualist and Cathar Churches of the Middle Ages. It remained unpersecuted, and its history, its inertia as a missionary force and the involvement of its churchmen in the secular world shows what happened when heretics had authority, freedom and a landed endowment. Their leaders became virtually indistinguishable from the wealthy and powerful hierarchies of either the Catholic or Orthodox Churches of the time.

The Bosnian Church survived in isolation: it faded as the country was opened up to the outside world. Bosnian tombstones, once identified as the work of Bogomils, give hardly any evidence on the Bosnian Church but a great deal more on the foreign influences which helped to kill it off. A handful of inscriptions link stones to the Bosnian Church, as in the case of *Gost* Milutin; examination of others has shown that styles of ornament and inscriptions developed irrespective of religious allegiance; stones are spread widely in areas where Orthodox, Catholics or the Bosnian Church had points of strength.[49] The proportion which depicts hunts, tournaments and dances shows how in the fourteenth and fifteenth centuries the interests of the nobles who commissioned them were running parallel to those of their Western counterparts. With the opening of mines in the interior west of the Drina a new prosperity reached the horsemen and stockbreeders who escorted caravans to and from the coast, the likeliest patrons of the more 'Western' tombstones. Contacts with the outside world could only work against the interests of the old Bosnian Church. The effectiveness of the major Churches grew and there were more conversions.

Stephen Thomas was the last effective ruler. The Turkish menace had grown and with it a pressing need for Western alliances to save Bosnia; it was natural to calculate that a full conversion to Catholicism might bring more effective military aid. Personal conviction may well have played a part; in 1446, the year he married his queen, Katarina, daughter of one of the

---

[47] It is Fine's achievement (*FBC*, pp. 226–7, 229–33, 238–44, 264–7) to have demonstrated this.

[48] *FBC*, pp. 236–7.

[49] See map facing p. 1, N. Miletić and O. Höckmann, *Mittelalterliche Grabmäler aus Bosnien* (Mainz, 1967). Search for Bogomil symbolism, Solovjev or G. Wild, *Bogomilen und Katharer in ihrer Symbolik* (Wiesbaden, 1970) cannot survive M. Wenzel, 'Bosnian and Herzegovinian tombstones: who made them and why', *Süd-Ost Forschungen* XXI (1962), pp. 102–43, list of Solovjev's articles, p. 103; her interpretations *Ukrasni motivi na stećcima* (Sarajevo, 1966); see O. Bihalji-Merin and A. Benac, *The Bogomils* (London, 1962) (Bihalji-Merin's views preferred). I am indebted for offprints to Dr Wenzel and Prof. Solovjev's executors.

greatest supporters of the old Church, Stephen Vukčić, but a devout Catholic convert and builder of churches, with Franciscans as her chaplains, he announced his own conversion.[50] Yet in the same year he had issued a charter to the Dragišić brothers which carries a guarantee from the *djed*. The grant made will not be revoked, the king assures the brothers, unless it seems just to the *djed*, the Bosnian Church and the 'Good Bosnians', that is, Bosnian nobles.[51] It was not easy to escape the power of the old Church.

In approximately 1459 Stephen Thomas took the final, drastic step and proscribed the old Church. He offered supporters a choice between conversion and exile. There were apparently no martyrs. Those who declined a forced conversion went into exile under Herceg Stephen Vukčić, where they found support at his court until the great man's death. Bosnia fell rapidly: the State barely outlived the Church. Stephen Thomas's son was unable to preserve his kingdom against the Turks and was executed by them in 1463: a brother and a sister accepted Islam. Katarina, still queen of Bosnia when in 1478 as a Franciscan tertiary in Rome she made out her testament, bequeathed the kingdom: if either her son or her daughter should return to Catholicism, she said, one or other should inherit; if not, she left Bosnia to the pope.[52]

Bosnia forms a curious codicil to the history of Catharism. Unique among the elite class of the perfect, Bosnian churchmen enjoyed centuries of freedom, living in tranquillity and ease while their co-religionists either died out or were crushed. Their Church faded after its last major patron died and *Gost* Radin and his followers made for the security of Dubrovnik. Radin died in peace; no doubt his entourage proved incapable of handing on their ecclesiastical inheritance to a new generation. Okić's researches on Turkish tax documents demonstrate a continuing existence of Bosnian Church members for a time under the Turks,[53] but they were only a small remnant facing the force of a triumphant Islam.

It was an anticlimatic ending to the heroic story of European Catharism. The elite of the Bosnian Church seem never to have been moved by the passionate evangelical zeal of their Western counterparts: only a section of the nobility were touched and little impact was made on the mass of the population. Perversion of historiography under the Austro-Hungarian Empire and nationalist emotions have given the Bosnian Church a prominence it has not deserved:[54] it never had the role in the Bosnian State which some writers have wished to attribute it. Certain churchmen carried

[50]   On Katarina, Džambo, *Franziskaner*, pp. 176–8. Diplomatic marriage, healing conflict (*FBC*, p. 302).
[51]   *FBC*, pp. 304–4, cautiously accepting authenticity. Power of Bosnian Church in fifteenth century, J. Šidak, 'O autentičnosti i znacenju jedne isprave Bosanskog "djeda" (1427)', *Slovo* (Zagreb) XV–XVI (1965), pp. 282–97 (German summary, pp. 296–7).
[52]   Džambo, *Franziskaner*, p. 179, n. 139; neither Džaja, *Islamisierungsproblem*, p. 95, nor Fine, *FBC*, p. 338, believes Bosnian Church significantly aided Turkish conquest; Bosnian Church survival, Džaja.
[53]   T. Okić, 'Les Kristians (Bogomiles Parfaits) de Bosnie d'après des documents turcs inédits', *Süd-Ost Forschungen* XIX (1960), pp. 108–33.
[54]   Devastating exposé, Wenzel, 'Bosnian history …'.

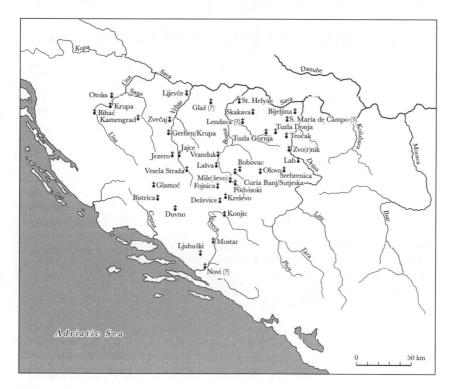

Map 11 Franciscan friaries in fifteenth-century Bosnia
Source: J. Džambo, *Die Franziskaner im mittelalterlichen Bosnien* (Werl/Westfalen, 1991),
p. 168

out important functions for the state; bans and kings had to reckon with its aristocratic membership; it had a wealth and power which the Western Cathars did not attain: but it was never dominant and its dualism, in the primitive circumstances of a backward land, was a dualism in inert solution, a half-understood inheritance, part of a set of rites and formularies which had come down from the past and were maintained out of local loyalty. The Church ended quietly. The story that Stephen Thomas's proscription created a reaction which facilitated the Turkish conquest is a legend: the Turks conquered because of their own ruthless military power.

While it lasted, the Bosnian Church provided for the Italian Cathars a legendary land of faith, a misty redoubt whither aspiring leaders could travel, continuing to Catharism's last days the attractions of the Eastern dualism of little known lands, on which the success and prestige of Nicetas had been built in the twelfth century. But the mainline story of Catharism is set in Western Europe, pre-eminently in parts of Languedoc and Northern and Central Italy. Here the heresy made its greatest impact and here it failed or was crushed.

Epilogue: the Legacy of Catharism

Catharism vanished in Western Europe in the course of the fourteenth century, leaving not a wraith behind. Waldensianism survived into the Reformation epoch, kept in being by a missionary elite hearing the confessions of their faithful and administering penance and instruction in secrecy within devoted families, a procedure so simple and flexible it could readily be concealed, in contrast to the chronic problems of timing and access faced by the Cathar perfect seeking to console the dying at the crucial moment.

Waldensian teaching stood close to the mainstream of Christian tradition, whereas Catharism had an exotic strand which came to seem increasingly alien as the thirteenth-century Church underwent a pastoral revolution and defended its faith more effectively, exposing the curiosities and illogicalities of Cathar belief.

It can never be forgotten that dualism is one of the perennial religions of mankind. In a gentle spoof, E. Turdeanu in his introduction to Bozóky's edition of the *Interrogation of John*, retold a creation myth, at first sight characteristic of the stock in trade of Bogomilism and Catharism alike, involving a struggle between a good and an evil God, only to reveal it was a twentieth-century legend from the Ivory Coast.[1] Cathars were sincere in believing they were bearers of an authentic apostolic tradition, but the scriptural texts and allusions which formed a large part of their instruction and the echoes of New Testament practice in their rites of blessing and breaking bread and the laying on of hands were outer husks of an inner core of belief which represented a profound distortion of central Christian tradition. As Guiraud long ago observed, the spiritual place of the perfect lay not with the leaders and teachers of the Christian Church but rather with Eastern religious teachers, the bonzes and fakirs of Japan and India or the adepts of the Orphic mysteries.[2]

The inquisitors who, with the bishops, rolled up Catharism were by and large not sadists but conscientious administrators and policemen dealing

---

[1] Bozóky, *Livre secret*, p. 10.
[2] J. Guiraud, *Cartulaire de Notre-Dame de Prouille* (Paris, 1907), I, pp. ccxxii–ccxxiii.

with the facts of heretical encounters rather than the beliefs of the suspect before them; but they were managing a system which rewarded and praised the sneak and the spy and only too readily corroded society with suspicion.[3] Force mattered, and though, in the early stages, the preliminary preaching and time of grace in an inquisition blended force with persuasion, and though popes in the thirteenth century may have believed inquisitional proceedings were but a temporary expedient to deal with a crisis of faith, they had in fact created a terrible engine which developed a life of its own.

Reared in the Anglo-Saxon tradition of jurisprudence, the flawed but still impressive pioneer of inquisition history, H. C. Lea, saw how grave were the dangers of injustice embedded in the procedure of *inquisitio*, all the more glaring when, in the interests of efficiency and speed, safeguards for defendants were stripped away. The immense discretionary power vested in the inquisitor, the absence of defence facilities or practicable rights of appeal, gave opportunities to the sadist and fanatic and, applied to the envenomed question of heresy, did in time spawn thought police and give occasion to conscious or unconscious fabrication of heresy, as in the case of the Free Spirit.

Pre-existing belief in Satan and his demons was reinforced by the tenets of Catharism and by churchmen who deduced that because they believed in the power of Satan, Lucifer or an evil principle, they therefore paid reverence to it. The struggle with Catharism helped to fabricate the image of a heretic as a servant of Satan, while Gregory IX's *Vox in Rama* gave a stamp of authority to the kind of obscene slander once deployed against the early Christians and now, in melancholy reversal, turned against Christian heretics. Witchcraft fell under the purview of inquisitors and a body of supposed information on the nature, powers and means of detection of witches and their dealings with demons was assembled. From *Vox in Rama* the way led down to the *Malleus maleficarum*, Bible of the witch-hunters, and to the witch craze which spanned the Reformation and blackens the reputations of Catholics and Protestants alike.[4] It was the most important legacy of the Cathar episode to the future – a legacy which the Cathars themselves would certainly have repudiated.[5]

---

[3]   Roquebert, *L'Epopée*, IV, pp. 245–7.

[4]   P. Segl, *Katharer: Lexikon für Theologie und Kirche* v (3rd edn, 1996), cols 1327–30; and *Als die Ketzer fliegen lernten: Über den Hexen-Wahn im Mittelalter* (Weltenburg, 1991) (popular pamphlet, linking witchcraft and medieval concept of heresy). See also J. B. Russell, *Lucifer: the Devil in the Middle Ages* (Ithaca, London, 1984); D. Müller, 'Hexenprozess und Frauenrepression', *Heresis* XXII (1989), pp. 33–51; *Der Hexenhammer*, ed. P. Segl (Cologne, Vienna, 1988).

[5]   Legacy of interest in Cathars, popular and history writing good and bad, L. Albaret, 'Recherche sur l'historiographie du Catharisme depuis 1970', Mémoire de Maitrise sous la direction de M. le Professeur André Vauchez (Paris-X, Nanterre, 1991–2), carrying on from *CF* XIV (1979), note esp. folklore, pp. 65–91, survey, pp. 142–50.

Abbreviations

Act. Fel.	*Les Actes du Concile Albigeoise de Saint Félix de Caraman*, ed. A. Dondaine, *Miscellanea Giovanni Mercati* V (*Studi e Testi* CXXV) (Rome, 1946)
AFH	*Archivum Franciscanum Historicum*
AFP	*Archivum Fratrum Praedicatorum*
AKG	*Archiv für Kulturgeschichte*
AM	*Annales du Midi*
ARBB	Académie royale de Belgique, *Bulletin de la classe des lettres et des sciences morales et politiques*
ASI	*Archivio storico Italiano*
BF	A. Brenon, *Les Femmes Cathares* (Paris, 1992)
BHL	*Heresy and Literacy, 1000–1530*, ed. P. Biller and A. Hudson (Cambridge, 1994)
BIHR	*Bulletin of the Institute of Historical Reserach*
BISIAM	*Bollettino dell' istituto storico Italiano per il Medio Evo e archivio Muratoriano*
Bouquet	*Recueil de historiens des Gaules et de la France*, ed. M. Bouquet
BPH	*Bulletin philologique et historique du comité des travaux historiques et scientifiques*
BSSV	*Bollettino della società di studi Valdesi*
CEC	*Cahiers des études Cathares*
CF	*Cahiers de Fanjeaux*
I	*Saint Dominique en Languedoc* (1966)
III	*Cathares en Languedoc* (1968)
IV	*Paix de Dieu et guerre sainte en Languedoc au XIIIe siècle* (1969)
V	*Les Universités du Languedoc au XIIe siècle* (1970)
VI	*Le Credo, la morale et l'inquisition* (1971)
VII	*Les Evêques, les clercs et le roi (1250–1300)* (1972)
VIII	*Les Mendiants au pays d'Oc au XIIIe siècle* (1973)
XI	*La Religion populaire en Languedoc du XIIIe siècle à la moitié du XIVe siècle* (1976)
XIV	*Historiographie du Catharisme* (1979)
XVI	*Bernard Gui et son monde* (1984)

xx   *Effacement du Catharisme? (XIIIe–XIVe s.)* (1985)
xxii   *La Femme dans la vie religieuse du Languedoc (XIIIe–XIVe s.)* (1988)
xxix   *L'Eglise et le droit dans le Midi (XIIIe–XIVe s.)* (1994)

CHR   *Catholic Historical Review*
DA   *Deutsches Archiv*
DHC   *De heresi catharorum in Lombardia,* ed. A. Dondaine, in 'La Hiérarchie Cathare en Italie', *AFP* xix (1949), pp. 250–312.
DLZ   *Deutsche Literaturzeitung*
EO   *Europe et Occitanie: les pays Cathares, Collection Heresis* v (Arques, 1995)
ETR   *Etudes théologiques et religieuses*
FBC   J. V. A. Fine Jr, *The Bosnian Church: a New Interpretation* (Boulder, 1975)
FF   *Forschungen und Fortschritte*
FS   *Franciscan Studies*
GA   A. Pales-Gobilliard, *L'Inquisiteur Geoffrey d'Ablis et les Cathares du comté de Foix (1308–1309)* (Paris, 1984)
GRK   G. Rottenwöhrer, Der Katharismus
   i   (1) *Quellen zum Katharismus,* (2) *Anmerkungen* (Bad Honnef, 1982)
   ii   *Der Kult, die religiöse Praxis, die Kritik am Kult und Sakramenten der Katholischen Kirche* (1) *Der Kult,* (2) *Die religiöse Praxis …* (Bad Honnef, 1982)
   iii   *Die Herkunft der Katharer nach Theologie und Geschichte* (Bad Honnef, 1990)
   iv   *Glaube und Theologie der Katharer 1–3* (Bad Honnef, 1993)
JDH   J. Duvernoy, *Le Catharisme:* ii *L'Histoire des Cathares* (Toulouse, 1979)
JDR   J. Duvernoy, *Le Catharisme:* i *La Religion des Cathares* (Toulouse, 1976)
JEH   *Journal of Ecclesiastical History*
JF   *Le Registre d'Inquisition de Jacques Fournier (1318–1325),* ed. J. Duvernoy, i–iii (Toulouse,1965)
JFD   *Le Registre d'Inquisition de Jacques Fournier (Evêque de Pamiers), 1318–1325,* trans. J. Duvernoy, i–iii (Paris, la Haye, New York, 1978)
JMH   *Journal of Medieval History*
L   P. van Limborch, *Historia inquisitionis cui subiungitur Liber Sententiarum inquisitionis Tholosanae ab anno Christi MCCCVII ad annum MCCCXXIII* (Amsterdam, 1692)
LRLM   E. Le Roy Ladurie, *Montaillou village occitan de 1294 à 1324* (Paris, 1975)
Mansi   J. D. Mansi, *Sacrorum conciliorum nova et amplissima collectio* (Florence and Venice, 1759–98), 31 vols.
ME   G. G. Merlo, *Eretici e inquisitori nella società piemontese del trecento* (Turin, 1977)
MGH   *Monumenta Germaniae Historica*

MOPH	*Monumenta Ordinis Praedicatorum Historica*
MS	*Medieval Studies*
PG	J. P. Migne, *Patrologia Graeca*
PL	J. P. Migne, *Patrologia Latina* (Paris, 1844–64)
RB	H. Grundmann, *Religiöse Bewegungen*, 2nd edn (Hildesheim, 1961) (1st edn, 1935)
RBPH	*Revue belge de philologie et d'histoire*
RHE	*Revue d'histoire ecclésiastique*
RHEF	*Revue de l'histoire de l'Eglise de France*
RHL	*Revue historique et littéraire du Languedoc*
RHR	*Revue de l'histoire des religions*
RQH	*Revue des questions historiques*
RS	*Chronicles and Memorials of Great Britain and Ireland during the Middle Ages* (London, 1858–97) (The Rolls Series)
RSCI	*Rivista di storia della chiesa in Italia*
SCH	*Studies in Church History*
	XII *Church, Society and Politics*, ed. D. Baker (Oxford, 1975)
	XV *Religious Motivation: Biographical and Sociological Problems for the Church Historian*, ed. D. Baker (Oxford, 1978)
	XXI *Persecution and Toleration*, ed. W. J. Sheils (Oxford, 1984)
	XXX *Martyrs and Martyrologies*, ed. D. Wood (Oxford, 1993)
	Subsidia IV *The Bible in the Medieval World*, ed. K. Walsh and D. Wood (Oxford, 1985)
	Subsidia IX *The Church and Sovereignty*, ed. D. Wood (Oxford, 1991)
SM	*Studi medievali*
TDH	*Tractatus de hereticis*, ed. A. Dondaine, in 'La Hiérarchie Cathare en Italie', *AFP* XX (1950), pp. 234–324.
WEH	W. L. Wakefield and A. P. Evans (ed.), *Heresies of the High Middle Ages* (New York, London, 1969)
WHC	W. L. Wakefield, *Heresy, Crusade and Inquisition in Southern France, 1100–1250* (London, 1974)
ZRGKA	*Zeitschrift der Savigny-Stiftung für Rechtgeschichte Kanonistische Abteilung*

Index